Unilateral Sanctions in International Law and the Enforcement of Human Rights

World Trade Institute Advanced Studies

VOLUME 9

The titles published in this series are listed at *brill.com/wtia*

Unilateral Sanctions in International Law and the Enforcement of Human Rights

The Impact of the Principle of Common Concern of Humankind

By

Iryna Bogdanova

BRILL
NIJHOFF

LEIDEN | BOSTON

Research for the book took place between 2016 and 2020, as a part of the Swiss National Science Foundation (SNSF) funded project "Towards a Principle of Common Concern of Humankind in Global Law."

Library of Congress Cataloging-in-Publication Data

Names: Bogdanova, Iryna, author.
Title: Unilateral sanctions in international law and the enforcement of human rights : the impact of the principle of common concern of humankind / Iryna Bogdanova.
Description: Leiden ; Boston : Brill/Nijhoff, 2022. | Series: World trade institute advanced studies, 2405-9331 ; vol.9 | Includes bibliographical references and index.
Identifiers: LCCN 2022012171 (print) | LCCN 2022012172 (ebook) | ISBN 9789004507883 (hardback) | ISBN 9789004507890 (ebook)
Subjects: LCSH: Sanctions (International law) | Economic sanctions. | International law and human rights.
Classification: LCC KZ6373 .B64 2022 (print) | LCC KZ6373 (ebook) | DDC 341.5/82–dc23/eng/20220531
LC record available at https://lccn.loc.gov/2022012171
LC ebook record available at https://lccn.loc.gov/2022012172

Typeface for the Latin, Greek, and Cyrillic scripts: "Brill." See and download: brill.com/brill-typeface.

ISSN 2405-9331
ISBN 978-90-04-50788-3 (hardback)
ISBN 978-90-04-50789-0 (e-book)

This book is printed on acid-free paper and produced in a sustainable manner.

Ця книга присвячена моїй родині

Де зараз ви, кати мого народу?

Де зараз ви, кати мого народу?
Де велич ваша, сила ваша де?
На ясні зорі і на тихі води
Вже чорна ваша злоба не впаде.

Народ росте, і множиться, і діє
Без ваших нагаїв і палаша.
Під сонцем вічності древніє й молодіє
Його жорстока й лагідна душа.

Народ мій є! Народ мій завжди буде!
Ніхто не перекреслить мій народ!
Пощезнуть всі перевертні й приблуди,
І орди завойовників-заброд!

Ви, байстрюки катів осатанілих,
Не забувайте, виродки, ніде:
Народ мій є! В його гарячих жилах
Козацька кров пульсує і гуде!

ВАСИЛЬ СИМОНЕНКО © 24 грудня 1962

Contents

PART 2
The International Enforcement of Human Rights and the Legality of Unilateral Human Rights Sanctions

PART 3
The Contribution of the Doctrine of Common Concern of Humankind to the International Protection of Human Rights

Acknowledgements

This book is an edited version of my doctoral dissertation, and it represents the culmination of a number of years of research, which was conducted at the World Trade Institute (WTI), University of Berne. It was a privilege to be a member of the research team working for the project "Towards a Principle of Common Concern in Global Law." This research was made possible by the extraordinary enthusiasm of Professor Thomas Cottier and with the generous financial support provided by the Swiss National Science Foundation (SNSF). The initial findings of this research project were presented during the 2018 conference and were later published in an edited volume *The Prospects of Common Concern of Humankind in International Law* by Cambridge University Press in 2021.

I would like to take this opportunity to thank Professor Thomas Cottier for his trust, invaluable support and encouragement over the years. I am equally grateful to Professor Michael Hahn for his guidance as a second supervisor of my work.

This work would not be possible without unstinting support and encouragement from my family, friends and colleagues. Throughout my work on this book, I benefited from guidance and support generously offered by my teammates – Zaker Ahmad, Alexander Beyleveld and Lucia Satragno. I was lucky to form a close friendship with Zaker and Alex and hopefully, the bonds of friendship will only strengthen with time. The valuable help and wholehearted support of my close friend and a fellow PhD colleague – Anqi Wang – should also be acknowledged. Moreover, I was privileged to obtain advice and insights from many other people, in particular, fellow PhD colleagues – Andrea Schlaepfer, Judith Schaeli, Rosa Maria Losada, Aylin Yildiz and María Vásquez Callo-Müller.

I thank the WTI doctoral school, under the guidance of Doris Oberdabernig and Octavio Fernandez, for providing me with the opportunity to learn from many leading experts in the course of my doctoral studies.

Many colleagues have guided and assisted me during this time, including Professor Peter Van den Bossche, Professor Manfred Elsig and Dr Rodrigo Polanco. I am grateful for their support and assistance.

Finally, the work of the WTI and researchers like me would not be possible without administrative and logistical support timely and professionally provided by Margrit Vetter and Sandra Joseph. Many thanks to both of them for being always there for the WTI researchers and students.

Thanks should also be extended to Pablo Das and Sophia Thompson for managing public communications and helping to spread the word about the research conducted at the WTI.

Thanks to language editor Chad Jorgenson for editing my manuscript and doing it on very short notice and under a significant time constraint, yet maintaining outstanding quality.

Thanks to the staff at Brill, especially Kelley Baylis and Dove Morissette for coordinating the publication process. Thanks to the designers, typesetters and the production staff for their patience and efforts.

A few words of gratitude are owed to my long-term friends, whose support is a great encouragement for me – Roman Prodayko, Artem Nikitin, and Daryna Koryagina.

This book is dedicated to my family.

This book will be available in open access due to the generous support of the SNSF (grant number: 10BP12_208113).

Iryna Bogdanova
Poltava, Ukraine
January 2022

Tables

Abbreviations

AB	Appellate Body
CAT	Convention against Torture and Other Cruel, Inhuman or Degrading Treatment or Punishment
CEDAW	Convention on the Elimination of All Forms of Discrimination against Women
CPED	International Convention for the Protection of All Persons from Enforced Disappearance
CRC	Convention on the Rights of the Child
CRPD	Convention on the Rights of Persons with Disabilities
Draft articles	Draft articles on Responsibility of States for Internationally Wrongful Acts
DSU	Understanding on rules and procedures governing the settlement of disputes
EU	European Union
GATS	General Agreement on Trade in Services
GATT 1947/1994	General Agreement on Tariffs and Trade
Genocide Convention	Convention on the Prevention and Punishment of the Crime of Genocide
ICCPR	International Covenant on Civil and Political Rights
ICERD	International Convention on the Elimination of All Forms of Racial Discrimination
ICESCR	International Covenant on Economic, Social and Cultural Rights
ICJ	International Court of Justice
ICMW	International Convention on the Protection of the Rights of All Migrant Workers and Members of Their Families
ILC	International Law Commission
MFN	Most-favoured-nation principle
NATO	North Atlantic Treaty Organization
OFAC	Office of Foreign Assets Control
PCIJ	Permanent Court of International Justice
R2P	Responsibility to Protect
Security Council	United Nations Security Council
UAE	United Arab Emirates
UN	United Nations
UN Charter	Charter of the United Nations

UN Convention	United Nations Convention on Jurisdictional Immunities of States and Their Property
VCLT	Vienna Convention on the Law of Treaties
WTO	World Trade Organization

Introduction

In the early spring of 2014, the silence of the blossoming Crimean gardens was shattered by the manoeuvres of Russian military forces. The Russian Federation seized control of the southernmost outpost of the once-mighty Russian empire – the Crimean Peninsula. The core principles enshrined in the Charter of the United Nations almost seventy years earlier were overturned in a single stroke. This illegal annexation was followed by military conflict in eastern Ukraine, which was fuelled and supported by the Russian Federation. Needless to say, these events triggered an international outcry. Official statements made by heads of states and governments condemned these flagrant violations of international law.[1] Soon, diplomatic notes were replaced by unilateral economic sanctions.[2]

These sanctions were unilateral acts on the part of states, which were introduced in line with their domestic laws and were not authorised by any international institution. However, these unilateral efforts to inflict economic pain did not go unanswered. The Russian Federation fired back with its own economic restrictions against the states that had imposed restrictive measures, calling these measures "countersanctions."[3]

---

1 "The sovereignty, territorial integrity and independence of Ukraine must be respected. The European Union does neither recognise the illegal and illegitimate referendum in Crimea nor its outcome. The European Union does not and will not recognise the annexation of Crimea and Sevastopol to the Russian Federation." 'Joint Statement on Crimea by President of the European Council Herman Van Rompuy and President of the European Commission José Manuel Barroso. Brussels, 18 March 2014. EUCO 63/14.'; On 3 March 2014, the House of Commons of Canada unanimously passed a motion to "strongly condemn Russia's provocative military intervention in Ukraine." 'Journals No. 55 – March 3, 2014 (41–2) – House of Commons of Canada' <https://www.ourcommons.ca/DocumentViewer/en/41-2/house/sitting-55/journals>.

2 The first wave of sanctions was imposed in March 2014. President of the United States of America. Executive Order 13660 of March 6, 2014. Blocking Property of Certain Persons Contributing to the Situation in Ukraine; President of the United States of America. Executive Order 13661 of March 16, 2014. Blocking Property of Additional Persons Contributing to the Situation in Ukraine; The European Union introduced Council Regulation (EU) No 269/2014 of 17 March 2014 concerning restrictive measures in respect of actions undermining or threatening the territorial integrity, sovereignty and independence of Ukraine 2014 (OJ L); Canada introduced the Special Economic Measures (Ukraine) Regulations. SOR/2014-60, on March 17, 2014.

3 The Decree of the President of the Russian Federation on 6 August 2014 No. 560 'On the application of certain special economic measures to ensure the security of the Russian Federation' (Указ Президента Российской Федерации от 06.08.2014 г. No. 560 О применении

The tensions between Ukraine and Russia and the ensuing sanctions led international legal scholars to be caught in the crossfire. The perennial legal debate over the legality of unilateral economic sanctions, which are not authorised by the Security Council of the United Nations, was given new momentum. Despite being voluminous, the literature on the subject does not provide much clarity beyond the mere recognition that it is a highly contentious topic.[4] Thus, even the basic question of whether unilateral economic sanctions are permitted under international law has not been firmly settled.

Furthermore, in light of the statements made by high-ranking Russian government officials pointing to the inconsistency of unilateral sanctions with World Trade Organization (WTO) law,[5] debates about whether national security considerations can justify such unilateral responses proliferated.[6] Subsequent developments, which resulted in a dispute initiated by Ukraine against the Russian Federation at the WTO, shed some light on the matter, yet did not clarify it fully.[7]

The dramatic unfolding of the war in Syria, along with the well-documented and widely reported large-scale human rights atrocities, prompted states to tighten the unilateral economic sanctions they had previously imposed. It is worth noting that the UN Security Council made numerous attempts to adopt a resolution condemning widespread violence and egregious human rights violations, as well as to impose collective sanctions, yet some of the permanent members, notably the Russian Federation and the People's Republic of China,

---

отдельных специальных экономических мер в целях обеспечения безопасности Российской Федерации).

4 Mergen Doraev, 'The "Memory Effect" of Economic Sanctions against Russia: Opposing Approaches to the Legality of Unilateral Sanctions Clash Again' (2015) 37 University of Pennsylvania Journal of International Law 355; Tom Ruys, 'Sanctions, Retorsions and Countermeasures: Concepts and International Legal Framework' in Larissa Van den Herik (ed), *Research Handbook on UN Sanctions and International Law* (Edward Elgar Publishing 2017).

5 Shawn Donnan and Kathrin Hille, 'Russia Threatens US with WTO Action over Crimea Sanctions' *Financial Times* (16 April 2014) <https://www.ft.com/content/5418ad46-c57c-11e3-97e4-00144feabdc0>; Benjamin Fox, 'Poland Demands WTO Challenge over Russia Food Ban' (20 August 2014) <https://euobserver.com/news/125295>.

6 Rostam J Neuwirth and Alexandr Svetlicinii, 'The Economic Sanctions over the Ukraine Conflict and the WTO: 'Catch-XXI' and the Revival of the Debate on Security Exceptions' (2015) 49 Journal of World Trade 891; Rostam J Neuwirth and Alexandr Svetlicinii, 'The Current EU/US–Russia Conflict over Ukraine and the WTO: A Preliminary Note on (Trade) Restrictive Measures' (2016) 32 Post-Soviet Affairs 237.

7 *Panel Report, Russia – Measures Concerning Traffic in Transit, WT/DS512/R and Add1, adopted 26 April 2019.*

vetoed all these attempts.[8] Hence, the proposed actions under Chapter VII of the UN Charter were blocked.

Individual states faced with the need to respond to this international crisis relied on unilateral economic sanctions.[9] These included economic restrictions imposed on the Central Bank of Syria and on the acting head of state, as well as on other high-ranking government officials.[10] These developments provoked a debate about the relationship between unilateral restrictive measures and the immunities granted under the international law to states, heads of states and other high-ranking government officials.[11]

Venezuela's attempts to call into question the legality of unilateral economic sanctions represent another convoluted legal twist. In January 2019, Venezuela aimed to challenge the consistency of the unilateral economic sanctions

---

8 The first attempt to adopt the Security Council resolution, in 2011, failed. 'Security Council Fails to Adopt Draft Resolution Condemning Syria's Crackdown on Anti-Government Protestors, Owing to Veto by Russian Federation, China' <https://www.un.org/press/en/2011/sc10403.doc.htm>; On 4 February 2012, the adoption of the draft resolution condemning the violence in Syria was vetoed by the Russian Federation and China. 'Security Council Fails to Adopt Draft Resolution on Syria as Russian Federation, China Veto Text Supporting Arab League's Proposed Peace Plan' <https://www.un.org/press/en/2012/sc10536.doc.htm>; On 19 July 2012, the adoption of another draft resolution was vetoed by the Russian Federation and China. 'Security Council Fails to Adopt Draft Resolution on Syria That Would Have Threatened Sanctions, Due to Negative Votes of China, Russian Federation' <https://www.un.org/press/en/2012/sc10714.doc.htm>; The General Assembly in its resolution that was adopted with an overwhelming majority condemned the Security Council's failure to act on Syria. UNGA Res 66/253 B The situation in the Syrian Arab Republic (7 August 2012) UN Doc A/RES/66/253 B.

9 The European Union and the United States have been levying various types of unilateral economic sanctions in order to end violence and grave human rights violations, as well as to encourage the Syrian government to negotiate a peaceful political settlement. Other states, such as the United Kingdom, have also imposed unilateral economic sanctions on Syria.

10 President of the United States of America. Executive Order 13573 of May 18, 2011. Blocking Property of Senior Officials of the Government of Syria; President of the United States of America. Executive Order 13582 of August 17, 2011. Blocking Property of the Government of Syria and Prohibiting Certain Transactions with Respect to Syria; Council Regulation (EU) No 168/2012 of 27 February 2012 amending Regulation (EU) No 36/2012 concerning restrictive measures in view of the situation in Syria 2012 (OJ L).

11 Natalino Ronzitti, 'Sanctions as Instruments of Coercive Diplomacy: An International Law Perspective' in Natalino Ronzitti (ed), *Coercive Diplomacy, Sanctions and International Law* (Brill Nijhoff 2016); Tom Ruys, 'Immunity, Inviolability and Countermeasures – A Closer Look at Non-UN Targeted Sanctions' in Tom Ruys and Nicolas Angelet (eds.), *The Cambridge Handbook of Immunities and International Law* (Cambridge University Press 2019).

imposed by the United States with WTO obligations.[12] The United States did not engage in consultations and contended that it was not obliged to do so, given that it did not recognise the legitimacy of the current Venezuelan government.[13] Under pressure from the other WTO Members, Venezuela withdrew its request to establish a WTO panel to resolve the dispute.[14] Yet, the matter did not rest there. In February 2020, the government of Venezuela filed a referral under Article 14 of the Rome Statute of the International Criminal Court regarding the situation in Venezuela. Venezuela argues that crimes against humanity are being committed "as a result of the application of unlawful coercive measures adopted unilaterally by the government of the United States of America against Venezuela, at least since the year 2014."[15] The prosecutor of the International Criminal Court was charged with taking a decision about this request.[16] As of this writing, the investigation is still ongoing. However, legal scholars argue that "Venezuela's expansive arguments do not find support in international law."[17]

The above-mentioned examples illustrate that states habitually rely upon unilateral economic sanctions in circumstances in which other means of recourse are either unfeasible or legally unavailable. This is the reality of state practice, which situates the debate about the legality of unilateral economic sanctions in a factual context. Furthermore, these examples demonstrate the diversity of the legal questions raised. What is noteworthy in this regard is that

---

12 WTO, 'United States – Measures Relating to Trade in Goods and Services. Request for Consultations by Venezuela. Document WT/DS574/1, G/L/1289, S/L/420, 8 January 2019.'

13 Tom Miles, 'U.S. Objection over Venezuela Threatens to Halt WTO Trade Disputes' *Reuters* (26 March 2019) <https://www.reuters.com/article/us-usa-trade-venezuela-wto/u-s-venuezela-spat-threatens-to-halt-wto-trade-disputes-idUSKCN1R71KJ>.

14 WTO, 'United States – Measures Relating to Trade in Goods and Services. Request for the Establishment of a Panel by Venezuela. Document WT/DS574/2, 15 March 2019'; The issue was included in the agenda for the Dispute Settlement Body meeting, but the United States rejected the proposed agenda and, as a result, the meeting was postponed. Miles (n 13).

15 Annex I to the Prosecution's Provision of the Supporting Document of the Referral Submitted by the Government of Venezuela, ICC Doc. ICC-01/20-4-AnxI, 04 March 2020 (Situation in the Bolivarian Republic of Venezuela II). https://www.icc-cpi.int/Pages/record.aspx?docNo=ICC-01/20-4-AnxI.

16 'Statement of the Prosecutor of the International Criminal Court, Mrs Fatou Bensouda, on the Referral by Venezuela Regarding the Situation in Its Own Territory' <https://www.icc-cpi.int/Pages/item.aspx?name=200217-otp-statement-venezuela>.

17 Dapo Akande, Payam Akhavan, and Eirik Bjorge, 'Economic Sanctions, International Law, and Crimes Against Humanity: Venezuela's ICC Referral' (2021) 115(3) American Journal of International Law 493, doi:10.1017/ajil.2021.20.

the legality of unilateral economic sanctions per se remains contested, irrespective of the objective pursued.

The primary focus of this book is question of the legality of unilateral economic sanctions, with particular emphasis on economic sanctions imposed in order to redress severe human rights violations. Moreover, the potential contribution of the doctrine of Common Concern of Humankind to the enhancement of the international protection of human rights will also be presented. To this end, I analyse the existing state practice of applying unilateral economic sanctions against the background of diverse principles and norms of international law. The subsequent discussion of the legality of unilateral economic sanctions imposed to redress human rights violations is preceded by an analysis of the international enforcement of human rights. This analysis is intended to reveal the shortcomings of the current system of human rights enforcement. Another objective of this study is to consider the potential contribution of the doctrine of Common Concern of Humankind to strengthening the international protection of human rights. In order to do so, I rely upon a three-pronged framing of this doctrine suggested by Professor Thomas Cottier and others.[18]

In this book, unilateral economic sanctions are defined as restrictive economic measures imposed by an individual state against another state and/or its government officials and bodies, legal entities and foreign nationals, in pursuance of political objectives and without any prior authorisation from an international or regional organisation. In other words, such economic restrictions are enacted on the basis of the domestic laws and regulations of the state that imposes them.

It is crucial to define what types of restrictive economic measures are not covered in this study. First and foremost, there will be no analysis of economic restrictions imposed by the United Nations Security Council under Chapter VII of the UN Charter (collective economic sanctions) or of measures taken by individual states insofar as they are merely implementing the binding

18 Thomas Cottier, 'The Principle of Common Concern of Humankind' in Thomas Cottier and Zaker Ahmad (eds.), *The Prospects of Common Concern of Humankind in International Law* (Cambridge University Press 2021); Iryna Bogdanova, 'Reshaping the Law of Economic Sanctions for Human Rights Enforcement: The Potential of Common Concern of Humankind' in Thomas Cottier and Zaker Ahmad (eds.), *The Prospects of Common Concern of Humankind in International Law* (Cambridge University Press 2021) doi:10.1017/9781108878739.008; Thomas Cottier and others, 'The Principle of Common Concern and Climate Change' (2014) 52 Archiv des Völkerrechts 293; Thomas Cottier and Krista Nadakavukaren Schefer, 'Responsibility to Protect (R2P) and the Emerging Principle of Common Concern' (2012) NCCR Working Paper 2012/29.

decisions of the Security Council. Collective economic sanctions are discussed only in order to describe the historical evolution of coercive economic measures and the role of the Security Council in enforcing human rights. Second, non-forcible measures introduced by a regional or international organisation against its member states in accordance with the provisions of their constituent documents fall outside the scope of this research project. Third, trade restrictions introduced to implement the suspension of concessions allowed in some instances under WTO law are excluded. Finally, there is no discussion of positive sanctions[19] or restrictions on the trade in arms.

The legality of unilateral economic sanctions is not well settled in international law. Paradoxically, although states habitually rely upon unilateral economic measures, this abundance of state practice has not resulted in legal certainty regarding their status. Even the use of the term "sanction" is not subject to agreement.[20]

Given the backlash against globalisation and international trade, as well as the fact that some scholars even argue that the international economic order is in the process of transition to a new geo-economic order,[21] we may witness increasing recourse to unilateral economic sanctions as instruments of unfolding geopolitical tensions. Hence, the discussion of the legality of unilateral economic sanctions, as well as the circumstances in which they can be legally employed, is a timely undertaking.

Alongside these recent developments, the perennial political rifts between developed and developing countries continue to haunt the debate on the legality of unilateral economic sanctions.[22] In parallel to the attempts on the part of developing countries to denounce the use of unilateral economic sanctions, attempts which are explicitly reflected in numerous documents adopted under the auspices of the United Nations,[23] individual states have moved

---

19 "Positive sanctions can involve a state promising to grant enhanced access to its markets or to increase its foreign aid to another country in return for it making specific policy changes or continuing to follow an existing policy." Kern Alexander, *Economic Sanctions: Law and Public Policy* (Palgrave Macmillan 2009) 10.

20 For a similar view, see Ruys (n 4).

21 Anthea Roberts, Henrique Choer Moraes and Victor Ferguson, 'Toward a Geoeconomic Order in International Trade and Investment' (2019) 22 Journal of International Economic Law 655.

22 Alexandra Hofer, 'The Developed/Developing Divide on Unilateral Coercive Measures: Legitimate Enforcement or Illegitimate Intervention?' (2017) 16 Chinese Journal of International Law 175.

23 ibid.

forward with enacting domestic laws authorising them to sanction not only other states, but also high-ranking government officials of the other states.[24]

The recent trend towards imposing unilateral human rights sanctions also warrants further discussion. The practice of justifying economic restrictions on the grounds of human rights violations dates back to the protection of religious minorities in medieval times. Indeed, Kern Alexander provides an example of trade restrictions imposed by Protestant Swiss cantons, led by Zurich, on Catholic cantons for violating their treaty obligation to tolerate their Protestant minorities.[25] Discussing the growing role of unilateral economic sanctions imposed on human rights grounds, the distinguished international lawyer Alain Pellet has accurately pointed out one of the reasons behind it: "the institutionalized sanctions machinery is all too often paralyzed not only by the veto, but also by the inexistence of a 'caring majority' – who really cares about the fate of the Moslem minority in Myanmar, or endemic slavery in many countries, or gross human rights violations in Saudi Arabia."[26]

Notwithstanding their increased use, the legality of imposing unilateral economic sanctions in order to redress grave human rights violations remains unclear. This uncertainty has inspired debates about the legality of such measures as third-party countermeasures, that is, countermeasures imposed by non-injured states. The recent trend towards sanctioning heads of states and other high-ranking government officials for gross human rights violations has provoked a debate about the consistency of such actions with the immunities granted under international law to states, heads of states and other senior government officials. With respect to WTO law, the debate concerning the relationship between trade restrictions justified on human rights grounds and the commitments undertaken by WTO Members is multifaceted. In particular, trade restrictions may be invoked as a protection against unfair trade practices. A frequently reported example of such measures are the trade restrictions imposed on products produced by forced labour. Pointing to such trade restrictions, Sarah Cleveland has noted: "The United States has restricted imports made with convict labor since 1890, and began barring imports made

24 Nienke van der Have, 'The Proposed EU Human Rights Sanctions Regime: A First Appreciation' (2020) 1 Security and Human Rights 1; Clara Portela, 'Targeted sanctions against individuals on grounds of grave human rights violations – impact, trends and prospects at EU level' (2018) Study commissioned by the European Parliament's Subcommittee of Human Rights 1.

25 Alexander (n 19) footnote 4, 8–9.

26 Alain Pellet, 'Unilateral Sanctions and International Law. A Proposal for a New Commission on Unilateral Sanctions and International Law.' (2015) 76 Yearbook of Institute of International Law 730.

with other forms of forced labor in 1930."[27] These trade restrictions prompted a vigorous dispute about whether the distinction between the two kinds of products, which is rooted in different production and processing methods, is permitted under WTO law. Thus far, WTO adjudicators have eschewed any direct pronouncements on the matter. Another group of trade restrictions can be characterised as general human rights sanctions. General human rights sanctions are a conventional foreign policy instrument which is channelled through trade prohibitions. Put differently, such trade prohibitions are levied in order to express dissatisfaction with the human rights policies of a given state, and they are not related to any particular product or production method. In this study, the WTO consistency of general human rights sanctions is analysed.

This book aims to answer the following research questions:

- Are unilateral economic sanctions legal under public international law? And how do they relate to various principles and norms of public international law?
- Can unilateral economic sanctions imposed to redress grave human rights violations be subjected to the same legal contestations as other unilateral sanctions?
- What potential contribution can the recently formulated doctrine of Common Concern of Humankind make to improving compliance with human rights, in particular by introducing substantive and procedural prerequisites to legitimise unilateral human rights sanctions?

The hypothesis of this study is that the legality of unilateral economic sanctions is contested even when these restrictions have as a goal to remedy gross human rights violations and that the suggested framework of the doctrine of Common Concern of Humankind provides pathways for legitimising unilateral human rights sanctions.

This study is divided into three sections:

In the first part, I discuss the legality of unilateral economic sanctions under public international law. This is accomplished by analysing their legality in light of different principles and norms of international law.

The second part is devoted to a discussion of the international enforcement of human rights and the role of unilateral economic sanctions in this enforcement. Here, the legality of unilateral human rights sanctions is analysed. In particular, I tackle the legal question of whether the purpose of such unilateral action – namely, redressing human right violations – supports their legality.

---

27 Sarah H Cleveland, 'Human Rights Sanctions and International Trade: A Theory of Compatibility' (2002) 5 Journal of International Economic Law 133, 134.

The third part discusses the potential contribution of the recently formulated doctrine of Common Concern of Humankind to the improvement of the international enforcement of human rights. This part concludes with a number of normative suggestions.

This study argues that deliberations about the legality or illegality of unilateral economic sanctions, in particular human rights sanctions, ought to be superseded by a discussion of the principles legitimising the use of economic coercion to promote community interests. With this consideration in mind, I demonstrate how the normative implications of the doctrine of Common Concern of Humankind could potentially constrain the use of politically motivated economic coercion and concurrently encourage states to respond to instances of grave human rights violations by legitimising such unilateral actions.

In this study, I apply the method of doctrinal research. Within the boundaries of this methodology, the following legal research techniques were employed: deductive reasoning, analogy, induction and legal formalism. These techniques aim to reconstruct what the law says about the use of unilateral economic sanctions. The use of this methodology conforms to the approach to international law as a rules-based system, in which the rules can be discerned from the sources of law duly recognised by the states (De lege lata).

This study also applies empirical methods, mainly observation, in order to summarise and describe the existing state practice of relying upon unilateral economic sanctions, including restrictions to redress grave human rights violations. Furthermore, empirical analysis is utilised to analyse the efficiency of the international protection of human rights. In particular, an enquiry into compliance with reporting obligations and the reliance upon interstate complaint mechanisms is conducted using this approach.

The chapter describing the historical evolution of economic coercion applies the method of historical analysis, whereas the part of the study in which the effectiveness of the economic coercive measures is reviewed relies upon interdisciplinary research. The effectiveness of economic sanctions has been vigorously debated by legal scholars, political scientists and economists. The discussion of the issue here includes references to studies in all these disciplines.

In the last chapter, this study is concerned with the normative dimension of the subject. The discussion of normative implications of the doctrine of Common Concern of Humankind in international human rights law entails a discussion of how the law should be developed (De lege ferenda).

The book consists of five chapters, in addition to an introduction and a conclusion.

Chapter 1 sets out the origins of the modern economic sanctions and briefly summarises the heated debate about their effectiveness. In order to do so, the relevant historical episodes are gathered, analysed and presented. The description of the main historical developments is also accompanied by an account of the legal discussions associated with particular events. Regarding the effectiveness of economic coercion, pertinent studies conducted by legal scholars, political scientists and economists are scrutinised. Drawing on the growing body of literature on the subject, the discussion evolves around the main theories and findings concerning the efficiency of sanctions.

Chapter 2 analyses the legal dimension of unilateral economic sanctions. The objective of this chapter is to provide an analysis of the legality of such sanctions under public international law. For this purpose, their legality is reviewed against the principles enshrined in the UN Charter before their legality as third-party countermeasures is addressed. The relationship between extraterritorial sanctions and the established principles of jurisdiction in international law are explored. The recent trend towards imposing sanctions on the central banks of states and heads of state, as well as other high-ranking government officials, warrants a further discussion of the compatibility of such measures with the immunities granted under international law to states, heads of state and senior government officials. The last section of the chapter is devoted to the assessment of the WTO consistency of unilateral economic sanctions.

Chapter 3 examines the international enforcement of human rights. It begins by providing a brief description of the core international human rights treaties. This description is followed by an analysis of the treaty-based mechanisms of human rights protection. These mechanisms include: a reporting obligation, interstate and individual complaint mechanisms, enquiry procedures and the possibility to bring a case before the International Court of Justice. The use and effectiveness of all these avenues of recourse are reviewed. This is then followed by a discussion on the enforcement of human rights as jus cogens and obligations erga omnes. Finally, the role of the Human Rights Council and the Security Council in the international protection of human rights is evaluated.

Chapter 4 discusses the legality of unilateral economic sanctions imposed on human rights grounds. It raises the question of whether human rights sanctions can be subject to the same legal contestations as any other type of unilateral economic sanctions. In seeking an answer to this question, I examine the relationship between human rights sanctions and the principle of non-intervention embedded in the UN Charter. The possibility of justifying human rights sanctions as legal third-party countermeasures is also considered. This is followed by a discussion of whether or not human rights sanctions encroach on the immunities guaranteed under international law to the heads of states and other senior government officials. The most intricate legal issue is the possibility of justifying human rights sanctions under the exceptions prescribed under WTO law. I analyse this possibility in relation to two exceptions: the public morals exception and the national security exception.

Chapter 5 explores the potential contribution of the recently emerged doctrine of Common Concern of Humankind to enhance the international protection of human rights. It starts with a discussion of the historical evolution of the doctrine, before addressing the normative implications of the doctrine of Common Concern of Humankind suggested by Thomas Cottier and others. The primary objective of this chapter is to introduce this doctrine into international human rights law, in order to assess its potential contribution to the enhancement of international protection of human rights and its role in legitimising unilateral human rights sanctions.

The Conclusion summarises the main findings of each chapter and emphasises the suggestions put forward as a result of this research.

PART 1

The History, Effectiveness and Legality of Unilateral Economic Sanctions

CHAPTER 1

The History and Effectiveness of Economic Coercion

1 The History of Economic Coercion: From Economic Warfare to the Enforcement of Community Interests

This chapter traces back the origins and historical evolution of economic coercion in international law and international relations. To this end, a brief review of the most significant developments is provided. Furthermore, this chapter highlights the significantly increased role of economic coercion and provides a glimpse into the debate about its effectiveness.

This chapter pursues two objectives. First, the historical overview provides evidence for the assertion that economic sanctions are conventional instruments of foreign policy, while also demonstrating their growing significance after World War II and outlining recent trends. Second, the discussion of the effectiveness of economic sanctions reveals the multifaceted nature of this debate, while acknowledging that economic sanctions can be effective if they are appropriately framed.

1.1 *Economic Coercion before the Twentieth Century*

The growing body of literature on economic coercion has largely overlooked the historical accounts of the early practice of economic policies used for political goals, and thus there is an apparent lack of a consistent narrative on the subject. Notwithstanding this shortcoming, a brief account of the major historical developments is provided here.

The first attempts to exercise economic pressure to achieve political goals date back to the times of ancient Greece.[28] These early attempts to deploy economic coercion were, as a rule, accompanied by the use of military force.

28 "The most celebrated occasion was Pericles's Megarian decree, enacted in 432 BC in response to the kidnapping of three Asparian women. Thucydides accords the decree only minor notice in The Peloponnesian War; by contrast, Aristophanes in his comedy The Acharnians assigns the Megarian decree a major role in triggering the war." Gary Clyde Hufbauer and others, *Economic Sanctions Reconsidered* (3rd ed, Peterson Institute for International Economics 2007) 9; "Indeed, Athens imposed economic sanctions in 432 BC when Pericles issued the Megarian import embargo against the Greek city-states which had refused to join the Athenian-led Delian League during the Peloponnesian

The historical records attest that until the early twentieth century, states relied upon economic coercion predominantly during times of military conflict and that these measures were aimed at undermining the economic strength of a belligerent state.[29] More specifically, naval blockades were frequently deployed at the end of the sixteenth and throughout the seventeenth century.[30] Later, the Napoleonic Wars unveiled the future potential of continental blockades.[31]

Trade embargoes were a common form of economic pressure. A number of studies shed light on the origins of trade embargoes, as well as on their deployment in the Middle Ages.[32] For example, Stefan Stantchev emphasises that strategic export controls, which forbade the export of wine, oil, defensive and offensive equipment, along with the raw materials necessary for their manufacture, were already enshrined in the Code of Justinian.[33] This fact by no means implies that those prohibitions operated as foreign policy tools. As Stantchev infers from the scant historical evidence: "there were embargoes as legislated realities, as export control systems, but not as relevant and frequently applied policy tools, except maybe – and the stress is on maybe – in the Byzantine Empire."[34] Stantchev further elucidates the evolution of the various forms of embargoes and enumerates the goals that were pursued by these measures, concluding: "Embargo emerged as a well-conceptualized and continuously employed policy tool in the central Middle Ages as a result of the sharp increase in trade volumes within a politically fragmented space."[35]

Boycotts represent another form of trade restriction imposed on political grounds. The term was coined in 1880 to describe an act of social ostracism

War." Barry E Carter, 'International Economic Sanctions: Improving the Haphazard U.S. Legal Regime' (1987) 75 California Law Review 1159.

29 One of the most comprehensive studies on the history and efficacy of economic sanctions by Hufbauer, Schott, and Elliott includes a list of economic sanctions used before the World War I, all the measures from the list were employed during a military confrontation between the states, in the authors' words "foreshadowed or accompanied warfare." Hufbauer and others (n 28) 40–41 Table 1A.3.

30 Wolff Heintschel von Heinegg, 'Blockade,' *Max Planck Encyclopedia of Public International Law* [*MPEPIL*] (2015) <http://opil.ouplaw.com/view/10.1093/law:epil/9780199231690/law-9780199231690-e252>.

31 Margaret Pamela Doxey, *Economic Sanctions and International Enforcement* (2nd ed., Macmillan Press 1980) 10.

32 Richard J Ellings, *Embargoes and World Power: Lessons from American Foreign Policy* (Westview Press 1985); Stefan Stantchev, 'The Medival Origins of Embargo as a Policy Tool' (2012) 33 History of Political Thought 373.

33 Stantchev (n 32) 379.

34 ibid 383.

35 ibid 399.

exercised by land tenants against Captain Charles Boycott, who was acting as a rent collector for Lord Erne.[36] As to the practice of imposing boycotts, Margaret Doxey observes: “Although the term ‘boycott’ dates only from the 1880s the practice of refusing to buy from, or sell to other merchants, or to have commercial relations with other political entities was well known in earlier times.”[37] One of the most celebrated examples is the United States’ boycott of British goods, which was imposed to express disagreement with the rules of the colonial administration.[38]

On numerous occasions, states have employed coercive economic measures as part of their military warfare.[39] The prohibition on trade with an enemy was a common practice,[40] yet such prohibitions did not restrict the right of neutral states to engage in commerce with belligerents. In order to inflict severe economic deprivation on an adversary state, states introduced restrictions on trade between a belligerent state and neutral states. During the Seven Years’ War, the military conflict between the major powers in Europe that lasted from 1756 until 1763, the kingdom of Great Britain unilaterally decreed that neutral states could not benefit from trade during wartime if that trade did not occur in peacetime (“The Rule of 1756” or “Rule of the War of 1756”).[41]

---

36 Christopher C Joyner, ‘Boycott,’ *Max Planck Encyclopedia of Public International Law* (2009) <https://opil.ouplaw.com/oxlaw/entryview/viewoxlawoxchap/10.1093$002flaw:epil$002f9780199231690$002flaw-9780199231690-e258>.

37 Doxey (n 31) 15.

38 Alexander (n 19) 12–13.

39 Hufbauer and others (n 28) 40–41.

40 “As economic development enabled nations to commit ever larger proportions of their total resources to war, it became increasingly logical, at least for the stronger antagonist, to cut off all intercourse with the enemy as a means of achieving the quickest possible victory. English law moved spasmodically toward the recognition and application of this logic. Glimmerings can be found as early as the reign of Edward II, when three merchants who had traded with Scotland, then at war with England, were arrested.” Ludwell H Johnson, III, ‘The Business of War: Trading with the Enemy in English and Early American Law’ (1974) 118(5) Proceedings of the American Philosophical Society 459.

41 “Up to that date each European nation had retained the exclusive right of trading with its colonies. During the Seven Years War, the English navy drove French commerce from the seas, practically isolating France from her colonies. France attempted to obviate this by granting colonial trade rights to the Dutch, but the English declared in the ‘Rule of 1756’ that neutrals in time of war could not enjoy a trade from which they were barred in time of peace and proceeded to seize and condemn Dutch ships plying between France and her colonies on the ground that they were virtually French ships.” ‘The Doctrine of Continuous Voyages’ [1916] St. Louis L. Rev. 259.

In an attempt to circumvent the application of the Rule of 1756, ships owned by neutral states would make a stopover at an intermediate port and then claim that these were two distinct voyages and therefore legal.[42] In their judgements, the English courts relied upon the notorious doctrine of the continuous voyage, about which Herbert Whittaker Briggs says: "as a principle of international law the doctrine has been said to apply 'whenever an intermediate port is fraudulently interjected into a voyage which, if direct, would by the law of nations be illegal.'"[43] The doctrine was amply used during the major military conflicts of the nineteenth century – including the maritime struggle between Great Britain and Napoleon's France in the early nineteenth century and the American Civil War – and was later applied to the cases of contraband and blockade.[44] The London Declaration Concerning the Laws of Naval War – a codification of relevant customary international law signed by the then-leading sea powers on 26 February 1909, pronounced that the doctrine of continuous voyage was not a part of blockade law.[45] Despite this, states heavily relied upon this doctrine during World War I.[46]

Having sketched the historical context, it is prudent to conclude that economic restrictions played a significant role even before the twentieth century, albeit a secondary one. Traditionally, economic pressure exercised during military conflicts aimed at other objectives than present-day measures of economic coercion do. The rationale that underlies the distinction between these objectives has been astutely captured by Margaret Doxey: "In conditions of war, the target is the enemy; the objective is to hasten its defeat, to reduce or eliminate its capacity to wage war, and to undermine morale. Humanitarian considerations may play some part, but destruction of life and property are priorities of war. When economic measures are used as sanctions, the objective should be to deter or dissuade states from pursuing policies which do not conform to accepted norms of international conduct. Compliance is considered to be in the general interest, and sanctions are penalties which relate specifically to acts which the international body condemns."[47]

42 ibid.

43 Herbert Whittaker Briggs, *The Doctrine of Continuous Voyage* (Johns Hopkins Press, 1926) 11.

44 ibid.

45 ibid.

46 ibid.

47 Doxey (n 31) 9.

1.2 *Economic Sanctions in the Covenant of the League of Nations and Their Application in the Interwar Period*

The beginning of World War I sparked a debate about the role of international law and the legal means used to promote peaceful coexistence between the nations. With the outbreak of the war in 1914, US political elites laid the foundations of the debate on the transformation of international law and its institutions.[48] Presidents Taft, Wilson and Roosevelt, along with Elihu Root, were the most influential contemporary intellectuals involved in the debate.[49] From 1914 to 1917, the debate revolved around the idea of developing an international legal code along with a judicial mechanism to settle future interstate disputes.[50] The newly established organisations to promote international peace, such as the League to Enforce Peace[51] and the League of Free Nations Association,[52] supported the proposal to intertwine international law and enforcement. This suggestion reveals the vision of the post-war world shared by leading US intellectuals, which Stephen Wertheim describes as follows: "[the] international realm was destined to transform from anarchy to community."[53] Despite harbouring transformative ambitions, neither of the scholars suggested transcending a voluntarist notion of international enforcement.[54]

President Wilson truly believed that economic pressure was a viable alternative to the use of force. As a prophet of economic coercion, Wilson assumed that: "the boycott is what is substituted for war."[55] Wilson described economic

48 For a detailed analysis, see Stephen Wertheim, 'The League That Wasn't: American Designs for a Legalist-Sanctionist League of Nations and the Intellectual Origins of International Organization, 1914–1920' (2011) 35 Diplomatic History 797.

49 ibid.

50 ibid.

51 Hamilton Holt, the editor of the *Independent*, talking about the establishment of the League to Enforce Peace, asserted: "The idea of the League to Enforce Peace, perhaps the one constructive idea that has been born out of this war's universal destruction, was first given to the world at Independence Hall, Philadelphia, on June 17, 1915, on the very spot where the United States of America was born. It may be that the little group of men who met there on that hot June day started a movement that will eventually lead to the united nations, just as their forefathers in the same place started a movement which led to the formation of the United States." Hamilton Holt, 'The League to Enforce Peace' (1917) 7 Proceedings of the Academy of Political Science in the City of New York 65.

52 The Association was reconstituted as the Foreign Policy Association in 1923. 'Foreign Policy Association' <https://www.fpa.org/features/index.cfm?act=feature&announcement_id=337&show_sidebar=0>.

53 Wertheim (n 48) 799.

54 Wertheim (n 48).

55 Woodrow Wilson and Hamilton Foley, *Woodrow Wilson's Case for the League of Nations* (Princeton University Press; Humphrey Milford/Oxford University Press 1923) 72.

sanctions as a "peaceful, silent, deadly remedy" and anticipating their efficiency called them a "hand upon the throat of the offending nation."[56]

The British elite favoured the idea of an institution authorised to resolve interstate disputes and to prevent military confrontations.[57] Diverse proposals were made about how to achieve this, ranging from the suggestion to establish a world federation to a proposal of introducing an international legislature.[58] The proposals drafted by the Fabian Society and the Bryce Group were among the most influential ones, both of which included economic sanctions as an enforcement instrument.[59]

Later, David Hunter Miller, a US lawyer actively involved in the drafting of the Covenant of the League of Nations, when discussing the early drafts of the Covenant, highlighted the contribution made by British intellectuals.[60] Miller praised the draft prepared by the Lord Phillimore's Committee.[61] It stipulated that if any state violates the peace, other states should either provide military and naval force or, as an alternative, impose financial and economic restrictions.[62] Other nations were also involved in those debates and their views were aligned with the ones expressed by the United States or the United Kingdom.[63]

The effectiveness of economic warfare during World War I encouraged statesmen to put significant faith in such measures as potential mechanisms for enforcing the rules of a new world order. In his book *After the Great War: Economic Warfare and the Promise of Peace in Paris 1919*, Phillip Dehne argues that the most significant success of the Paris Peace Conference concerned economic warfare.[64] Dehne contends that the successful use of measures of economic warfare in the course of the war informed the negotiations of the relevant provisions for the lasting peace: "These economic lessons of the Great War were then embedded in the League of Nations, with the hope

56 ibid 71.

57 Henry R Winkler, 'The Development of the League of Nations Idea in Great Britain, 1914–1919' (1948) 20 The Journal of Modern History 95.

58 ibid.

59 ibid.

60 David Hunter Miller and Nicholas Murray Butler, *The Drafting of the Covenant* (G P Putnam's sons 1928).

61 ibid.

62 ibid 6.

63 Margaret Mack Chandler, 'The Interpretation and Effect of Article 16 of the Covenant of the League of Nations. Dissertation University of Chicago' (1936) 13–14.

64 Phillip A Dehne, *After the Great War: Economic Warfare and the Promise of Peace in Paris 1919* (Bloomsbury Academic 2019) 2.

that the threat of facing universal economic sanctions would lead countries to reconsider before launching the war."[65]

Early discussions of the text of the Covenant of the League of Nations and the role attributed to economic sanctions revealed the diversity of opposing views.[66] Although the debate was premised on the assumption that "the primary means of coercion should be economic and that armed force should be used only as a secondary resort,"[67] there existed strong opposition to coercive economic measures, mainly due to their negative impact on civilian populations.[68]

The idea of relying upon economic coercion to promote peaceful coexistence between the nations was reflected in Article 16 of the Covenant of the League of Nations. Article 16 entitled members of the League to impose economic sanctions.[69] Yet this entitlement was not without constraints: only a member of the League could be subjected to such measures and only if the member in question resorted to war.[70] Interpretative resolutions adopted in 1921 further narrowed down the instances in which Article 16 could be invoked.[71] Moreover, the necessary procedural steps preceding the imposition of such coercive economic measures remained undefined.[72]

Even after the Covenant acknowledged the legality of economic sanctions, their legal nature remained unsettled. More specifically, the issue that remained unresolved was whether economic sanctions constituted war measures or not. In an article published in 1931, Anton Bertram poses the following question: are economic sanctions an instrument of war or an instrument of peaceful pressure?[73] In his view, even the drafters of the Covenant had divergent opinions on the matter: President Wilson was convinced that economic sanctions are "something more tremendous than war" and Lord Robert Cecil

65 ibid 3.

66 Chandler (n 63) 7–8.

67 ibid 8. In a similar vein, Phillip Dehne emphasises that the drafters of the Covenant of the League of Nations intended economic coercion to be independent of the use of force: "Economic blockade might work not just as an adjunct to military conflict but also as a decisive coercive tool on its own." Dehne (n 64) 7.

68 Chandler (n 63) 8–9.

69 Article 16 League of Nations, Covenant of the League of Nations, 28 April 1919.

70 Article 16 ibid.

71 "[I]t was no longer a question of automatic response to a breach of the Covenant; each member was henceforth to decide for itself whether a breach of the Covenant had been committed." Doxey (n 31) 43–44.

72 Chandler (n 63).

73 Anton Bertram, 'The Economic Weapon as a Form of Peaceful Pressure' (1931) 17 Transactions of the Grotius Society 139, 140.

argued that "blockade was a war measure."[74] Yet, the subsequent work of the International Blockade Committee confirmed that economic sanctions were considered "a form of 'peaceful pressure.'"[75]

Although the interwar period witnessed numerous instances of confrontation among the members of the League, Article 16 was not invoked as often as one may expect. Discussing the League's practice in applying Article 16, Margaret Mack Chandler concluded: "It is to be expected that the victim will ask, in more or less open terms, for the application of Article 16 and that its fellow-members will apparently be struck deaf whenever such a request is made. In general, they do not even try to explain why they believe it is inappropriate or impossible to apply Article 16."[76]

The economic and financial sanctions prescribed by Article 16 were imposed for the first time during the Italian-Ethiopian conflict.[77] Describing these sanctions, Doxey acknowledges: "this was not the severance of communication and intercourse laid down in Article 16 of the Covenant, but a much more limited programme of denial."[78] It is noteworthy that the members of the League were allowed to deviate from even such a half-hearted programme of economic deprivation.[79]

In sum, the economic sanctions prescribed by the Covenant were framed as a part of a broader effort to promote the peaceful coexistence between nations, yet they crumbled under the weight of the states' parochial interests. Indeed, the economic sanctions imposed by the League of Nations were ineffective at reaching their goals.[80] Notwithstanding these deficiencies, the Covenant and the subsequent practice acknowledged economic coercion as a policy option distinct from military force.[81] The Covenant of the League of Nations

74 ibid 146.

75 ibid 150.

76 Chandler (n 63) 88.

77 "Italy had invaded Ethiopia, in violation of her obligations under the Covenant and other international treaties, and was subjected to economic sanctions by the great majority of League members." Doxey (n 31) 45.

78 ibid 48.

79 Chandler (n 63) 102.

80 Alexander (n 19) 23; Doxey (n 31) 42–55; Phillip Dehne concludes: "In the cases of the Italian invasion of Ethiopia and the Japanese occupation of Manchuria, the League provided incapable of forcing recalcitrant members to do the League's bidding and thus was fundamentally unable to enforce international law as embodied in the League Covenant." Dehne (n 64) 6.

81 "Since 1919, in many cases, these sanctions have been entirely economic, with no real military component, and no real expectation that they would lead to military action." Dehne (n 64) 7.

rebranded economic sanctions: subsequently, they were no longer considered a part of a military strategy.

1.3 *Economic Sanctions after World War II*

With the outbreak of World War II, states started to employ various economic measures to undermine the economic strength of the belligerents. These measures included the prohibition on the re-export of certain goods to adversary states, the blacklisting of individuals and entities from neutral states involved in trade with the enemy and the coordination of sanctioning efforts between the British and the US governments.[82] These measures of economic deprivation imposed significant economic pressure on the belligerents. For example, the United States imposed various sanctions on Japan, which – according to the then-Japanese ambassador to the United States – had a significant detrimental effect.[83]

In the aftermath of World War II, states were driven by the idea of preventing the devastation caused by military conflicts, leading them to introduce rules governing the use of force.[84] The UN Charter thus limited the circumstances under which states may legitimately refer to military coercion.[85] The implications have been far-reaching. As Elizabeth Zoller concludes: "the legal ban on physical coercion meant that states had to turn to milder forms of coercion."[86]

Since its inception, the Security Council has been entrusted with the function of maintaining international peace and security.[87] In line with this mandate, Article 41 of the UN Charter confers on it the following special rights: "The Security Council may decide what measures not involving the use of armed force are to be employed to give effect to its decisions, and it may call upon the Members of the United Nations to apply such measures. These may include complete or partial interruption of economic relations and of rail, sea, air, postal, telegraphic, radio, and other means of communication, and the severance of diplomatic relations." The final text contains an illustrative list of the

82 For a detailed discussion, see Alexander (n 19) 14–20.

83 Juan C Zarate, *Treasury's War: The Unleashing of a New Era of Financial Warfare* (Public Affairs 2013) 5.

84 Article 2(4) Charter of the United Nations (adopted 26 June 1945, entered into force 24 October 1945) UNTS 1 XVI (UN Charter).

85 Article 51 ibid.

86 Elisabeth Zoller, *Peacetime Unilateral Remedies: An Analysis of Countermeasures* (Transnational Publishers 1984) 4–5.

87 Article 24 UN Charter.

possible coercive measures, and the wording is the result of the compromise reached between the negotiating parties.[88]

Although the UN Charter authorises the Security Council to impose compulsory economic sanctions, it does not address the issue of violations of international law that do not pose a threat to international peace and security. In light of this, Elizabeth Zoller observes: "It is therefore no exaggeration to say that nothing has ever been collectively decided about the casual violation [meaning a violation that does not threaten international peace and security] of law in peacetime. Apart from excluding the use of force, the system still fails to provide a clear answer as to what a state can actually do against an offending state."[89] This statement was made in a book published in 1984, yet it is still pertinent. While the Draft articles partly resolve this issue, it is worth emphasising that they are ambiguous with respect to the countermeasures imposed by non-injured states to protect community values.[90]

The period between 1945 and 1990 was characterised by embargoes and export controls imposed by the Western states against the Soviet-bloc countries and vice versa, although some economic restrictions were gradually lifted.[91] The United States measures against the Dominican Republic (1960–1962) and Cuba (from 1960) exemplify such attempts at coercion.[92]

On a number of occasions, the Soviet Union targeted other communist states whose interests were less aligned with those of the Soviet Union than the latter expected. For example, the Soviet-sponsored boycotts of Yugoslavia (1948–1955) and Albania (1961–1965),[93] as well as restrictions imposed on

88 "Long discussions arose over the question as to whether a conclusive catalogue of non-military sanctions should be included in the Charter. The Soviet Union advocated such a catalogue, and it had already drawn up a detailed list of graduated, increasingly severe reactions. In contrast, the United States and Great Britain regarded this as an inappropriate limitation on the authority of the SC [Security Council]. Agreement was finally reached on a compromise formula with an illustrative, non-exhaustive enumeration." Bruno Simma and Nikolai Wessendorf (eds.), *The Charter of the United Nations: A Commentary* (3rd ed., Oxford University Press 2012) 1307.

89 Zoller (n 86) xv.

90 Regarding the right of non-injured states to impose countermeasures, the commentary to the Draft articles makes the following stipulation: "Occasions have arisen in practice of countermeasures being taken by other States, in particular those identified in Article 48, where no State is injured or else on behalf of and at the request of an injured State. Such cases are controversial and the practice is embryonic." ILC, 'Draft Articles on Responsibility of States for Internationally Wrongful Acts, (2001), UN Doc. A/56/10' 129.

91 Doxey (n 31) 16–18.

92 Anna P Schreiber, 'Economic Coercion as an Instrument of Foreign Policy: U.S. Economic Measures Against Cuba and the Dominican Republic' (1973) 25 World Politics 387.

93 Doxey (n 31) 29–33.

China in the period 1960–1970,[94] bear witness to this. Another example of such politically tainted coercive diplomacy is the Arab states' oil embargo against Israel and its allies, which was introduced in 1973.[95]

Starting from the 1970s, the United States framed sanctions as a part of a broader effort to promote human rights abroad. In 1974, the United States enacted a provision in federal law, which became known as the Jackson-Vanik amendment.[96] This amendment prescribed the suspension of trade relations with the non-market economies, mainly the communist bloc states, if they restricted free emigration and failed to respect other human rights.[97] Human rights continued to play a significant role in economic aid and military assistance programmes provided by the United States. States demonstrating a consistent pattern of human rights violations were excluded from participation in such programmes.[98] In particular, a number of events in Latin America triggered the elimination of proposed military aid to Argentina, Brazil, El Salvador, Guatemala, Nicaragua and Paraguay in 1977.[99] Moreover, economic aid programmes, including loan decisions, were also subject to compliance with basic human rights obligations.[100]

These human rights considerations paved the way for the United States' economic sanctions against Idi Amin's brutal regime in Uganda in the late 1970s. Despite the hesitancy of President Jimmy Carter's administration to impose economic sanctions on Amin's regime, Congress proceeded with a vote in favour of a trade embargo.[101] Ralph Nurnberger notes that: "October 10, 1978, embargo of United States' trade with Uganda established new precedents in America's commitment to human rights."[102]

In the 1970s–1980s, states imposed economic sanctions in response to various political crises. For example, Turkey was sanctioned for its invasion of

94 "The open conflict of mid-1960, climaxed by the U.S.S.R.'s withdrawal of technical aid, prompted China to seek new trading partners in the early 1960's; P.R.C. trade with the U.S.S.R. declined from $1.7 billion in 1960 to only $450 million in 1964." Liang-Shing Fan, 'The Economy and Foreign Trade of China' (1973) 38 Law and Contemporary Problems 249, 256.

95 Doxey (n 31) 20–28.

96 Trade Act of 1974, Public Law 93–618, January 3, 1975, 88 Stat. Title IV, Section 402.

97 ibid Section 402.

98 Lisa L Martin, *Coercive Cooperation: Explaining Multilateral Economic Sanctions* (Princeton University Press 1992) 101–111.

99 ibid 110.

100 ibid 101–111.

101 Ralph D Nurnberger, 'The United States and Idi Amin: Congress to the Rescue' (1982) 25 African Studies Review 49.

102 ibid 49.

northern Cyprus in 1974.[103] The Iran hostage crisis of 1979–1981 sowed the seeds of a longstanding confrontation between Iran and the United States, which also resulted in various economic sanctions against Iran.[104] A similar fate had befallen Pakistan for its nuclear policy and the violations of non-proliferation agreements.[105] In response to the Soviet Union's invasion of Afghanistan, the United States imposed a grain embargo,[106] which was harshly criticised for its ineffectiveness and its detrimental effect on the US farmers.[107] Another oft-quoted example are the restrictive measures invoked in the midst of the Falklands crisis.[108] As one of the parties directly involved in the conflict over the Falkland Islands, the United Kingdom not only imposed severe economic and financial restrictions on Argentina, but also convinced other members of the European Economic Community to follow suit.[109]

The imposition of martial law in Poland in 1981, an act of the communist government aimed at suppressing the opposition, and "the Soviet Union's heavy and direct responsibility for the repression in Poland" triggered a wave of US economic sanctions against both states.[110] As a part of those sanctions, the United States embargoed US products and technology for oil and gas transmission equipment, which significantly undermined the Soviet Union's plans to construct the Trans-Siberian Pipeline that would enable the export

103 The United States imposed an arms embargo following the Turkish occupation of Northern Cyprus in 1974. For more, see Richard C Campany, 'U.S.-Turkish Relations in the Arms Embargo Period 1974–1980' (ProQuest Dissertations Publishing 1984).

104 "Within ten days of the US Embassy being seized, the US had embargoed Iranian oil and placed an unprecedented financial block on billions of Iran's dollar assets. The US also began to pressure its European allies, who were amongst Iran's largest trading partners, to cooperate in sanctioning Iran. Despite a Soviet veto of UN sanctions, the European Economic Community (EEC) states eventually acquiesced in late April 1980, two weeks after the US applied a total trade embargo and suspended diplomatic relations with Iran." Christian Emery, 'The Transatlantic and Cold War Dynamics of Iran Sanctions, 1979–80' (2010) 10 Cold War History 371, 372.

105 Hufbauer and others (n 28) Case 79–2.

106 "Grain was an obvious target for disruption, not only because of poor harvests and the increased importance of imported grain to the Soviet Union but also because grain dominated the West's economic intercourse with the USSR." Kim Richard Nossal, 'Knowing When to Fold: Western Sanctions against the USSR 1980–1983' (1988) 44 International Journal 698, 703–704.

107 Robert L Paarlberg, 'Lessons on the Grain Embargo' (1980) 59 Foreign Affairs 144.

108 Martin (n 98) 131–153.

109 ibid 132–135.

110 Gary H Perlow, 'Taking Peacetime Trade Sanctions to the Limit: The Soviet Pipeline Embargo' (1983) 15 Case Western Reserve Journal of International Law 253.

of the Soviet gas to the Central and Western European states.[111] In June 1982, a dramatic expansion of the sanctions followed: the export prohibition was extended to foreign subsidiaries of US companies, as well as to equipment manufactured abroad under a license received from the US companies.[112] The European states sharply criticised these unilateral sanctions and questioned their legality.[113] After successful negotiations and what President Reagan announced as a "substantial agreement" with the Europeans, the sanctions were lifted in November 1982.[114]

The United States trade embargo against Nicaragua imposed by then-President Ronald Reagan prepared the terrain for exploring the legal status of this type of economic restriction.[115] Indeed, Nicaragua initiated parallel proceedings before both the ICJ and the GATT 1947 panel challenging the legality of the embargo. Those proceedings raised vexed legal questions such as: can economic coercion violate the principle of non-intervention? When can economic sanctions be justified as measures necessary for the protection of national security interests? The ICJ discussed these issues and concluded that while, in this particular instance, the trade embargo did not violate the principle of non-intervention, it did violate obligations under the bilateral trade agreement and this violation was not justified on national security grounds.[116] The GATT panel was prevented by its terms of reference from presenting findings on the possibility of justifying such measures under the GATT 1947 national security clause,[117] and its report was not even adopted.[118]

During the same period – between 1945 and 1990 – the Security Council authorised economic sanctions only in two cases: against Rhodesia in 1966 and South Africa in 1977.

111 ibid.

112 ibid 255–256.

113 "European indignation exploded. In their view, legitimate American opposition to the pipeline project had now become outright interference in their sovereign affairs. Moreover, the potential economic cost being imposed by the Americans was significant, particularly in the midst of a severe recession." ibid 255.

114 ibid 257.

115 President of the United States of America. Executive Order No. 12,513, 50 Fed. Reg. 18,629 (May 1, 1985). Prohibiting Trade and Certain Other Transactions Involving Nicaragua.

116 *Military and Paramilitary Activities in and against Nicaragua (Nicaragua v. United States of America) Merits, Judgment ICJ Reports 1986, p 14* 148.

117 *United States – Trade measures affecting Nicaragua, Report by the Panel (unadopted), Doc L/6053, 13 October 1986.*

118 ibid.

1.3.1 UN Sanctions against Rhodesia

On 11 November 1965, the Rhodesian prime minister Ian Smith announced the Unilateral Declaration of Independence. This decision was preceded by several attempts to convince the British government to grant independence to its internally self-governing colony.[119] Yet the Rhodesian claims were denied based on the demand of guaranteeing access to the government for the country's black majority.[120]

The Security Council kept the question of Southern Rhodesia on its agenda even before the unilateral declaration was proclaimed and insisted on a constitutional transition to independence.[121] On 12 November 1965, the Security Council condemned the Unilateral Declaration of Independence and called upon all UN Member States to not recognise the "illegal, racist minority regime in Southern Rhodesia."[122] The condemnation was repeated one week later in the subsequent resolution, which also called upon all states "to do their utmost in order to break all economic relations with Southern Rhodesia, including an embargo on oil and petroleum products."[123] The Security Council Resolution adopted in April 1966 determined that the illegal regime in Southern Rhodesia constituted "a threat to the peace" and reinforced its prohibition on supplying oil to Southern Rhodesia, by demanding cooperation from Portugal, which was a known ally of the new Rhodesian government.[124] Furthermore, the Security Council encouraged other UN Members to enforce the oil embargo and to provide special enforcement rights to the United Kingdom.[125]

Opinions on the economic sanctions against Rhodesia, published shortly after their imposition, reveal a certain scepticism about their usefulness. In March 1966, Dennis Austin pointed out the weak points that could undermine sanctioning efforts against Rhodesia.[126] In his view, sanctions ought not to be divorced from military force. Moreover, sanctioning efforts can bring results only in the long term and if they are universally enforced.[127] Austin also voiced concerns about the detrimental effect of sanctions on the civilian

119 Douglas G Anglin, 'Unilateral Independence in Southern Rhodesia' (1964) 19 International Journal 551.

120 ibid.

121 UNSC Res 202 (6 May 1965) UN Doc S/RES/202.

122 UNSC Res 216 (12 November 1965) UN Doc S/RES/216.

123 UNSC Res 217 (20 November 1965) UN Doc S/RES/217.

124 UNSC Res 221 (9 April 1966) UN Doc S/RES/221.

125 ibid.

126 Dennis Austin, 'Sanctions and Rhodesia' (1966) 22 World Today 106.

127 ibid.

population and their impact on the economies of neighbouring countries.[128] In 1967, it became obvious that sanctions were not an expeditious means of realizing the expected political outcomes, even though economic deprivation was observed.[129] Their efficacy was partly undermined by South Africa and Portugal, which continued to cooperate economically with Rhodesia.[130] Notwithstanding the long-lasting debate on the efficacy and detrimental effects of sanctions, they were lifted only after the agreement with the United Kingdom was reached in 1979.[131]

1.3.2 UN Sanctions against South Africa

The apartheid regime was on the Security Council's agenda long before the mandatory sanctions were authorised. The Security Council called upon the government of South Africa "to abandon its policies of apartheid and racial discrimination."[132] In August 1963, a voluntary arms embargo was imposed.[133] Eventually, a mandatory arms embargo was introduced in November 1977.[134] Anticipating the Security Council's next move, policies to establish domestic self-sufficiency were promoted by the South African government.[135] For example, in order to counteract the negative consequences of the arms embargoes the Armaments Productions Board and the Armaments Development and Production Corporation were established in 1964 and 1976, respectively.[136]

In 1985, the Security Council urged the UN Member States to adopt a wide range of economic measures against South Africa.[137] In particular, the Resolution of the Security Council reads as follows: "the Security Council urges States Members of the United Nations to adopt measures against South Africa, such as the following: (a) Suspension of all new investment in South Africa; (b) Prohibition of the sale of krugerrands and all other coins minted in South Africa; (c) Restrictions on sports and cultural relations; (d) Suspension of guaranteed export loans; (e) Prohibition of all new contracts in the nuclear field;

128 ibid.

129 Colin Harris, 'Note of the Month. Political and Economic Effects of Sanctions on Rhodesia.' (1967) 23 The World Today 1.

130 Doxey (n 31) 73–79.

131 UNSC Res 460 (21 December 1979) UN Doc S/RES/460.

132 UNSC Res 134 (1 April 1960) UN Doc S/RES/134.

133 UNSC Res 181 (7 August 1963) UN Doc S/RES/181.

134 UNSC Res 418 (4 November 1977) UN Doc S/RES/418.

135 Lee Jones, *Societies under Siege: Exploring How International Economic Sanctions (Do Not) Work* (First edition, Oxford University Press 2015) 69.

136 ibid.

137 UNSC Res 569 (26 July 1985) UN Doc S/RES/569.

(f) Prohibition of all sales of computer equipment that may be used by the South African army and police."[138]

The literature on the economic sanctions against South Africa suggests that the majority of scholars consider them to have been effective.[139] In this regard, a distinguished human rights activist Aryeh Neier observes: "Acknowledgment of the role of sanctions in helping to end apartheid is not universal, but it is widespread."[140]

1.4 *The "Sanctions Decade" and the Quest for "Smart" Sanctions*

The end of the Cold War coincided with or, as some scholars argue, instigated,[141] the phenomenon known as the "sanctions decade." The term "sanctions decade" denotes the increased use of economic sanctions since the end of the Cold War, which was accompanied by an expansion of the purposes for which sanctions were employed.[142]

Indeed, the overwhelming majority of UN sanctions have been authorised since 1990.[143] Notwithstanding these developments, many attempts to impose sanctions were sacrificed at the altar of political interests. As Sarabeth Egle accurately acknowledges: "The Security Council has therefore been criticized as going too far in defining a threat to international security in some sanctions (e.g. the period following the invasion of Kuwait by Iraq), and not doing enough in other cases (e.g. during the Bosnia/Kosovo crisis)."[144]

The Security Council imposed comprehensive economic sanctions on a number of occasions – against Iraq,[145] the Federal Republic of Yugoslavia[146] and Haiti.[147] While the effectiveness of these sanctions has not been determined

138 ibid.

139 Jones (n 135) 52–53.

140 Aryeh Neier, 'Sanctions and Human Rights' (2015) 82:4 Social research 875, 878.

141 Jones (n 135) 2–3.

142 David Cortright, George A Lopez and Richard W Conroy, *The Sanctions Decade: Assessing UN Strategies in the 1990s* (L Rienner 2000) 2.

143 Kimberly Ann Elliott, 'Assessing UN Sanctions after the Cold War: New and Evolving Standards of Measurement (UN Sanctions: New Dilemmas and Unintended Consequences)' (2009) 65 International Journal 85, 90.

144 Sarabeth Egle, 'The Learning Curve of Sanctions – Have Three Decades of Sanctions Reform Taught Us Anything Chester James Taylor Award 2011' (2010) 19 Currents – International Trade Law Journal 34.

145 UNSC Res 661 (6 August 1990) UN Doc S/RES/661; UNSC Res 665 (25 August 1990) UN Doc S/RES/665; UNSC Res 666 (13 September 1990) UN Doc S/RES/666; UNSC Res 670 (25 September 1990) UN Doc S/RES/670; UNSC Res 700 (17 June 1991) UN Doc S/RES/700.

146 UNSC Res 757 (30 May 1992) UN Doc S/RES/757.

147 UNSC Res 917 (6 May 1994) UN Doc S/RES/917.

with great precision, their detrimental effect on the civilian population of the targeted states became evident by the mid-1990s.[148] For example, the comprehensive sanctions against Iraq were debated at length within the international community. Their dreadful aftermath is well captured by the following observation: "No one knows with any precision how many Iraqi civilians have died as a result, but various agencies of the United Nations, which oversees the sanctions, have estimated that they have contributed to hundreds of thousands of deaths."[149]

Furthermore, comprehensive economic sanctions were criticised for creating opportunities for non-democratic regimes to benefit from them.[150] Since the majority of economic sanctions – one study suggests more than 78% in the past three decades[151] – are imposed against non-democratic states, the possibility that a targeted country's elite benefits from them has undermined their legitimacy even further. Another consideration behind the shift towards targeted sanctions is a decrease in the domestic costs incurred by the sanctioning states.

To curtail the negative impact of comprehensive sanctions on civilians, humanitarian exemptions were introduced as a partial solution. However, the public release of Paul Volcker's reports on "The Management of the United Nations Oil for Food Programme" was a turning point in the history of comprehensive sanctions and the celebrated humanitarian exemptions.[152] Illusions

148 "By the mid-1990[s], it was no longer enough for sanctions to achieve foreign policy goals, they had to do so without excessive harm to civilians in the target country, or third countries, as in Yugoslavia." Elliott (n 143) 92.

149 John Mueller and Karl Mueller, 'Sanctions of Mass Destruction' (1999) 78 Foreign Affairs 43.

150 "Comprehensive sanctions created the opportunity for target governments to allocate rent-seeking opportunities to those supporters." Daniel W Drezner, 'Sanctions Sometimes Smart: Targeted Sanctions in Theory and Practice' (2011) 13 International Studies Review 96.

151 Susan Hannah Allen, 'Political Institutions and Constrained Response to Economic Sanctions' (2008) 4 Foreign Policy Analysis 255, 269.

152 Paul A Volcker, Richard J Goldstone and Mark Pieth, 'Independent Inquiry Committee into the United Nations Oil-for-Food Programme. Interim Report. February 3, 2005.'; Paul A Volcker, Richard J Goldstone and Mark Pieth, 'Independent Inquiry Committee into the United Nations Oil-for-Food Programme. Second Interim Report. March 29, 2005.'; Paul A Volcker, Richard J Goldstone and Mark Pieth, 'Independent Inquiry Committee into the United Nations Oil-for-Food Programme. Third Interim Report. August 8, 2005.'; Paul A Volcker, Richard J Goldstone and Mark Pieth, 'Independent Inquiry Committee into the United Nations Oil-for-Food Programme. The Management of the United Nations Oil-For-Food Programme. September 7, 2005.'; Paul A Volcker, Richard J Goldstone and Mark Pieth, 'Independent Inquiry Committee into the United Nations Oil-for-Food Programme. Manipulation of the Oil-For-Food Programme by the Iraqi Regime. October 27, 2005.'

about humanitarian exemptions were dispelled: they came under fire for reported mismanagement and serious allegations of corruption inside the UN system.[153]

After the legitimacy of comprehensive economic sanctions had been undermined, "smart" or "targeted" sanctions – sanctions directed against individuals, groups or entities – loomed on the horizon. Ironically, when writing about economic sanctions in 1967, Johan Galtung was only able to imagine that economic sanctions might be imposed on individuals: "nevertheless, let us imagine for a moment that international society was structured in such a way that sanctions could be *aimed at responsible individuals*."[154]

Smart or targeted sanctions differ from comprehensive sanctions in two respects – they penalise political or economic elites and protect vulnerable social groups.[155] As Daniel Drezner notes, targeted economic sanctions have gained substantial support from policymakers, as well as from scholars.[156]

Since a simple distinction between comprehensive and targeted sanctions does not always capture the whole gamut of such measures, Thomas Biersteker and others have introduced a classification of sanctions according to their degree of discrimination.[157] These categories are:[158]

- Comprehensive sanctions (e.g. comprehensive trade embargo)
- Relatively non-discriminating measures (sanctions affecting core economic sectors, e.g. the oil sector)
- Moderately discriminating measures (sanctions that target either key export commodities or several large companies, which are crucial for a state's economy)

153 Ewen MacAskill, 'Oil-for-Food Report Condemns "corrupt" UN' *The Guardian* (7 September 2005) <https://www.theguardian.com/world/2005/sep/07/iraq.ewenmacaskill>; Carola Hoyos, 'Big Oil Groups Implicated in Oil-for-Food Scandal' (28 October 2005) <https://www.ft.com/content/1f250dd4-47de-11da-a949-00000e2511c8>; 'Opinion | The Oil-for-Food Failures' *The New York Times* (8 September 2005) <https://www.nytimes.com/2005/09/08/opinion/the-oilforfood-failures.html>.

154 Johan Galtung, 'On the Effects of International Economic Sanctions: With Examples from the Case of Rhodesia' (1967) 19 World Politics 378, 415.

155 Arne Tostensen and Beate Bull, 'Are Smart Sanctions Feasible?' (2002) 54 World Politics 373, 373–374.

156 Drezner, 'Sanctions Sometimes Smart' (n 150).

157 Thomas J Biersteker and others, *Thinking about United Nations Targeted Sanctions* §1 in Thomas Biersteker, Sue E Eckert, and Marcos Tourinho (eds.), *Targeted Sanctions: The Impacts and Effectiveness of United Nations Action*, (Cambridge University Press 2016), 27.

158 ibid.

- Relatively discriminating measures (sanctions that target specific sectors of government or non-government targets, e.g. arms embargo, restrictions on trade in luxury goods)
- Most targeted measures (sanctions against individuals and entities, e.g. asset freezes)

A number of international conferences have been organised to discuss targeted sanctions. Two conferences dedicated to targeted financial sanctions, collectively known as the "Interlaken Process," were held in Switzerland in 1998 and 1999.[159] The next series in the international debate, the "Bonn-Berlin Process," took place in Germany in 1999 and 2000. These meetings were devoted to targeted arms embargoes and travel restrictions.[160] The last international meetings, "Stockholm Process," focused on the implementation and monitoring of targeted sanctions.[161]

1.5 *The War against Terrorism and the UN Security Council's Targeted Sanctions*

In the post-9/11 era, the Security Council was actively involved in the war against terrorism, with its participation culminating in the UN sanctions targeting individuals for their alleged involvement in terrorist networks. The targeted individuals were not only political or governing elites, but also individuals whose involvement in terrorist activities, including financing of terrorism, was questionable.

The Security Council sanctions directed against individuals faced a barrage of stinging criticism for their inconsistency with minimum human rights standards.[162] Their legitimacy has been questioned by the national and regional

159 As a part of the "Interlaken Process," the Watson Institute for International Studies prepared a handbook on the targeted sanctions. *Targeted Financial Sanctions: A Manual for Design and Implementation: Contributions from the Interlaken Process* (Thomas J Watson Jr Institute for International Studies 2001).

160 Michael Brzoska, 'Design and Implementation of Arms Embargoes and Travel and Aviation Related Sanctions' (BICC Publications 2001) <https://www.bicc.de/publications/publicationpage/publication/design-and-implementation-of-arms-embargoes-and-travel-and-aviation-related-sanctions-results-of-t/>.

161 The Final Report puts forward recommendations on strengthening the role of the UN in implementing targeted sanctions, recommendations on improving the UN Member States' capacity to implement targeted sanctions, as well as measures to improve accuracy and manage sanctions evasion. Peter Wallensteen and others (eds.), *Making Targeted Sanctions Effective: Guidelines for the Implementation of UN Policy Options,* (Uppsala University, Department of Peace and Conflict Research 2003).

162 Devika Hovell, 'Due Process in the United Nations' (2016) 110 The American Journal of International Law 1; Marko Milanovic, 'Norm Conflict in International Law: Whither

judicial and quasi-judicial bodies, UN Member States and legal scholars based on the lack of procedural due process rights guaranteed to the targeted individuals.[163] Paradoxically, human rights concerns triggered the shift towards targeted sanctions, but targeted measures were subsequently called into question for the lack of procedural fairness in the related decision-making.[164]

Since the UN's targeted sanctions came under fire for their inconsistency with human rights, the United Nations Office of Legal Affairs commissioned a study to explore whether due process rights were being violated by contemporary sanctions-authorisation procedures.[165] Bardo Fassbender was charged with preparing the study. In the meantime, the Commission on Human Rights appointed a special rapporteur on the promotion and protection of human rights and fundamental freedoms while countering terrorism.[166] The mandate of the special rapporteur, which includes *inter alia* fact-finding country visits and annual reports to the Human Rights Council and General Assembly, has been extended several times, with the last extension running until March 2022.[167]

Human Rights?' (2009) 20 Duke Journal of Comparative & International Law 69; Daniel Halberstam and Eric Stein, 'The United Nations, the European Union, and the King of Sweden: Economic Sanctions and Individual Rights in a Plural World Order' (2009) 46 Common Market Law Review 13.

163 The most discussed cases are: *Case T-306/01 Ahmed Ali Yusuf and Al Barakaat International Foundation v. Council of the European Union and Commission of the European Communities* [2005] *European Court Reports 2005 II-03533 ECLI identifier: ECLI:EU:T:2005:331; Case T-315/01 Yassin Abdullah Kadi v. Council of the European Union and Commission of the European Communities* [2005] *European Court Reports 2005 II-03649 ECLI identifier: ECLI:EU:T:2005:332; Joined cases C-402/05 P and C-415/05 P Yassin Abdullah Kadi and Al Barakaat International Foundation v. Council of the European Union and Commission of the European Communities* [2008] *European Court Reports 2008 I-06351 ECLI identifier: ECLI:EU:C:2008:461; Case T-253/02 Chafiq Ayadi v. Council of the European Union* [2006] *European Court Reports 2006 II-02139 ECLI identifier: ECLI:EU:T:2006:200; Case T-49/04 Faraj Hassan v. Council of the European Union and Commission of the European Communities* [2006] *European Court Reports 2006 II-00052 ECLI identifier: ECLI:EU:T:2006:201; Joined cases C-399/06 P and C-403/06 P Faraj Hassan v. Council of the European Union and European Commission (C-399/06 P) and Chafiq Ayadi v. Council of the European Union (C-403/06 P)* [2009] *European Court Reports 2009 I-11393 ECLI identifier: ECLI:EU:C:2009:748.*

164 Hovell (n 162) 8.

165 Bardo Fassbender, 'Targeted Sanctions and Due Process: The Responsibility of the UN Security Council to Ensure That Fair and Clear Procedures Are Made Available to Individuals and Entities Targeted with Sanctions under Chapter VII of the UN Charter, Study Commissioned by the United Nations Office of Legal Affairs.' (2006).

166 UNCHR Res 2005/80 (21 April 2005) UN Doc E/CN.4/RES/2005/80.

167 UNHRC Res 40/16 (8 April 2019) UN Doc A/HRC/RES/40/16.

In his study, Bardo Fassbender relied on the internationally accepted minimum standards as the benchmark for assessing compliance with due process rights. This analysis revealed the following problems:[168]

- Designated individuals were not informed before being listed and, consequently, were deprived of the right to challenge their listing
- Listed individuals were deprived of the right to request de-listing directly from the sanctions committee
- Listed individuals were not granted a hearing after a de-listing request was filed
- The absence of legal rules that would oblige the sanctions committee to approve a de-listing request if specific conditions were met

According to the report, the UN's engagement in "supranational" law-making with a direct effect on individuals ought to be blamed for these problems.[169]

Following these developments, a group of UN Member States – the Group of Like-Minded States on Targeted Sanctions, in which Switzerland has played an active role – prepared and submitted a number of proposals to establish fair and clear procedures for a more effective UN sanctions system.[170]

As a result of the constant criticism of the UN sanctions regime, the Office of the Ombudsperson was established in 2009.[171] The primary responsibility of the Ombudsperson is to review de-listing requests submitted by designated individuals.[172] It appears, though, that not all designated individuals are entitled to file de-listing requests before the Ombudsperson: this mechanism was developed only for individuals listed under the ISIL (Da'esh) and Al-Qaida sanctions regimes.[173] Individuals designated under other sanctions regimes

168 Fassbender (n 165) 4.

169 ibid 18.

170 "[...] in May of 2008, the representatives of Denmark, Germany, Liechtenstein, the Netherlands, Sweden, and Switzerland wrote to the president of the security council about the idea of establishing an expert panel to assist security council sanctions committees in the consideration of delisting requests." Thomas J Biersteker, 'Targeted Sanctions and Individual Human Rights' (Winter 2009–10) 65(1) International Journal 99, 114. The Group of Like-Minded States on Targeted Sanctions has been taking an active part in preparing new proposals for further improvements of the UN sanctions system. For example, UNSC Enclosure (9 November 2012) Improving fair and clear procedures for a more effective United Nations sanctions system. UN Doc A/67/557, S/2012/805 https://www.un.org/ga/search/view_doc.asp?symbol=A/67/557.

171 UNSC Res 1904 (17 December 2009) UN Doc S/RES/1904.

172 ibid.

173 ibid.

can file their de-listing requests with the focal point that was specifically established for this purpose.[174]

1.6 *The Increased Use of Unilateral Economic Sanctions and a New Geo-economic World Order*

The increased deployment of unilateral economic sanctions deserves attention as well. In the last decades, states have made ample use of unilateral economic sanctions.[175] It follows that in the decentralised system of public international law enforcement, unilateral measures play a significant role.[176] To this end, states even introduce laws and regulations to respond to violations of public international law.[177]

The following examples illustrate the use of economic sanctions for international law enforcement:

The Russian annexation of part of Ukraine – i.e. the Crimean peninsula – and its military support of the pro-Russian separatists in the eastern part of Ukraine paved the way for the wide range of unilateral economic sanctions imposed by other states.[178] Canadian regulations justify such restrictive

---

174 UNSC Res 1730 (19 December 2006) UN Doc S/RES/1730.

175 Gabriel Felbermayr and others, 'The Global Sanctions Data Base' (4 August 2020) https://voxeu.org/article/global-sanctions-data-base.

176 Monica Hakimi, 'Unfriendly Unilateralism' (2014) 55 Harvard International Law Journal 105.

177 Have (n 24); Portela (n 24).

178 On March 17, 2014, Canada adopted the Special Economic Measures (Russia) Regulations. These regulations were amended several times, with the last update in 2019. Canadian sanctions include restrictions on the financial and energy sectors, as well as the asset freeze and dealings prohibition on designated individuals and entities. Special Economic Measures (Ukraine) Regulations. SOR/2014-60. March 17, 2014.; The United States has introduced economic sanctions based on four executive orders (EOs 13660, 13661, 13662, and 13685) that President Obama issued in 2014 and two acts establishing sanctions in response to Russia's invasion of Ukraine: the Support for the Sovereignty, Integrity, Democracy, and Economic Stability of Ukraine Act of 2014 (SSIDES; P.L. 113-95/H.R. 4152) and the Ukraine Freedom Support Act of 2014 (UFSA; P.L. 113-272/H.R. 5859). In 2017, the US sanctions were further strengthened. For more on the US sanctions, see Cory Welt and others, 'U.S. Sanctions on Russia. Congressional Research Service, Report R45415' (2020); In 2014, Australia announced and implemented an autonomous sanctions regime in relation to Russia. These autonomous sanctions include restrictions on the export or supply of goods; restrictions on the export or provision of services; restrictions on the import, purchase or transport of goods; restrictions on commercial activities; targeted financial sanctions; and travel bans. 'Autonomous Sanctions (Russia, Crimea and Sevastopol) Specification 2015 Made under Regulations 4, 5B and 5C of the Autonomous Sanctions Regulations 2011.'; In 2014, the Council of the European Union adopted Council Decision concerning restrictive measures in view of Russia's actions destabilising the

measures in virtue of "the gravity of Russia's violation of the sovereignty and territorial integrity of Ukraine."[179] The reasons for the imposition of sanctions by the United States were enumerated as follows: "The United States has imposed sanctions on Russia mainly in response to Russia's 2014 invasion of Ukraine, to reverse and deter further Russian aggression in Ukraine, and to deter Russian aggression against other countries."[180] The European Union has emphasised that its restrictive measures were taken "in response to Russia's actions destabilising the situation in Ukraine."[181]

The Russian Federation fired back with its own sanctions. These restrictive measures targeted food imports from (i.e. constituted a food embargo against) the states that introduced sanctions against the Russian Federation.[182] Furthermore, senior government officials expressed their intention to challenge the legality of unilateral economic sanctions against Russia at the WTO.[183] These official statements provoked a scholarly debate on the WTO consistency

situation in Ukraine. On the same date, the Council Regulation concerning restrictive measures in view of Russia's actions destabilising the situation in Ukraine was enacted. Both acts were amended and remain in force. Council Decision 2014/512/CFSP of 31 July 2014 concerning restrictive measures in view of Russia's actions destabilising the situation in Ukraine 2014 (OJ L) A number of countries that are not the EU Member states, but maintain strong economic relations with the EU aligned with the EU sanctions against Russia – for example, Norway and Liechtenstein. Ukraine introduced economic sanctions in alignment with the EU measures. Despite being hesitant to undermine its relations with the Russian Federation, Japan joined the sanctioning efforts as well. Maria Shagina, 'Japan's Sanctions Policy Vis-à-Vis Russia' 1; Switzerland also implemented economic sanctions against Russia. For more details, please see 'SR 946.231.176.72 Verordnung Vom 27. August 2014 Über Massnahmen Zur Vermeidung Der Umgehung Internationaler Sanktionen Im Zusammenhang Mit Der Situation in Der Ukraine' <https://www.admin.ch/opc/de/classified-compilation/20142202/index.html>.

179 Special Economic Measures (Ukraine) Regulations. SOR/2014-60. 17 March 2014.

180 Welt and others (n 178) 1.

181 Council Decision 2014/512/CFSP of 31 July 2014 concerning restrictive measures in view of Russia's actions destabilising the situation in Ukraine.

182 The Decree of the President of the Russian Federation on 6 August 2014, No. 560 'On the application of certain special economic measures to ensure the security of the Russian Federation' (Указ Президента Российской Федерации от 06.08.2014 г. No. 560 'О применении отдельных специальных экономических мер в целях обеспечения безопасности Российской Федерации'); Resolution of the Government of the Russian Federation No. 778 of 7 August 2014 'On measures concerning the implementation of the Presidential Decree as of 6 August 2014 No. 560 On the application of certain special economic measures to ensure safety of the Russian Federation.' (Постановление Правительства Российской Федерации N 778 от 7 августа 2014 года 'О мерах по реализации указа Президента Российской Федерации от 6 августа 2014 года N 560'). Later additional trade restrictions were enacted.

183 Donnan and Hille (n 5).

of these unilateral restrictions and the possible invocation of the national security clause.[184] Yet, these sanctions were not scrutinised by the WTO dispute settlement system.

Another recent development is the imposition of targeted economic sanctions against individuals and legal entities involved in serious human rights violations abroad, known as Magnitsky-style sanctions. Sergei Magnitsky, who uncovered a major corruption scheme in Russia enabling senior tax officials to steal funds from a number of private companies and illegally obtain fraudulent tax refunds, was arrested, tortured, denied adequate medical assistance and died in a pre-trial detention.[185] In 2012, the United States enacted the Sergei Magnitsky Rule of Law Accountability Act of 2012, which asserts that Sergei Magnitsky's experience "appears to be emblematic of a broader pattern of disregard for the numerous domestic and international human rights commitments of the Russian Federation and impunity for those who violate basic human rights and freedoms."[186] This act authorises the US president to identify individuals responsible for serious human rights violations committed in the Russian Federation and to impose sanctions against them, provided that these individuals have not been prosecuted appropriately for the activities in which they engaged.[187] These sanctions include travel bans, the freezing of assets and a complete prohibition on any transactions with the sanctioned individuals, as well as entities owned by them.[188]

In 2016, Congress enacted the Global Magnitsky Human Rights Accountability Act.[189] This act entitles the US president to impose sanctions

184 Neuwirth and Svetlicinii, 'The Economic Sanctions over the Ukraine Conflict and the WTO' (n 6); Neuwirth and Svetlicinii, 'The Current EU/US–Russia Conflict over Ukraine and the WTO' (n 6).

185 The European Court of Human Rights in its 2019 decision unanimously found that the Russian Federation violated Article 3 of the Convention (prohibition of torture) on account of the conditions of Magnitskiy's detention; Article 5 § 3 of the Convention (right to liberty and security); Article 3 of the Convention (prohibition of torture) on account of Magnitskiy's ill-treatment by the prison guards and the lack of an effective investigation in that regard; Article 2 of the Convention (right to life) on account of the authorities' failure to protect Magnitskiy's right to life and ensure an effective investigation into the circumstances of his death; Article 6 § 1 of the Convention as well as Article 6 § 2 of the Convention (right to a fair trial). *Magnitskiy and Others v. Russia App no 32631/09 and 53799/12* (ECtHR, 27 August 2019).

186 The Sergei Magnitsky Rule of Law Accountability Act of 2012, Public Law 112–208, title IV, Dec. 14, 2012, 126 Stat. 1502.

187 ibid.

188 ibid.; 31 C.F.R. § 584 Magnitsky Act Sanctions Regulations.

189 The Global Magnitsky Human Rights Accountability Act, Public Law 114–328, title XII, Dec. 23, 2016, 130 Stat. 2533.

against any foreign national if there is credible evidence that this person committed or is complicit in gross violations of internationally recognised human rights and against any foreign government official responsible for acts of significant corruption.[190] The prescribed sanctions include travel bans and the freezing of assets, as well as a general ban on any transactions with the sanctioned persons and entities owned by them.[191] In December 2020, the US Department of State announced that 243 individuals and entities from 28 countries have been designated under this sanctions regime.[192]

A number of other states followed this example and imposed similar human rights sanctions. Among the states that have enacted such legislation, we find the United Kingdom[193] and Canada.[194] The Australian government launched an inquiry into whether Australia should enact similar legislation.[195] As a consequence of this inquiry, the Parliament's Joint Standing Committee on Foreign Affairs, Defence and Trade recommended introducing legislation allowing the imposition of human rights sanctions.[196] To this end, the International Human Rights and Corruption (Magnitsky Sanctions) Bill was introduced in the Senate in August 2021.[197]

---

190 ibid.

191 ibid.; 31 C.F.R. § 583 Global Magnitsky Sanctions Regulations.

192 U.S. Department of State, 'Infographics: December 9–10 2020 Global Magnitsky Program Designations' (2020) https://www.state.gov/wp-content/uploads/2020/12/Infographic_v1.8-508.pdf.

193 The Global Human Rights Sanctions Regulations 2020 No. 680 (2020) https://www.legislation.gov.uk/uksi/2020/680/made.

194 Justice for Victims of Corrupt Foreign Officials Act (Sergei Magnitsky Law) (S.C. 2017, c. 21) 2017; In December 2019, the prime minister of Canada, Justin Trudeau, published a letter to Francois-Philippe Champagne, Canada's foreign minister, with a request to "build on the Magnitsky sanctions regime to ensure increased support for victims of human rights violations by developing a framework to transfer seized assets from those who commit grave human rights abuses to their victims, with appropriate judicial oversight." 'Minister of Foreign Affairs Mandate Letter' <https://pm.gc.ca/en/mandate-letters/2019/12/13/minister-foreign-affairs-mandate-letter>.

195 On 3 December 2019, the minister for foreign affairs and the minister for women requested the Joint Standing Committee on Foreign Affairs, Defence and Trade to inquire into the use of targeted sanctions to address human rights abuses. 'Inquiry into Whether Australia Should Examine the Use of Targeted Sanctions to Address Human Rights Abuses.' <https://www.aph.gov.au/Parliamentary_Business/Committees/Joint/Foreign_Affairs_Defence_and_Trade/MagnitskyAct>.

196 Abhijnan Rej, 'Australian Parliamentary Committee Recommends Global Magnitsky Type Legislation' *The Diplomat* (7 December 2020) https://thediplomat.com/2020/12/australian-parliamentary-committee-recommends-global-magnitsky-type-legislation/.

197 Commonwealth of Australia. Senate. Hansard. Tuesday, 3 August, 2021. Available at: https://parlinfo.aph.gov.au/parlInfo/download/chamber/hansards/cc2b3d91-d8ca-4ed3-a179-cce9561bc86e/toc_pdf/Senate_2021_08_03_8996.pdf;fileType=application%2Fpdf.

Following this global trend, the EU's High Representative for Foreign Affairs and Security Policy, Josep Borrell, announced in December 2019 that: "under the request of several member states we have agreed to launch the preparatory work for a global sanctions regime to address serious human rights violations which will be the European Union equivalent of the so-called Magnitsky Act of the United States."[198] In December 2020, the European Union established a framework to impose sanctions (restrictive measures) against individuals, legal persons, entities or bodies responsible for grave human rights violations.[199]

Failed international attempts to negotiate rules of conduct in cyberspace leave states with a limited number of options to respond to the growing number of cyber-attacks and other malicious cyber-enabled activities,[200] which have not only become more frequent, but also more destructive, as has been seen during the COVID-19 pandemic.[201] In order to prevent and punish various malicious actions in cyberspace, states have introduced regulations enabling them to target actors responsible for malicious activities, as well as those who facilitate such actions or benefit from them.[202] The United States has been employing cyber sanctions since 2015,[203] and their application has been extended several times.[204] The European Union has followed this example,

---

198 Jacopo Barigazzi, 'EU to Prepare Magnitsky-Style Human Rights Sanctions Regime' *POLITICO* (9 December 2019) <https://www.politico.eu/article/eu-to-prepare-magnitsky-style-human-rights-sanctions-regime/>; Have (n 24).

199 Council Decision (CFSP) No 2020/1999 of 7 December 2020 concerning restrictive measures against serious human rights violations and abuses, 2020 (OJ L); Council Regulation (EU) No 2020/1998 of 7 December 2020 concerning restrictive measures against serious human rights violations and abuses, 2020 (OJ L).

200 For more on the international efforts to establish rules of conduct in the cyberspace, see Iryna Bogdanova and María Vásquez Callo-Müller, 'Unilateral Cyber Sanctions: Between Questioned Legality and Normative Value' (2021) 54 Vanderbilt Journal of Transnational Law 911; Iryna Bogdanova and María Vásquez Callo-Müller, 'Unilateral Economic Sanctions to Deter and Punish Cyber-Attacks: Are They Here to Stay?' (*EJIL: Talk!*, 7 December 2021), https://www.ejiltalk.org/unilateral-economic-sanctions-to-deter-and-punish-cyber-attacks-are-they-here-to-stay/.

201 Marko Milanovic and Michael N Schmitt, 'Cyber Attacks and Cyber (Mis)information Operations During a Pandemic' (2020) 11 Journal of National Security Law & Policy 247.

202 For more on the relevant legislation and state practice, see Bogdanova and Callo-Müller (n 200).

203 President of the United States of America. Executive Order 13694 of April 1, 2015. Blocking the Property of Certain Persons Engaging in Significant Malicious Cyber-Enabled Activities.

204 President of the United States of America. Executive Order 13757 of December 28, 2016. Taking Additional Steps to Address the National Emergency with Respect to Significant Malicious Cyber-Enabled Activities.

enacting a legal framework for cyber sanctions in 2019[205] and imposing its first sanctions in 2020.[206] Several non-EU states expressed their intention to align themselves with the EU cyber sanctions.[207] For example, Norway is considering amending its laws to fully implement the EU unilateral sanctions, including cyber sanctions.[208] The United Kingdom has also implemented cyber sanctions regulations.[209] Thus, cyber sanctions are gaining momentum.

The various types of unilateral economic sanctions described above could be applied *inter alia* to government bodies and government officials. For example, human right sanctions may target government officials and thus might infringe on the immunities to which such officials are entitled under public international law.[210] Similarly, US and EU cyber sanctions punish not only individuals engaged in malicious cyber-enabled activities, but also government officials and government bodies.[211] The interrelations between such unilateral

205 Council Regulation (EU) No 2019/796 of 17 May 2019 concerning restrictive measures against cyber-attacks threatening the Union or its Member States, 2019 (OJ L); Council Decision (CFSP) No 2019/797 of 17 May 2019 concerning restrictive measures against cyber-attacks threatening the Union or its Member States, 2019 (OJ L).

206 Council Decision (CFSP) No 2020/1127 of 30 July 2020 Amending Decision (CFSP) 2019/797 concerning restrictive measures against cyber-attacks threatening the Union or its Member States, 2020 (OJ L); Council Regulation (EU) No 2020/1125 of 30 July 2020 Implementing Regulation (EU) 2019/796 concerning restrictive measures against cyber-attacks threatening the Union or its Member States, 2020 (OJ L).

207 Council of the EU, 'Declaration by the High Representative on behalf of the EU on the alignment of certain third countries concerning restrictive measures against cyber-attacks threatening the Union or its member states' (2 July 2019) http://www.consilium.europa.eu/en/press/press-releases/2019/07/02/declaration-by-the-high-representative-on-behalf-of-the-eu-on-the-alignment-of-certain-third-countries-concerning-restrictive-measures-against-cyber-attacks-threatening-the-union-or-its-member-states/.

208 *Press Release*, Government proposes new sanctions act (18 December 2020) https://www.regjeringen.no/en/aktuelt/new-sanctions-act/id2815141/.

209 The Cyber (Sanctions) (EU Exit) Regulations 2020 No. 597 (2020).

210 For example, in August 2018, the United States Office of Foreign Assets Control added Turkey's minister of justice, Abdulhamit Gul, and minister of the interior, Suleyman Soylu, to the Global Magnitsky sanctions list. President of the United States of America. Executive Order 13818 of December 20, 2017. Blocking the Property of Persons Involved in Serious Human Rights Abuse or Corruption. In November 2018, both were removed from the US Global Magnitsky sanctions list after the US pastor Andrew Brunson was returned to the United States, since this was the reason for the imposition of the sanctions. Yet, this example illustrates that such restrictive measures may apply to government officials as well.

211 Some of the US cyber sanctions are directed against government bodies of the Russian Federation. For example, the list of sanctioned entities includes the following government agencies: Main Intelligence Directorate (Glavnoe Razvedyvatel'noe Upravlenie)

restrictive measures and the immunities accorded to senior government officials and government bodies under international law are discussed in the next chapter of this book.[212]

There are a number of reasons for the increasing use of economic sanctions. First and foremost, as the former US Deputy National Security Advisor for Combating Terrorism, Juan Zarate, has accurately pointed out: "Economic sanctions and financial influence are now the national security tools of choice when neither diplomacy nor military force proves effective or possible."[213] Second, the ample use of unilateral economic sanctions can also be explained by the mounting evidence against the usefulness of military interventions. In his book *The Sanctions Paradox,* the distinguished political scientist Daniel Drezner observes: "Bosnia, Chechnya, and Somalia have highlighted the costs of military intervention for the great powers. Unless the use of force is quick and successful, militarized disputes sap a nation's resourses and create a domestic political backlash against the sender government. As public resistance to military interventions increases, and as foreign aid budgets are slashed, policy-makers are turning more and more to economic coercion as an attractive substitute to advance the national interest."[214]

In a similar vein, Michael Reisman argues that economic sanctions are "politically cheap" and that this explains their substantially increased use.[215] In his view, society is more willing to accept economic measures than military intervention in a foreign state.[216] Moreover, the domestic costs of such coercive measures are hardly noticeable, except for in the industries that bear these costs.[217]

In view of the ongoing trade war between the United States and the People's Republic of China,[218] in the context of which both sides have introduced

---

(GRU); Federal Security Service (Federalnaya Sluzhba Bezopasnosti) (FSB). Holders of high-ranking government positions are also targeted. Executive Order 13757 (n 204); Council Decision (CFSP) No 2020/1127 and Council Regulation (EU) No 2020/1125 (n 206).

212 Chapter 2, 6. Unilateral economic sanctions and the immunities of states and state officials.

213 Zarate (n 83) 11.

214 Daniel W Drezner, *The Sanctions Paradox: Economic Statecraft and International Relations* (Cambridge University Press 1999) 7–8.

215 W Michael Reisman, 'Sanctions and International Law. Keynote Address: The Cuban Embargo and Human Rights.' (2008) 4 Intercultural Human Rights Law Review 13.

216 ibid.

217 ibid.

218 Chad P Bown, 'The US-China Trade War and Phase One Agreement' (2021) Peterson Institute for International Economics Working Paper 21–2 https://www.piie.com/sites/default/files/documents/wp21-2.pdf.

additional import tariffs,[219] and the growing use of unilateral trade restrictions to implement policies pursuing the goal of technological supremacy,[220] the international relations and legal scholars have been arguing that we are entering a new geo-economic world order. This argument will now briefly be considered.

The term geo-economics is not a new one. In fact, the term was coined at the end of the Cold War. Edward Luttwak, who published an essay with the title *From Geopolitics to Geo-Economics: Logic of Conflict, Grammar of Commerce*, is frequently named as the author of the concept.[221] Luttwak described the rationale behind this new concept as follows: "This neologism is the best term I can think of to describe the admixture of the logic of conflict with the methods of commerce."[222]

The current interest in geo-economics is motivated by the policies pursued by the major world powers – specifically by the United States and China.[223] Some scholars even argue that we are entering into a new geo-economic world order.[224] The crux of their argument rests on the growing evidence of the increased convergence between economic and security thinking.[225] The prophets of a new geo-economic world order contend: "The new order is characterized by a higher degree of convergence between security and economics; a greater focus on relative economic gains given their implications for security; and increased concern over the security risks posed by interdependence in terms of undermining state control, self-sufficiency and resilience."[226]

The logic underpinning the position regarding the disentanglement of economic policies from politics over the last several decades is well illustrated by

---

219 "[...] each country increased its average duty on imports from the other to rates of roughly 20 percent, with the new tariffs and counter-tariffs covering more than 50 percent of bilateral trade." ibid.

220 Graham Webster and others, 'Mapping U.S. – China Technology Decoupling' (27 August 2020) Stanford Freeman Spogli Institute for International Studies White Paper.

221 Edward N Luttwak, 'From Geopolitics to Geo-Economics: Logic of Conflict, Grammar of Commerce' (1990) The National Interest 17.

222 ibid 19.

223 Mark Beeson, 'Geoeconomics Isn't Back – It Never Went Away' (22 August 2018) <https://www.lowyinstitute.org/the-interpreter/geoeconomics-isnt-back-never-went-away>.; Peter A Petri, 'United States – China Technological Rivalry' (22 August 2019) https://ssrn.com/abstract=3441035.

224 Anthea Roberts, Henrique Choer Moraes and Victor Ferguson, 'The Geoeconomic World Order' (*Lawfare*, 19 November 2018) <https://www.lawfareblog.com/geoeconomic-world-order>.; Roberts, Choer Moraes and Ferguson (n 21).

225 ibid.

226 ibid.

the following quote: "The heart of politics is power; the aim of economics is wealth. Power is inherently limited. The quest for power is therefore competitive. It is a 'zero-sum game' […] . Wealth, by contrast, is limitless, which makes economics a 'positive-sum game.'"[227]

Those scholars who argue that the shift towards a new geo-economic order has occurred emphasise that the period of hegemonic stability has been superseded by the period of strategic rivalry between the United States and China.[228] This rivalry is characterised by the use of economic interdependence as a weapon against the potential military competitor.[229] There is an abundance of current state practice to substantiate this assertion. In particular, export control policy might serve as a good example to focus on. The restrictive measures imposed by the United States on Chinese technology companies such as Huawei and ZTE are illustrative of how US export controls can be operationalised to target a strategic competitor and its technology companies.[230] For its part, China has also enacted a new law on export controls.[231]

Worries regarding a new geo-economic world order are not being voiced in a vacuum. As history tends to repeat itself, we observe pendular swings towards and away from the idea of globalisation and economic interdependence. One might ponder the implications of this new world order on the use of unilateral economic sanctions. The implications might be far-reaching. The strategy of inflicting economic pain on rival states in pursuit of a national security agenda, which is not aligned with the enforcement of public international law, can potentially undermine the legitimacy of such measures.

2 The Effectiveness of Economic Sanctions

This section starts with a description of the goals that states pursue by imposing economic sanctions. A discussion of their effectiveness follows. While any

---

227 Robert D Blackwill and Jennifer M Harris, *War by Other Means: Geoeconomics and Statecraft* (The Belknap Press of Harvard University Press 2016) 6.

228 Roberts, Choer Moraes and Ferguson (n 21).

229 ibid.

230 Iryna Bogdanova, 'Targeted Economic Sanctions and WTO Law: Examining the Adequacy of the National Security Exception' (2021) 48(2) Legal Issues of Economic Integration 171.

231 The Export Control Law of the People's Republic of China was passed on 17 October 2020. This new law permits the imposition of retaliatory export controls against the states that unilaterally restrict their strategic exports to China. Maya Lester, 'China adopts new export control law' (*EU Sanctions*, 19 October 2020) https://www.europeansanctions.com/2020/10/china-adopts-new-export-control-law/.

detailed analysis of existing theories or theoretical models described in the voluminous literature would go beyond the ambit of our enquiry, the discussion below highlights the major findings on the effectiveness of economic sanctions. Finally, strategies for circumventing the negative implications of economic coercion are outlined.

Before we proceed with the analysis, a few clarifications are warranted. The literature displays a lack of consistency in the use of the term "economic sanctions," as well as a lack of a settled approach to measuring the effectiveness of sanctions. Despite ambiguity and inconsistency, all the definitions of economic sanctions share a common core: these measures entail restrictions on economic transactions and, for the most part, pursue political objectives. The second deficiency – the lack of a settled standard in evaluating efficiency – is addressed by explicit indication of the criteria that were relied upon to assess the economic sanctions' efficiency.

2.1 *The Objectives Pursued by Economic Sanctions*

Economic sanctions may be imposed for a variety of reasons and, indeed, the majority of them pursue multiple goals.[232] Barry Carter points out that the rationales for imposing economic sanctions might include: influencing, punishing or demonstrating opposition to another country's policies.[233] By the same token, Kern Alexander identifies the following objectives of economic sanctions: behaviour modification, punishment and sending a signal to a targeted country or a third country.[234] Additionally, some scholars argue that the goal of sanctions is not only behaviour modification, but also impairing a targeted state's ability to inflict further damage.[235]

David Baldwin contends that the extensive literature on the subject reveals three justifications for the use of economic sanctions: cognitive, expressive and instrumental.[236] The essence of the cognitive explanation is that economic

232 One recent study identifies the following possible reasons for a decision to impose sanctions: "[…] the desire to demonstrate the sender's willingness and capacity to act, to anticipate or deflect criticism, to maintain certain patterns of behaviour in international affairs, to deter further engagement in the objectionable actions by the target and third parties, to support international institutions, to promote subversion in the target or to assuage domestic audiences." Tobias Stoll and others, 'Extraterritorial sanctions on trade and investments and European responses' (2020) Study requested by the European Parliament's Committee on International Trade, 15.

233 Carter (n 28) 1170.

234 Alexander (n 19) 10.

235 Tostensen and Bull (n 155) 377.

236 David A Baldwin, 'Prologamena to Thinking about Economic Sanctions and Free Trade' (2003) 4 Chicago Journal of International Law 271.

sanctions do not bring positive results, and thus the decision to impose them flows either from ignorance or from bad judgement.[237] The expressive explanation considers economic sanctions as an end in themselves: they are used to release the internal tensions of the state that imposes them.[238] The instrumental approach focuses on the desired effects of economic coercion, implying that these actions are purposive.[239]

Since he is convinced of the accuracy of the instrumental approach, Baldwin argues that this explanation, combined with what he calls "logic of choice," captures the rationale behind the use of economic sanctions.[240] A brief rehearsal of Baldwin's argument on the "logic of choice" is warranted here: "The logic of choice applies to situations in which policymakers must choose to allocate scarce resources among competing needs. In such situations, policymakers must consider the opportunity costs of their actions. In such situations, choosing a low-cost policy alternative with a low probability of success may not be foolish at all if the likely cost-effectiveness of other policy alternatives is even less attractive."[241]

More recent studies on the effectiveness of economic sanctions also demonstrate that the existing literature on the subject can be grouped into three categories. In particular, Jean-Marc Blanchard and Norrin Ripsman distinguish three schools of thought depending on their views on the effectiveness of economic sanctions.[242] The representatives of the realist school argue that economic sanctions cannot be effective, given that states give preference to political and strategic considerations and thus would not sacrifice them for the economic ones.[243] By contrast, the economic liberal approach views economic sanctions as an effective instrument assuming that economic gains or losses are of significance for each state.[244] The third approach – the conditionalist approach – considers sanctions effective only if certain preconditions are met and this body of literature discusses the impact of both international environment, as well as domestic processes.[245]

---

237 ibid 274.

238 ibid 274–275.

239 ibid 275.

240 ibid.

241 ibid.

242 Jean-Marc F Blanchard and Norrin M Ripsman, 'A Political Theory of Economic Statecraft' (2008) 4 Foreign Policy Analysis 371.

243 ibid.

244 ibid.

245 ibid.

2.2 *The Debate on the Effectiveness of Economic Sanctions*

The effectiveness of economic sanctions has been debated at length. Political scientists and economists have been the main contributors to the voluminous literature on the subject, while the contributions of legal scholars are mostly descriptive.

The effectiveness of economic sanctions became a subject of a vigorous debate in the 1960s and 1970s. One of the first studies on the effects and efficiency of economic sanctions was conducted by Johan Galtung in the 1960s.[246] Johan Galtung analysed the psychological and social mechanisms of economic sanctions, using examples drawn from the economic sanctions against Rhodesia.[247] In his analysis, the following factors were taken into consideration: the country's import-export structure, the possibility of substituting imported/exported goods and markets, the country's size and geography, and the country's reliance on a certain product or trading partner.[248] Johan Galtung distinguished naïve and revised theories of the sanctions' effectiveness.[249] The underlying assumption of the naïve theory is that the severity of the economic suffering inflicted is directly proportional to the desired political changes.[250] In Galtung's view, this theory completely disregards the principle of adaptation.[251] The revised theory of the sanctions' efficacy, which is derived from the naïve theory, acknowledges the target's willingness to sacrifice and thus admits that political changes would take longer.[252] Overall, Galtung concluded that comprehensive economic sanctions are not effective.[253] Alternatively, Galtung suggested exploring the potential of positive sanctions (incentives), as well as sanctions against individuals (what later became known as targeted sanctions).[254]

In the late 1960s and through the 1970s, the predominant view was that economic sanctions were not as effective as military force.[255] George Tsebelis points out that the academic community was sceptical about the effectiveness

246 Galtung (n 154).
247 ibid.
248 ibid.
249 ibid.
250 ibid.
251 ibid.
252 ibid.
253 ibid.
254 ibid.
255 Robert Anthony Pape, 'Why Economic Sanctions Do Not Work' (1997) 22 International Security 90, 91.

of economic sanctions, even though during the same period, the number of sanctions incidents increased.[256] In this vein, Lee Jones notes that "sanctions scholarship was sparse and pessimistic until the late 1980s."[257]

In the 1980s, the fundamental tenets of the conventional wisdom crumbled under the weight of new evidence about the effectiveness of economic sanctions.[258] A few studies laid down the foundations for a new belief in the economic sanctions' effectiveness. Later, this shift was reinforced by the geopolitical changes as well.[259]

David Baldwin's book *Economic Statecraft*, published in 1985, questioned the conventional wisdom about the effectiveness of economic sanctions.[260] Baldwin summarised the prevailing sentiment as follows: "The overall impression one derives from the literature is that economic statecraft is so obviously useless as to raise questions about the good judgement of any policy maker who gives serious consideration to using such techniques."[261]

At the outset, Baldwin argues that since 1945, political scientists and scholars have devoted much of their research efforts to evaluating and analysing policy-making processes, but have ignored the policy content.[262] Thus, scholars have frequently misinterpreted the intentions of the states that invoke economic sanctions and, as a result, wrongly argued that economic sanctions are ends in themselves.[263] Baldwin underlines the idea that policymakers choose from a limited number of alternatives.[264] From this, it flows logically that the cost-benefit analysis is of the utmost importance.[265] In this regard, Baldwin

---

256 George Tsebelis, 'Are Sanctions Effective? A Game-Theoretic Analysis' (1990) 34 Journal of Conflict Resolution 3, 5.

257 Jones (n 135) 2.

258 Pape (n 255) 91.

259 "With the end of the Cold War, the ascendancy of United States (US) 'unipolarity,' and widespread liberal triumphalism, there was apparently a historical opportunity for what President George H.W. Bush dubbed a 'new world order,' in which the United Nations Security Council (UNSC) would be harnessed to a new, liberal-interventionist agenda of democracy promotion, human rights protection, conflict resolution, and statebuilding." Jones (n 135) 2–3.

260 Baldwin defined economic statecraft as economic sanctions in the broad meaning of the term. David A Baldwin, *Economic Statecraft* (Princeton University Press 1985).

261 ibid 115.

262 ibid 9–12.

263 ibid 97–98.

264 ibid.

265 ibid.

observes: "Costs always matter to the rational decision maker, and costs estimates must be made no matter how difficult that may be."[266]

The quantitative study conducted by Hufbauer and others that was published in 1985 is considered to be one of the most influential empirical analyses of the effectiveness of economic sanctions.[267] The authors applied their model to 115 cases of economic sanctions imposed after 1914, concluding that in 34 per cent of the cases, sanctions achieved one of the four policy objectives (for their model four policy objectives were identified for each sanctioning episode).[268] In the third edition of the book, published in 2007, this conclusion was confirmed: "we found sanctions to be at least partially successful in 34 per cent of the cases that we documented."[269] The latter study included an analysis of more than 200 sanctions episodes imposed between 1914 and 2000.[270] The success was determined based on two criteria: the extent to which the policy objectives pursued by economic sanctions were achieved and the contribution to success made by economic sanctions.[271]

In the 1990s, the "pain-gain" formula – an assumption that economic deprivation would lead to political changes[272] – predominated.[273] One of the most cited examples where this logic proved to be wrong is the UN-authorised comprehensive sanctions against Iraq introduced in the 1990s.[274] Daniel Drezner described the dreadful aftermath of these sanctions as follows: "As a result, infant mortality rates have increased sevenfold, annual inflation rose to over 4,000 per cent, and per capita income has fallen to less than half pre-war levels."[275]

There is no unanimity on whether the "pain-gain" formula is a valid assumption. A number of studies have concluded that the severity of economic

266 ibid 120.

267 Gary Clyde Hufbauer, Jeffrey J Schott and Kimberly Ann Elliott, *Economic Sanctions Reconsidered: History and Current Policy* (Institute for International Economics 1985).

268 ibid.

269 Hufbauer and others (n 28).

270 ibid.

271 ibid.

272 In Lee Jones's words: "altering the welfare of people in the targeted society – whether many with comprehensive sanctions, or few with targeted measures – will somehow generate political changes desired by the 'senders.'" Jones (n 135) 13.

273 Tostensen and Bull (n 155) 375.

274 UNSC Res 661 (6 August 1990) UN Doc S/RES/661 The sanctions were further elaborated in subsequent resolutions and remained in force until 2003.

275 Drezner, *The Sanctions Paradox* (n 214) 1.

sanctions is proportional to their success in achieving policy goals,[276] whereas other surveys are more sceptical about the existence of a causal relationship.[277]

Various studies have scrutinised the effectiveness of economic sanctions from different angles:

David Cortright and George Lopez analysed twelve sanctioning episodes authorised by the UN in the 1990s.[278] According to their study, the effectiveness rate of the UN-authorised economic sanctions is 36 per cent.[279] Furthermore, the authors contend that the UN sanctions could substantially benefit from improved cooperation and enhanced enforcement.[280]

George Tsebelis attempted to apply game theory to the problem of explaining the effectiveness of sanctions, along with the interaction between a sanctioning state and a targeted state.[281] Tsebelis introduced six theoretical scenarios depicting economic sanctions as a game played between a sender and a target.[282] Six different scenarios led to the same equilibrium,[283] and Tsebelis contends that this demonstrates that the strategy of both the sender state and the target state depends on the opponent's pay-offs.[284]

---

276 "I conclude that the most effective economic sanctions are those that hurt the target countries' GNP most" San Ling Lam, 'Economic Sanctions and the Success of Foreign Policy Goals: A Critical Evaluation' (1990) 2 Japan & The World Economy 239; "the cost to the target as a portion of their GNP has a positive significant effect on success" A Cooper Drury, 'Revisiting Economic Sanctions Reconsidered' (1998) 35 Journal of Peace Research 497; "Conventional wisdom holds that increasing costs should increase the probability a sanction succeeds, and Drezner's (1998) conflict expectation model hypothesizes that targets that have cordial prior relations with the sender should be more likely to concede. While neither variable is significant at conventional levels, in both cases the confidence interval lies in the correct directions (positive for both)." Irfan Nooruddin, 'Modeling Selection Bias in Studies of Sanctions Efficacy' (2002) 28 International Interactions 57.

277 "Sanctions that impose less harm on the target can sometimes be more effective than those that impose great harm." Jonathan Eaton and Maxim Engers, 'Sanctions' (1992) 100 Journal of Political Economy 899.

278 Cortright, Lopez and Conroy (n 142).

279 "We judge sanctions as a success if they had a positive, enduring impact on bargaining dynamics or if they helped isolate or weaken the power of an abusive regime." ibid 204.

280 Cortright, Lopez and Conroy (n 142).

281 Tsebelis (n 256).

282 ibid.

283 The following conclusion is reached: "Six different scenarios led to the same equilibrium. Some assumed simultaneous, others sequential moves; some assumed perfect rationality, others simple adaptive behaviour; some perfect information, and others incomplete information by one or both sides; and in some scenarios the countries had simple dichotomous choices; in others a continuum of strategies was available. The convergence of all these models to the same equilibrium should be interpreted as an indication of the robustness of this equilibrium to different plausible specifications of the sanctions problem." ibid 11.

284 Tsebelis (n 256).

Yet not all scholars were swept along in the wave of sanction euphoria that came with the studies published in the 1980s. For example, Robert Pape, in his study published in 1997, made an effort to challenge the prevailing optimism about the effectiveness of economic sanctions.[285] Pape argued that only five cases out of 40 reported by Hufbauer and others as successful qualify for the analysis.[286] In his response in the article "Evaluating Economic Sanctions," David Baldwin criticised Pape's narrowly constructed definition of economic sanctions and argued that it should be defined in terms of means, not ends.[287] Baldwin pointed out that Pape's criteria suggest that success has only two possible values – 1 or 0.[288] Furthermore, the costs of imposing economic sanctions were not accounted for. All these deficiencies, in Baldwin's view, invalidate the conclusions.[289]

In his later article "The Sanctions Debate and the Logic of Choice," David Baldwin suggested that a rational decision-maker evaluates costs and benefits of all available policy options and then makes a decision ("the logic of choice").[290] Moreover, Baldwin identified five dimensions measuring the success of economic sanctions: effectiveness, costs to the user, costs to the target, stakes for the user and stakes for the target.[291] Baldwin is convinced that

285 Pape (n 255).

286 In his study, Pape used a narrow definition of "economic sanctions" – namely, coercive economic measures imposed by one state on another to change its political behaviour – and distinguished between economic sanctions, trade wars and economic warfare. Moreover, Pape introduced his criteria to measure the "success" of economic sanctions. In Pape's view, alternative explanations of the state's behaviour (for instance, threat to use military force) were not considered in the empirical analysis of Hufbauer, Schott, and Elliot, which he sees as a huge failure. Pape concludes: "HSE routinely fail to control for the role of force. This is the most serious possible methodological error in a study of economic sanctions, because the principal policy usefulness claimed for economic sanctions is as an alternative to force." ibid.

287 David A Baldwin and Robert A Pape, 'Evaluating Economic Sanctions' (1998) 23 International Security 189, 191.

288 ibid.

289 Baldwin argues: "If one's principal interest is to determine the relative 'policy usefulness' of force and economic sanctions, however, the failure to consider the relative costliness of both instruments is a 'methodological error' of equal importance." ibid 194.

290 "When economic sanctions are being considered, the question of whether they will 'work' in the sense of achieving their goals is only one of several important considerations. What rational policymakers really want to know is: How effective will they be, with respect to which goals and targets, at what cost, and in comparison with which policy alternatives? Scholarly discussions that fail to address all of these questions do not provide a basis for advising policymakers and can be quite misleading if they purport to do so." David A (David Allen) Baldwin, 'The Sanctions Debate and the Logic of Choice' (1999) 24 International Security 80, 86.

291 ibid.

economic sanctions may pursue multiple goals and that their contribution to achieving any of those goals may vary, without this implying that they fail.[292]

2.2.1 Openness to International Trade and Its Impact on the Effectiveness of Economic Sanctions

The earliest studies on the effectiveness of economic sanctions, i.e. Johan Galtung's research, already emphasised the role of a state's participation in international trade for the ability of economic sanctions to achieve results. Recent studies have in general confirmed the previous conclusions, while expounding further on the intricate relationship between the two.

David Lektzian and Dennis Patterson contend that economic sanctions can either increase or decrease support for the existing political regime.[293] The outcome hinges on a country's openness to trade and the effects sanctions may create on the abundant and scarce factors such as land, labour and capital.[294] More precisely, depending on a country's specific abundance of factors and its openness to international trade, ruling elites could either benefit from the imposition of sanctions or suffer losses.[295]

Lektzian and Patterson argue that if sanctions change the relative wealth of the owners of the principal factors – land, labour and capital – a change in the distribution of political power is unavoidable.[296] Yet economic sanctions can also contribute to the stability of the existing regime, if the returns on factors favouring the existing political regime grow.[297] Overall, they conclude that economic sanctions, when accurately designed and implemented, could impact internal political dynamics and consequently, contribute to policy change.[298]

The recent study prepared at the request of the EU also confirms that the effectiveness of trade sanctions depends on two factors – the relative importance of international trade and the relative importance of the affected sectors for a targeted country.[299]

292 ibid.

293 David Lektzian and Dennis Patterson, 'Political Cleavages and Economic Sanctions: The Economic and Political Winners and Losers of Sanctions' (2015) 59 International Studies Quarterly 46.

294 ibid.

295 ibid.

296 ibid.

297 ibid.

298 ibid.

299 Stoll and others (n 232) 41.

2.2.2 Multilateral Cooperation and Its Impact on the Effectiveness of Economic Sanctions

The existing literature on the effectiveness of institutionally imposed economic sanctions is not uniform. While the predominant view is that economic sanctions backed up by international organisations solve a coordination problem between states,[300] the implementation, monitoring and enforcement of such sanctions might be undermined by a broader participation.[301]

Daniel Drezner analysed the reasons behind failed multilateral cooperation.[302] In order to do so, he identified three different stages in the sanctioning process.[303] The first stage is bargaining between a primary sender and a target: if the parties are reluctant to concede and both sides consider an issue as important, then increased pressure will not translate into concessions.[304] The next stage is bargaining between a primary sender and secondary senders.[305] At this stage, a coalition of sender countries is formed, and goals are identified.[306] Inflexible demands formulated by a coalition of states could potentially contribute to a continuing deadlock, as well as a lack of any effort to resolve the issue.[307] Finally, the last stage is the enforcement of multilateral cooperation.[308] The enforcement problem resembles the prisoner's dilemma: individual actors might be better off if they defect while others cooperate.[309] Daniel Drezner argues that enforcement difficulties, not bargaining problems, undermine the efficiency of multilateral economic sanctions.[310]

Discussing the problems with the enforcement of economic sanctions,[311] Margaret Doxey emphasises that "a system of international enforcement

300 Daniel W Drezner, 'Bargaining, Enforcement, and Multilateral Sanctions: When Is Cooperation Counterproductive?' (2000) 54 International Organization 73, 76–77.

301 Collective economic sanctions suffer from the following deficiencies: lack of enforcement and monitoring, a prisoner's dilemma, and the lack of clear and transparent rules on the suspension and termination of sanctions. For more on this, see UNGA Res 51/242 (26 September 1997) UN Doc A/RES/51/242.

302 Drezner, 'Bargaining, Enforcement, and Multilateral Sanctions' (n 300).

303 ibid.

304 ibid 79–80.

305 ibid.

306 ibid.

307 ibid 81–83.

308 ibid.

309 ibid.

310 ibid.

311 According to Margaret Doxey, the following problems in the international enforcement of economic sanctions exist: the identification of collective goals as distinct from the separate goals of participants, selecting the measures that could be the most effective in each particular case, the scope of sanctions (existence of participating and non-participating

might function successfully in a genuinely international community with a cohesive social base."[312] Her idea has been further developed in recent research. Bryan Early and Robert Spice contend that the members of small homogeneous international organisations are more committed to supporting and enforcing institutionally imposed economic sanctions than members of international organisations with broad, heterogeneous membership.[313] These scholars assert that sanctions increase the economic rents gained from economic transactions, thereby nourishing a desire to deviate.[314] To the contrary, the effectiveness of economic sanctions imposed by small homogeneous international organizations can be explained by the possibility to engage in deeper commitments and the enhanced ability to monitor members' compliance.[315]

2.2.3 Financial Sanctions as a New Frontier in the Effectiveness of Economic Sanctions

Currently, a significant share of both collective and unilateral sanctions is financial, as exemplified by the practice both of the Security Council and of individual states. The Security Council has been playing an active role in demonstrating the potency of financial sanctions. In particular, it has authorised collective economic sanctions that are mandatory for UN Member States, in order to pursue objectives as diverse as countering terrorism, preventing conflict, promoting peace, protecting the civilian population, supporting democracy, improving resource governance and preventing the proliferation of nuclear weapons.[316] The Security Council has utilised this financial leverage in targeting individuals[317] and governments.[318]

---

states and the problem of secondary enforcement – although Article 25 of the UN Charter makes decisions of the Security Council obligatory, the automatic penalty for non-compliance does not exist), the costs to a sanctioning state and the internal opposition from the groups that will bear the costs of sanctions, lack of effective policing and supervising mechanisms. Doxey (n 31) 80–106.

312 ibid 81.

313 Bryan R Early and Robert Spice, 'Economic Sanctions, International Institutions, and Sanctions Busters: When Does Institutionalized Cooperation Help Sanctioning Efforts?' (2015) 11 Foreign Policy Analysis 339.

314 ibid.

315 ibid.

316 Biersteker and others (n 157) 12.

317 "The second most frequent type of sanctions comprises measures against individuals, such as [...] asset freezes (63 per cent)." Francesco Giumelli, 'Understanding United Nations Targeted Sanctions: An Empirical Analysis' (2015) 91(6) International affairs 1351, 1361.

318 "National assets were targeted with sanctions on the central bank and sovereign wealth funds in the case of Libya 2, investment into Iran was prohibited, and financial services were targeted in the DPRK." ibid 1362.

The effectiveness of financial sanctions is determined by market forces: banks and other financial institutions are aware of the reputational and financial costs of non-compliance and thus comply with such restrictions.[319] As has been accurately pointed out: "[…] the effects of restrictive financial measures rely, in part, on the specific behavior of financial institutions with respect to sanctioned counterparties."[320] In particular, empirical research suggests that financial sanctions have a negative impact on the provision of credit to banks and other financial institutions based in the sanctioned countries.[321] This conclusion was reached in a study that focused on the behaviour of German banks in the period 2002–2015. Yet the same result does not hold for foreign subsidiaries and branches of the German banks.[322]

Unilateral financial sanctions might be successful in achieving their goals as well. One recent example are the unilateral financial sanctions imposed on Iran by the United States.[323] In discussing the efficacy[324] of these financial sanctions, Suzanne Katzenstein concludes that three factors, which should be considered together, influence the effectiveness of US financial sanctions.[325] These factors are: the structure of the industry targeted by sanctions, the

319 This argument was expressed in different ways in the existing literature. Zarate (n 83); Daniel Drezner, 'Targeted Sanctions in a World of Global Finance' (2015) 41 International Interactions 755.

320 Matthias Efing, Stefan Goldbach, and Volker Nitsch, 'Freeze! Financial Sanctions and Bank Responses' (2018) Deutsche Bundesbank Discussion Paper No 45/2018, 1.

321 This conclusion was reached in a study that focused on the behaviour of German banks and their subsidiaries between 2002 and 2015. ibid.

322 "We find that financial sanctions have a strong negative effect on the external positions of German banks. The estimated decline in the provision of credit to counterparties in sanctioned countries, however, is exclusively driven by banks located in Germany. Whereas domestic banks reduce their external positions by 38%, sanctions have, on average, no statistically significant effect on positions held by subsidiaries and branches of German banks abroad. As a result, a sizable portion of German positions in targeted countries remains partly unaffected by sanctions." ibid.

323 "Soon after the imposition of the United States' unilateral secondary sanctions, Chinese trade and investment with Iran noticeably reversed course. In the first four months of 2012, China's oil imports from Iran dropped roughly 23 percent. […] More dramatically, new Chinese capital investment in Iran shrunk from almost US $3 billion in 2011 to US $400 million in 2012." Cameron Rotblat, 'Weaponizing the Plumbing: Dollar Diplomacy, Yuan Internationalization, and the Future of Financial Sanctions' (2017) 21 UCLA J Int'l L Foreign Aff 311, 328–329.

324 Suzanne Katzenstein uses a narrow definition of efficacy "focusing on the government's ability to influence foreign banks, and foreign firms more generally." Suzanne Katzenstein, 'Dollar Unilateralism: The New Frontline of National Security' (2015) 90 Indiana Law Journal 293.

325 ibid.

international acceptability of the policy goals that the government is pursuing and the bargaining asymmetries between the government and the industry.[326] In her view, financial sanctions imposed by the United States against Iran proved to be effective in isolating Iranian banks and businesses.[327] This conclusion has been buttressed by the work of other scholars.[328]

2.3 *Strategies for Circumventing the Negative Effects of Economic Sanctions*

Johan Galtung observed that the implicit features of economic sanctions determine possible circumvention strategies.[329] According to him, the following strategies may be discerned: acceptance of sacrifice, adaptation (i.e. restructuring of the economy) and smuggling.[330] He argues that a moral element – a very strong identification with a sending nation and a strong disapproval of its sanctions – could also have an impact on a decision to comply with sanctions.[331] The example of Rhodesia proves how manipulating facts and government propaganda could misrepresent the demands of a sanctioning state and depict compliance with such demands as unacceptable.[332]

Margaret Doxey identifies the following strategies for circumventing the negative effects of economic sanctions:

- anticipatory actions (e.g. stockpiling, development of alternative external sources of supply, stimulation and diversification of production)
- defence of the economy under sanctions (e.g. measures to increase self-sufficiency, development of economic links with non-participating states and countermeasures against sanctioning states)
- evasion of sanctions[333]

More recent studies identify other strategies that sanctioned states may pursue in order to diminish the negative impact of economic sanctions on their economy. For example, Patrick Weber and Beata Stępień provide the example of the Russian Federation enacting domestic regulation promising additional

326 ibid 341.
327 ibid.
328 Joanna Diane Caytas, 'Weaponizing Finance: U.S. and European Options, Tools, and Policies' (2017) 23 Columbia Journal of European Law 441.
329 Galtung (n 154).
330 ibid 393.
331 ibid 399.
332 For more details, see ibid 399–404.
333 Doxey (n 31) 106–124.

incentives for foreign firms that establish their production on Russian soil.[334] This regulation was introduced as a part of a broader import-substitution programme established by the Russian government.[335] The example reflects a general practice engaged in by sanctioned states, in order to cope with the negative effects of economic sanctions by providing economic incentives.[336]

3 Conclusion

Economic sanctions initially emerged as a constituent element of military strategy, as the historical record clearly shows. The evolution of the system of collective security, first attempted via the Covenant of the League of Nations and later through the UN Charter, encompassed a shift in the role attributed to economic sanctions. Indeed, after World War I and even more so after World War II, economic sanctions evolved as measures to promote collective security. Eventually, with an increased number of international legal obligations and the lack of centralised institutional enforcement, measures of economic pressure have acquired value as a tool to enforce international law.

The end of the Cold War breathed new life into economic sanctions. The UN Security Council relied upon economic pressure to achieve its main goal – to maintain international peace and security. Furthermore, targeted sanctions gained momentum. The proliferation of unilateral economic sanctions and the diversity of the policy objectives pursued by such measures provide sufficient ground to argue that, in the last decades, states have relied excessively upon economic coercion.

The effectiveness of economic sanctions cannot be evaluated separately from their intended objectives and the domestic dynamics of a sanctioned state. Furthermore, the specific outcome of economic sanctions also depends

334 Regulation of the Russian Federation Government of 16 July 2015 No. 708 'On special investment contracts for certain industries.' Patrick Maximilian Weber and Beata Stępień, 'Conform or Challenge? Adjustment Strategies of Sanction-torn Companies' (2020) 43 The World Economy 3006, 3008.

335 Hayk Safaryan, 'Implementation of the Import Substitution Policy – Further Developments' (2015) https://cms.law/en/rus/publication/implementation-of-the-import-substitution-policy-further-developments.

336 "[…] targeted nations under sanctions are likely to provide economic goodies to attract FDI." Glen Biglaiser and David Lektzian, 'The Effect of Sanctions on U.S. Foreign Direct Investment' (2011) 65(3) International Organization, 531, 535.

on the targeted country's openness to international trade. Studies of the effectiveness of economic sanctions demonstrate that they can be a viable policy response only if they are accurately framed and implemented.

CHAPTER 2

The Legality of Unilateral Economic Sanctions under Public International Law

This chapter discusses the legality of coercive economic measures imposed by individual states – unilateral economic sanctions – under public international law. At the outset, the terminology used to define coercive economic measures is clarified. Subsequently, the legality of unilateral economic sanctions is reviewed in light of the principles embedded in the UN Charter, the authority to impose countermeasures stipulated in the Draft articles, established principles of jurisdiction in international law and the immunities that international law accords to states, as well as to state officials. In the last section, the consistency of unilateral economic sanctions with WTO law is examined.

This chapter addresses two questions: First, what norms of public international law might be infringed by the states that impose unilateral economic sanctions? Second and more implicitly, to what extent does public international law constrain powerful states from overusing economic coercion? In order to answer the first question, I analyse the legality of unilateral economic sanctions against the background of various norms and principles of public international law. As regards the second question, the assumption is that the questionable legality of unilateral economic sanctions, reinforced by the decentralised system of public international law enforcement, enables more powerful states not only to use, but also to misuse economic sanctions. In order to illustrate this assumption, I discuss extraterritorial economic sanctions and the emergence of the correspondent-bank account jurisdiction that allows US domestic courts to ascertain jurisdiction over the conduct of foreign nationals that occurred abroad and thus enforce US unilateral financial sanctions by bringing criminal charges against them.

One minor clarification: I will not explore the legal questions brought up by the imposition of unilateral economic sanctions in the context of international investment disputes and international commercial arbitration, since this lies beyond the scope of the present study.

1 Unilateral Economic Sanctions: In Search of Definitional Clarity

There is no one well-accepted definition of economic sanctions. Yet what is agreed is that economic sanctions lie at the crossroads between economic and political rationales. Perry Bechky claims that "sanctions are a political tool – but a political tool that operates through economic regulation."[337] By the same token, Andreas Lowenfeld, in his numerous publications on the subject, argues that economic sanctions are "economic controls for political ends."[338]

In this book, unilateral economic sanctions are defined as restrictive economic measures imposed by an individual state against another state and/or its government officials, legal entities and nationals in pursuit of political objectives and without any prior authorisation from an international or regional organisation. Unilateral economic sanctions, which are the subject matter of this study, may be imposed for a variety of reasons and take different forms.

Unilateral economic sanctions do not fall squarely within a single existing legal category in international law. As such, several different legal categories might be used to characterise such restrictions. In particular, this diversity is exemplified by categories such as retorsion, reprisals, countermeasures, third-party countermeasures (solidarity measures) and sanctions. Each of these categories is discussed below.

1.1 *Retorsion*

Retorsions are defined as "acts which are wrongful not in the legal but only in the political or moral sense, or a simple discourtesy."[339] In the same vein, Elizabeth Zoller describes retorsion as "an unfriendly but nevertheless lawful act by the aggrieved party against the wrongdoer."[340] The concept of retorsion hinges on the incompleteness of public international law. In other words, states are entitled to freedom of action if no rule constrains them. The rationale behind this conclusion has been well expressed by Elizabeth Zoller: "the

337 Perry S Bechky, 'Sanctions and the Blurred Boundaries of International Economic Law' (2018) 83 Missouri Law Review 1, 1.

338 Andreas F Lowenfeld, *International Economic Law* (2nd ed., Oxford University Press 2008) VIII; Andreas F Lowenfeld, 'Trade Controls for Political Ends: Four Perspectives' (2003) 4 Chicago Journal of International Law 355.

339 Thomas Giegerich, 'Retorsion,' *Max Planck Encyclopedia of Public International Law* [*MPEPIL*] (2011) <http://opil.ouplaw.com/view/10.1093/law:epil/9780199231690/law-9780199231690-e983>.

340 Zoller (n 86) 5.

scope of retorsion is basically as wide as that of the nonregulated conduct of states."[341]

Retorsion belongs to the instruments of self-help deployed unilaterally by states. These instruments may be punitive or may aim at goals such as retribution or deterrence.[342] Scholars provide numerous examples of the acts that fall under the definition of retorsion: "terminating the payment of development aid or the provision of military assistance; unilaterally imposing legally permissible economic sanctions such as an arms embargo; recognition of a situation (the sovereignty of a third State over territory also claimed by the target State); suspending, terminating, or refusing to prolong a treaty; and withdrawing from an international organization in order to protest this organization's political activities."[343] The proportionality requirement, which is of significance for countermeasures, does not apply to acts of retorsion.[344]

Unilateral economic sanctions may, in some circumstances, be characterised as acts of retorsion. For instance, the withdrawal of voluntary aid programmes constitutes an act of retorsion.[345] Trade embargoes and other restrictions on trade might represent retorsions or be tantamount to countermeasures, depending on the scope of such restrictions and states' membership at the WTO.[346] Indeed, states that are not WTO Members and are not bound by international obligations under the multilateral or bilateral trade agreements may restrict trade with each other. However, in reality, such instances are very rare.

1.2 *Reprisals*

Reprisals are defined as "measures undertaken by one subject of public international law to coerce another subject of public international law to abide by its legal obligations towards the first of the subjects mentioned."[347] Another definition of reprisals can be found in the Naulilaa arbitration: "acts of self-help by the injured State, acts in retaliation for acts contrary to international law on the part of the offending State, which have remained unredressed after

341 ibid 6.

342 Giegerich (n 339).

343 ibid.

344 ibid.

345 ibid.; Ruys (n 4) 24.

346 Ruys (n 4) 25.

347 Matthias Ruffert, 'Reprisals,' *Max Planck Encyclopedia of Public International Law* [*MPEPIL*] (2015) <http://opil.ouplaw.com/view/10.1093/law:epil/9780199231690/law-9780199231690-e1771>.

a demand for amends."[348] Thus, the right to enact reprisals is conditional upon the existence of an earlier violation of international law.

The classical law of reprisals predated the law of state responsibility, the emergence of which mirrored the evolution of international law as a more coherent system. The eighteenth-century luminary Emer de Vattel mentioned reprisals as a possible alternative to war.[349] Vattel not only pointed out the term, but also provided a detailed description of the circumstances under which recourse to reprisals was lawful.[350]

With time, the term "reprisal" evolved and changed its meaning.[351] Elizabeth Zoller observes: "there seems to be very little in common between what reprisals originally were, i.e. acts of armed violence, and what they legally are taken for today, namely the right for the wronged state not to perform a rule of international law in dealings between itself and the wrongdoer."[352] James Crawford contends that recent developments in public international law have deprived the concept of its meaning.[353] More specifically, it was replaced by two concepts: self-defence, which is allowed under certain circumstances, and non-forcible countermeasures.[354] Indeed, after the ILC adopted the Draft articles, the concept of countermeasures overshadowed that of reprisals. Suffice it to say that "most authors consider reprisals either to fall within the concept of countermeasures or to equal that concept."[355]

Another point of view is that the present-day concept of reprisals denotes only countermeasures taken in times of war.[356] The commentary to the Draft articles stipulates: "More recently, the term 'reprisals' has been limited to action taken in time of international armed conflict; i.e. it has been taken as equivalent to belligerent reprisals."[357]

---

348 *Responsibility of Germany arising out of damage caused in the Portuguese colonies of southern Africa (Naulilaa incident), 2 RIAA 1025 (Award of July 31, 1928).*

349 Emer de Vattel, *The Law of Nations, or, Principles of the Law of Nature, Applied to the Conduct and Affairs of Nations and Sovereigns, with Three Early Essays on the Origine and Nature of Natural Law and on Luxury* (Béla Kapossy and Richard Whatmore eds., Indianapolis, Liberty Fund 2008) §342–§354.

350 ibid.

351 Ruffert (n 347).

352 Zoller (n 86) 35–36.

353 James Crawford, *State Responsibility: The General Part* (Cambridge University Press 2013) 586.

354 ibid.

355 Math Noortmann, *Enforcing International Law: From Self-Help to Self-Contained Regimes* (Ashgate 2005) 38.

356 Ruffert (n 347).

357 ILC, 'Draft articles' (n 90) 128.

The distinction between the concepts of retorsion and reprisals remains hazy. Thomas Giegerich buttresses this conclusion: "Retorsion and reprisals can be placed on a sliding scale of self-help measures with a grey area instead of a precise line between the two."[358] Giegerich sets out the following reasons for this: "One reason for this uncertainty is that the illegality of the initial act of the target State (opening the possibility of using reprisals instead of retorsion) and/or the compatibility of the reacting State's measures with its own international legal obligations (compelling it to invoke reprisals and not only retorsion as a justification) will often be disputed, the allocation of the burden of proof uncertain, and compulsory third-party dispute settlement unavailable."[359]

Unilateral economic sanctions can be invoked as a response to a previous violation of international law and may be contrary to international obligations of the imposing state. Thus, they might potentially fall under the definition of reprisals. Yet, more often unilateral economic sanctions are considered to be tantamount to countermeasures or third-party countermeasures, as the concept of reprisals has been less used in recent years.

1.3 *Countermeasures*

The term countermeasures came to the forefront of international law in the 1970s.[360] In the 1980s and 1990s, the ICJ followed this trend, relying upon the concept of countermeasures in a number of its decisions.[361] Elizabeth Zoller, writing after the concept was acknowledged in the *Air Services Agreement arbitration* and the ICJ dispute *United States Diplomatic and Consular Staff in Tehran*, identified two core attributes of the newly introduced concept of countermeasures: they are "unilateral in form and remedial in purpose."[362]

358 Giegerich (n 339).

359 ibid.

360 *Case concerning the Air Service Agreement of 27 March 1946 between the United States of America and France* [*1978*] *18 RIAA 417* [80]. In this respect, Math Noortmann points out: "The Tribunal in the Air Services Agreement case copied the term 'countermeasures' from the memorial of the US, which used 'countermeasures' to describe its measures against French airlines. Reuter, a member of the abovementioned Tribunal, held, at a meeting of the International Law Commission on Article 30 of Part One of the Commission's Draft on State Responsibility, that the term 'countermeasures meant nothing.' He revealed that the Tribunal was merely "seeking to avoid the words 'reciprocal obligations' and 'reprisals.'" Noortmann (n 355).

361 *United States Diplomatic and Consular Staff in Tehran, Judgment, ICJ Reports 1980, p 3*; *Military and Paramilitary Activities in and against Nicaragua* (n 116); *Gabcikovo-Nagymaros Project (Hungary/Slovakia), Judgment, ICJ Reports 1997, p 7*.

362 Zoller (n 86) 3.

The normative content of the concept was framed as a part of the broader effort to codify international rules concerning the responsibility of states. The Draft articles define the ambit of countermeasures as follows: "Countermeasures are limited to the non-performance for the time being of international obligations of the State taking the measures towards the responsible State."[363] International law scholars define countermeasures as "unilateral measures adopted by a State in response to the breach of its rights by the wrongful act of another State that affect the rights of the target State and are aimed at inducing it to provide cessation or reparations to the injured State."[364]

The right to impose countermeasures is not an absolute right, and the exercise of this right is restricted in several ways. The Draft articles distinguish between injured and non-injured states, and the entitlement to impose countermeasures is granted only to injured states.[365] The final text reflects the then-prevailing traditional theory: only states whose subjective rights were violated could invoke the state responsibility of another state.[366] The legality of countermeasures imposed by non-injured states – third-party countermeasures – is discussed in more detail in section 3 of this chapter. The question of whether the Draft articles reflect customary international law is a part of that discussion.

The conditions for the use of countermeasures are enlisted in Articles 49 and 51 of the Draft articles.[367] The former article stipulates object and limits of countermeasures, while the latter prescribes that such measures should be proportional to the injury suffered by the state imposing them. Furthermore, countermeasures may not affect international obligations enumerated in Article 50 of the Draft articles.[368]

363 Article 49(2) ILC, 'Draft articles' (n 90).

364 Federica I Paddeu, 'Countermeasures,' *Max Planck Encyclopedia of Public International Law* [*MPEPIL*] <https://opil.ouplaw.com/view/10.1093/law:epil/9780199231690/law-9780199231690-e1020?prd=OPIL>.

365 Article 42 lays out the definition of an injured state for the purposes of invoking state responsibility of another state. This definition is narrow and excludes states that are not directly affected by the violation. Article 48 stipulates the rules for an invocation of responsibility by a state other than an injured state. According to this article, non-injured states are not allowed to resort to countermeasures. ILC, 'Draft articles' (n 90).

366 Crawford (n 353) 542.

367 ILC, 'Draft articles' (n 90).

368 Article 50 of the Draft articles reads as follows: "1. Countermeasures shall not affect: (a) the obligation to refrain from the threat or use of force as embodied in the Charter of the United Nations; (b) obligations for the protection of fundamental human rights; (c) obligations of a humanitarian character prohibiting reprisals; (d) other obligations under peremptory norms of general international law. 2. A State taking countermeasures is not relieved from fulfilling its obligations: (a) under any dispute settlement procedure

State practice bears witness to the fact that unilateral economic sanctions are frequently used as countermeasures. Describing the state practice of applying countermeasures, Antonios Tzanakopoulos contends that "countermeasures are predominantly economic in nature."[369]

1.4 *Third-Party Countermeasures (Solidarity Measures, Countermeasures in the Collective Interest)*

Third-party countermeasures (solidarity measures, countermeasures in the collective interest) are countermeasures imposed by a non-injured state or a group of states.[370] The Draft articles prescribe a narrow and rigid definition of an injured state.[371] As a result, a significant portion of the imposed countermeasures fall under the definition of third-party countermeasures.[372] Put differently, the majority of the third-party countermeasures have been imposed against states that violated the norms of international law, which protect community interests.

The debate concerning whether states should be allowed to act as representatives of humankind and protect certain common values goes back to the seventeenth century.[373] Martin Dawidowicz provides an excellent historical overview of this long-lasting discussion.[374] Initially, two opposing views dominated the debate: one emphasising the necessity to protect community interests and another focusing on the negative aspects of granting such power to individual states.[375] In the twentieth century, the third approach emerged: it

---

applicable between it and the responsible State; (b) to respect the inviolability of diplomatic or consular agents, premises, archives and documents." ibid.

369 Antonios Tzanakopoulos, 'The Right to Be Free from Economic Coercion' (2015) 4 Cambridge International Law Journal 616, 617.

370 The Draft articles do not employ terms such as third-party countermeasures, solidarity measures or countermeasures in the collective interest. All these terms were introduced by international legal scholars.

371 Article 42 ILC, 'Draft articles' (n 90).

372 Martin Dawidowicz, *Third-Party Countermeasures in International Law* (Cambridge University Press 2017); Martin Dawidowicz, 'Third-Party Countermeasures: A Progressive Development of International Law?' (2016) Questions of International Law; Martin Dawidowicz, 'Public Law Enforcement without Public Law Safeguards? An Analysis of State Practice on Third-Party Countermeasures and Their Relationship to the UN Security Council' (2007) 77 British Yearbook of International Law 333; Elena Katselli Proukaki, *The Problem of Enforcement in International Law: Countermeasures, the Non-Injured State and the Idea of International Community* (Routledge 2011).

373 Dawidowicz, *Third-Party Countermeasures in International Law* (n 372); Dawidowicz, 'Public Law Enforcement without Public Law Safeguards?' (n 372).

374 Dawidowicz, 'Public Law Enforcement without Public Law Safeguards?' (n 372) 337–348.

375 Dawidowicz, 'Public Law Enforcement without Public Law Safeguards?' (n 372).

was argued that the enforcement of community interests and values should be exercised through international institutions.[376] Despite these theoretical debates and the proposal made by the special rapporteur James Crawford to recognise third-party countermeasures,[377] the final text of the Draft articles leaves the question of the legality of third-party countermeasures uncertain.[378]

The legality of third-party countermeasures is discussed in section 3 of this chapter, while the characterisation of unilateral economic sanctions imposed to redress human rights violations and their legality are discussed in chapter 4.

1.5 *Sanctions*

The term sanction is not a legal term of art and has a certain notoriety. Moreover, the use of the term by political scientists and economists provides little clarity regarding its definition and ambit. The term was initially used by the ILC in its work on the Draft articles,[379] but it was then decided to replace it with the more neutral concept of countermeasures.[380]

Tom Ruys discerns three approaches to defining the term "sanction": a purpose-oriented definition, an author-oriented definition and a definition focused on the types of measures imposed.[381] The purpose-oriented approach focuses on the measure's objective of responding to a breach of a legal norm.[382] The author-oriented approach is related to the identity of the sanction's author, thus narrowing down the definition of sanctions to actions undertaken by international organisations.[383] The third approach equates sanctions with economic restrictions.[384]

International legal scholars do not always agree on whether the term "sanction" can be used to denote unilateral restrictions imposed by individual

---

376 ibid.

377 In 2000, the Drafting Committee of the ILC had provisionally adopted Article 54 suggested by James Crawford, which recognised the countermeasures imposed by the non-injured states and established rules for their use. ibid.

378 Article 48 ILC, 'Draft articles' (n 90). For more on this debate, see Section 3 of this chapter.

379 Dawidowicz, 'Public Law Enforcement without Public Law Safeguards?' (n 372).

380 Martin Dawidowicz, in this context, states: "In 1979 the ILC rejected Special Rapporteur Ago's proposed term 'sanction' and replaced it with the concept of 'countermeasures.' The reason for this change was that modern international law 'reserve[d] the term 'sanction' for reactive measures applied by virtue of a decision taken by an international organization.'" Dawidowicz, 'Public Law Enforcement without Public Law Safeguards?' (n 372) Footnote 1.

381 Ruys (n 4) 19.

382 ibid 19–20.

383 ibid 20–21.

384 ibid 21–22.

states. For example, a distinguished international lawyer, Alain Pellet, once contended that the term should be only used to denote restrictions authorised by the Security Council under Chapter VII of the UN Charter.[385] Yet, recently he seems to be less convinced by this position and has even argued the opposite.[386] Other scholars employ the term, but qualify it. In particular, Tom Ruys calls such measures "non-UN sanctions,"[387] while Devika Hovel identifies them as "autonomous sanctions."[388] The recent study prepared at the request of the European Parliament's Committee on International Trade also makes use of the term "sanction" to describe unilateral economic restrictions of individual states.[389]

The convincing argument advanced by the supporters of the broad definition of the term sanction, which also encompasses unilateral measures adopted by states, is the abundance of pertinent state practice.[390] Indeed, unilateral coercive measures are frequently imposed by the United States, Canada, Australia, the European Union member states and other states.[391] As a rule, such restrictive measures are invoked without any prior authorisation from regional or international organisations, and the domestic laws regulate their invocation.[392] The states that impose these measures have different names for them: the United States refers to such measures as "sanctions," the European Union as "restrictive measures," Canada as "special economic measures" and Australia as "autonomous measures."[393]

---

385 Alain Pellet and Alina Miron, 'Sanctions,' *Max Planck Encyclopedia of Public International Law* [*MPEPIL*] <https://opil.ouplaw.com/view/10.1093/law:epil/9780199231690/law-9780199231690-e984?prd=OPIL>. A similar view was expressed by the ILC in the commentary to the Draft articles. In particular, the ILC has made the following observation: "The term 'sanctions' has been used for measures taken in accordance with the constituent instrument of some international organization, in particular under Chapter VII of the Charter of the United Nations – despite the fact that the Charter uses the term 'measures,' not 'sanctions.'" ILC, 'Draft articles' (n 90) 75.

386 Pellet (n 26).

387 Ruys, 'Immunity, Inviolability and Countermeasures – A Closer Look at Non-UN Targeted Sanctions' (n 11).

388 Devika Hovell, 'Unfinished Business of International Law: The Questionable Legality of Autonomous Sanctions' (2019) 113 AJIL Unbound 140.

389 Stoll and others (n 232).

390 "[..] such attempt to distinguish between the two terms [sanctions and countermeasures] on the basis of the identity of the author of the measures concerned is legally inaccurate, and moreover ignores the fact that the 'sanction' label is also commonly used to refer to measures adopted by States." Ruys (n 4) 21.

391 Bogdanova, 'Targeted Economic Sanctions and WTO Law' (n 230).

392 ibid.

393 ibid.

The fine line distinguishing the concepts of retorsion, countermeasures, third-party countermeasures and sanctions is not self-evident. According to Tom Ruys, enforcement through non-forcible measures "remains plagued by a variety of delicate controversies and grey areas."[394] The rationale behind the current predicament has been well formulated by Ruys: "Efforts to clear the grey area by means of an in-depth assessment of State practice are complicated by the fact that States adopting economic sanctions often leave open whether the measures concerned are deemed to qualify as retorsions or as countermeasures."[395] Furthermore, states rely on their domestic laws and impose various economic restrictions as a response to the behaviour of other states, but hardly ever elucidate whether such restrictions are countermeasures or third-party countermeasures.

2 The Legality of Unilateral Economic Sanctions under the Charter of the United Nations

Political and ideological rifts continue to haunt the debate on the legality of unilateral economic sanctions. The crux of the debate revolves around the scope of the prohibition of the use of force and the scope of the principle of non-intervention. Both principles are engrained in the UN Charter – yet the question whether these principles restrain states' ability to impose unilateral economic sanctions remains unsettled.

The fierce opposition to unilateral economic sanctions has traditionally come from the Russian Federation and the People's Republic of China.[396] Ironically, both of these states frequently rely upon unilateral coercive measures to advance their political agenda abroad. For example, the Russian Federation often imposes unilateral trade restrictions on neighbouring countries in pursuit of its foreign policy goals.[397] Mergen Doraev provides the

394 Ruys (n 4) 23–24.

395 ibid 31–32.

396 'The Declaration of the Russian Federation and the People's Republic of China on the Promotion of International Law' (2016) <https://www.mid.ru/foreign_policy/news/-/asset_publisher/cKNonkJE02Bw/content/id/2331698>.

397 Mergen Doraev provides an extensive analysis of the Russian practice in applying unilateral trade restrictions on neighbouring states in pursuit of its foreign policy agenda. Part 4.3 of the article is devoted to the examination of Russia's trade wars with neighbouring countries. The general conclusion of this analysis is the following: "while on political and diplomatic levels the United States and Russia demonstrate opposing views toward the legality of unilateral economic sanctions, the actual activity of these powerful

following explanation for the discrepancy between the official position of the Russian Federation and its practice: "Russia's strong opposition to U.S. unilateral economic coercion measures is based on its desire (1) to increase the role of the U.N. Security Council and, thereby, the powers of its permanent members, (2) to maintain moral ascendancy over opponents, getting support of developing countries in debates on the legitimacy of unilateral sanctions, and (3) to keep strong legal arguments contesting potential economic sanctions against Russia and its allies."[398]

Regarding Chinese practice, James Reilly describes the increasing use of unilateral sanctions by China as follows: "Over the past few years, Chinese experts have begun to clear some of the legal, moral, ideological, and practical hurdles to Beijing's use of unilateral sanctions."[399] In their 2016 book *War by Other Means: Geoeconomics and Statecraft*, Robert Blackwill and Jennifer Harris provide a long list of the examples of how Chinese government relies upon the unilateral measures of economic coercion to advance its foreign policy agenda. It is worth quoting some of these examples: "China curtails the import of Japanese autos to signal its disapproval of Japan's security policies. It lets Philippine bananas rot on China's wharfs because Manila opposes Chinese policies in the South China Sea. It rewards Taiwanese companies that march to Beijing's cadence, and punishes those that do not. It promises trade and business with South Korea in exchange for Seoul rejecting a U.S. bid to deploy the Terminal High-Altitude Area Defence (THAAD) missile defense system."[400] The distinguishing characteristics of Chinese unilateral sanctions are an absence of official threats or public admissions of sanctions and their targeted nature (i.e. sanctions were frequently targeted at specific sectors, thus avoiding affecting broader patterns of trade and investment).[401]

Other studies that have analysed China's use of economic instruments, including unilateral economic sanctions, to pursue its national objectives abroad confirm the increasing use of economic coercion as a foreign-policy tool.[402] For example, Cameron Rotblat not only emphasises that "over the

---

Security Council permanent members in the international arena tends to make unilateral sanctions more recognizable as a part of customary international law." Doraev (n 4).

398 ibid 358–359.

399 James Reilly, 'China's Unilateral Sanctions' (2012) 35 The Washington Quarterly 121.

400 Blackwill and Harris (n 227) 4.

401 Angela Poh, *Sanctions with Chinese Characteristics: Rhetoric and Restraint in China's Diplomacy* (Amsterdam University Press 2021).

402 "[…] while opposition to sanctions has long been considered to be a core principle of Chinese foreign policy, since 2010, China has imposed unilateral sanctions more often than ever before." Vida Macikenaite, 'China's economic statecraft: the use of economic

past decade, China increasingly used narrowly targeted unilateral sanctions in order to advance its foreign policy interests," but also analyses the writings of Chinese scholars to demonstrate that they endorse the legality of such unilateral economic sanctions.[403]

This development has been further enhanced by recently enacted laws. To take one example, in October 2020, China enacted a new export control law.[404] The law makes possible the introduction of export restrictions as a response to the policies of other states that have unilaterally restricted their strategic exports to China.[405]

It is also worth mentioning numerous resolutions adopted by the UN General Assembly condemning unilateral coercive measures and their implications.[406] The special rapporteur on the negative impact of the unilateral coercive measures Idriss Jazairy called into question the legality of unilateral coercive measures and even contended that a general prohibition on their use has emerged.[407] Against this backdrop, Alexandra Hofer analysed the UN resolutions on the subject and deliberations between the UN Member States, as well as the opinions of legal scholars.[408] Hofer concludes that such a general prohibition has not emerged.[409] Similar conclusions have been reached by

power in an interdependent world' (2020) 9(2) Journal of Contemporary East Asia Studies 108, 119.

403 Rotblat (n 323).

404 Lester, 'China adopts new export control law' (n 231).

405 ibid.

406 There are two types of UN resolutions that condemn unilateral economic sanctions: (1) human rights and unilateral coercive measures and (2) unilateral economic measures as a means of political and economic coercion against developing countries. Resolutions on human rights and unilateral coercive measures have been adopted annually since 1996. Resolutions on economic measures as a means of political and economic coercion against developing countries were adopted annually from 1983 until 1987. Since 1987, these resolutions have been referred to as unilateral economic measures, representing a means of political and economic coercion against developing countries, and are adopted biannually. Hofer (n 22).

407 UNHRC, 'Report of the Special Rapporteur on the Negative Impact of Unilateral Coercive Measures on the Enjoyment of Human Rights' (2015) UN Doc A/HRC/30/45; Idriss Jazairy, 'Unilateral Economic Sanctions, International Law, and Human Rights' (2019) 33 Ethics & International Affairs 291.

408 Hofer (n 22).

409 According to Alexandra Hofer, twenty-one resolutions condemning unilateral coercive measures for their negative impact on human rights have been adopted since 1996, and nineteen resolutions entitled 'Unilateral economic measures as a means of political and economic coercion against developing countries' have been adopted since 1993. In both resolutions, it was argued that unilateral coercive measures constitute a violation

other scholars.[410] Thus, there is no general prohibition on employing coercive economic measures, even if they are imposed unilaterally.

2.1 *Unilateral Economic Sanctions as a Use of Force under Article 2(4)*

Prior to the twentieth century, states could freely rely upon the use of force without any legal constraints.[411] The Drago-Porter Convention, which restricted the use of armed force for recovering contractual debts, was the first attempt to change the contemporary status quo.[412] The next attempt to restrict the use of force in interstate relations was the Covenant of the League of Nations.[413] However, the Covenant fell short of establishing an absolute prohibition on the use of force.[414] Several years later, the Kellogg-Briand Pact introduced a general prohibition on the use of force.[415] The further developments of the prohibition of the use of force culminated in the incorporation of Article 2(4) in the UN Charter.[416] The ICJ acknowledged the

---

of international law. Despite this, Hofer argues that the general prohibition on the use of such measures has not yet emerged. ibid.

410 Tzanakopoulos (n 369).

411 Simma and Wessendorf (n 88) 204.

412 Art. 1 of the 1907 Hague Convention II, which came to be known as the Drago-Porter Convention, provided: "The Contracting Powers agree not to have recourse to armed force for the recovery of contract debts claimed from the Government of one country by the Government of another country as being due to its nationals. This undertaking is, however, not applicable when the Debtor State refuses or neglects to reply to an offer of arbitration, or, after accepting the offer, prevents any 'compromis' from being agreed on, or, after the arbitration, fails to submit to the award." For more details, please, see Wolfgang Benedek, 'Drago-Porter Convention (1907),' *Max Planck Encyclopedia of Public International Law* [*MPEPIL*] (2007) <https://opil.ouplaw.com/view/10.1093/law:epil/9780199231690/law-9780199231690-e733>.

413 League of Nations, Covenant of the League of Nations, 28 April 1919.

414 Simma and Wessendorf (n 88) 205.

415 Randall Lesaffer has written the following about the pact: "The Pact counted only two substantive articles. Art. 1 contained a solemn declaration by the States to 'condemn recourse to war for the solution of international controversies, and [to] renounce it as an instrument of national policy in their relations with one another.' In Art. 2, the signatories agreed that 'the settlement or solution of all disputes or conflicts of whatever nature or of whatever origin they may be, which may arise among them, shall never be sought except by pacific means.'" For more details, please, see Randall Lesaffer, 'Kellogg-Briand Pact (1928),' *Max Planck Encyclopedia of Public International Law* [*MPEPIL*] <https://opil.ouplaw.com/view/10.1093/law:epil/9780199231690/law-9780199231690-e320>.

416 The text of Article 2(4) reads as follows: "All Members shall refrain in their international relations from the threat or use of force against the territorial integrity or political independence of any state, or in any other manner inconsistent with the Purposes of the United Nations."

significance of this principle by calling it "a cornerstone of the United Nations Charter."[417]

The claim that unilateral economic sanctions fall under the prohibition of the use of force is not new. During the UN General Assembly meeting in 1970, the representative of Pakistan stated the following: "There had been some disagreement in the Special Committee as to whether the duty to refrain from the use of force included the duty to refrain from economic, political and other forms of pressure, and whether a definition of the term 'force' should be included in the statement of that principle."[418] Elaborating further on this point, the Pakistani representative cited General Assembly resolution 2160 (XXI), which "had recognized that the term 'force' included not only armed attacks but also other forms of coercion contrary to international law."[419] Yet, a closer examination of the text of General Assembly resolution 2160 (XXI) reveals that the text as such does not provide any satisfactory definition of the exact scope of the term "force."[420]

The Arab oil embargo was the spark that lit the fuse: after oil-producing Arab countries temporary restricted oil shipments to several countries, including the United States, scholars started to vigorously argue that economic coercion is tantamount to the use of force prohibited under the UN Charter.[421] In the following years, a long-lasting debate on the scope of the term "force" in Article 2(4) of the UN Charter was triggered by the claims made by the developing countries, together with the Soviet bloc states, and became the symbol of the lingering tensions between developed states and the developing world.[422]

417 *Armed Activities on the Territory of the Congo (Democratic Republic of the Congo v. Uganda), Judgment, ICJ Reports 2005, p 168* [148].

418 UNGA Sixth Committee (25th Session) Summary record of the 1179th meeting (24 September 1970) UN Doc A/C.6/SR.1179 para 19.

419 ibid.

420 With respect to the prohibition of the use of force, the UN General Assembly Resolution reads as follows: "States shall strictly observe, in their international relations, the prohibition of the threat or use of force against the territorial integrity or political independence of any State, or in any other manner inconsistent with the purposes of the United Nations. Accordingly, armed attack by one State against another or the use of force in any other form contrary to the Charter of the United Nations constitutes a violation of international law giving rise to international responsibility." UNGA Res 2160 (30 November 1966) UN Doc A/RES/2160 (XXI).

421 Hartmut Brosche, 'The Arab Oil Embargo and United States Pressure against Chile: Economic and Political Coercion and the Charter of the United Nations' (1974) 7 Case Western Reserve Journal of International Law 3.

422 James A Delanis, '"Force" under Article 2(4) of the United Nations Charter: The Question of Economic and Political Coercion' (1979) 12 Vanderbilt Journal of Transnational Law.

Writing on the subject in the wake of the notorious Arab oil embargo, James Delanis provided a comprehensive summary of the legal claims advanced by both sides of the debate.[423] Delanis pointed out that the traditional view is reflected in a narrow definition of "force" as only military force, whereas the view favoured by developing countries expands the definition to include economic and political force.[424]

More recent discussions on whether economic coercion violates the prohibition of the use of force reveal a diversity of opinions. The prevailing international sentiment in this regard can be framed as follows: "The term does not cover any possible kind of force, but is, according to the correct and prevailing view, limited to armed force."[425] The rationale underlying this conclusion has been captured by the following counterfactual scenario: "were this provision to extend to other forms of force, States would be left with no means of exerting pressure on other States which act in violation of international law."[426] The negotiating history of the UN Charter buttresses this conclusion: the proposal submitted by the representative of Brazil to include a general prohibition on the use of economic force in interstate relations was dismissed during the San Francisco Conference.[427] Furthermore, Nikolas Stürchler discussing the wording of Article 2(4) of the UN Charter has emphasised: "The new wording in the UN Charter was created to overcome the deficiency that governments could deny the existence of a state of war by simply omitting to attribute that word to their military actions. The terms 'threat' and 'force' were designed to describe a single wrong and put an end to self-declaratory formalism."[428]

---

423 ibid 103–114.

424 ibid.

425 Simma and Wessendorf (n 88) 208; Omer Y Elagab, 'Coercive Economic Measures Against Developing Countries' (1992) 41 International and Comparative Law Quarterly 682, 688.

426 Simma and Wessendorf (n 88) 209.

427 "The Brazilian delegation proposed to extend the prohibition of article 2(4) to cover 'the threat or use of economic measures in any manner inconsistent' with the United Nations purposes. The amendment was rejected, but the reasons for its disapproval are not clear." 'The Use of Nonviolent Coercion: A Study in Legality under Article 2(4) of the Charter of the United Nations' (1974) 122 University of Pennsylvania Law Review 983; The opposing view has gained some support as well. For example, as Maziar Jamnejad and Michael Wood have pointed out: "An argument is still occasionally heard that the reason for the rejection of the Brazilian proposal was that Art. 2(4) as it stands extends to economic force." Maziar Jamnejad and Michael Wood, 'The Principle of Non-Intervention' (2009) 22 Leiden Journal of International Law 345, Footnote 12.

428 Nikolas Stürchler, *The Threat of Force in International Law* (1st publ., Cambridge University Press, 2007) 2.

Yet, the contrary opinion on the subject is also defended. In his research, Mergen Doraev has analysed the views expressed by Soviet and Russian legal scholars.[429] Some of these commentators argued that unilateral economic sanctions violate the prohibition of the use of force,[430] while others viewed them as a violation of the principle of non-intervention.[431] Additionally, several Russian scholars contend that unilateral economic sanctions are illegitimate, since they violate the principle of the sovereign equality of states.[432]

Discussing the possibility that unilateral economic sanctions fall squarely within the prohibition of the use of force, Krista Schefer offers the most plausible explanation: "In the politicized context of the United Nations, it is unlikely that anything less than an armed blockade will be deemed to reach the severity of a 'use of force' deserving condemnation under Article 2(4) (and even that is likely to depend on the military enforcement of the blockade than the economic effects of it)."[433]

While acknowledging that unilateral economic sanctions are most likely not covered by the prohibition of the use of force embedded in Article 2(4) of the UN Charter, such measures might violate the general principle of non-intervention.[434] Thus, this matter is discussed in the subsequent part.

2.2 *Unilateral Economic Sanctions as a Violation of the Principle of Non-intervention*

Maziar Jamnejad and Michael Wood describe the principle of non-intervention as "[o]ne of the most potent and elusive of all international principles."[435] While the exact contours of the principle of non-intervention have not been determined with great precision in the UN Charter or any other international treaty, they have been moulded by international tribunals and legal scholars. The extensive literature on the subject deals mainly with the principle of non-intervention either in the context of Articles 1(2) and 55 of the UN Charter[436] – the principle of friendly relations among nations and the principle of equal rights, or in the context of the use of force prohibited under Article 2(4) or

429 Doraev (n 4) 388–393.

430 Reference to Grigori Tunkin, ibid 388–389.

431 ibid footnote 149.

432 ibid footnote 162.

433 Krista Nadakavukaren Schefer, *Social Regulation in the WTO: Trade Policy and International Legal Development* (Edward Elgar 2010) 39.

434 Simma and Wessendorf (n 88) 209.

435 Jamnejad and Wood (n 427).

436 Elagab (n 425) 687.

alternatively Article 2(7) of the UN Charter,[437] which reads: "Nothing contained in the present Charter shall authorize the United Nations to intervene in matters which are essentially within the domestic jurisdiction of any state."

The UN General Assembly has adopted more than thirty-five resolutions specifically addressing the principle of non-intervention.[438] While highlighting the existence of these resolutions, Maziar Jamnejad and Michael Wood contend that only a few of them have received broad support and are endowed with sufficient authority,[439] namely the Declaration on the Inadmissibility of Intervention in the Domestic Affairs of States and the Protection of Their Independence and Sovereignty (1965),[440] the Declaration on Principles of International Law Concerning Friendly Relations and Cooperation among States in Accordance with the Charter of the United Nations (1970),[441] and the Declaration on the Inadmissibility of Intervention and Interference in the Internal Affairs of States (1981).[442] The declarations adopted in 1965 and 1970 lay down a prohibition on "us[ing] or encourage[ing] the use of economic political or any other type of measures to coerce another State in order to obtain from it the subordination of the exercise of its sovereign rights and to secure from it advantages of any kind."[443] The declaration of 1981 imposes the following duty on the states: "The duty of a State, in the conduct of its international relations in the economic, social, technical and trade fields, to refrain from measures which would constitute interference or intervention in the internal or external affairs of another State, thus preventing it from determining freely its political, economic and social development; this includes, inter alia, the duty of a State not to use its external economic assistance programme or adopt any multilateral or unilateral economic reprisal or blockade and to prevent the use of transnational and multinational corporations under its jurisdiction and

437 Jamnejad and Wood (n 427) 357.

438 Jamnejad and Wood (n 427).

439 ibid 350–351.

440 Declaration on the Inadmissibility of Intervention in the Domestic Affairs of States and the Protection of Their Independence and Sovereignty, UNGA Res 2131 (21 December 1965) UN Doc A/RES/2131(XX) (UNGA Res 2131).

441 Declaration on Principles of International Law concerning Friendly Relations and Cooperation among States in accordance with the Charter of the United Nations, UNGA Res 2625 (24 October 1970) UN Doc A/RES/2625(XXV) (UNGA Res 2625).

442 Declaration on the Inadmissibility of Intervention and Interference in the Internal Affairs of States, UNGA Res 36/103 (December 1981) UN Doc A/RES/36/103 (UNGA Res 36/103).

443 UNGA Res 2131 para 2; UNGA Res 2625 the principle concerning the duty not to intervene in matters within the domestic jurisdiction of any State, in accordance with the Charter.

control as instruments of political pressure or coercion against another State, in violation of the Charter of the United Nations."[444]

The ICJ made a number of influential assertions on the scope of the principle of non-intervention. It was confronted with the need to adjudicate the scope of the principle of non-intervention in its first dispute, *Corfu Channel*.[445] At that time, the court denied restrictions on the principle of non-intervention, even when they were justified by the necessity of securing evidence.[446] The next occasion upon which the court had to elaborate on this principle at length was the *Military and Paramilitary Activities in and against Nicaragua* dispute.[447] The court not only acknowledged that the principle of non-intervention "is part and parcel of customary international law,"[448] but also defined its contours. It is worth quoting the court at length on what constitutes a prohibited intervention under international law: "A prohibited intervention must accordingly be one bearing on matters in which each State is permitted, by the principle of State sovereignty, to decide freely. One of these is the choice of a political, economic, social and cultural system, and the formulation of foreign policy. Intervention is wrongful when it uses methods of coercion in regard to such choices, which must remain free ones."[449]

This observation is of particular interest for our discussion. Unilateral economic sanctions might be considered a form of coercion. Does this then imply that unilateral economic sanctions infringe the principle of non-intervention irrespective of their objectives and consequences?

It should be emphasised that coercion does not equal intervention. Only coercion that intervenes in the *domaine réservé* of a state, for example, by impeding that state's freedom of choice of a political, economic, social and cultural system, can constitute a prohibited intervention. This conclusion echoes ICJ findings on whether a trade embargo imposed by the United States against Nicaragua violated the principle of non-intervention: "the Court

444 UNGA Res 36/103 para. 2 II (k).

445 *Corfu Channel case, Judgment of April 9th, 1949: ICJ Reports 1949, p 4.*

446 The court declared: "Between independent States, respect for territorial sovereignty is an essential foundation of international relations. The Court recognizes that the Albanian Government's complete failure to carry out its duties after the explosions, and the dilatory nature of its diplomatic notes, are extenuating circumstances for the action of the United Kingdom Government. But to ensure respect for international law, of which it is the organ, the Court must declare that the action of the British Navy constituted a violation of Albanian sovereignty." ibid 35.

447 *Military and Paramilitary Activities in and against Nicaragua* (n 116).

448 ibid [202].

449 ibid [205].

has merely to say that it is unable to regard such action on the economic plane as is here complained of as a breach of the customary-law principle of non-intervention."[450]

The question of whether economic coercion constitutes a potential violation of the principle of non-intervention was debated at length. In this connection, Yehuda Blum noted that "while the meaning of the term 'force' seems to be controversial, it is possible to deduce the impermissibility of at least certain forms of economic pressure by reference to the doctrine of nonintervention, as elaborated in various international instruments in recent years."[451] A decade later, Omer Yousif Elagab contended that the principle of non-intervention "did not seem to have crystallized into a clear rule prohibiting economic coercion."[452] In 1993, the Secretary-General of the UN reiterated the following claim: "There is no clear consensus in international law as to when coercive economic measures are improper, despite relevant treaties, declarations and resolutions adopted in international organizations which try to develop norms limiting the use of such measures."[453]

More recent studies support the view that only extreme forms of economic coercion might infringe the principle of non-intervention. According to Hofer, the prevalent view among the academics is that economic sanctions exemplify illegal coercion only if they constitute an intervention in the *domaine réservé* of a targeted state.[454] Antonios Tzanakopoulos puts forward the similar argument to the effect that economic coercion amounts to intervention only if it encroaches on a state's sphere of freedom, which is defined by the fact that a state did not undertake any international obligations in this particular sphere.[455]

---

450 ibid [245].

451 Yehuda Z Blum, 'Economic Boycotts in International Law' (1977) 12 Texas International Law Journal.

452 Omer Yousif Elagab, *The Legality of Non-Forcible Counter-Measures in International Law* (Clarendon Press 1988) 542–544.

453 Note by the Secretary-General, 'Economic Measures as a Means of Political and Economic Coercion against Developing Countries.' (1993) UN Doc A/48/535.

454 Alexandra Hofer draws the following conclusion: "As we saw in Part 2 of this paper, the majority opinion in doctrine is that there is no autonomous norm prohibiting economic coercion. Such practice is considered permissible to the extent that it does not violate the principle of non-intervention or that it does not violate other rules of customary international law or applicable treaty rules." Hofer (n 22) 192.

455 Antonios Tzanakopoulos distinguishes coercion from intervention in the following way: "Seeking to coerce a state within its sphere of freedom is wrongful; it constitutes intervention. Merely interfering with a state's choices within its sphere of freedom and applying relevant pressure without breaching any obligations is lawful, as long as it does not amount to coercion and, thus, intervention." Tzanakopoulos (n 369) 620.

Other actions irrespective of their coercive nature might be "mere pressure or interference."[456]

Notwithstanding the growing body of literature on relations between unilateral economic sanctions and the principle of non-intervention, the matter is far from settled. Indeed, it appears that the lengthy discussions merely serve a rhetorical purpose. In this regard, Tom Ruys observes: "In the end, it remains altogether unclear to what exact extent the principle of non-intervention prohibits certain economic sanctions."[457] Numerous international law scholars have echoed this view.[458]

3 The Legality of Unilateral Economic Sanctions under the Draft Articles on Responsibility of States for Internationally Wrongful Acts

In this section, the legality of economic countermeasures is discussed. More specifically, our analysis touches upon economic countermeasures imposed by injured states, as well as non-injured states – third-party countermeasures – in the meaning of the Draft articles. This choice is not a coincidence: the rigid definition of an injured state contained in the Draft articles entails that the majority of the present-day unilateral economic sanctions fall under the definition of third-party countermeasures.

The earliest attempts to distinguish between violations of bilateral obligations and violations of rights owed to all nations in the context of state responsibility were made in the late seventeenth century.[459] These discussions re-emerged in the nineteenth century. In this context, Robert Kolb refers to the work of A.G. Heffter, published in 1883.[460] James Crawford references the original German edition of the Heffter's book and asserts that: "it is not before the second half of the nineteenth century that a recognizably modern conception of responsibility appeared."[461] Along with Heffter, the Swiss jurist Johann

---

456 ibid 623.

457 Ruys (n 4).

458 "there are no rules of international law which categorically pronounce either on the prima-facie legality or prima-facie illegality of economic coercion" Elagab (n 452) 212–213; Tzanakopoulos (n 369).

459 Dawidowicz, 'Public Law Enforcement without Public Law Safeguards?' (n 372).

460 Robert Kolb, *The International Law of State Responsibility: An Introduction* (Edward Elgar Publishing 2017) 10.

461 Crawford (n 353) 4.

Caspar Bluntschli and the English lawyer William Edward Hall contributed to the debate on the rules of state responsibility.[462]

The subsequent evolution of the law of state responsibility was substantially influenced by the dominance of legal positivism. The general theory of responsibility developed by Dionisio Anzilotti is of particular interest in this context. A prominent Italian lawyer and judge of the PCIJ, Anzilotti grounded his inferences on the nature and scope of the state's responsibility in his firm belief in the bilateral nature of international law.[463] Therefore, his attitude to state responsibility can be equated with the responsibility arising out of bilateral contractual relations between states.[464] George Nolte advances various arguments to justify the views expressed by Anzilotti, including that he "wrote at a time when the use of force between states was not yet prohibited and in which community interests could lawfully be pursued by powerful states without having to invoke a specific right."[465]

The League of Nations undertook an attempt to codify international law on the responsibility of states.[466] These first attempts at codification are broadly considered to have been unsuccessful.[467] In the interwar period, several prominent legal scholars contributed to the debate on the international responsibility of states. According to James Crawford, Edwin Borchard and Clyde Eagleton were "two of the most significant systematizers" of the time.[468] Nolte also points out the valuable contribution made by Hersch Lauterpacht to this discussion.[469]

Those early endeavours revealed the pertinence of the rules for state responsibility, and, consequently, this matter was included in the ILC agenda following its establishment.[470] In Robert Kolb's view, the progressive development

462 Georg Nolte, 'From Dionisio Anzilotti to Roberto Ago: The Classical International Law of State Responsibility and the Traditional Primacy of a Bilateral Conception of Inter-State Relations' (2002) 13 European Journal of International Law 1083, 1085–1086.

463 ibid.

464 "[...] only the violation by a state of a true subjective right of another state can give rise to state responsibility and not the mere violation of general or more specific interests." ibid 1087.

465 ibid.

466 Crawford (n 353) 28–32.

467 ibid 28–32.

468 ibid 24–28.

469 Nolte (n 462) 1091–1093.

470 ILC, 'Report of the International Law Commission on the Work of Its First Session' (12 April 1949) UN Doc A/CN.4/13 and Corr. 1–3; UNGA Res 799 Request for the codification of the principles of international law governing State responsibility (7 December 1953) UN Doc A/RES/799.

of the law of state responsibility was closely intertwined with an attempt to outlaw the unilateral use of force and to promote the peaceful settlement of disputes.[471] Extensive discussions of general international rules on state responsibility under the auspices of the ILC are associated with Roberto Ago. James Crawford referred to Ago's contribution as "prodigious."[472] Overall, the codification process took more than half of a century, eventually culminating in the adoption of the Draft articles in 2001.[473] The rules prescribed by the Draft articles were not codified in an international treaty. Despite this, international courts and tribunals frequently cite them as a reflection of customary international law.[474]

3.1 *Unilateral Economic Sanctions as Countermeasures*

Unilateral economic sanctions can fall under the category of economic countermeasures, which are subject to the same preconditions and restrictions as any other type of countermeasures. There are two categories of such restrictions or preconditions: substantive and procedural. The substantive prerequisites are enumerated in Articles 49–51 of the Draft articles,[475] while the procedural ones are listed in Article 52.[476]

First and foremost, countermeasures can be imposed only as a response to a prior violation of an international obligation[477] and "are limited to the

471 Kolb (n 460) 8–9.

472 Crawford (n 353) footnote 187.

473 ILC, 'Draft articles' (n 90).

474 UNGA, 'Responsibility of States for Internationally Wrongful Acts. Compilation of Decisions of International Courts, Tribunals and Other Bodies' (2016) UN Doc A/71/80.

475 Among the most important restrictions are: countermeasures can be taken only against a state which is responsible for an internationally wrongful act (Article 49), there is a defined group of international obligations that cannot be affected by countermeasures (Article 50), and countermeasures must be proportional (Article 51). ILC, 'Draft articles' (n 90).

476 Procedural preconditions include: a duty to call upon the responsible state to fulfil its obligations, a duty to notify the responsible state of a decision to take countermeasures, a duty to suspend countermeasures either if the wrongful act has ceased or if there is a pending dispute before the tribunal. ibid.

477 The commentary to the Draft articles clarifies this prerequisite as follows: "A fundamental prerequisite for any lawful countermeasure is the existence of an internationally wrongful act which injured the State taking the countermeasure. This point was clearly made by ICJ in the Gabcíkovo Nagymaros Project case, in the following passage: In order to be justifiable, a countermeasure must meet certain conditions [...] In the first place it must be taken in response to a previous international wrongful act of another State and must be directed against that State." ibid 130.

non-performance for the time being of international obligation of the State taking the measures towards the responsible State."[478] It ought to be noted that there is no requirement that the countermeasures and the initial obligation, the breach of which provided the justification for imposing such countermeasures, should be of the same or of a closely related nature.[479] Second, countermeasures can be directed only against a state responsible for an internationally wrongful act.[480] Third, countermeasures should be temporary in character[481] and proportionate to the initial violation of the international obligation.[482] The prerequisite of proportionality has been formulated as follows: "Countermeasures must be commensurate with the injury suffered, taking into account the gravity of the internationally wrongful act and the rights in question."[483] Thomas Cottier and others emphasise that the principle of proportionality applicable to countermeasures "first entered international law by the application of the principle of equity by international tribunals" and quoted the pertinent discussion in Naulilaa Arbitration between Portugal and Germany (1928).[484]

Article 50 of the Draft articles places further constraints on the types of obligations that might be impacted by countermeasures. More specifically, this article enumerates the international obligations of states that shall not be affected by countermeasures. Accordingly, countermeasures shall not affect: "(a) the obligation to refrain from the threat or use of force as embodied in the Charter of the United Nations; (b) obligations for the protection of fundamental human rights; (c) obligations of a humanitarian character prohibiting reprisals; (d) other obligations under peremptory norms of general international law."[485] Moreover, a state relying upon such measures is not relieved from fulfilling the following obligations: "(a) under any dispute settlement procedure applicable between it and the responsible State; (b) to respect the inviolability of diplomatic or consular agents, premises, archives and documents."[486]

---

478 Article 49(2) ILC, 'Draft articles' (n 90).
479 ibid 129.
480 Article 49(1) ILC, 'Draft articles' (n 90).
481 Articles 49 and 53 ibid.
482 Article 51 ibid.
483 Article 51 ibid.
484 Thomas Cottier and others, 'The Principle of Proportionality in International Law: Foundations and Variations' (2017) 18 The Journal of World Investment & Trade 628, 636.
485 Article 50(1) ILC, 'Draft articles' (n 90).
486 Article 50(2) ibid.

A number of procedural preconditions apply to countermeasures, such as the requirement to call on the responsible state to fulfil its obligations,[487] the requirement to notify the responsible state of a decision to take countermeasures and offer to negotiate,[488] and a prohibition on imposing countermeasures if an internationally wrongful act has ceased[489] or if there is a pending dispute before a court or tribunal which is authorised to issue a binding decision.[490] Additionally, a state that has imposed countermeasures is obliged to terminate them as soon as the responsible state has complied with its obligations.[491]

Unilateral economic sanctions often do not fall under the definition of legitimate countermeasures. This is due, first of all, to the rigid definition of an injured state[492] and, second, to the fact that the illegality of the prior conduct that served to justify the countermeasures and the proportionality of the imposed countermeasures are often called into question.[493]

3.2 *Unilateral Economic Sanctions as Third-Party Countermeasures*

The final text of the Draft articles entitles an injured state to rely upon countermeasures, including economic countermeasures.[494] Article 42 stipulates under what conditions a state might be considered as an injured state. A state may qualify as an injured state if a breached obligation is owed either to this state or to a group of states (which includes this state), or even to the international community as a whole.[495] Despite the explicit right to invoke the responsibility of a state that violated obligations owed to a group of states or the international community as a whole, the application of this right is permitted only if the breach either affects the state or is of such a character as to be able to radically change the position of all the other states to which the obligation is owed with respect to the further performance of the obligation.[496]

When it comes to the rights of a non-injured state, Article 48 of the Draft articles is a reference point. Article 48 prescribes the rules for invocation of state responsibility by a state other than an injured state.[497] According to this

487 Article 52(1)(a) ibid.
488 Article 52(1)(b) ibid.
489 Article 52(3)(a) ibid.
490 Article 52(3)(b) ibid.
491 Article 53 ibid.
492 For more, see footnote 365.
493 Ruys (n 4) 35.
494 Article 49 ILC, 'Draft articles' (n 90).
495 Article 42 ibid.
496 ibid.
497 Article 48 ibid.

article, state responsibility can be invoked by a non-injured state only in relation to certain obligations, namely obligations for the protection of community interests.[498] What is even more pivotal is that the remedies offered to a non-injured state are confined to claims of cessation, assurances and guarantees of non-repetition, or reparations in the interests of an injured state.[499] Thus, the right of a non-injured state to impose countermeasures is not explicitly enshrined in the Draft articles.[500]

The commentary to the Draft articles provides the following explanation for this outcome: "Occasions have arisen in practice of countermeasures being taken by other States, in particular, those identified in Article 48, where no State is injured or else on behalf of and at the request of an injured State. Such cases are controversial and the practice is embryonic."[501] The conclusion that the practice is embryonic has been questioned by legal scholars.[502] I discuss some of these studies below.

Article 54 of the Draft articles makes matters even more complicated, particularly when it states: "This chapter does not prejudice the right of any State, entitled under article 48, paragraph 1, to invoke the responsibility of another State, to take lawful measures against that State to ensure cessation of the breach and reparation in the interest of the injured State or of the beneficiaries of the obligation breached." The article does not refer to countermeasures, yet it explicitly mentions "lawful measures." Christian Hillgruber points out: "As shown by the official commentaries, this provision is seen as a safeguard clause designed to leave the issue of whether and how third States may have recourse to 'countermeasures' (which presumably primarily means 'reprisals') to be decided in the course of further developments in international law."[503]

Before the Draft articles were adopted, the ICJ categorically objected to the possibility of acknowledging the legality of third-party countermeasures: "The

498 The relevant section, reads as follows: "1. Any State other than an injured State is entitled to invoke the responsibility of another State in accordance with paragraph 2 if: (a) the obligation breached is owed to a group of States including that State, and is established for the protection of a collective interest of the group; or (b) the obligation breached is owed to the international community as a whole." ibid.

499 Article 48 ibid.

500 For a similar conclusion, see Dawidowicz, 'Third-Party Countermeasures' (n 372).

501 ILC, 'Draft articles' (n 90) 129.

502 Dawidowicz, *Third-Party Countermeasures in International Law* (n 372); Dawidowicz, 'Third-Party Countermeasures' (n 372); Dawidowicz, 'Public Law Enforcement without Public Law Safeguards?' (n 372); Katselli Proukaki (n 372).

503 Christian Hillgruber, 'The Right of Third States to Take Countermeasures' in Christian Tomuschat and Jean-Marc Thouvenin (eds.), *The Fundamental Rules of the International Legal Order* (Martinus Nijhoff Publishers 2006).

acts of which Nicaragua is accused, even assuming them to have been established and imputable to that State, could only have justified proportionate counter-measures on the part of the State which had been the victim of these acts, namely El Salvador, Honduras or Costa Rica. They could not justify counter-measures taken by a third State, the United States, and particularly could not justify intervention involving the use of force."[504]

A significant share of unilateral economic sanctions imposed by individual states fall under the category of third-party countermeasures, since states that impose such measures are not always injured states in the sense laid out in the Draft articles. This discrepancy between state practice and the existing legal rules has received sufficient attention in the literature. International law scholars provide numerous accounts of state practice when countermeasures were relied upon by non-injured states, thus making them third-party countermeasures.[505]

Martin Dawidowicz examined the state practice of imposing unilateral countermeasures to establish whether international law recognises a system of public law enforcement for the most serious breaches of international law.[506] After analysing twenty-two instances of coercive measures imposed by non-injured states, Dawidowicz concluded that all of these measures are third-party countermeasures.[507] On this basis, Dawidowicz criticises the view expressed by the ILC concerning third-party countermeasures, arguing that "international practice could thus hardly be described as still being in a formative stage of development."[508] Moreover, Dawidowicz challenges the premise that western states dominate the state practice, declaring that "as many as 108 states, from all but the Latin American region, have adopted third-party countermeasures at any one time since 1950."[509]

Elena Katselli has made a list with numerous examples of third-party countermeasures,[510] containing more than thirty instances.[511] Overall, Katselli's research buttresses the conclusions reached by Dawidowicz.[512]

---

504 *Military and Paramilitary Activities in and against Nicaragua* (n 116) [249].

505 Dawidowicz, *Third-Party Countermeasures in International Law* (n 372); Dawidowicz, 'Third-Party Countermeasures' (n 372); Dawidowicz, 'Public Law Enforcement without Public Law Safeguards?' (n 372); Katselli Proukaki (n 372); Christian J Tams, *Enforcing Obligations 'Erga Omnes' in International Law* (Cambridge University Press 2005).

506 Dawidowicz, 'Public Law Enforcement without Public Law Safeguards?' (n 372).

507 ibid.

508 ibid 410.

509 ibid 411.

510 Katselli Proukaki (n 372).

511 ibid Chapter 3.

512 ibid.

A study prepared at the request of the European Parliament's Committee on International Trade in 2020 emphasises that sanctions imposed against a state responsible for a violation of international law might be justified under the emerging customary international law on state responsibility.[513] That being said, the study highlights that it is doubtful whether a general right to impose sanctions exists.[514] In a similar vein, Chinese scholars argue that sanctions imposed in response to a previous violation of international law may be permitted, thus legitimising third-party countermeasures.[515]

To conclude our discussion on the legality of third-party countermeasures, the suggestion put forward by Tom Ruys should be quoted: "the time may ultimately be ripe to shift the debate from the binary question whether third-party countermeasures are permissible or not, to defining the possible boundaries to their use."[516] In light of this proposition, in chapter 4 of this book, I analyse whether unilateral economic sanctions imposed on human rights grounds constitute permissible countermeasures in the sense outlined in the Draft articles. Subsequently, in chapter 5, the possible preconditions for recognition the legality of unilateral economic sanctions imposed on human rights grounds are defined.

4 Unilateral Economic Sanctions and Established Principles of Jurisdiction in International Law

The extraterritorial application of unilateral economic sanctions faces a barrage of criticism from the affected states,[517] practitioners[518] and international legal scholars.[519] From the perspective of public international law, such an

513 Stoll and others (n 232) 55.

514 ibid 55.

515 Rotblat (n 323) 350–351.

516 Ruys (n 4) 47.

517 Traditionally, the EU has been active in condemning unilateral economic sanctions that are unlawfully extraterritorial. The recent study prepared at the request of the European Parliament's Committee on International Trade emphasises the following point: "The impact of such extraterritorial sanctions driven by political considerations poses new, if indirect, challenges to the EU." Stoll and others (n 232) 18.

518 Meredith Rathbone, Peter Jeydel and Amy Lentz, 'Sanctions, Sanctions Everywhere: Forging a Path through Complex Transnational Sanctions Laws' (2013) 44 Georgetown Journal of International Law 1055.

519 Susan Emmenegger and Thirza Döbeli, 'Extraterritorial Application of US Sanctions Law' in Andrea Bonomi and Krista Nadakavukaren Schefer (eds.), *US Litigation Today: Still a Threat For European Businesses or Just a Paper Tiger? Conference proceedings from the 29th*

extraterritorial application may contradict established principles of jurisdiction developed in international law.[520]

Thus, it is warranted to discuss the relationship between jurisdiction and unilateral economic sanctions, as well as to examine what types of unilateral economic sanctions might be unlawfully extraterritorial. This section starts with a brief review of the principles on the basis of which states are allowed to ascertain jurisdiction. I then proceed with a discussion of secondary sanctions, which have attracted mounting criticism for their alleged inconsistency with the principles on ascertaining jurisdiction, before briefly considering what strategies states implement to offset the negative implications of extraterritorial economic sanctions. Finally, the analysis focuses on defining the types of economic sanctions that run the risk of being classified as unlawfully extraterritorial.

4.1 *Jurisdiction in International Law*

Despite being one of the essential building blocks of international law, the doctrine of jurisdiction remains conceptually blurry and, in practice, often illusory. Yet it is of the utmost importance for states, since, as Cedric Ryngaert points out: "Jurisdiction becomes a concern of international law when a State, in its eagerness to promote its sovereign interests abroad, adopts laws that govern matters of not purely domestic concern."[521] This observation explains why jurisdiction is closely related to the principles of non-intervention and of the sovereign equality of states.[522]

The term "jurisdiction" denotes three competences exercised by a state: prescriptive jurisdiction, adjudicative jurisdiction and enforcement jurisdiction. The most authoritative pronouncements on the doctrine of jurisdiction date back to the judgement in the *Lotus case*,[523] where the PCIJ observed that

Journée de droit International privé du 23 juin 2017, vol 85 (Schulthess Verlag 2018); Susan Emmenegger, 'Extraterritorial Economic Sanctions and Their Foundation in International Law' (2016) 33 Arizona Journal of International and Comparative Law 631.

520 Emmenegger and Döbeli (n 519); Charlotte Beaucillon, 'Practice Makes Perfect, Eventually? Unilateral State Sanctions and the Extraterritorial Effects of National Legislation' in Natalino Ronzitti (ed), *Coercive Diplomacy, Sanctions and International Law* (Brill Nijhoff 2016); Emmenegger (n 519); Cedric Ryngaert, 'Extraterritorial Export Controls (Secondary Boycotts)' (2008) 7 Chinese Journal of International Law 625.

521 Cedric Ryngaert, *Jurisdiction in International Law* (Second edition, Oxford University Press 2015) 5.

522 ibid 6.

523 *The case of the SS Lotus (France v. Turkey) (Merits) PCIJ (1927) Rep Series A No 10.*

prescriptive jurisdiction is not restricted unless there is a prohibitive rule.[524] Notwithstanding the court's pronouncements, customary international law has taken the opposite stand on the issue of prescriptive jurisdiction. The majority of states favour the permissive principle of ascertaining jurisdiction, which entails that states are required to justify their jurisdictional assertions.[525] Yet, this permissive principle has been formulated rather broadly: "States are generally considered to be authorized to exercise jurisdiction if they can advance a legitimate interest based on personal or territorial connections of the matter to be regulated."[526]

Discussing the relevance of both approaches for jurisdiction over economic matters, one conclusion deserves particular attention. As Ryngaert has emphasised: "States – in particular the United States and the European Union and its Member States – have never primarily substantiated their claims of economic jurisdiction in Lotus terms. Instead, they relied upon the classical principles of jurisdiction, although such required stretching them at times."[527] In other words, in economic matters states favour the principle of permissive jurisdiction over an idea of unrestricted jurisdiction unless there is a prohibitive rule.

The territoriality principle is one of the most authoritative grounds for establishing a state's jurisdiction over a particular matter.[528] Brownlie distinguishes between subjective and objective territorial jurisdiction – while the former relates to the conduct that materialised in a state's territory, the latter concerns

524 "Such a view would only be tenable if international law contained a general prohibition to States to extend the application of their laws and the jurisdiction of their courts to persons, property and acts outside their territory, and if, as an exception to this general prohibition, it allowed States to do so in certain specific cases. But this is certainly not the case under international law as it stands at present. Far from laying down a general prohibition to the effect that States may not extend the application of their laws and the jurisdiction of their courts to persons, property and acts outside their territory, it leaves them in this respect a wide measure of discretion which is only limited in certain cases by prohibitive rules; as regards other cases, every State remains free to adopt the principles which it regards as best and most suitable." ibid 19.

525 Ryngaert (n 521) 29. In the similar vein, Susan Emmenegger points out: "Today's conventional view is more restrictive: states are required to justify their jurisdictional assertion under generally accepted rules or principles of international law (permissive principles approach)." Emmenegger (n 519) 644.

526 Ryngaert (n 521) 30.

527 ibid 38.

528 Bruno Simma and Andreas Th Müller, 'Exercise and Limits of Jurisdiction' in James Crawford and Martti Koskenniemi (eds.), *The Cambridge Companion to International Law* (Cambridge University Press 2012) 137; Cedric Ryngaert asserts that: "The primacy of territorial jurisdiction is usually premised on the principle of sovereign equality of States and the principle of non-intervention (or non-interference)." Ryngaert (n 521) 36.

the results.[529] The effects doctrine, which evolved in US antitrust law, is considered as a variation of objective territorial jurisdiction.[530] The International Bar Association has acknowledged that "virtually all jurisdictions apply some form of an 'effects' test."[531] Thus, states recognise objective territorial jurisdiction in one way or another. However, the effects doctrine should not be conflated with jurisdiction as a territorial extension of domestic law. Jurisdiction as a territorial extension can be defined in the following way: "Jurisdiction via territorial extension is typically exercised by conditioning access to domestic territory and markets, on an economic operator satisfying certain standards also when it operates outside the domestic sphere, and by including performance abroad in assessing whether the operator meets domestic regulatory targets."[532]

The personality or nationality principle endows a state with jurisdiction over its nationals, and a distinction is made between active and passive embodiments of this principle.[533] The active personality principle entitles a state to exercise jurisdiction over its nationals abroad, including having jurisdiction over crimes committed by its nationals abroad.[534] The passive personality principle, the existence of which is often questioned, is triggered when a national of a given state is the victim of a crime.[535]

In addition to these principles, the protective principle has also been fully acknowledged.[536] The rationale underlying the need for such a principle has been expressed as follows: "acts that severely jeopardise a state's government functions are considered a sufficient basis for jurisdiction."[537] While the exact contours of this principle have not been determined with great precision, numerous measures might be justified on the basis of it. Bruno Simma and Andreas Müller have identified the following tendency: "In the post-2001 atmosphere where 'security' appears to have become to some a catch-all concept, a sweeping application of the protective principle may present itself as highly opportune, but this is far from being a commonly accepted position."[538]

529 Ian Brownlie, *Principles of Public International Law* (7th ed., Oxford University Press 2008) 301.

530 Simma and Müller (n 528) 140.

531 Ryngaert (n 521) 84.

532 ibid 94.

533 Simma and Müller (n 528) 142.

534 ibid.

535 ibid.

536 ibid 143.

537 ibid 144.

538 ibid.

The universality principle, commonly known as universal jurisdiction, authorises a state to assert jurisdiction over a crime irrespective of the existence of any other grounds for jurisdiction.[539] This broad discretion is warranted by the unique nature of the crimes that are of concern to the international community.[540] This principle has been embedded in numerous international conventions, mainly in the fields of international humanitarian law and international human rights law.[541]

4.2 *Secondary Sanctions and Their Extraterritorial Reach*

In this book, secondary sanctions are defined as "economic restriction imposed by a sanctioning or sending state (e.g., the United States) that is intended to deter a third-party country or its citizens and companies (e.g., France, the French people and French companies) from transacting with a sanctions target (e.g., a rogue regime, its high government officials)."[542]

Perry Bechky quotes Senator Alfonse D'Amato to illustrate the rationale behind secondary sanctions: "Now the nations of the world will know they can trade with them [i.e. Iran and Libya] or trade with us. They have to choose."[543] Notorious historical examples of secondary sanctions include the Arab League Boycott against Israel,[544] the United States sanctions against the Soviet Union imposed in relation to the construction of the pipeline in 1982[545] and the Helms-Burton Act of 1996.[546]

The United States is known for implementing unilateral economic restrictions with broad extraterritorial reach. An example that has received

539 ibid.

540 ibid.

541 ibid 145.

542 Jeffrey A Meyer, 'Second Thoughts on Secondary Sanctions' (2009) 30 University of Pennsylvania Journal of International Law 905, 926. Other scholars define secondary sanctions as "extraterritorial sanctions, also called secondary sanctions, that subject foreign persons to sanctions for actions that they take wholly outside the sanctioning state." Rathbone, Jeydel and Lentz (n 518) 1070; or as "a 'secondary sanction,' adapting Lowenfeld's definition of an economic sanction to this context, is an economic measure taken for the political end of inducing third states or non-state actors in third states to change their policies or practices concerning economic dealings with the target of the sending state's 'primary sanctions.'" Bechky (n 337) 10.

543 Bechky (n 337) 10–11.

544 Nancy Turck, 'The Arab Boycott of Israel' (1977) 55 Foreign Affairs 472.

545 Perlow (n 110).

546 Robert L Muse, 'A Public Internation Law Critique of the Extraterritorial Jurisdiction of the Helms-Burton Act (Cuban Liberty and Democratic Solidarity (Libertad) Act of 1996)' (1996) 30 The George Washington Journal of International Law and Economics 207.

considerable critical attention is the Helms-Burton Act, which was discussed under the auspices of the WTO.[547] Among recent sanctioning programmes, the secondary financial sanctions imposed on Iran by the United States are vehemently condemned as extraterritorial.[548] Even China and its financial institutions had to comply with the US secondary sanctions against Iran, despite China's close economic cooperation with Iran.[549]

Secondary sanctions are frequently criticized for overstepping jurisdictional boundaries. In particular, it is argued that secondary sanctions "impinge on the rights of neutral states to regulate their own citizens and companies."[550] The literature abounds in claims that secondary sanctions are illegal.[551] In this regard, Sarah Cleveland notes: "The use of trade sanctions or foreign assistance limitations to impose secondary boycotts has been criticized for violating international law principles regarding state jurisdiction."[552] Cedric Ryngaert contends that secondary sanctions, or secondary boycotts as he calls them, "raise serious public international law concerns."[553] Ryngaert emphasises that such measures "subject corporations that are not incorporated in the boycotting State to the latter's regulations in the absence of a direct and clearly discernable effect on that State."[554] In their most recent study, Tom Ruys and Cedric Ryngaert argue that secondary sanctions limit the sovereignty of third states by curtailing their right to freely conduct external economic relations with other states.[555] A study prepared at the request of the European Parliament's Committee on International Trade reveals the following negative repercussions of secondary

547 The European Communities formally initiated a dispute at the WTO. Furthermore, Canada and Mexico engaged in a dispute under the NAFTA. For more details, see Harvey Oyer, 'The Extraterritorial Effects of U.S. Unilateral Trade Sanctions and Their Impact on U.S. Obligations under NAFTA' (1997) 11 Florida Journal of International Law 429.

548 Emmenegger and Döbeli (n 519); Emmenegger (n 519); Katzenstein (n 324).

549 Chinese scholars writing on the subject have reached the following conclusion: "China had no choice but to cooperate with the sanctions regime against Iran." Rotblat (n 323) 329.

550 Meyer (n 542) 932–933.

551 Sarah Cleveland, 'Norm Internalization and U.S. Economic Sanctions' (2001) 26 Yale Journal of International Law 1, 56–57; Lowenfeld, *International Economic Law* (n 338) 926. Chinese scholars contest the legality of secondary sanctions on various grounds. Their overall conclusion is that "Chinese legal scholars and diplomats have steadfastly held that secondary sanctions violate international law." Rotblat (n 323) 348.

552 Cleveland (n 551) 48.

553 Ryngaert (n 520) 626.

554 ibid.

555 Tom Ruys and Cedric Ryngaert, 'Secondary Sanctions: A Weapon out of Control? The International Legality of, and European Responses to, US Secondary Sanctions' (2021) British Yearbook of International Law 1, 4.

sanctions: "The extraterritorial reach of sanctions does not only affect EU businesses but also puts into question the political independence and ultimately the sovereignty of the EU and its Member States."[556]

However, other scholars evince little sympathy for these arguments. Jeffrey Meyer argues that a distinction must be drawn between various types of secondary sanctions.[557] Following Meyer's line of reasoning, the prohibition on conducting business with third-country nationals or entities that do business with the sanctioned state or its enterprises is a legitimate exercise of the "terrinational jurisdiction" – a combination of territorial and nationality principles.[558] Other types of secondary sanctions that directly target foreign nationals or legal enterprises, in Meyer's view, are more susceptible to jurisdictional challenges.[559] Hence, Meyer contends that narrowly defined secondary sanctions – i.e. those that are connected either with a territory or with a nationality – are legal and should not be conflated with other secondary sanctions.[560]

States have invoked various justifications for their extraterritorial sanctions. On some occasions, the classical territorial or nationality principles of jurisdiction were extended.[561] On others, the protective jurisdiction or effects doctrine were relied upon.[562]

The application of the nationality principle might be particularly burdensome if a multinational legal entity is involved.[563] For example, the United States was known for extending the reach of its unilateral sanctions to any legal entity "controlled" by US nationals.[564] These legal entities were required

556 Stoll and others (n 232) 9.

557 Meyer (n 542).

558 "[...] the fact that the United States may lack a proper prescriptive jurisdictional basis to regulate business deals between China and Sudan does not dispel U.S. authority to regulate the conduct of U.S. companies in U.S. territory to prohibit them from doing business with Sudan's Chinese business partners." ibid 957.

559 Meyer (n 542).

560 ibid.

561 Ryngaert (n 520).

562 Meyer (n 542) 909. Regarding the possibility of justifying secondary sanctions under the protective principle, Susan Emmenegger emphasises that there is a lack of unanimity on this issue among the legal scholars. Emmenegger (n 519) 651–652.

563 "In the field of economic law, additional difficulties surrounding the application of the nationality principle may arise, since the nationality of a corporation may not always be readily established. Corporations could have different nationalities, as their nationality could be based on the State of incorporation, shareholder nationality or other corporate links to the forum." Ryngaert (n 520) 627.

564 In this vein, Cedric Ryngaert provides the following examples: "In the 1960s, it [the United States] attempted to prohibit Fruehauf, a French corporation under U.S. control, from exporting to China under the U.S. Trading with the Enemy Act. In the 1980s then, it

to comply with unilateral US sanctions even though they might have been incorporated under the laws of another state. The predominant international sentiment in this regard is that this practice oversteps the limits of the principle of nationality used for ascertaining jurisdiction.[565]

States that suffer from the negative consequences of secondary sanctions may implement blocking statutes to hinder domestic legal entities or individuals from complying with these secondary sanctions.[566] The history of blocking statutes goes back to the Arab Oil Embargo, when the United States prohibited its nationals from complying with the secondary embargo against Israel.[567] Later the enactment of the Helms-Burton Act resulted in the adoption of the blocking statute by the European Union.[568] Businesses from both sides of the Atlantic were confronted with a dilemma – what set of rules should they comply with and at what cost?[569] Fortunately, this tension was resolved by diplomatic means.[570]

The most recent example is the EU blocking statute enacted after the United States withdrew from participation in the Joint Comprehensive Plan of Action, an agreement signed between a number of states and Iran.[571] The

prohibited the export to Russia of equipment produced abroad by foreign subsidiaries of U.S. undertakings and by any company using technology licenses granted by U.S. undertakings. In the 1990s, in a last volley of secondary boycotts, the United States prohibited foreign corporations, even if not owned by U.S. corporations, from trading in goods confiscated from U.S. nationals by the Cuban government in the 1960s, and from trading with such 'terrorist' States as Iran and Libya." ibid 626.

565 Susan Emmenegger discussed this issue and concluded as follows: "Moreover, a state cannot premise nationality jurisdiction on control of a foreign corporation by its citizens. The US practice of exercising jurisdiction over companies that are incorporated outside the United States but are owned by a US parent corporation is not legal under international law." Emmenegger (n 519) 650; Ryngaert (n 521) 110.

566 Other available responses to unilateral economic sanctions include: challenging the legality of such measures before international and national courts, issuing diplomatic statements condemning such sanctions, taking countermeasures, implementing measures with the objective of reducing the economic vulnerability of the economy and businesses to such measures. Stoll and others (n 232) 51.

567 For a detailed discussion of the United States blocking statutes and the several court cases which were initiated by the US government to reinforce these blocking statutes, see Ryngaert (n 520) 641.

568 Council Regulation (EC) No 2271/96 of 22 November 1996 protecting against the effects of the extra-territorial application of legislation adopted by a third country, and actions based thereon or resulting therefrom 1996 (OJ L).

569 Rathbone, Jeydel and Lentz (n 518) 1072–1074.

570 ibid.

571 In 2015, Iran, the five permanent members of the UN Security Council, Germany and the European Union reached a landmark decision on Iran's nuclear programme (the Joint

updated blocking statute in support of Iran's nuclear deal entered into force on 7 August 2018.[572] Despite these laudable efforts, practitioners are sceptical of the ability of blocking statutes to impact the decisions of private entities to comply with the reinstated unilateral US sanctions.[573] Confirming this view, the devastating effects of these sanctions on the EU-Iran bilateral trade have been reported: "imports from Iran to the EU dropped 92.8% in 2019, while exports to Iran dropped nearly 50%."[574]

History provides successful examples of blocking statutes, including the Canadian blocking statute, which prohibited companies incorporated in Canada from complying with the unilateral economic sanctions imposed on Cuba by the United States.[575] In 1997, the Canadian subsidiary of the US parent company Walmart put pyjamas made in Cuba on sale. This minor action triggered a forceful response from both the US and Canadian sides. The US OFAC claimed that the Canadian subsidiary was subject to US economic sanctions

---

Comprehensive Plan of Action). This agreement, which was unanimously endorsed by the UN Security Council, paved the way for subsequent sanction relief. UNSC Res 2231 (20 July 2015) UN Doc S/RES/2231. After the United States announced its withdrawal from the Joint Comprehensive Plan of Action, the European Union issued a press release to confirm its support for the deal and its desire to oppose the reimposition of US sanctions. 'European Commission Acts to Protect the Interests of EU Companies Investing in Iran as Part of the EU's Continued Commitment to the Joint Comprehensive Plan of Action' (*European Commission*) <https://ec.europa.eu/commission/presscorner/detail/en/IP_18_3861>. A few weeks later, the European Commission adopted a blocking statute. Commission Delegated Regulation (EU) 2018/1100 of 6 June 2018 amending the Annex to Council Regulation (EC) No 2271/96 protecting against the effects of extra-territorial application of legislation adopted by a third country, and actions based thereon or resulting therefrom 2018 (OJ L).

572 'Updated Blocking Statute in Support of Iran Nuclear Deal Enters into Force' (*European Commission*) <https://ec.europa.eu/commission/presscorner/detail/en/IP_18_4805>; Commission Implementing Regulation (EU) 2018/1101 of 3 August 2018 laying down the criteria for the application of the second paragraph of Article 5 of Council Regulation (EC) No 2271/96 protecting against the effects of the extra-territorial application of legislation adopted by a third country, and actions based thereon or resulting therefrom 2018 (OJ L).

573 "In recent cases involving US sanctions violations by European companies, Ms Bradshaw says compliance with the EU blocking regulation even seems to have been treated as an aggravating factor, justifying greater punishment. 'Evidence of steps taken to follow the EU regime could be invoked as proof of how a company is violating the US regulations,' she says." Bruce Love, 'Companies Caught in EU-US Sanctions Crossfire' *Financial Times* (30 January 2020) <https://www.ft.com/content/97a75318-16a8-11ea-b869-0971bffac109>.

574 Stoll and others (n 232) 31.

575 John W Boscariol, 'An Anatomy of a Cuban Pyjama Crisis: Reconsidering Blocking Legislation in Response to Extraterritorial Trade Measures of the United States' (1999) 30 Law and Policy in International Business 439.

against Cuba and should comply with them by sending the pyjamas back to Cuba.[576] By contrast, Canada asserted that the Canadian subsidiary was subject to the blocking statutes introduced against Cuban extraterritorial sanctions.[577] After evaluating the relevant risks and losses, the Canadian subsidiary of Walmart complied with the Canadian laws, while the parent company was forced to pay fines in the United States.[578]

4.3 *Types of Primary and Secondary Unilateral Sanctions That Face a Significant Risk of Being Classed as Extraterritorial*

The categories of measures described below have been chosen due to a significant risk of their being found inconsistent with the established principles of jurisdiction. One more clarification is warranted here. The examples mostly represent the unilateral economic sanctions imposed by the United States, and thus we analyse them in light of the jurisdictional justifications invoked by the United States, namely the effects doctrine and protective jurisdiction.

4.3.1 Restrictions Imposed on Foreign Persons

Unilateral economic sanctions may prescribe restrictions applicable to foreign persons or foreign legal entities. One such example is the Iran and Libya Sanctions Act of 1996 (ISA),[579] as amended by certain provisions of the Comprehensive Iran Sanctions, Accountability, and Divestment Act of 2010 (CISADA)[580] and the Iran Threat Reduction and Syria Human Rights Act (ITRA).[581]

Initially, the ISA required the president to impose at least two out of a menu of six sanctions on foreign companies, entities and persons that made an investment in Iran's energy sector of more than $40 million in one year.[582] This act explicitly stipulated that it applies to "any person the President determines

576 H Scott Fairley, 'Between Scylla and Charybdis: The U.S. Embargo of Cuba and Canadian Foreign Extraterritorial Measures Against It' (2010) 44 The International Lawyer 887.

577 ibid.

578 David E Sanger, 'Wal-Mart Canada Is Putting Cuban Pajamas Back on Shelf' *The New York Times* (14 March 1997) <https://www.nytimes.com/1997/03/14/business/wal-mart-canada-is-putting-cuban-pajamas-back-on-shelf.html>.

579 Iran and Libya Sanctions Act of 1996, Public Law 104–172, August 5, 1996, 110 Stat. 1541 (Iran and Libya Sanctions Act of 1996).

580 Comprehensive Iran Sanctions, Accountability, and Divestment Act of 2010, Public Law 111–195, July 1, 2010, 124 Stat. 1312 (Comprehensive Iran Sanctions, Accountability, and Divestment Act of 2010).

581 Iran Threat Reduction and Syria Human Rights Act of 2012, Public Law 112–158, August 10, 2012, 126 Stat. 1214 (Iran Threat Reduction and Syria Human Rights Act of 2012).

582 Iran and Libya Sanctions Act of 1996 Section 5 (a) Sanctions With Respect to Iran.

has carried out the activities described" or its successor, subsidiary or affiliate if they engaged in such activities with the actual knowledge.[583] The sanctions menu included: (1) denial of Export-Import Bank loans, credits or credit guarantees for US exports to the sanctioned entity; (2) denial of licenses for the US export of military or militarily useful technology to the entity; (3) denial of US bank loans exceeding $10 million in one year to the entity; (4) if the entity is a financial institution, a prohibition on its service as a primary dealer in US government bonds and/or a prohibition on its serving as a repository for US government funds (each counts as one sanction); (5) prohibition on US government procurement from the entity; and (6) restriction on imports from the entity, in accordance with the International Emergency Economic Powers Act.[584]

Regarding the imposition of unilateral economic sanctions of this kind on foreign persons, the Act prescribes that the president should engage in consultations with "the government with primary jurisdiction over that foreign person with respect to the imposition of sanctions under this Act."[585] Following such consultations, the president should impose sanctions "unless the President determines and certifies to the Congress that the government has taken specific and effective actions, including, as appropriate, the imposition of appropriate penalties, to terminate the involvement of the foreign person in the activities" which triggered the imposition of sanctions.[586]

After the ISA was amended by the Comprehensive Iran Sanctions, Accountability, and Divestment Act of 2010 (CISADA), the president was required to impose at least three out of six possible sanctions on any person investing $20 million in one year, if this investment "is an investment that directly and significantly contributes to the enhancement of Iran's ability to develop petroleum resources."[587] The application of these economic sanctions to subsidiaries and affiliates was replaced by the application to the persons who own or control or are owned and controlled by the person that engaged in sanctioned conduct.[588]

The Iran Threat Reduction and Syria Human Rights Act (ITRA), which amended the ISA, significantly tightened sanctions by expanding their

583 ibid Section 5 (c) Persons Against Which the Sanctions Are To Be Imposed.
584 ibid Section 6. Description of Sanctions.
585 ibid Section 9. Duration of Sanctions; Presidential Waiver; (a) Delay of Sanctions.
586 ibid.
587 Comprehensive Iran Sanctions, Accountability, and Divestment Act of 2010 Section 102. Expansion of sanctions under the Iran Sanctions Act of 1996.
588 ibid Section 102. Expansion of sanctions under the Iran Sanctions Act of 1996.

application to other activities, as well as by requiring that the president impose five possible sanctions from a list against anyone engaged in sanctionable activities.[589]

The expansive extraterritorial reach of these sanctions was strongly opposed by the European Union, and the United States agreed to a partially diplomatic solution with respect to EU-incorporated entities that continued doing business with Iran.[590] Yet these acts were not repealed, and their application to other foreign individuals or foreign-based entities is permitted.

These prohibitions serve as a good example of the sanctions that require justification under the existing principles for ascertaining jurisdiction, in order not to be considered unlawfully extraterritorial. These restrictions could be potentially justified under the effects doctrine or the protective principle of jurisdiction. The effects doctrine emerged in the context of applying antitrust law extraterritorially.[591] In order to be able to rely upon the effects doctrine to ascertain jurisdiction over foreign nationals, the state must prove that the conduct of the foreign nationals in question has a direct, substantial and reasonably predictable effect on the state invoking the effects doctrine.[592] The unilateral economic sanctions described above pursue the objective of

589 Iran Threat Reduction and Syria Human Rights Act of 2012.

590 "Traditionally skeptical of imposing economic sanctions, European Union states opposed ISA as an extraterritorial application of U.S. law and threatened counter-action in the World Trade Organization (WTO). In April 1997, the United States and the EU agreed to avoid a trade confrontation over it (and a separate 'Helms-Burton' Cuba sanctions law, P.L. 104–114). This agreement contributed to a May 18, 1998, decision by the Clinton Administration to waive ILSA sanctions ('national interest' grounds – Section 9[c]) on the first project determined to be in violation: a $2 billion contract, signed in September 1997, for Total SA of France and its partners, Gazprom of Russia and Petronas of Malaysia to develop phases 2 and 3 of the 25-phase South Pars gas field. In exchange, the EU pledged to increase cooperation with the United States on non-proliferation and counterterrorism, and the Administration indicated that EU firms would likely receive waivers for future similar investments in Iran." Kenneth Katzman, 'The Iran Sanctions Act (ISA)' (2007) CRS Report for Congress RS20871.

591 "It is settled law […] that any State may impose liabilities, even upon persons not within its allegiance, for conduct outside its borders that has consequences within its borders which the State reprehends; and these liabilities other States will ordinarily recognise." *United States v. Aluminum Co of America 148 F2d 416 (1945)* (Circuit Court of Appeals, 2nd Cir).

592 "[…] the US Department of Justice ('DOJ') prosecutes 'foreign conduct that was meant to produce, and did produce some substantial effect in the United States,' while the European Commission extends extraterritorial jurisdiction to cartel cases where the economic effects in the European Union are 'direct, immediate, reasonably foreseeable and substantial.'" International Bar Association, 'Report of the IBA Task Force on Extraterritorial Jurisdiction' (2009) 12.

reinforcing the effectiveness of such restrictions by expanding their application extraterritorially. It appears though that non-compliance on the part of foreign nationals with such sanctions cannot produce the direct, substantial and reasonably predictable effect required to justify their extraterritorial application under the effects doctrine.

By contrast, the boundaries of protective jurisdiction are not well defined. Thus, the United States might argue that Iran is engaged in the development of the nuclear weapons and thus that sanctions that undermine the economic viability of Iran's industries aim to cut the financial support for nuclear weapons development. However, the validity of this argument can be challenged: it is debatable whether extraterritorial unilateral economic sanctions can be justified under the principle of protective jurisdiction, if the potential threat does not emanate from the conduct of particular economic operators abroad, but rather from their partners in third countries.

4.3.2 Restrictions Imposed on Domestic Legal Entities and Individuals to Penalise Third-Country Nationals That Do Not Comply with a State's Unilateral Sanctions

Early examples of this type of restrictions include the prohibition on trading with the enemy and third parties engaged in such trade.[593] The existing sanctions regimes may urge third-country nationals to comply with unilateral sanctions, either by conditioning market access or by penalising domestic constituencies for dealing with the non-compliant third parties. Examples of both types of restrictions are provided below.

The Comprehensive Iran Sanctions, Accountability, and Divestment Act of 2010 (CISADA) includes several provisions that restrict access to the US financial market for foreign-based financial institutions that fail to comply with the US financial sanctions against Iran.[594] This Act followed the unprecedented (and futile) efforts on the part of President Obama and his administration to improve relations between the two countries.[595] It was adopted as a means of enforcing the provisions of the Iran Sanctions Act of 1996 by imposing additional restrictions.[596] For example, CISADA enlists a number of prohibited financial transactions and prohibits the US-based financial institutions

593 Alexander (n 19) 14–20.

594 Comprehensive Iran Sanctions, Accountability, and Divestment Act of 2010.

595 Ian Black, 'Barack Obama Offers Iran "New Beginning" with Video Message' *The Guardian* (20 March 2009) <https://www.theguardian.com/world/2009/mar/20/barack-obama-video-iran>.

596 Comprehensive Iran Sanctions, Accountability, and Divestment Act of 2010.

from opening or maintaining a correspondent account or a payable-through account for a foreign-based financial institution that "knowingly" engages in prohibited transactions.[597] In fact, a correspondent account or payable-through account in a US-incorporated bank is the only possible way in which foreign financial institutions can maintain access to the US financial market, without incorporating their branch or subsidiary in the United States. Thus, all financial institutions irrespective of the country in which they are incorporated are bound by these unilateral financial sanctions, if they are interested in preserving market access to the US financial market.

The regulation that was adopted to implement CISADA authorises the secretary of the treasury either to impose strict restrictions on opening and maintaining a correspondent or a payable-through account for a foreign-based financial institution or to prohibit domestic financial institutions from opening such an account.[598] Furthermore, the regulation stipulates that a special list of the financial institutions to which the aforesaid restrictions apply shall be maintained and made publicly accessible.[599] These restrictions demonstrate how compliance with unilateral economic sanctions can be leveraged as a precondition for market access.

The relationship between unilateral financial sanctions and jurisdiction is discussed in detail in the next part of this chapter. However, one observation is warranted here. Conditioning market access on compliance with unilateral economic sanctions does not pose a significant risk of being extraterritorial, if it is channelled through the regulation of the conduct of domestically incorporated companies.[600] Yet, it might be extremely expansive if the state that imposes such restrictions has dominant market power.[601]

Other potentially extraterritorial unilateral economic sanctions are restrictions imposed on domestic persons for dealing with foreign third parties that

597 ibid Sec. 104. Mandatory sanctions with respect to financial institutions that engage in certain transactions.

598 The Iranian Financial Sanctions Regulations 31 CFR part 561.

599 ibid.

600 Tom Ruys and Cedric Ryngaert reached a similar conclusion: "It is argued that sanctions which limit foreign persons' access to the targeting state's economic or financial system fall within that state's territorial sovereignty, and in principle do not raise concerns under the law of jurisdiction." Ruys and Ryngaert (n 555) 9.

601 Chinese scholars discussing this type of unilateral US sanction emphasise its extraterritorial reach: "While admitting that the actual implementation of the sanctions is done by regulating the actions of financial institutions under the jurisdiction of the United States, 'the effect, purpose, and implementation, is to sanction legal foreign exchange in the energy and financial sectors.'" Rotblat (n 323) 350.

fail to comply with a state's unilateral sanctions. One such example is the extremely expansive interpretation of the prohibition to "facilitate" business transactions with the sanctioned entities adopted by the Office of Foreign Assets Control (OFAC), a US agency responsible for administering US sanctions. The prohibition on "facilitating" transactions between the sanctioned entities and third parties outside of the US jurisdiction has been incorporated in a number of economic sanctions regimes administered by the OFAC.[602] Legal commentators have emphasised that "[b]y virtue of OFAC's prohibitions on facilitation, a U.S. company may be exposed to sanctions risks when dealing with a completely legitimate non-U.S. business partner if that foreign entity in turn does business with a sanctioned destination."[603]

The prohibition on a US person's "approval" or "facilitation" of conduct by a foreign subsidiary might have the same effect as the application of sanctions on companies incorporated abroad.[604] The complexity of this prohibition is further exacerbated by the different definitions of what constitutes "facilitation" under numerous US sanctions regimes.[605] In light of this issue, practising lawyers observe that "it is the concept of prohibited 'facilitation' of transactions by non-U.S. persons that is most apt to keep compliance counsel up at night."[606]

The conditioning of market access and the prohibition on "facilitating" business transactions between sanctioned entities and third parties imposed on domestic constituencies appear to be a purely territorial exercise of jurisdiction.[607] However, the situation is more complex than it seems. Prohibitions of this kind, reinforced by severe civil penalties or even criminal prosecution, may lay the foundations for risk-based compliance, and, as a result, extend the reach of unilateral economic sanctions far beyond the territorial borders of a state.

The effect of such regulations is that legal entities or individuals with respect to whom the United States has no right to either prescribe rules of

---

602 Rathbone, Jeydel and Lentz (n 518).

603 ibid 1102.

604 Terence J Lau, 'Triggering Parent Company Liability under United States Sanctions Regimes: The Troubling Implications of Prohibiting Approval and Facilitation' (2004) 41 American Business Law Journal 413, 438.

605 Rathbone, Jeydel and Lentz (n 518) 1102–1103.

606 ibid 1102.

607 Discussing unilateral US sanctions that restrict market access, Tom Ruys and Cedric Ryngaert note: "As international law does not entitle foreign persons to financial, economic, or physical access to the US, such measures do not, in principle, raise jurisdictional problems." Ruys and Ryngaert (n 555) 12.

conduct or enforce them are, in reality, bound by them. In this regard, Suzanne Katzenstein has accurately pointed out that "even when the U.S. lacks adjudicative jurisdiction over a foreign party, the government is able to penalize the foreign party through directing U.S. companies to refrain from engaging in business with it."[608]

4.3.3 Restrictions Imposed on Foreign Subsidiaries "Controlled" by the State's Nationals

Unilateral economic sanctions could apply to foreign subsidiaries of domestically incorporated entities or foreign legal entities over which the national of a given state exercises control. The following examples illustrate these restrictions.

The first example is the unilateral economic sanctions imposed on Cuba by the US. According to the regulations, these sanctions apply to "persons subject to the jurisdiction of the United States," which includes "(a) Any individual, wherever located, who is a citizen or resident of the United States; (b) Any person within the United States as defined in § 515.330; (c) Any corporation, partnership, association, or other organization organized under the laws of the United States or of any State, territory, possession, or district of the United States; and (d) Any corporation, partnership, association, or other organization, wherever organized or doing business, that is owned or controlled by persons specified in paragraphs (a) or (c) of this section."[609] This definition of "persons subject to the jurisdiction of the United States" covers any legal entity, regardless of where it is established, that is owned or controlled by US citizens, residents or legal entities. Legal commentators have emphasised that the meaning of the terms "owned" and "controlled" has been interpreted differently in various sanctions regimes, thus contributing to the uncertainty regarding the exact scope of such ownership or control.[610]

The second example is provided by the unilateral economic sanctions imposed on Iran that apply to the entities "controlled" by US persons. For instance, the pertinent regulation stipulates: "An entity that is owned or controlled by a United States person and established or maintained outside the United States is prohibited from knowingly engaging in any transaction, directly or indirectly, with the Government of Iran or any person subject to the jurisdiction of the Government of Iran that would be prohibited pursuant to

608 Katzenstein (n 324) 315.

609 Cuban Assets Control Regulations 31 CFR Part 515 §515.329 – Person subject to the jurisdiction of the United States; person subject to U.S. jurisdiction.

610 Rathbone, Jeydel and Lentz (n 518).

this part if engaged in by a United States person or in the United States."[611] In this particular example, an entity should not only be "owned" or "controlled" by a US person, but also engage in a certain conduct "knowingly."

These examples should be distinguished from the anti-circumvention provisions incorporated into primary sanctions. For example, the EU Guidelines on the Implementation and Evaluation of Restrictive Measures (Sanctions) prescribe the following rule: "An entity incorporated in an EU Member State may not, inter alia, use a company that it controls as a tool to circumvent a prohibition, including where that company is not incorporated in the EU, nor may this entity give instructions to such effect."[612] The difference between this rule and the previous examples is that the former curtails evasion practices by prohibiting certain behaviour on the part of domestically incorporated entities, while the latter expands the prescriptive jurisdiction of a state enacting such unilateral sanctions.

Unilateral economic sanctions, compliance with which was mandatory for foreign-based entities if they were controlled by US persons, came in for stinging criticism. A number of states, including the European Union and Canada, expressed their opposition to such measures, arguing that these restrictions deprive them of their legitimate right to regulate the conduct of the entities established in their respective territories.[613] Indeed, this extraterritorial expansion of the prescriptive jurisdiction deprives the states under whose laws legal entities are established of their legitimate right to prescribe norms of conduct. Whether such extraterritorial expansion can be permitted under the effects doctrine or the protective principle of jurisdiction is doubtful. The adverse impact of non-compliance with unilateral economic sanctions by foreign-based entitles may be too insignificant to be justified under the effects doctrine. The protective principle of jurisdiction is related to the state's national security. Thus, it is necessary for sanctions that are enforced via such expansive extraterritorial restrictions to be imposed on a state that represents a genuine threat to the sanctioning state. This is a high threshold that can be met only by a subset of existing sanctions.

Additionally, the possibility of justifying such extraterritorial sanctions by an expansive interpretation of the nationality principle is doubtful. In this

---

611 Iranian Transactions and Sanctions Regulations 31 CFR Part 560 § 560.215 – Prohibitions on foreign entities owned or controlled by U.S. persons.

612 Council of the EU, 'Guidelines on Implementation and Evaluation of Restrictive Measures (Sanctions) in the Framework of the EU Common Foreign and Security Policy' (Annex to Doc No 5664/18, 4 May 2018) para 54.

613 Muse (n 546).

regard, Tom Ruys and Cedric Ryngaert observe: "From a jurisdictional perspective, this 'control theory' appears to be an improper application of the nationality principle, as in international law the nationality of a corporation is based on its place of incorporation rather than the nationality of its shareholders."[614]

4.3.4 Restrictions on Exports of Goods, Services and Technology That Incorporate Components or Technology Originated in a State, If Such Exports Are Destined to Designated Entities

Since May 2019, the United States has been imposing various restrictions on the Chinese-based technology companies, mainly Huawei and its affiliates incorporated globally.[615] As a result, US exports, reexports and in-country transfers to Huawei and its affiliates are subject to a compulsory export license requirement, which is issued under the presumption of denial (i.e. it is assumed that the majority of license requests will be denied).[616] These restrictions have been tightened several times: the number of entities to which export licensing requirement applies, as well as categories of goods, were expanded.[617]

In May 2020, the application of the export licensing requirement was expanded to include foreign-produced goods, if these goods were produced using US technology (Foreign-Produced Direct Product Rule) and if they are destined for Huawei and its non-US affiliates.[618] These restrictions that *inter alia* completely prevent Huawei from obtaining foreign-produced chips

---

614 Ruys and Ryngaert (n 555) 18.

615 On 16 May 2019, the US Bureau of Industry and Security (BIS) included Huawei and sixty-eight non-U.S. affiliates of Huawei in twenty-six locations on the so-called Entity List. This listing entails the imposition of additional license requirements on the listed entities for exports, reexports and in-country transfers, as well as exclusion from most license exceptions. U.S. Department of Commerce, Bureau of Industry and Security, 15 C.F.R. § 744 Addition of Entities to the Entity List, Final Rule (16 May 2019).

616 ibid.

617 U.S. Department of Commerce, Bureau of Industry and Security, 15 C.F.R. § 744 Addition of Certain Entities to the Entity List and Revision of Entries on the Entity List, Final Rule (19 Aug. 2019); U.S. Department of Commerce, Bureau of Industry and Security, 15 C.F.R. § 736, 744 and 762, Addition of Huawei Non-U.S. Affiliates to the Entity List, the Removal of Temporary General License, and Amendments to General Prohibition Three (Foreign-Produced Direct Product Rule).

618 U.S. Department of Commerce, Bureau of Industry and Security, 15 C.F.R. § 730, 732, 736 and 744 Export Administration Regulations: Amendments to General Prohibition Three (Foreign-Produced Direct Product Rule) and the Entity List, Interim final rule (15 May 2020).

developed or produced from the US software or technology were revised and further tightened in August 2020.[619]

The latter restrictions are of particular interest for our discussion. In particular, the relevant rules stipulate that certain categories of foreign-produced goods can be subject to the US Export Administration Regulation (EAR).[620] The foreign-produced goods that fall into this category are: (1) goods that contain a certain percentage of controlled US-origin content which is more than the *de minimis* amount[621] and (2) foreign-produced goods that are subject to §736.2(b)(3) of the EAR (the foreign-produced direct product rule).[622] The foreign-produced direct product rule applies to two types of goods: (1) foreign-made items that are direct products of "controlled" technology or software[623] and (2) foreign-made items that are direct products of a complete plant or any major component of a plant, if this plant or component is the direct product of "controlled" technology.[624] These rules imply that legal entities incorporated in other jurisdictions may be obligated to comply with unilateral US sanctions, even if they produce goods abroad, and, as a result of these unilateral sanctions, are prohibited from exporting goods that are considered to be subject to the EAR and are destined for sanctioned states and/or legal entities.

The reasons lying behind these severe restrictions are formulated as follows: "they [Huawei Technologies Co., Ltd. and its affiliates] pose a significant risk of involvement in activities contrary to the national security or foreign policy interests of the United States."[625] Notably, tightening of the restrictions was justified on the following grounds: "These revisions promote U.S. national security by limiting access to, and use of, U.S. technology to design and produce items outside the United States by entities that pose a significant risk

619 U.S. Department of Commerce, Bureau of Industry and Security, 15 C.F.R. § 736, 744 and 762 (n 617).

620 U.S. Department of Commerce, Bureau of Industry and Security, 15 C.F.R. § 730, 732, 736 and 744 (n 618).

621 The rules on the *de minimis* content are prescribed by 15 C.F.R. § 734.4 – De minimis U.S. content.

622 General Prohibition Three – Foreign-produced direct product of specified "technology" and "software" (Foreign-Produced Direct Product Rule), 15 C.F.R. § 736.2 General prohibitions and determination of applicability.

623 (A) Conditions defining direct product of technology. 15 C.F.R. § 736.2 General prohibitions and determination of applicability.

624 (B) Conditions defining direct product of a plant. 15 C.F.R. § 736.2 General prohibitions and determination of applicability.

625 U.S. Department of Commerce, Bureau of Industry and Security, 15 C.F.R. § 730, 732, 736, and 744 (n 618).

of involvement in activities contrary to the national security or foreign policy interests of the United States."[626]

In light of this, it is clear that the protective principle on ascertaining jurisdiction may be invoked to justify unilateral sanctions that prescribe rules of conduct for foreign-based legal entities, provided that they use US-origin technology and/or software. In the present case, the threat that Huawei and its affiliates pose to the US national security is ambiguous and revolves around the potential threat that may emanate from the alleged close links between Huawei and the Chinese military. Such an all-embracing use of the protective principle would probably be opposed by other countries and would not justify these unilateral sanctions, which are unlawfully extraterritorial.

4.3.5 Restrictions on the Re-export of Goods, Services and Technology That Originated in a State

Export control laws are common for many jurisdictions.[627] For instance, the US Export Control Act laid the foundation for the GATT 1947 dispute between Czechoslovakia and the United States, in which the latter relied upon the national security exception embedded in the GATT 1947.[628]

Unilateral economic sanctions may be framed as restrictions on the re-export of goods and services. Indeed, such restrictions are entrenched in the US sanctions regimes against Cuba, Iran, Sudan and Syria.[629] Foreign entities are prohibited from exporting goods, services, software and technology that are of US origin or that contain more than a *de minimis* amount of the US content from third countries to the sanctioned states.[630]

These prohibitions on re-export may raise concerns regarding their extraterritorial application. The prohibition on re-export entails that the government must regulate the conduct of foreign-based entities, entities that potentially

626 U.S. Department of Commerce, Bureau of Industry and Security, 15 C.F.R. Parts 736, 744 and 762 (n 617).

627 For example, the United Kingdom adopted an export control law in 2002. *Export Control Act 2002, Chapter 28, 2002.*

628 Contracting Parties to the GATT 1947, 'Twenty-Second Meeting, GATT/CP.3/SR.22, p. 9; II/28, Request of Czechoslovakia for Decision under Article XXIII' (1949); The Export Control Act of 1949 raised a number of questions regarding its extraterritorial application. For more, see Paul H Silverstone, 'The Export Control Act of 1949: Extraterritorial Enforcement' (1959) 107 University of Pennsylvania Law Review 331.

629 "OFAC's sanctions regimes broadly prohibit the export of goods, services, software, and technology from the United States or by U.S. persons to Cuba, Iran, Sudan, and Syria, including exports that are 'transshipped' through third countries." Rathbone, Jeydel and Lentz (n 518) 1107.

630 ibid.

have no connection to that particular state, by requiring them to refrain from engaging in certain business transactions. In other words, the government of one state prescribes and enforces rules with respect to subjects over which it has no jurisdiction.

The extraterritorial reach of these sanctions explains why enforcement agencies, while enforcing such prohibitions, allege that the violators were involved in unlawful indirect export from the United States instead of claiming a violation of re-export rules. In this regard, commentators have pointed out: "The fact patterns in these cases suggest that OFAC could have alleged 'reexport' violations [...] , but instead chose to allege unlawful indirect export 'from the United States' [...] . Presumably, this is because the extraterritorial application of the sanctions regulations is less controversial when the relevant activity is alleged to have occurred 'from the United States,' rather than entirely overseas."[631]

The penalties for violations of sanctions of this kind can be severe. For instance, in 2018 Ericsson Inc (located in Texas) and Ericsson AB (located in Sweden), both subsidiaries of Telefonaktiebolaget LM Ericsson, agreed to pay a $145,893 settlement for violations of the economic sanctions against Sudan.[632] In 2018, the Chinese corporation ZTE (Zhongxing Telecommunications Equipment Corporation) and ZTE Kangxun Telecommunications Ltd pled guilty to violating US re-export sanctions against Iran.[633] The initial ban which was imposed against the corporation was lifted by the United States only after the company agreed to a number of penalties, including a $1 billion fine.[634] This fine, along with other restrictions wilfully undertaken by the corporation, might be considered as the most severe punishment for violation of the prohibition to re-export US-origin goods and technologies.

5 Jurisdiction and the Imposition of Unilateral Financial Sanctions

The recent proliferation of unilateral financial sanctions has resulted in a number of ongoing disputes before US domestic courts, in which foreign nationals

631 ibid 1109.

632 'The Settlement Agreement between Ericsson Inc. and Ericsson, and the U.S. Department of the Treasury Office of Foreign Assets Control (OFAC).' <https://www.treasury.gov/resource-center/sanctions/CivPen/Documents/20180606_ericsson_settlement.pdf>.

633 Karen Freifeld, 'U.S. Reveals ZTE Settlement Details, Ban Still in Place' *Reuters* (11 June 2018) <https://www.reuters.com/article/us-usa-trade-china-zte-idUSKBN1J72GK>.

634 ibid.

have been charged with violating these restrictions. In light of these developments, this section is devoted to the discussion of unilateral financial sanctions, their extraterritorial application and public international law principles on establishing jurisdiction.

5.1 *The Era of Financial Warfare*

In his book *Treasury's War: The Unleashing of a New Era of Financial Warfare*, Juan Zarate posits: "We are now living in a new era of financial warfare."[635] He explains that: "This new warfare is defined by the use of financial tools, pressure, and market forces to isolate rogue actors from the international financial and commercial systems and gain leverage over our enemies."[636] This new financial warfare, in Zarate's view, has been channelled in three directions: the expansion of the international anti-money-laundering regime, the development of financial tools and intelligence geared to national security and a new understanding of the role of the international financial system, as well as the private sector, for national security.[637]

One of the outcomes of this new era of financial warfare is the ever expanding role of financial sanctions in international relations.[638] The development of the instruments of financial warfare was instigated by the 9/11 attacks in the United States and the subsequent warfare against terrorism financing.[639] Consequently, the United States[640] and the European Union,[641] as well as the

635 Zarate (n 83) 2. Suzanne Katzenstein defines this development as "dollar unilateralism." Katzenstein (n 324); Tom Lin describes it as "financial weapons of war." Tom CW Lin, 'Financial Weapons of War' (2016) 100 Minnesota Law Review 1377.

636 Zarate (n 83) 2–3.

637 ibid 8.

638 The Security Council has been playing an active role in demonstrating the potential of financial sanctions. In particular, it has authorised mandatory, collective economic sanctions for UN Member States, in order to pursue objectives as diverse as countering terrorism, preventing conflicts, promoting peace, protecting the civilian population, supporting democracy, improving resource governance and preventing the proliferation of nuclear weapons. Biersteker and others (n 157) 12.

639 Zarate (n 83).

640 The United States frequently relies upon unilateral financial sanctions. For more, see Katzenstein (n 324); Sue E Eckert, 'The Use of Financial Measures to Promote Security' (2008) 62 Journal of International Affairs 103;

641 For more details on the use of financial sanctions by the European Union, see Caytas (n 328).

United Kingdom, Canada, Australia, Japan and Switzerland,[642] all became aware of a significant potential of financial restrictions.

Explaining the efficiency of financial sanctions, Zarate points out that "the policy decisions of governments are not nearly as persuasive as the risk-based compliance calculus of financial institutions."[643] Indeed, he highlights the necessity to comply with the United States' unilateral financial sanctions: "If you want to be a serious international institution with the ability to work globally, you have to access New York and the American banking system."[644] This assertion ought to be considered in the context of the international financial system in its current form.

The modern international financial system is described as "a globalized, high-tech, American-centric system."[645] Two peculiarities of this system – its globalized and American-centric nature – play a particular role in the increased use of financial sanctions and will be discussed in more detail.

Over the last few decades, the world has witnessed significantly increased interdependence between financial markets.[646] Thus, sovereign states and their financial institutions find it beneficial to integrate into this system. This integration necessarily implies that the financial institution's ability to operate effectively within the broader system hinges on its access to the US financial market and to the US dollar as a currency.

The special status of the US dollar as a reserve currency and as the currency of international trade, including commodity trade, provides the US Department of the Treasury with a valuable policy instrument.[647] In his book

---

642 Sanctions imposed by all these states on the Russian Federation following its annexation of Crimea and involvement in destabilising the situation in Ukraine bear witness to the accuracy of this assertion.

643 Zarate (n 83) 8. The advantage of such measures has been well articulated by Suzanne Katzenstein: "In theory at least, a Russian or Chinese veto of U.N. sanctions is a moot point if foreign banks – including those in Russia and China – are implementing U.S. policy." Katzenstein (n 324) 311. Political scientists also emphasize the tendency of private entities to comply with complex sanctions. In particular, it is highlighted that: "In fact, overcompliance is a typical phenomenon for companies that hesitate 'to invest in the complex due diligence required to ensure that their [...] counterparts are not linked to sanctioned entities.'" Patrick Maximilian Weber and Beata Stępień (n 334) 3008.

644 Zarate (n 83) 25.

645 Lin (n 635) 1379–1388.

646 ibid.

647 "Its [the United States] most important weapon is one available to no other state – the dollar's status as the global reserve currency. The rationale rests on the premise that foreigners often use the American financial system and so become vulnerable to prosecution under US law. Concomitantly the US can threaten foreign companies and individuals with financial sanctions, wherever they are." Stoll and others (n 232) 19.

Exorbitant Privilege, Barry Eichengreen, an eminent economist, has emphasised the unique role of the US currency as follows: "For more than half a century the dollar has been the world's monetary lingua franca."[648] Indeed, the preeminent role of the US dollar as a currency cannot be overestimated or exaggerated, as a few examples show. To start with, oil and other commodities are priced in dollars, which "require[es] countries that are oil consumers to accumulate dollars to pay for oil – mostly by exporting their goods and services to receive dollars as payment."[649] The majority of transactions between the states involved in international trade is invoiced in dollars, even if the United States is neither the country of origin nor the destination country.[650] The US dollar is also the currency of international debt securities.[651] Finally, the US dollar is an international reserve currency, even though the US dollar has not been convertible into gold since 1971, when the United States unilaterally ended previous arrangements on dollar-gold convertibility.[652] According to Barry Eichengreen, the US dollar "is the form in which central banks hold more than 60 percent of their foreign currency reserves."[653] Notwithstanding critiques of the dominance of the US dollar[654] and potential threats of currency erosion,[655] the dollar-based system is today's reality.

Legal scholars acknowledge the far-reaching implications of the current international financial system on the use of financial restrictions. In this regard, Zarate has perceptively pointed out: "The reach of this kind of US financial power derives as well from the predominance of the US dollar as the principal reserve and trading currency around the world. [...] Countries, companies, and individuals keep dollars or accounts in dollars as security against the uncertainties of other currencies."[656] In a similar vein, Suzanne Katzenstein, in

648 Barry Eichengreen, *Exorbitant Privilege: The Rise and Fall of the Dollar* (Oxford University Press 2011) 1–2.

649 Lan Cao, 'Currency Wars and the Erosion of Dollar Hegemony' (2016) 38 Michigan Journal of International Law 58.

650 ibid.; "Eighty-one percent of the global trade financing is conducted using the American dollar." Lin (n 635) 1387.

651 "Half of international debt securities are in dollars." Cao (n 649) 58.

652 Eichengreen (n 648).

653 ibid 2.

654 Eichengreen (n 648); Cao (n 649) 60–61.

655 Other countries have undertaken attempts to destabilise and erode the preeminent role of the US currency. Cao (n 649) 64–67. Cameron Rotblat has described Chinese efforts to internationalise the yuan. Among the factors that contributed to this decision he emphasised that: "[...] US financial sanctions on Iran (as well as those against Russia, Zimbabwe, and Belarus) have pushed sanctioned nations towards using the yuan as a partial replacement for hard-to-access US dollars." Rotblat (n 323) 339.

656 Zarate (n 83) 25–26.

her discussion of the unique efficacy of US financial restrictions, defines this development as a "dollar unilateralism,"[657] arguing that unilateral US financial sanctions are effective due to industry structure, policy acceptability and bargaining asymmetry.[658] Joanna Diane Caytas highlights the increased reliance upon financial sanctions, emphasising that: "For reasons that include critical mass and size, global interconnectedness, and a lack of comparable reserve currency options, coercive financial measures have thus far proved to be a near-monopoly of the United States, the EU, and their allies, which serve their policy objectives extraterritorially."[659]

5.2 *Unilateral Financial Sanctions and Jurisdiction*

The expanded use of unilateral financial sanctions raises a number of vexed questions concerning their relationship with the established principles for ascertaining jurisdiction. As has been mentioned before, access to the US financial market is so vital for any financial institution worldwide that even the theoretical possibility of being denied such access encourages compliance with sanctions.[660] The risk-based compliance introduced by private financial institutions is at the core of compliance with financial sanctions. For instance, the recent historical record demonstrates that financial institutions are willing to pay exorbitant financial penalties for sanctions violations simply in order to avoid potential losses stemming from loss of access to the US financial market. Thus, BNP Paribas agreed to pay a record $8.9 billion in penalties in 2014 for conspiring to violate US sanctions,[661] while in 2015, OFAC settled with the UBS on the allegations of sanctions violations with the payment of $1.7 million.[662] That same year, Deutsche Bank AG paid a $258 million penalty for

657 "Dollar unilateralism occurs when the government uses the unique status of the U.S. dollar in global financial markets to pursue policy goals independently, rather than work through traditional inter-governmental and multilateral channels." Katzenstein (n 324) 294–295.

658 "The dominance of U.S. currency gives the U.S. government 'the power to persuade and coerce.' At any moment, the government can choose to cut off a foreign bank's access to U.S. financial markets and thus push it to the periphery of global trade and finance." ibid 314.

659 Caytas (n 328) 442–443.

660 "Regardless of a bank's capitalization and financial soundness, it would be fatal for any financial institution involved in international payments to lose access to dollars." ibid 454.

661 Emmenegger (n 519) 632.

662 Jason Lange and Yeganeh Torbati, 'UBS to Pay $1.7 Mln Settlement over Sanctions Case – U.S. Treasury' *Reuters* (27 August 2015) <https://www.reuters.com/article/ubs-group-settlement-idUSL1N1121WN20150827>.

doing business on behalf of entities in countries subject to US sanctions.[663] The most recent examples include Standard Chartered's settlement of $1 billion[664] and the French Société Générale's global settlement agreement to the tune of $1.34 billion.[665] Additionally, several settlement agreements went so far as to demand the appointment of an independent compliance monitor to improve the financial institution's compliance with the US sanctions, as was the case with the Standard Chartered PLC in 2012.[666]

The incentives to comply with US financial sanctions are so high that European banks are willing to withhold their services from sanctioned individuals. The recent attempts of the Russian billionaire Boris Rotenberg to file a suit against several European banks that complied with US financial sanctions against him illustrate this.[667] Despite being a Finnish citizen and arguing that he faced discrimination owing to the financial institutions' refusal to process his payments, he lost the case.[668] In its last decision, issued in January 2020, the court ruled against him: "Helsinki District Court has rejected Boris Rotenberg's complaint over the right to banking services and damages for discrimination."[669] What is noteworthy here is that the court argued that "the banks were entitled to refuse him banking services given the risk of violating US sanctions."[670]

663 Suzanne Barlyn, 'Deutsche Bank to Pay $258 Million to Settle U.S. Sanctions Case – NYDFS' *Reuters* (4 November 2015) <https://www.reuters.com/article/us-deutsche-bank-penalty-idUSKCN0ST2J720151104>.

664 'Standard Chartered to Pay $1bn for Breaching Iran Sanctions' *BBC News* (9 April 2019) <https://www.bbc.com/news/business-47872318>.

665 Katanga Johnson, Karen Freifeld and Inti Landauro, 'Societe Generale to Pay $1.4 Billion to Settle Cases in the U.S.' *Reuters* (19 November 2018) <https://www.reuters.com/article/us-usa-fed-socgen-idUSKCN1NO26B>.

666 'Standard Chartered Agrees Settlement with New York Regulator' *BBC News* (14 August 2012) <https://www.bbc.com/news/business-19253666>.

667 Frances Schwartzkopff, Kati Pohjanpalo and Henry Meyer, 'Russian Oligarch Rotenberg Files Lawsuit Against Nordic Banks' *Bloomberg.com* (19 October 2018) <https://www.bloomberg.com/news/articles/2018-10-19/russian-oligarch-rotenberg-files-lawsuit-against-nordic-banks>.

668 A Savin, 'In Finland, the Court Rejected the Claim of Billionaire Boris Rotenberg to Scandinavian Banks' *24-my.info* (14 February 2019) <https://www.24-my.info/in-finland-the-court-rejected-the-claim-of-billionaire-boris-rotenberg-to-scandinavian-banks/>.

669 'Finnish Court Rejects Rotenberg's Suit against Nordic Banks' *Reuters* (13 January 2020) <https://www.reuters.com/article/finland-russia-sanctions-idUSL8N29I26o>.

670 Maya Lester, 'Helsinki Court Dismisses Boris Rotenberg's Sanctions Case' *EU Sanctions* (15 January 2020) <https://www.europeansanctions.com/2020/01/helsinki-court-dismisses-boris-rotenbergs-sanctions-case/>.

The intricate question concerning the relationship between such unilateral financial sanctions and the law of jurisdiction has been well formulated by Susan Emmenegger: "The common denominator between these cases is the US assertion of domestic authority over conduct that occurred abroad: banks outside the US providing banking services to entities outside the US."[671]

In justifying its extraterritorial sanctions, the United States traditionally relies upon the effects doctrine or, alternatively, the principle of protective jurisdiction. Yet such invocations might be without merit. Emmenegger contends that the effects doctrine cannot serve as a jurisdictional ground for unilateral financial sanctions.[672] In her view, the application of the effects doctrine to conduct that is legal in the state where a financial institution is incorporated is highly controversial.[673] Furthermore, the effects doctrine implies that the conduct that gives rise to ascertaining jurisdiction should have a direct, substantial and foreseeable effect on the state invoking it.[674] The majority of financial institutions proven to have violated US financial sanctions were providing payment services to sanctioned clients.[675] The clearing of the prohibited transaction by a US-based bank does not, according to Emmenegger, constitute a substantial effect on the US payment system.[676] Thus, Emmenegger is sceptical of the possibility to justify unlawfully extraterritorial financial sanctions as legal under the effects doctrine.[677]

Concerning the possibility of justifying extraterritorial financial sanctions under the principle of protective jurisdiction, it must be noted that legal scholars favour the narrow interpretation of the concept of national threat under the protective principle.[678] For example, as Cedric Ryngaert has noted with respect to the possibility of justifying the Helms-Burton Act under the principle of protective jurisdiction: "It is difficult to sustain that a vaguely defined threat to the political independence or territorial integrity of the United States falls within the scope of the protective principle."[679] Emmenegger expressed similar doubts about the application of the protective principle: "For activities not directly linked to the cause of the national security threat, the protective

671 Emmenegger (n 519) 632.
672 Emmenegger (n 519).
673 ibid 656–657.
674 International Bar Association (n 592).
675 Lange and Torbati (n 662); Barlyn (n 663); Johnson, Freifeld and Landauro (n 665).
676 Emmenegger (n 519).
677 ibid.
678 ibid.; Ryngaert (n 520).
679 Ryngaert (n 520) 642.

principle does not provide a sufficient basis for jurisdiction."[680] Thus, both principles – the effects doctrine and the protective jurisdiction – fail to provide sufficient grounds for justifying extraterritorial financial sanctions.

5.3 *Correspondent Account-Based Jurisdiction: A New Rule for Ascertaining Jurisdiction*

In the previous subsection, it was shown that unilateral financial sanctions face a significant risk of being unlawfully extraterritorial and could violate the principles for ascertaining jurisdiction developed in international law. Against this backdrop, the United States invokes correspondent account-based jurisdiction to establish its jurisdiction over the conduct of the foreign-based financial institutions. US authorities have been invoking correspondent account-based jurisdiction for at least a decade.[681] Notwithstanding its questionable legality, private actors, mainly financial institutions, have opted for settlement agreements with the US Department of the Treasury instead of bringing legal challenges before US courts.[682]

The court case discussed below deviates from previous practice in two respects. First and foremost, this is a case in which non-US residents faced criminal charges for violating unilateral US sanctions by engaging in conduct that occurred outside the territory of the United States. Second, this case provided an opportunity for a US domestic court to examine the legality of the correspondent account-based jurisdiction.

For this reason, the arrest and detention of the Turkey-based businessman Reza Zarrab and of another Turkish national Mehmet Atilla on the charges of violating the US unilateral financial sanctions against Iran are of the utmost importance for our discussion. Indeed, these two arrests demonstrate that sanctions may apply not only to foreign corporations, but also to foreign natural persons who are neither US nationals nor reside in the United States. Additionally, these proceedings have revealed the stance of the US courts on the jurisdictional reach of the US unilateral financial sanctions, which seems to be extremely far-reaching.

5.3.1 Factual Background

The name "Reza Zarrab" became known to the media during the Turkish corruption scandal, which unfolded when the Turkish customs officials

680 Emmenegger (n 519) 658.

681 ibid 655.

682 For examples, see above: subsection 5.2 Unilateral financial sanctions and jurisdiction.

accidentally found three thousand pounds of gold bars in a cargo plane.[683] The notorious investigation unveiled extensive corruption among the high-ranking government officials in Turkey.[684] According to the investigators, Reza Zarrab masterminded a scheme to undermine US sanctions against Iran by exchanging Iranian gas and oil for gold.[685] Consequently, Zarrab was arrested and charged.[686] In spite of the laudable efforts of Turkish investigators, the charges against Zarrab were dropped, and the "gas for gold" scandal, as it was dubbed by the media, lost most of its steam.[687]

Yet the matter was not laid to rest. In 2016, Reza Zarrab was arrested in the United States and charged with violating US unilateral financial sanctions against Iran.[688] In a nutshell, Zarrab had ordered several payments to be processed on behalf of Iranian legal entities, and since these payments were denominated in US dollars, they were cleared through US banks.[689] US prosecutors initially charged Zarrab with four counts: conspiracy to defraud the United States, conspiracy to violate the International Emergency Economic Powers Act, conspiracy to commit bank fraud and conspiracy to commit money laundering.[690] In the most recent superseding indictment, Reza Zarrab and other defendants were charged with six counts:[691] conspiracy to defraud the United States, conspiracy to violate the International Emergency Economic Powers Act, bank fraud, conspiracy to commit bank fraud, money laundering and conspiracy to commit money laundering.[692] The charges brought by the prosecutors placed the discussion of the extraterritorial reach of US financial sanctions at the forefront of international law.[693]

683 Dexter Filkins, 'A Mysterious Case Involving Turkey, Iran, and Rudy Giuliani' *The New Yorker* (14 April 2017) <https://www.newyorker.com/news/news-desk/a-mysterious-case-involving-turkey-iran-and-rudy-giuliani>.

684 ibid.

685 ibid.

686 ibid.

687 ibid.

688 'United States of America, Government v. Reza Zarrab, et al., Defendant No. S1 15 Cr. 867 (RMB) Sealed Indictment, December 15, 2015.'

689 ibid.

690 ibid.; 'United States of America, Government v. Reza Zarrab, et al., Defendant No. S2 15 Cr. 867 (RMB) Superseding Indictment, November 7, 2016'; 'United States of America, Government v. Reza Zarrab, et al., Defendant No. S3 15 Cr. 867 (RMB) Superseding Indictment, April 7, 2017.'

691 'United States of America, Government v. Reza Zarrab, et al., Defendant No. S4 15 Cr. 867 (RMB) Superseding Indictment, September 6, 2017.'

692 ibid.

693 Emmenegger and Döbeli (n 519); Scott M Flicker, Jason Fiebig and Kwame Manley, 'United States of America v. Reza Zarrab: The Long Reach of U.S. Sanctions May Have Just

5.3.2 The Findings of the Court on the Extraterritorial Application of US Financial Sanctions

The charges deriving from the violation of US sanctions laws have proved to be highly controversial. In the motion to dismiss the indictment, Reza Zarrab's lawyers emphasised the extraterritoriality of US unilateral sanctions as follows: "Zarrab stands accused of violating U.S. law for agreeing with *foreign* persons in *foreign* countries to direct *foreign* banks to send funds transfers from *foreign* companies to other *foreign* banks for *foreign* companies."[694] Such extraterritoriality has far-reaching implications, which are elucidated in the motion to dismiss: "It is as unprecedented as it is problematic. These transactions are fundamentally foreign, and they are entirely legal under the foreign law that directly governs foreign persons and foreign transactions."[695]

Furthermore, the motion to dismiss the indictment alludes to the only connection that exists between Zarrab's actions and the United States. This connection originates "out of the incidental involvement of a U.S. bank at some mid-point in the payment chain of a transaction that originated from a foreign country and occurred between two foreign entities."[696] This argument was advanced by the defence team to contend that the mere fact that all payments in US dollars are cleared via US-based banks do not constitute "export from the United States" for the purposes of the sanctions regulation.[697]

The government filed its opposition to the Zarrab's motion to dismiss, underlining that the defendant used the US financial system to process US-dollar transactions and thus helped a nation that presents "a significant threat to this country's national security."[698]

Judge Richard Berman reached several conclusions that have a bearing on the extraterritorial application of US unilateral financial sanctions. Discussing the allegations of conspiracy to defraud the United States, Judge Berman entertained the defendant's arguments that the law, on which allegations of

---

Gotten Longer' *Paul Hastings* LLP <https://casetext.com/analysis/united-states-of-america-v-reza-zarrab-the-long-reach-of-us-sanctions-may-have-just-gotten-longer-1>.

694 'United States of America, Government v. Reza Zarrab, et al., Defendant No. S1 15 Cr. 867 (RMB) Memorandum of Law in Support of Defendant Reza Zarrab's Motion to Dismiss the Superseding Indictment, July 19, 2016' 4.

695 ibid.

696 ibid 5.

697 ibid.

698 'United States of America, Government v. Reza Zarrab, et al., Defendant No. S1 15 Cr. 867 (RMB) Government's Memorandum of Law in Opposition to Defendant Reza Zarrab's Motions to Dismiss the Indictment and to Suppress Evidence, August 8, 2016.' 6.

conspiracy were grounded, does not apply to foreign conduct.[699] The judge took previous case law into account to substantiate his findings.[700] In particular, two cases were referenced – *United States v. Budovsky* and *Licci v. Lebanese Canadian Bank, SAL*.[701] In *United States v. Budovsky* district judge found that a sufficient nexus existed between a foreigner operating an online currency exchange incorporated in Costa Rica and the territory of the United States.[702] This sufficient nexus was established, among other factors, based on the fact that the defendant moved 13.5 million US dollars from a Costa Rican account through a correspondent bank account in the Southern District of New York.[703] In an even more controversial court case, *Licci v. Lebanese Canadian Bank, SAL*, the judge accepted the plaintiffs' argument that the conduct of the foreign-incorporated bank – which did not operate in the United States, yet conducted payments through a New York bank account – was "both specific and domestic."[704] Thus, the judge found a justification for displacing the presumption against extraterritoriality.[705] In the present case, Judge Berman found the defendant's argument that his conduct is foreign since it involved only transfers through the US banks *en route* to other banks as unpersuasive.[706]

Regarding violations of the Iran sanctions regulation, the defendant claimed that his actions – i.e. the transfer of payments denominated in US dollars from one foreign bank to another, cleared through the US correspondent bank account – did not constitute exports "from the United States, or by a United States person, wherever located" as was stipulated in the pertinent

699 *United States of America, Government, v. Reza Zarrab, et al., Defendant Decision & Order* [2016] SDNY No. S1 15 Cr. 867 (RMB).

700 ibid.

701 ibid.

702 The court asserted: "A jurisdictional nexus exists 'when the aim of that activity is to cause harm inside the United States or to U.S. citizens or interests.'" *United States v. Budovsky* [2015] SDNY 13-cr-368 (DLC).

703 ibid.

704 *Licci v. Lebanese Canadian Bank, SAL* [2016] Court of Appeals for the Second Circuit No. 15-1580.

705 The court observed: "Unlike the Kiobel plaintiffs, who only alleged extraterritorial conduct, Plaintiffs allege, inter alia, that LCB used its correspondent banking account in New York to facilitate dozens of international wire transfers for the Shahid, an entity alleged to be an 'integral part' of Hezbollah. Thus, Plaintiffs allege sufficient connections with the United States to require 'further analysis.'" Upon further analysis, the court dismissed the presumption against extraterritoriality. ibid.

706 *United States of America, Government, v. Reza Zarrab, et al., Defendant. Decision & Order* (n 699).

sanctions regulations.[707] Against this, the US government argued that financial transactions performed by a US bank are a "service" that is exported or supplied from the United States or by a US person.[708] The court sided with the US government and found the defendant's claims unpersuasive.[709] Judge Berman relied upon previous case law in which the court ruled that "the execution of money transfers from the United States to Iran on behalf of another, whether or not performed for a fee, constitutes the exportation of a service."[710] Further support for this argument was found in *United States v. Homa International Trading Corp.*, where the court, in interpreting the same Iranian sanctions statutes, declared that "the execution on behalf of others of money transfers from the United States to Iran is a 'service' under the terms of the Embargo."[711]

In the course of discussing this particular argument, the court considered the question of extraterritoriality.[712] Despite acknowledging that there is a sufficient nexus between the defendant's conduct and the United States, the court proceeded with the discussion of the extraterritoriality on arguendo basis.[713] Before delving into the analysis of the relevant jurisprudence, the court preliminarily concluded that "any presumption against extraterritoriality would be overcome by the United States' interest in defending itself."[714] The court went on to say that the criminal liability for the violation of the Iranian sanctions "is not limited to individuals who are subject to the jurisdiction of the United States" and that "Congress intended the statute to be applied extraterritorially."[715] Buttressing its preliminary conclusions, the court rejected the arguments about the applicability of the case law presented by the defendant and concluded that the defendant could be charged under the Iranian sanctions

707 'United States of America, Government v. Reza Zarrab, et al., Defendant No. S1 15 Cr. 867 (RMB) Memorandum of Law in Support of Defendant Reza Zarrab's Motion to Dismiss the Superseding Indictment, July 19, 2016' (n 694).

708 'United States of America, Government v. Reza Zarrab, et al., Defendant No. S1 15 Cr. 867 (RMB) Government's Memorandum of Law in Opposition to Defendant Reza Zarrab's Motions to Dismiss the Indictment and to Suppress Evidence, August 8, 2016.' (n 698).

709 *United States of America, Government, v. Reza Zarrab, et al., Defendant. Decision & Order* (n 699).

710 *United States v. Banki* [2012] 2d Cir 685 F.3d 99.

711 *United States v. Homa International Trading Corp* [2004] 2d Cir 387 F.3d 144.

712 *United States of America, Government, v. Reza Zarrab, et al., Defendant. Decision & Order* (n 699).

713 ibid.

714 ibid.

715 ibid.

statutes "which encompass conduct emanating 'from the United States' and/ or involves 'property [...] subject to the jurisdiction of the United States.'"[716]

These findings are of the utmost importance for the present discussion. The court asserted that unilateral financial sanctions imposed by the United States have extraterritorial reach. More specifically, the court ruled that the execution of a money transfer constitutes the exportation or supply of services. This determination holds even if the payment originated from abroad and was made by a foreign national, with the only link to US territory being that the clearing operation was conducted in the United States. The other justification for the extraterritorial application of US domestic law is the motivation for imposing sanctions against Iran, which was described as "reflect[ing] the United States' interest in protecting and defending itself against, among other things, Iran's sponsorship of international terrorism, Iran's frustration of the Middle East peace process, and Iran's pursuit of weapons of mass destruction, which implicate the national security, foreign policy, and the economy of the United States."[717] Put differently, the court relied upon the protective principle of jurisdiction, the contours of which remain elusive not only in law, but also in state practice.

5.3.3 Subsequent Developments of the Case

The case took an unprecedented turn after the Turkish banker Mehmet Hakan Atilla was arrested while in transit in the United States.[718] He was charged with the same offences as Reza Zarrab and, in fact, was accused of conspiring with Zarrab.[719]

Facing criminal charges for violating US sanctions against Iran, Atilla and his defence team fruitlessly attempted to have the indictment dismissed.[720]

716 ibid.

717 ibid 19.

718 Nathan Vardi, 'Feds Arrest Turkish Banker For Conspiring With Trader Reza Zarrab To Violate Sanctions Against Iran' *Forbes* (28 March 2017) <https://www.forbes.com/sites/nathanvardi/2017/03/28/feds-arrest-turkish-banker-for-violating-u-s-sanctions-against-iran/>.

719 Elias Groll, 'Turkish Gold Dealer Pleads Guilty in Politically Explosive Sanctions Trial' *Foreign Policy* (28 November 2017) <https://foreignpolicy.com/2017/11/28/turkish-gold-dealer-pleads-guilty-in-politically-explosive-sanctions-trial-iran-zarrab-erdogan/>.

720 The defence team filed a motion to dismiss the indictment; after the superseding indictment was issued a new motion to dismiss was filed before the court. The defence team argued in the memorandum of law in support of this motion that if their client were to be prosecuted "it would be an unprecedented exercise of authority by the US." 'United States of America, Government v. Reza Zarrab, et al., Defendant No. S4 15 Cr. 867 (RMB) Memorandum of Law in Support of Defendant Mehmet Hakan Atilla's Motion to Dismiss Superseding Indictment S4, or Alternatively for Severance, October 9, 2017.'

The essence of the defendant's arguments was the lack of a sufficient nexus between Atilla's conduct – i.e. the facilitation of the financial transactions for the sanctioned Iranian enterprises – and the territory of the United States.[721] The defendant submitted that "the Sanctions Regime [meaning the Iranian Sanctions Regime] has never authorized the prosecution of a foreigner for entirely foreign activity that does not involve or affect a US person or entity, even when that activity displeases the US and is otherwise subject to sanctions under the statutory/regulatory scheme."[722] Another argument advanced by Atilla's defence team was that the sanctions regime does not prescribe criminal penalties applicable to the conduct of a foreigner.[723] Emphasising the findings of the US Supreme Court in *Morrison v. National Australian Bank, Ltd.*[724] and the presumption against the extraterritorial application of the US law, which can only be overturned by Congress, the defendant contended that: "The Sanctions Regime generally does not express an intention to apply its criminal reach to foreigners conducting their activity abroad."[725]

In response to the defendant's motion to dismiss, the US government submitted a memorandum of law, notably highlighting that Mehmet Hakan Atilla "personally was warned about the United States' concerns about what appeared to be happening at Halk Bank and nonetheless misled U.S. regulators about the sanctions evasion activity occurring at his bank."[726] The government once again emphasised that the existing Iranian sanctions regime reflects the United States' interest in protecting and defending itself.[727] Furthermore, it was submitted that the International Emergency Economic Powers Act, which is the core legal basis for the economic sanctions against Iran, applies extraterritorially.[728]

721 ibid.

722 ibid 3.

723 ibid.

724 "It is a long-standing principle of American law that legislation of Congress, unless a contrary intent appears, is meant to apply only within the territorial jurisdiction of the United States." *Morrison v. National Australia Bank Ltd 561 US 247* [2010] Supreme Court of the United States No. 08–1191.

725 'United States of America, Government v. Reza Zarrab, et al., Defendant No. S4 15 Cr. 867 (RMB) Memorandum of Law in Support of Defendant Mehmet Hakan Atilla's Motion to Dismiss Superseding Indictment S4, or Alternatively for Severance, October 9, 2017' (n 720) 9.

726 'United States of America, Government v. Mehmet Hakan Atilla, Defendant No. S4 15 Cr. 867 (RMB) Government's Memorandum of Law in Opposition to Defendant Mehmet Hakan Atilla's Motions to Dismiss the Superseding Indictment and for Severance, October 16, 2017' 3.

727 ibid 6.

728 ibid 9–10.

Despite the dedicated efforts of the defence team to prove the lack of a sufficient nexus to ascertain US jurisdiction over Mehmet Hakan Atilla's conduct, the case proceeded to jury trial. In 2018, Atilla was found guilty[729] and sentenced to 32 months in prison.[730] Attila's subsequent efforts to challenge the legality of this ruling did not bring any results. In July 2020, a US court of appeals upheld his convictions.[731]

5.3.4 The Views of Legal Scholars and Practitioners on the Correspondent Account-Based Jurisdiction

Susan Emmenegger published an article before the US court made its pronouncements on whether correspondent account relations constitute a substantial threshold for ascertaining jurisdiction,[732] concluding that: "Indeed, it would not satisfy the conditions set by the subjective territoriality principle, as this principle requires that a substantial part of the conduct takes place within the territory. Here, two entities outside of the United States contract for banking services that include payment services. The fact that the dollar portion of such payments (e.g. from an Iranian entity to a Swedish entity) passes through US territory via the clearing system does not meet the 'substantial part' threshold."[733] Furthermore, the effects doctrine cannot justify such extraterritorial sanctions and criminal responsibility applicable to foreign nationals. In particular, the clearing of transactions denominated in US dollars does not have a substantial effect on the US payment system, as is required under the effects doctrine.[734] Whether it is possible to justify this new correspondent account-based jurisdiction under the protective principle of jurisdiction is also questionable. More specifically, the payments that were cleared in this case were commercial transactions, and these payments as such did not pose any threat to the US payment system or to the United States.

---

729 'Turkish Banker Convicted of Conspiring to Evade U.S. Sanctions Against Iran and Other Offenses' (*The United States Department of Justice*, 3 January 2018) <https://www.justice.gov/opa/pr/turkish-banker-covicted-conspiring-evade-us-sanctions-against-iran-and-other-offenses>.

730 'Turkish Banker Mehmet Hakan Atilla Sentenced to 32 Months for Conspiring to Violate U.S. Sanctions Against Iran and Other Offenses' (*The United States Department of Justice*, 16 May 2018) <https://www.justice.gov/usao-sdny/pr/turkish-banker-mehmet-hakan-atilla-sentenced-32-months-conspiring-violate-us-sanctions>.

731 Adam Klasfeld, 'Bygone US Sentence of Turkish Banker Hakan Atilla Affirmed,' *Courthouse News Service* (20 July 2020) https://www.courthousenews.com/bygone-us-sentence-of-turkish-banker-hakan-atilla-affirmed/.

732 Emmenegger (n 519).

733 ibid.

734 ibid.

In a similar vein, Tom Ruys and Cedric Ryngaert observe that "grounding jurisdiction on the mere routing of (financial) messages via US servers without any other link with the US whatsoever, cannot be considered to be compatible with the international law of jurisdiction."[735]

Practising lawyers have also expressed their views on the outcome of the case. Some commentators, discussing the court's finding that the transfer of funds through a US-based bank counts as the exportation of services from the United States, note: "This sets the bar to establishing a domestic nexus in a case against a foreign national as low as it has ever been."[736] The general conclusion was that "the reach of U.S. sanctions law has never extended so far."[737]

5.3.5 The Arrest of the Huawei's CFO Meng Wanzhou for an Alleged Violation of US Financial Sanctions: A New Instance of Correspondent Account-Based Jurisdiction?

A similar case, which recently became prominent, is the arrest of the Huawei's Chief Financial Officer Meng Wanzhou for alleged violations of the unilateral US sanctions against Iran. Meng was arrested in December 2018, while in transit in Canada.[738] Canadian authorities arrested her based on an extradition request issued by the United States,[739] where an eleven-count indictment against Huawei, its Iran-based subsidiary Skycom and Meng, Huawei's Chief Financial Officer, was filed in August 2018.[740]

According to the indictment, in her capacity as Chief Financial Officer of Huawei, as well as an alleged member of the board of directors of Skycom, a company that functioned as a Huawei's Iran-based subsidiary, Meng deceived financial institutions and thus, enabled the clearing of financial transactions worth millions of US dollars, which would otherwise have been impossible as a consequence of the US sanctions against Iran.[741] More specifically, the indictment describes occasions on which Meng misrepresented the nature of the relationship between Huawei and Skycom, convincing financial institutions

735 Ruys and Ryngaert (n 555) 22.

736 Flicker, Fiebig and Manley (n 693).

737 ibid.

738 'Huawei finance chief Meng Wanzhou arrested in Canada,' *BBC News* (6 December 2018), https://www.bbc.com/news/business-46462858.

739 Daisuke Wakabayashi and Alan Rappeport, 'Huawei C.F.O. Is Arrested in Canada for Extradition to the U.S.,' *The New York Times* (5 December 2018) https://www.nytimes.com/2018/12/05/business/huawei-cfo-arrest-canada-extradition.html.

740 '*United States of America v. Huawei Technologies Co., LTD, Huawei Device USA Inc., Skycom Tech Co. LTD., Wanzhou Meng*, No 1:18-cr-00457, Indictment, August 22, 2018.'

741 ibid.

that there was no relationship of "control" between the two, a claim that contradicts the findings presented by US investigators.[742] After Meng's arrest, a superseding indictment was filed in January 2019.[743] Similar to the previous indictment, the document lists occasions on which financial institutions cleared financial transactions that violated US financial sanctions against Iran.[744] According to the indictment, these transactions were cleared as a result of the false statements and misrepresentations made *inter alia* by Meng to the financial institutions involved.[745]

Meng fought in Canadian court against extradition to the United States and a potential criminal trial there.[746] If Meng had faced a criminal trial in the United States, she would have been accused of violating the US unilateral financial sanctions against Iran by enabling the clearance of financial transactions, with the involvement of the Iran-based company Skycom. In September 2021, Meng entered into a deferred prosecution agreement to resolve charges of conspiracy to commit bank fraud and conspiracy to commit wire fraud, bank fraud and wire fraud.[747] As a result, the US government agreed to withdraw its extradition request.[748]

6 Unilateral Economic Sanctions and the Immunities of States and State Officials

As we saw in chapter 1, since the late 1990s, both collective and unilateral sanctions have become targeted.[749] This shift serves the dual purposes of avoiding the detrimental negative effect on the civilian population and of increasing the effectiveness of sanctions. The rationale behind targeted sanctions is to ratchet up pressure on groups or individuals in a position of power.

742 ibid.

743 '*United States of America v. Huawei Technologies Co., LTD, Huawei Device USA Inc., Skycom Tech Co. LTD., Wanzhou Meng*, No 1:18-cr-00457, Superseding Indictment, January 24, 2019.'

744 ibid.

745 ibid.

746 'Canada Judge Delays Extradition Hearings in Win for Huawei Executive,' *The Guardian* (21 April 2020) https://www.theguardian.com/world/2021/apr/21/meng-wanzhou-extradition-hearings-huawei-cfo.

747 'Huawei CFO Wanzhou Meng Admits to Misleading Global Financial Institution' (*The United States Department of Justice*, 24 September 2021) https://www.justice.gov/opa/pr/huawei-cfo-wanzhou-meng-admits-misleading-global-financial-institution.

748 ibid.

749 For more details, see chapter 1, subsection 1.4. The "sanctions decade" and the quest for "smart" sanctions.

From the perspective of public international law, unilateral targeted sanctions may encroach on the immunities of states and of high-ranking government officials. Thus, the discussion will now turn to an analysis of whether this type of sanction is compatible with the immunities that international law accords to states and state officials.

Legal scholars emphasise that the immunity of states should be carefully distinguished from diplomatic immunity and the immunity of heads of states.[750] Thus, I provide separate analyses of unilateral economic sanctions imposed on central banks and state-owned enterprises and unilateral economic sanctions imposed on high-ranking government officials.

6.1 *Blocking the Property of Central Banks and State-Owned Enterprises*

In recent years, states have increasingly imposed sanctions on the central banks and state-owned enterprises of other states. For example, the European Union and the United States introduced unilateral sanctions against the Central Bank of Iran and the Central Bank of Syria.[751] The Central Bank of Venezuela (Banco Central de Venezuela) has been targeted by the unilateral US sanctions, as a result of which all its assets and other property on the territory of the United States, as well as under the control of the United States persons, are "blocked and may not be transferred, paid, exported, withdrawn, or otherwise dealt in."[752] Additionally, the state-owned Venezuelan oil company (Petróleos de Venezuela, S.A.) has been sanctioned.[753] In addition to these restrictions,

---

750 Peter-Tobias Stoll, 'State Immunity,' *Max Planck Encyclopedia of Public International Law* [*MPEPIL*] <https://opil.ouplaw.com/view/10.1093/law:epil/9780199231690/law-9780199231690-e1106>.

751 For example, the EU froze the assets of the central banks of Iran and Syria. The Central Bank of Syria was included in the list of sanctioned enterprises for "providing financial support to the regime." Council Regulation (EU) No 168/2012 of 27 February 2012 amending Regulation (EU) No 36/2012 concerning restrictive measures in view of the situation in Syria 2012 (OJ L); The restrictive measures against the Central Bank of Iran were justified by "involvement in activities to circumvent sanctions." Council Decision 2012/35/CFSP of 23 January 2012 amending Decision 2010/413/CFSP concerning restrictive measures against Iran 2012 (OJ L). In the ICJ dispute – Certain Iranian Assets (Islamic Republic of Iran v. United States of America) – Iran questions the legality of the various US legislative acts that allowed blocking of the assets of the Iranian Central Bank (Bank Markazi) and the use of these assets to pay compensations to the alleged victims of the terrorist acts. *Certain Iranian Assets (Islamic Republic of Iran v. United States of America), Preliminary Objections, Judgment, ICJ Reports 2019, p 7.*

752 President of the United States of America. Executive Order 13884 of August 5, 2019. Blocking Property of the Government of Venezuela.

753 "In January 2019, the United States recognized Juan Guaidó, president of the democratically elected, opposition-led National Assembly, as interim president. The Trump

sanctions that undermine the state-owned sectors of the economy are also frequent.[754]

There is no unanimity among the legal scholars as to whether these restrictions violate state immunity. Pierre-Emmanuel Dupont argues that this type of unilateral economic sanction violates state immunity,[755] while Tom Ruys challenges this conventional account.[756] Given that economic sanctions of this kind are becoming more common, this discussion is very timely.

To start with, it is necessary to clarify a few points. The starting point of our inquiry is whether central banks and state-owned enterprises are entitled to the immunities guaranteed under international law. If the answer is affirmative, the scope of this immunity ought to be defined. These preliminary enquiries will allow us to establish whether unilateral economic sanctions imposed against the central banks and/or state-owned enterprises encroach on state immunity.

Discussing the beneficiaries of state immunity, Peter-Tobias Stoll has observed: "State immunity protects the State as an international legal personality as well as its organs, components, entities, and representatives."[757] Stoll has buttressed this conclusion with reference to the relevant provisions of the

---

Administration then imposed sanctions on Venezuela's state oil company (Petróleos de Venezuela, S.A., or PdVSA), central bank, and government to pressure Maduro to leave power." Clare Ribando Seelke, 'Venezuela: Overview of U.S. Sanctions,' Congressional Research Service (CRS) updated 22 January 2021; 'Factbox: U.S. Sanctions on Venezuela's Oil Industry' *Reuters* (30 January 2019) <https://www.reuters.com/article/us-venezuela-politics-usa-sanctions-fact-idUSKCN1PN34I>.

754 "As of January 2020, OFAC has placed 13 Russian companies and their subsidiaries and affiliates on the SSI List. The SSI List includes major state-owned companies in the financial, energy, and defense sectors; it does not include all companies in those sectors. The parent entities on the SSI List, under their respective directives, consist of the following: i. Four large state-owned banks (Sberbank, VTB Bank, Gazprombank, Rosselkhozbank) and VEB (rebranded VEB.RF in 2018), which 'acts as a development bank and payment agent for the Russian government'; ii. State-owned oil companies Rosneft and Gazpromneft, pipeline company Transneft, and private gas producer Novatek; iii. State-owned defense and hi-tech conglomerate Rostec; and iv. For restrictions on transactions related to deepwater, Arctic offshore, or shale oil projects, Rosneft and Gazpromneft, private companies Lukoil and Surgutneftegaz, and state-owned energy company Gazprom (Gazpromneft's parent company)." Welt and others (n 178).

755 Pierre-Emmanuel Dupont, 'Countermeasure and Collective Security: The Case of the EU Sanctions against Iran' (2012) 17 Journal of Conflict and Security Law 301.

756 Ruys (n 11).

757 Stoll (n 750).

UN Convention on Jurisdictional Immunities of States and Their Property (UN Convention).[758]

According to Stoll, central banks enjoy general immunity.[759] Furthermore, he argues that "the protection of the property of central banks from execution appears to be stronger than that afforded to other entities."[760] This conclusion is grounded on the textual interpretation of the UN Convention, which explicitly exempts "(c) property of the central bank or other monetary authority of the State" from post-judgement measures of constraint.[761] Notwithstanding this explicit recognition of the central banks' entitlement, commentators are sceptical of its universality, asserting that: "there is seemingly no general acceptance in State practice for the higher degree of immunity" granted to the central banks.[762] Indeed, upon closer examination, the unconstrained entitlement to state immunity granted to central banks might seem controversial in light of recent developments. In this connection, Ingrid Wuerth has observed: "During the middle of the 20th century, central banks became more independent from the state, making it more difficult to characterize central banks as foreign states or other entities entitled to immunity. Although that issue has largely been resolved in favour of immunity, central banks today conduct many of their operations on the open market, for example by purchasing government debt from commercial banks or by purchasing foreign currency. As mentioned above, they may also administer sovereign wealth funds. In these contexts, the actions of central banks are identical to those of private commercial actors, though the purpose may differ. This raises doctrinal and policy questions as to the optimal scope of central bank immunity."[763]

758 Stoll refers to Article 2 (1)(b) of the United Nations Convention on Jurisdictional Immunities of States and Their Property, which provides the definition of "state" and Article 6 (2)(b), which reads as follows: "A proceeding before a court of a State shall be considered to have been instituted against another State if that other State: (b) is not named as a party to the proceeding but the proceeding in effect seeks to affect the property, rights, interests or activities of that other State." ibid.

759 ibid.

760 ibid.

761 Article 21 United Nations Convention on Jurisdictional Immunities of States and Their Property (adopted 2 December 2004, not yet in force), UN Doc A/RES/59/38.

762 Hazel Fox and Philippa Webb, *The Law of State Immunity* (Revised and Updated Third Edition, Oxford University Press 2015) 529.

763 Ingrid Wuerth, 'Immunity from Execution of Central Bank Assets' in Tom Ruys and Nicolas Angelet (eds.), *The Cambridge Handbook of Immunities and International Law* (Cambridge University Press 2019) 269.

The question of the immunity of state-owned enterprises is less controversial, since the latter do not benefit from state immunity.[764] Thus, we may conclude that the central banks benefit from state immunity, while state-owned enterprises are not entitled to immunity guarantees.

State immunity originates in customary international law.[765] The efforts to codify rules on state immunity have not yet borne fruit: the UN Convention has not entered into force.[766] Nonetheless, the convention is widely acknowledged to represent an accurate reflection of the field and is used as a basis for scholarly deliberation.[767] State immunity embodies jurisdictional immunity as well as enforcement immunity,[768] while other commentators distinguish between immunity from adjudication and immunity from enforcement.[769]

Unilateral economic sanctions that entail the blocking of the central bank's property are imposed by the legislative or executive branches of government. In other words, these restrictions are not adopted in the course of judicial proceedings. Hence, jurisdictional immunity – immunity from adjudication – cannot be triggered.[770] However, such unilateral restrictive measures may conflict with enforcement immunity (i.e. immunity from enforcement). It is, however, debatable whether unilateral sanctions can be classified as measures of constraint in order to benefit from enforcement immunity.[771]

---

764 "True, many financial sanctions are targeted against State-owned companies that engage in commercial activities of a jure gestionis nature. 'Popular' targets include, for instance, companies that are active in the oil and gas sectors, or national airlines (think, e.g. of the Syrian Arab Airlines or the Syrian Petroleum Company). Inasmuch as the property, including the bank accounts, of these entities is not 'specifically in use or intended for use by the State for other than government non-commercial purposes' (in the sense of Article 19[c] of the 2004 UN Convention on State Immunity [UNCSI]), it does not enjoy immunity from execution under customary international law." Ruys (n 11) 671.

765 Stoll (n 750).

766 United Nations Convention on Jurisdictional Immunities of States and Their Property was adopted during the 65th plenary meeting of the General Assembly on 2 December 2004. As of today, the convention has 22 parties, and according to Article 30 of the convention, it will enter into force after thirty states ratify it. Thus, the convention is not yet in force.

767 Stoll (n 750).

768 ibid.

769 Fox and Webb (n 762) chapters 13–17.

770 For a similar view, see Ronzitti (n 11); Ruys (n 11).

771 The question of whether the freezing of the central bank's assets is covered by enforcement immunity under customary international law remains controversial. In the same volume, Jean-Marc Thouvenin and Victor Grandaubert argue in the affirmative – see Jean-Marc Thouvenin and Victor Grandaubert, 'The Material Scope of State Immunity from Execution' in Tom Ruys and Nicolas Angelet (eds.), *The Cambridge Handbook of*

Pierre-Emmanuel Dupont has argued that the unilateral restrictive measures taken against the Central Bank of Iran infringe upon the rules governing the immunities and privileges of foreign states under international law.[772] Other scholars are sceptical of such a conclusion. Natalino Ronzitti analysed the relations between unilateral sanctions and the entitlements granted under jurisdictional immunity and enforcement immunity.[773] Ronzitti has contended that jurisdictional immunity is a procedural norm, while asset freezing is a restrictive measure imposed either by executive or legislative order and, as such, is not subject of court proceedings.[774] Thus, in Ronzitti's view, restrictive measures against central banks and jurisdictional immunity are not commensurable.[775] Moreover, elaborating on the relations between unilateral sanctions and enforcement immunity, Ronzitti has gone as far as to suggest that enforcement immunity might cover "not only acts of constraints that are the continuation of a judgment, but also measures autonomously dictated by the legislative or the executive branch" and, as a result, unilateral economic sanctions may encroach on the principle of sovereign immunity.[776] Despite this, he concludes that even this violation might be justified, since these restrictions may constitute countermeasures.[777] In this regard, it is crucial to note that it is questionable whether the state that denied the protection granted under the customary international law of state immunity may invoke its right to rely upon countermeasures as a justification.[778]

Tom Ruys argues that unilateral sanctions – and more precisely asset freezes – do not give rise to a breach of immunities.[779] In support of this

Immunities and International Law (Cambridge University Press 2019). By contrast, Tom Ruys contends exactly the opposite. Ruys (n 11).

772 "In addition, as regards the measures taken against the Iranian Central Bank, they may be deemed to conflict with rules governing immunities and privileges of foreign States under international law, and in particular of the 2004 UN Convention on Jurisdictional Immunities of States and their Property, which is widely considered as reflecting customary international law, and provides for immunity of property of a central bank or other monetary authority from execution." Dupont (n 755) 314.

773 Ronzitti (n 11).

774 ibid 22.

775 ibid.

776 ibid.

777 Ronzitti (n 11).

778 Fox and Webb (n 762) 16.

779 Tom Ruys, 'Non-UN Financial Sanctions against Central Banks and Heads of State: In Breach of International Immunity Law?' (*EJIL: Talk!*, 12 May 2017) https://www.ejiltalk.org/non-un-financial-sanctions-against-central-banks-and-heads-of-state-in-breach-of-international-immunity-law/; Ruys (n 11).

conclusion, he argues that even though asset freezes are "measures of constraint" for the purposes of immunity from execution, the imposition of restrictive measures of this kind on a state or its central banks does not suffice to trigger the application of immunity.[780] Ruys claims that court proceedings serve as a necessary prerequisite for the application of state-immunity rules.[781] Thus, unilateral economic sanctions – in this instance, asset freezes – cannot trigger the application of state immunity rules, since they are either legislative or executive measures.[782] Ruys further discusses the interrelation between the concept of inviolability and unilateral economic sanctions, concluding that the latter does not interfere with the rules of inviolability.[783]

The argument that the central banks' assets cannot benefit from state immunity entitlements if they are targeted by unilateral sanctions is particularly interesting in light of the recent trends. Ingrid Wuerth has analysed domestic regulations and court practice in several states, concluding that the majority of jurisdictions afford protection from execution to the central bank assets of other states, if such assets are located within their territory.[784] Thus, it seems that private individuals or legal entities seeking to enforce a decision against the state might be denied this opportunity owing to the enforcement immunity provided for central bank assets, while unilateral sanctions, such as the freezing of the central bank's assets, do not fall squarely within the scope of the immunities accorded to states under international law. The paradoxical conclusion of this analysis has been well captured by Timor-Leste in a contrario argument before the ICJ: "State property would be in the absurdly paradoxical position of being inviolable and immune from judicial measures, but at the mercy of administrative or executive actions."[785]

Our analysis reveals that the scholarly debate does not provide an unequivocal answer whether unilateral sanctions imposed against central banks impede state immunity. ICJ jurisprudence does not shed much light on the

780 Ruys (n 11) 5–18.

781 Ruys distinguishes between the immunity from jurisdiction and immunity from execution, yet argues that both types of immunity apply only in the context of the court proceedings. ibid 7–10.

782 ibid.

783 ibid.

784 "The general development in state practice is towards greater and greater protection of foreign central bank assets." The only exception to this general tendency is the decision of the United States to allow the execution of terrorism-related judgements against the assets of the Central Bank of Iran. Wuerth (n 763).

785 'International Court of Justice. Questions Relating to the Seizure and Detention of Certain Documents and Data (Timor-Leste v. Australia). Memorial of Timor-Leste.' 39.

matter either. Nonetheless, a few of the court's pronouncements should be discussed here.

In *Jurisdictional Immunities of the State*, the ICJ has emphasised the distinction between jurisdictional immunity and immunity from enforcement.[786] As the court pointed out: "the immunity from enforcement enjoyed by States in regard to their property situated on foreign territory goes further than the jurisdictional immunity enjoyed by those same States before foreign courts."[787] In its further analysis, the ICJ emphasised that different rules apply to state property which is used for governmental non-commercial purposes and property which is used for other purposes.[788]

In the *Certain Iranian Assets* dispute, Iran claims that the freezing of the assets of the Central Bank of Iran (Bank Markazi),[789] along with the decision of US domestic courts to use these assets as compensation for victims of terrorism,[790] infringes upon customary international law of immunity.[791] Iran asserted the court's jurisdiction based on the relevant provisions of the Treaty of Amity, Economic Relations, and Consular Rights 1955.[792] The United States raised several preliminary objections to the court's jurisdiction, as well as to the admissibility of the claims.[793] Among the three preliminary objections

786 *Jurisdictional Immunities of the State (Germany v. Italy: Greece intervening), Judgment, ICJ Reports 2012, p 99* [113].

787 ibid.

788 ibid [116]–[118].

789 The immunity of the assets of the Central Bank of Iran was recognised until 2012. Executive Order 13599 blocked property, as well as interests in property, of the Central Bank. In addition, The Iran Threat Reduction and Syria Human Rights Act of 2012 expanded the scope of assets that can be used to satisfy judgements against Iran. Iran Threat Reduction and Syria Human Rights Act of 2012.

790 The Iran Threat Reduction and Syria Human Rights Act enacted in 2012 abrogated the immunity from execution of the assets of the Central Bank of Iran. These amendments coincided temporally with the court proceedings initiated by the victims of the 1983 bombing of the US Marine barracks in Beirut, Lebanon, which sought to satisfy their damage claims via the blocked assets of the Central Bank of Iran. *Deborah D Peterson, et al., Plaintiffs-Appellees, v. Islamic Republic of Iran, et al., Defendants-Appellants, 758 F3d 185* [2014] United States Court of Appeals, Second Circuit No. 13-2952-CV.

791 The main thrust of Iran's legal claims rests on the alleged violations of the 1955 Treaty of Amity, Economic Relations, and Consular Rights. Yet Iran argued that the relevant obligations under this treaty should be interpreted as incorporating, both explicitly and implicitly, customary international law of state immunity. 'International Court of Justice. Certain Iranian Assets (Islamic Republic of Iran v. United States of America). Application Instituting Proceedings.'

792 ibid.

793 'International Court of Justice. Certain Iranian Assets (Islamic Republic of Iran v. United States of America). Preliminary Objections Submitted by the United States of America.'

to the court's jurisdiction, the second objection relates to the possibility of distilling customary international law of state immunity from the relevant provisions of the Treaty of Amity, Economic Relations, and Consular Rights.[794] The ICJ analysed the provisions of the treaty invoked, only to conclude that the preliminary objection should be upheld.[795] Hence, the court unfortunately abstained from examining the legal claim that freezing of the central bank's assets infringes state immunity. As a result, the nature of the relationship between unilateral economic sanctions that target the property of central banks and state immunity remains open.

6.2 *Blocking of Property and Travel Restrictions Applicable to Heads of States and Other High-Ranking Government Officials*

Heads of states and other senior government officials are increasingly being targeted by unilateral economic sanctions, such as asset freezes and travel bans. For instance, the restrictive measures put in place by the EU against then-acting heads of states include restrictions imposed on the president of Syria and president of Zimbabwe.[796] US sanctions against Iran obligate the president to freeze the assets of individuals who meet the criteria laid down by the International Emergency Economic Powers Act.[797] This rule applies to any person "including an Iranian diplomat or representative of another government or military or quasi-governmental institution of Iran."[798] Current US sanctions against the Russian Federation cover many high-ranking government officials, who are targets of various restrictions.[799] The new wave of sanctions imposed by Ukraine against the Russian Federation target senior government officials.[800]

---

794 *Certain Iranian Assets, Preliminary Objections, Judgment* (n 751).

795 ibid.

796 Commission Implementing Regulation (EU) 2016/218 of 16 February 2016 amending Council Regulation (EC) No 314/2004 concerning certain restrictive measures in respect of Zimbabwe 2016 (OJ L) 218; Council Regulation (EU) No 36/2012 of 18 January 2012 concerning restrictive measures in view of the situation in Syria and repealing Regulation (EU) No 442/2011 2012 (OJ L).

797 Comprehensive Iran Sanctions, Accountability, and Divestment Act of 2010 Section 103. Economic sanctions relating to Iran.

798 ibid.

799 President of the United States of America. Executive Order 13660 of March 6, 2014. (n 2); President of the United States of America. Executive Order 13661 of March 16, 2014. (n 2).

800 On 15 May 2017, the president of Ukraine enacted the decision of the National Security and Defence Council of Ukraine (NSDC) of 28 April 2017 "On the Application of Personal Special Economic and Other Restrictive Measures (Sanctions)." 'President of Ukraine by His Decree Put into Effect the Decision of the National Security and Defense Council of Ukraine "On the Imposition of Personal Special Economic and Other Restrictive

The immunity of the head of state is primarily regulated by customary international law.[801] This immunity derives both from international rights and duties of states, as well as from the head of state's personal entitlements.[802] However, the scope of this immunity remains contestable.[803]

A number of principles, which constitute such immunity, can be distilled from the ICJ judgements in *Arrest Warrant of 11 April 2000* and *Certain Questions of Mutual Assistance in Criminal Matters*.[804] To start with, the ICJ observed that: "certain holders of high-ranking office in a State, such as the Head of State, Head of Government and Minister for Foreign Affairs, enjoy immunities from jurisdiction in other States, both civil and criminal."[805] Furthermore, the court decided that an arrest warrant infringes on the inviolability of the minister of foreign affairs[806] and that the same level of protection is guaranteed to

---

Measures (Sanctions)" – National Security and Defense Council of Ukraine' <https://www.rnbo.gov.ua/en/Diialnist/2764.html?PRINT>; Subsequently, on 14 May 2018, the president of Ukraine enacted a new decision of the NSDC of 2 May 2018 "On the Application and Repealing of Personal Special Economic and Other Restrictive Measures (Sanctions)." Указ Президента України від 14.05.2018 No. 126/2018, 'Про Рішення Ради Національної Безпеки і Оборони України Від 2 Травня 2018 Року "Про Застосування Та Скасування Персональних Спеціальних Економічних Та Інших Обмежувальних Заходів (Санкцій)"' (*Законодавство України*) <https://zakon.rada.gov.ua/go/126/2018>; In 2019, the Ukrainian president has enacted a decision by the NSDC from 19 March 2019 "On the use, revocation and introduction of amendments to the personal special economic and other restrictive measures (sanctions)." Указ Президента України No. 82/2019, 'Про Рішення Ради Національної Безпеки і Оборони України Від 19 Березня 2019 Року' (*Офіційне інтернет-представництво Президента України*) <https://www.president.gov.ua/documents/822019-26290> These decisions along with the other acts adopted by the Ukrainian government impose sanctions against listed individuals.

801 Sir Arthur Watts, 'Heads of State,' *Max Planck Encyclopedia of Public International Law* [*MPEPIL*] <https://opil.ouplaw.com/view/10.1093/law:epil/9780199231690/law-9780199231690-e1418?prd=EPIL>.

802 ibid.; "The immunity of a Head of State divides into immunity in the public capacity or 'as the State' and personal immunity. Article 2 (1)(b)(i) and (iv) of UNCSI includes heads of States within the definition of the State. By doing so it extends to such persons in the public capacity the immunities which the State itself enjoys under the Convention." Fox and Webb (n 762) 544.

803 Fox and Webb (n 762) Chapter 18.

804 *Arrest Warrant of 11 April 2000 (Democratic Republic of the Congo v. Belgium), Judgment, ICJ Reports 2002, p 3*; *Certain Questions of Mutual Assistance in Criminal Matters (Djibouti v. France), Judgment, ICJ Reports 2008, p 177*.

805 *Arrest Warrant of 11 April 2000 (Democratic Republic of the Congo v. Belgium), Judgment* (n 804) [51].

806 ibid [70–71].

a head of state.[807] This finding implies that the acting head of state should be entitled to an exemption from criminal prosecution during his time in office. Moreover, the court's pronouncement that an arrest warrant hinders the ability of the minister of foreign affairs to perform his functions implies that travel bans that prohibit the minister of foreign affairs, as well as acting head of state, from entering a territory of any other state, violate immunities guaranteed under international law.

Another well-established principle is the inviolability of a head of state's person, residence and property in a visited state. In the words of Arthur Watts, such inviolability implies that "officials of that State may not inspect his [the head of state's] person or property or enter upon the premises occupied by him."[808] It remains unclear how the principle of inviolability constrains states from imposing unilateral economic sanctions, in particular asset freezes, on a foreign head of state. In this regard, Tom Ruys contends that asset freezes do not encroach upon the inviolability conferred upon states or their officials under international law.[809]

When it comes to the immunity of other high-ranking government officials, the problem of determining its scope is even more intricate. To begin with, there is no clear rule about who is entitled to be called "high-ranking government official."[810] The analysis of the ICJ jurisprudence demonstrates that ministers can be considered as "holders of high-ranking office."[811]

---

807 *Certain Questions of Mutual Assistance in Criminal Matters (Djibouti v. France), Judgment* (n 804) [170].

808 Watts (n 801).

809 "Inviolability of residence and property during a (senior) State official's visit to a third country is ultimately of little relevance in the context of the adoption of targeted financial sanctions, for the simple reason that non-UN sanctions, such as those against President al-Assad of Syria, are normally adopted while the senior official concerned is in his/her home State. It follows that an inviolability of residence and property that is analogous to that of 'special missions' offers no meaningful protection whatsoever (from the perspective of the targeted official) and constitutes no significant obstacle (from the perspective of the sanctioning State) preventing the adoption of such sanctions." Ruys (n 11) 25.

810 Sir Arthur Watts, 'Heads of Governments and Other Senior Officials,' *Max Planck Encyclopedia of Public International Law* [*MPEPIL*] <https://opil.ouplaw.com/view/10.1093/law:epil/9780199231690/law-9780199231690-e1417>; "Ministers of central government other than the Head of State or government and the Minister for Foreign Affairs when performing official functions enjoy immunities as individuals acting as representatives of the State. The extent to which they enjoy additional immunities by reason of their membership of central government is not clear." Fox and Webb (n 762) 565.

811 Watts (n 810); "The tendency in practice has, however, been to expand the categories of high-ranking officials benefiting from immunity ratione personae. The ICJ in Congo v.

The extent of the immunity enjoyed by senior government officials is similar to that accorded to a head of state, at least with respect to their property.[812] Concerning the property of a head of state, Arthur Watts has asserted the following: "A Head of State probably enjoys extensive immunity in relation to property owned or held by him in a foreign State for private or non-official purposes, particularly in so far as measures of execution against such property are prohibited when he is in the foreign State in the exercise of his official functions."[813]

This rule applies only to the measures of execution, which should be related to the court proceedings, as described above. Whether asset freezes are measures of constraint for the purposes of enforcement immunity is debatable, and thus it is unclear how this rule can protect holders of high-ranking office from unilateral financial sanctions, such as asset freezes.

Tom Ruys contends that the immunity of the foreign officials cannot be broader in scope than state immunity and argues that this immunity arises only with a nexus to particular court proceedings.[814] In light of the ICJ findings in *Arrest Warrant of 11 April 2000*, Ruys argues that performance of the duties of the senior government officials might be hindered if travel bans were to prevent these officials from performing their functions, and thus such bans might be considered illegal.[815] For this reason, countries that frequently impose restrictions like travel bans introduce exemptions to allow even targeted senior officials to participate in international events and meetings.[816]

Our analysis demonstrates that the relationship between unilateral economic sanctions and immunities that international law accords to states, as

Rwanda after noting that Heads of State and of government and Ministers for Foreign Affairs are deemed to represent the State stated that: with increasing frequency in the modern time other persons representing a State in specific fields may be authorized by that State to bind it by their statements in respect of matters falling within their purview. This may be true, for example, of holders of technical ministerial portfolios exercising powers in their field of competence in the area of foreign relations, and even of certain officials." Fox and Webb (n 762) 565.

812 Watts (n 810).

813 ibid.

814 "While the scope (rather than substance) of 'individual' immunities accorded to specific persons (such as diplomats, visiting forces, special missions, or, more generally, State officials) has so far not been addressed in any detail, there is a priori no reason why the required nexus to court proceedings would not apply in this context as well." Ruys (n 11) 16.

815 ibid 26–27.

816 ibid. Tom Ruys provides as an example the practice of the European Union in this regard. Yet other states, like the United States, have also introduced similar exemptions.

well as to state officials, raise many intricate questions for which there are not yet definitive answers.

7 Unilateral Economic Sanctions and WTO Law

The renowned international lawyer Hersch Lauterpacht, writing in 1933 about the legality of economic boycott under international law, reached the following conclusion: "In the absence of explicit conventional obligations, particularly those laid down in commercial treaties, a state is entitled to prevent altogether goods from a foreign state from coming into its territory. It may – and frequently does – do so under the guise of a protective tariff or of sanitary precautions or in some other manner. The foreign state may treat such an attitude as an unfriendly act and retort accordingly. But it cannot legitimately regard it as a breach of international law."[817]

International law has changed drastically since 1933. International trade law has evolved to a level where international trade commitments are enforced through the institutionalised system of dispute settlement.[818] Moreover, states are allowed to retaliate against a state that fails to abide by a decision of the adjudicators.[819] Thus, it should come as no surprise that economic sanctions are frequently considered as inconsistent with WTO law and WTO Members attempt to challenge them.[820]

I analyse various types of unilateral economic sanctions and their potential inconsistency with WTO law below. The possibility of justifying such restrictive measures under the exceptions embedded in the WTO Agreements is discussed in chapter 4 (illustrated by the example of human rights economic sanctions).

817 Hersch Lauterpacht, 'Boycott in International Relations' (1933) 14 British Yearbook of International Law 125, 130.

818 DSU, Dispute Settlement Rules: Understanding on Rules and Procedures Governing the Settlement of Disputes, Marrakesh Agreement Establishing the World Trade Organization, Annex 2, 1869 UNTS 401 (DSU).

819 Article 22.6 ibid.

820 As a result of the military tension between Ukraine and Russia, several states imposed unilateral economic sanctions against Russia. Russia retaliated by implementing its restrictive measures, including a food embargo. These restrictions revived the debate on the consistency of such measures with the WTO law, in particular, the possibility to justify them under the national security exception. Neuwirth and Svetlicinii, 'The Economic Sanctions over the Ukraine Conflict and the WTO' (n 6); Neuwirth and Svetlicinii, 'The Current EU/US–Russia Conflict over Ukraine and the WTO' (n 6); Ji Yeong Yoo and Dukgeun Ahn, 'Security Exceptions in the WTO System: Bridge or Bottle-Neck for Trade and Security?' (2016) 19 Journal of International Economic Law 417.

7.1 *Import Restrictions*

7.1.1 Import Restrictions on Goods

Import restrictions are one of the most frequently deployed instruments of economic coercion. These restrictions can take various forms, such as a complete or partial import ban. The scope of the products covered by the ban is, as a rule, determined by the goals pursued by economic sanctions. For instance, a sanctioning state may decide to target a product that is of crucial importance for the targeted state's revenues or it may restrict the importation of the product for which its own market is the main importing market.

The principal objective of the multilateral trading system is to promote trade liberalisation by removing trade barriers. Thus, since the early days of the GATT 1947, the core principles have been the most-favoured-nation principle (MFN principle) and the prohibition of quantitative restrictions. Import restrictions run counter to both of these principles.

7.1.1.1 *Potential Violation of the MFN Principle*

The MFN principle is set out in Article I:1 of the GATT 1994 and reads as follows: "With respect to customs duties and charges of any kind imposed on or in connection with importation or exportation or imposed on the international transfer of payments for imports or exports, and with respect to the method of levying such duties and charges, and with respect to all rules and formalities in connection with importation and exportation, and with respect to all matters referred to in paragraphs 2 and 4 of Article III, any advantage, favour, privilege or immunity granted by any contracting party to any product originating in or destined for any other country shall be accorded immediately and unconditionally to the like product originating in or destined for the territories of all other contracting parties."[821]

WTO adjudicators elucidated the sequence of the analysis under Article I:1. In particular, the AB explains that: "Based on the text of Article I:1, the following elements must be demonstrated to establish an inconsistency with that provision: (i) that the measure at issue falls within the scope of application of Article I:1; (ii) that the imported products at issue are 'like' products within the meaning of Article I:1; (iii) that the measure at issue confers an 'advantage, favour, privilege, or immunity' on a product originating in the territory of any country; and (iv) that the advantage so accorded is not extended 'immediately' and 'unconditionally' to 'like' products originating in the territory of

821 GATT 1994: General Agreement on Tariffs and Trade 1994, April 15, 1994, Marrakesh Agreement Establishing the World Trade Organization, Annex 1A, 1867 UNTS 187 (GATT 1994).

all Members. Thus, if a Member grants any advantage to any product originating in the territory of any other country, such advantage must be accorded 'immediately and unconditionally' to like products originating from all other Members."[822]

A prohibition on the importation of goods that applies only to one WTO Member, while exempting other Members, faces a significant risk of being inconsistent with the MFN obligation. The MFN obligation applies to "all rules and formalities in connection with importation." What is more, under such circumstances, the "likeness" of the goods can be presumed. Seen in this way, an import prohibition of this type grants an 'advantage, favour, privilege, or immunity'[823] to WTO Members that can export goods and deprives goods from a sanctioned WTO Member of this opportunity. Furthermore, the finding that Article I:1 is violated does not require any actual trade effect to take place.[824]

Import restrictions discriminate against goods that originated in a particular country by granting market access to goods from other countries. The panel in *EC – Seal Products* explicitly pronounced that "the advantage granted by the EU Seal Regime is in the form of market access; it is granted to seal products that meet the conditions under the IC exception."[825] On the basis of the further finding that this advantage in the form of market access was not extended "immediately and unconditionally" to the other WTO Members, the panel concluded that the measure is inconsistent with the obligation under Article I:1 of the GATT 1994.[826]

---

822 *Appellate Body Reports, European Communities – Measures Prohibiting the Importation and Marketing of Seal Products, WT/DS400/AB/R / WT/DS401/AB/R, adopted 18 June 2014, DSR 2014:I, p 7* [5.86].

823 The WTO tribunals interpreted the term "advantage" in the context of the MFN obligation as referring to those advantages that create "more favourable import opportunities" or affect the commercial relationship between products of different origins. *Panel Reports, European Communities – Regime for the Importation, Sale and Distribution of Bananas, WT/DS27/R/ECU (Ecuador) / WT/DS27/R/GTM, WT/DS27/R/HND (Guatemala and Honduras) / WT/DS27/R/MEX (Mexico) / WT/DS27/R/USA (US), adopted 25 September 1997, as modified by Appellate Body Report WT/DS27/AB/R, DSR 1997:II, p 695 to DSR 1997:III, p 1085* [7.239].

824 The AB explained that "Article I:1 protects expectations of equal competitive opportunities for like imported products from all Members. ... it is for this reason that an inconsistency with Article I:1 is not contingent upon the actual trade effects of a measure." *Appellate Body Reports, European Communities – Measures Prohibiting the Importation and Marketing of Seal Products* (n 822) [5.87].

825 *Panel Reports, European Communities – Measures Prohibiting the Importation and Marketing of Seal Products, WT/DS400/R and Add1 / WT/DS401/R and Add1, adopted 18 June 2014, as modified by Appellate Body Reports WT/DS400/AB/R / WT/DS401/AB/R, DSR 2014:II, p 365* [7.596].

826 ibid [7.600].

In light of the above, unilateral economic sanctions in the form of import restrictions are inconsistent with Article I:1.

7.1.1.2 *Potential Violation of the Prohibition on Quantitative Restrictions*

The general prohibition on quantitative restrictions is embedded in Article XI:1 of the GATT 1994: "No prohibitions or restrictions other than duties, taxes or other charges, whether made effective through quotas, import or export licences or other measures, shall be instituted or maintained by any contracting party on the importation of any product of the territory of any other contracting party or on the exportation or sale for export of any product destined for the territory of any other contracting party."

In several disputes, the WTO adjudicators discussed import prohibitions and their compatibility with Article XI. A brief recapitulation of the tribunals' conclusions is warranted here. The panel in *Canada – Periodicals* concluded that a complete ban on imports of certain magazines was inconsistent with Article XI:1 of GATT.[827] The panel pointed out that: "Since the importation of certain foreign products into Canada is completely denied under Tariff Code 9958, it appears that this provision by its terms is inconsistent with Article XI:1 of GATT 1994."[828] The US import ban on shrimp and shrimp products harvested in a way that endangers sea turtles and causes their incidental killing sowed the seeds for one of the most oft-quoted WTO disputes, namely *US – Shrimp*. In the context of this dispute, the panel considered the terms "prohibitions or restrictions" entrenched in Article XI:1 and concluded as follows: "the United States bans imports of shrimp or shrimp products from any country not meeting certain policy conditions. We finally note that previous panels have considered similar measures restricting imports to be 'prohibitions or restrictions' within the meaning of Article XI."[829] Later the panel in *Brazil – Retreaded Tyres* emphasised that: "There is no ambiguity as to what 'prohibitions' on importation means: Members shall not forbid the importation of any product of any other Member into their markets."[830]

827 *Panel Report, Canada – Certain Measures Concerning Periodicals, WT/DS31/R and Corr1, adopted 30 July 1997, as modified by Appellate Body Report WT/DS31/AB/R, DSR 1997:I, p 481.*

828 ibid [5.5].

829 *Panel Report, United States – Import Prohibition of Certain Shrimp and Shrimp Products, WT/DS58/R and Corr1, adopted 6 November 1998, as modified by Appellate Body Report WT/DS58/AB/R, DSR 1998:VII, p 2821* [7.16].

830 *Panel Report, Brazil – Measures Affecting Imports of Retreaded Tyres, WT/DS332/R, adopted 17 December 2007, as modified by Appellate Body Report WT/DS332/AB/R, DSR 2007:V, p 1649* [7.11].

In light of the previous jurisprudence on the ambit of the prohibition on quantitative restrictions, there is no doubt that economic sanctions in the form of import restrictions on goods violate Article XI:1 of the GATT 1994.

7.1.2 Import Restrictions on Services

Restrictions on the importation of services have emerged as part of a broader effort to make sanctions more efficient. Given that international trade in services plays an increasingly important role, such prohibitions have significant potential to inflict economic grief on a targeted state. There are myriad ways in which this endeavour might be undertaken. Hence, restrictions on the importation of services might fall into all four modes of supply, as they are inscribed in the GATS.[831]

To illustrate this possibility, we compiled a table with the examples relevant for each mode of supply (Table 1).

The ultimate objective of the GATS is the liberalisation of trade in services. Against this backdrop, during the Uruguay Round negotiators agreed to a number of principles concerning the liberalisation of trade in services. These fundamental principles are conceptually distinct from the similar precepts of the GATT 1994. Since unilateral economic sanctions may encroach upon these fundamental principles, we examine below the consistency of import restrictions on services with the relevant disciplines of the GATS.

7.1.2.1 *Potential Violation of the MFN Principle*

Notwithstanding the significant flexibility granted to WTO Members with respect to their commitments on trade in services, the general MFN clause was embedded in Article II of the GATS. Article II:1 reads as follows: "With respect to any measure covered by this Agreement, each Member shall accord immediately and unconditionally to services and service suppliers of any other Member treatment no less favourable than that it accords to like services and service suppliers of any other country." This MFN obligation is an umbrella clause that guarantees that the commitments undertaken by any WTO Member

831 Article 1, in the relevant part, reads as follows: "supply of a service: (a) from the territory of one Member into the territory of any other Member; (b) in the territory of one Member to the service consumer of any other Member; (c) by a service supplier of one Member, through commercial presence in the territory of any other Member; (d) by a service supplier of one Member, through presence of natural persons of a Member in the territory of any other Member." GATS: General Agreement on Trade in Services, April 15, 1994, Marrakesh Agreement Establishing the World Trade Organization, Annex 1B, 1869 UNTS 183 (GATS).

TABLE 1 Types of import restrictions and modes of supply under the GATS

Modes of supply	Types of import restrictions
Cross-border trade	Prohibition on buying services that originated in a particular (sanctioned) state or from service suppliers incorporated under the laws of the sanctioned state
Consumption abroad	Prohibition on travel by nationals of a sanctioning state to a sanctioned state – for instance, the United States' unilateral economic sanctions against Cuba include such a travel prohibition (Cuban Assets Control Regulations 31 CFR Part 515)[a]
Commercial presence	Prohibition on the right of establishment that applies to foreign entities that are incorporated under the laws of a sanctioned state
Presence of natural persons	Prohibition on the nationals of a sanctioned state providing services on a territory of a sanctioning state, either as an individual supplier or as an employee of a foreign-incorporated legal entity

a "The prohibition on dealing in property in which Cuba or a Cuban national has an interest set forth in §515.201(b)(1) includes a prohibition on the receipt of goods or services in Cuba, even if provided free-of-charge by the Government of Cuba or a national of Cuba or paid for by a third-country national who is not subject to U.S. jurisdiction. The prohibition set forth in §515.201(b)(1) also prohibits payment for air travel by a person subject to U.S. jurisdiction to Cuba on a third-country carrier unless the travel is pursuant to an OFAC general or specific license." Cuban Assets Control Regulations 31 CFR Part 515 §515.420 Travel to Cuba.

are extended to the whole membership, irrespective of the Member's market size and other considerations.

The bulk of unilateral economic sanctions against foreign services or service suppliers are implemented in the form of discriminatory restrictions based exclusively on their origin. This peculiarity might enable a complainant to rely upon the presumption of "likeness" as developed in WTO jurisprudence. The AB explains the presumption of "likeness" in the context of trade in services as follows: "In our view, where a measure provides for a distinction based exclusively on origin, there will or can be services and service suppliers that are the same in all respects except for origin and, accordingly, 'likeness' can be presumed and the complainant is not required to establish 'likeness' on the basis of the relevant criteria set out above. Accordingly, we consider that, under Articles II:1 and XVII:1 of the GATS, a complainant is not required in all cases to establish 'likeness' of services and service suppliers on the basis of the relevant criteria for establishing 'likeness.' Rather, in principle, a complainant may establish 'likeness' by demonstrating that the measure at issue makes a distinction between services and service suppliers based exclusively on origin."[832]

As a result, if a WTO Member inserted a commitment for a specific sector and mode of supply into its schedule of concessions under the GATS and subsequently introduced economic sanctions in the form of import restrictions on services, which are exclusively based on the origin of the services or service supplier, these restrictions would be inconsistent with Article II:1 of the GATS.

7.1.2.2 *Potential Violation of Market Access Commitments*

Article XVI of the GATS prescribes a general obligation for a WTO Member to abide by the market access commitments it has inscribed for each services sector and mode of supply. Paragraph 1 of Article XVI reads as follows: "With respect to market access through the modes of supply identified in Article I, each Member shall accord services and service suppliers of any other Member treatment no less favourable than that provided for under the terms, limitations and conditions agreed and specified in its Schedule." Thus, if a WTO Member has liberalised a certain sector and mode of supply and subsequently imposes import restrictions on services and service suppliers that discriminate against a particular WTO Member, this Member thereby accords the services and service suppliers of another Member less favourable treatment. Consequently, import restrictions on services violate Article XVI of the GATS, provided a WTO Member has undertaken relevant commitments.

7.2 *Export Restrictions*

7.2.1 Export Restrictions on Goods

Restrictions on the export of goods are frequently used to advance foreign-policy objectives.[833] These restrictions may take different forms and pursue

832 *Appellate Body Report, Argentina – Measures Relating to Trade in Goods and Services, WT/DS453/AB/R and Add1, adopted 9 May 2016, DSR 2016:II, p 431* [6.38]. In the subsequent paragraphs of the report, the AB discusses the differences between the presumption of "likeness" in the context of trade in goods and trade in services. The AB points out the peculiarities of applying this presumption to the trade in services (paras. 6.38–6.40) and thus its limited applicability in the context of trade in services (para. 6.40), yet it did not disregard it as such and confirmed its applicability.

833 Barry Carter described in his book how the export controls were framed as a part of a broader effort to restrict trade with the communist bloc countries and their allies during

diverse objectives. Traditionally, dual-use goods are subject to elaborate export requirements.[834] Other forms of export restrictions include prohibitions on the export of goods, materials or services which are in high demand in a targeted state.[835]

The term "export restrictions" is broad enough to cover a range of measures. For example, quantitative export restrictions, such as quotas, export duties (export taxes)[836] and export licensing requirements, represent the diversity of export restrictions. While the WTO Members frequently rely upon these measures,[837] this study focuses on unilateral economic sanctions which take the form of export bans. Export bans might be complete or partial – yet irrespective of their form, they fall under the definition of quantitative restrictions and thus become subject to the disciplines contained in Article XI:1 of the GATT 1994. Furthermore, the imposition of such export restrictions against a particular WTO Member or a group of Members runs the risk of being inconsistent with the MFN principle embedded in Article I:1 of the GATT 1994.

Various forms of export restrictions might fall foul of the WTO Members' commitments, as embedded in WTO Agreements and the Members' Protocols of Accession.[838] For the subsequent analysis, I focus on the relevant provisions

---

the Cold War. In fact, at the end of World War II, the US president was granted extensive power over export controls. Barry E Carter, *International Economic Sanctions: Improving the Haphazard U.S. Legal Regime* (Cambridge University Press 1988).

834 Many countries have implemented internal control regimes to deal with the exports of dual-use goods. For instance, the European Union had such a regime in place and the EU Council has recently modernised the current regime. Regulation (EU) 2021/821 of the European Parliament and of the Council of 20 May 2021 setting up a Union regime for the control of exports, brokering, technical assistance, transit and transfer of dual-use items (recast) 2021 (OJ L). https://eur-lex.europa.eu/legal-content/EN/TXT/?uri=CELEX%3A32021R0821.

835 Mina Pollmann, 'What's Driving Japan's Trade Restrictions on South Korea?' *The Diplomat* (29 July 2019) <https://thediplomat.com/2019/07/whats-driving-japans-trade-restrictions-on-south-korea/>.

836 As Gabrielle Marceau has mentioned, both terms are used interchangeably in the literature. Gabrielle Marceau, 'WTO and Export Restrictions' (2016) 50 Journal of World Trade 563, Footnote 1.

837 Ilaria Espa, *Export Restrictions on Critical Minerals and Metals: Testing the Adequacy of WTO Disciplines* (Cambridge University Press 2015); Marceau (n 836).

838 Some WTO Members that joined the organisation after 1995 have incorporated commitments to eliminate or phase out export restrictions. In fact, WTO disputes brought against China were based on the allegations of the inconsistency of export restrictions with China's commitments contained in its Protocol of Accession. *Appellate Body Reports, China – Measures Related to the Exportation of Various Raw Materials, WT/DS394/AB/R / WT/DS395/AB/R / WT/DS398/AB/R, adopted 22 February 2012, DSR 2012:VII, p 3295; Appellate Body Reports, China – Measures Related to the Exportation of Rare Earths,*

of the WTO Agreements and examine the consistency of export bans with these provisions, drawing on WTO jurisprudence, as developed by the panels and the AB.

7.2.1.1 *Potential Violation of the MFN Principle*

An export ban on any category of goods has a high chance of running afoul of the MFN obligation contained in Article I:1 of the GATT 1994. The MFN treatment guarantees that "any advantage, favour, privilege or immunity granted by any contracting party to any product originating in or destined for any other country shall be accorded immediately and unconditionally to the like product originating in or destined for the territories of all other contracting parties." Thus, the MFN obligation is formulated broadly enough to cover any discrimination between the exports destined for different WTO Members, and thus any export ban inevitably falls foul of this commitment.

7.2.1.2 *Potential Violation of the Prohibition on Quantitative Restrictions*

The general prohibition on quantitative export restrictions is contained in Article XI:1 of the GATT 1994. The text of Article XI:1 outlaws "prohibitions or restrictions" on exportation or sale for export. The AB interpreted this prohibition as follows: "Article XI of the GATT 1994 covers those prohibitions or restrictions that have a limiting effect on the quantity or amount of a product being imported or exported."[839] Thus, an export ban, whether complete or partial, falls under this definition of "prohibition or restriction" on exportation and impedes compliance with the obligations under Article XI:1 of the GATT 1994.

In light of the above, it is evident that export bans on goods are inconsistent with Articles I:1 and XI:1 of the GATT 1994.

7.2.2 Export Restrictions on Services

While the relations between export restrictions and the disciplines contained in the GATT 1994 have been explored in the literature,[840] no similar analysis for the export restrictions on services and their compatibility with the GATS

Tungsten, and Molybdenum, WT/DS431/AB/R / WT/DS432/AB/R / WT/DS433/AB/R, adopted 29 August 2014, DSR 2014:III, p 805.

839 *Appellate Body Reports, China – Measures Related to the Exportation of Various Raw Materials* (n 838) [320].

840 Espa (n 837); Marceau (n 836). The policy of Chinese government and the subsequent WTO disputes inspired scholars to explore the WTO disciplines on export restrictions in more detail. Mark Wu, 'China's Export Restrictions and the Limits of WTO Law' (2017) 16 World Trade Review 673; Another complicated type of export restriction are restrictions on the export of agricultural products, particularly at times when the international prices

TABLE 2 Types of export restrictions and modes of supply under the GATS

Modes of supply	Types of export restrictions
Cross-border supply	A prohibition imposed on domestic industries and their subsidiaries on providing (export) financial services to foreign legal entities, including foreign banks
Consumption abroad	A prohibition imposed on foreign individuals preventing them from travelling to the country imposing the restriction, thus preventing targeted individuals from receiving medical treatment, education or travelling around
Commercial presence	Restrictions on domestic industries investing in a particular country or in a certain sector of that country's economy
Presence of natural persons	Prohibition preventing the nationals of the state from providing any professional services to a targeted state or to particular industries/legal entities in a targeted state

disciplines has been undertaken. The only exception is the research conducted by Rudolf Adlung.[841]

The focus of the GATS disciplines is on granting market access for foreign services and service providers, as well as on securing national treatment for foreign services and service providers. In other words, disciplines on the export of services have attracted little attention from negotiators.

Nonetheless, a plethora of economic sanctions may take the form of export restrictions on services. What is noteworthy is that some of these restrictions are extremely effective. For instance, the United States' prohibitions on the export of financial services, which also include the clearing of transactions denominated in US dollars, are so efficient that they are sometimes called "dollar unilateralism."[842]

In Table 2, I provide examples of export restrictions on services under the four modes of supply.

are unstable. Ryan Cardwell and William A Kerr, 'Can Export Restrictions Be Disciplined Through the World Trade Organisation?' (2014) 37 The World Economy 1186.

841 Rudolf Adlung, 'Export Policies and the General Agreement on Trade in Services' (2015) 18 Journal of International Economic Law 487.

842 Katzenstein (n 324).

A few observations on the consistency of export restrictions on services with the relevant provisions of the GATS are warranted here. First and foremost, the GATS does not prescribe a general prohibition on quantitative restrictions similar to Article XI:1 of the GATT 1994. Second, the wording of the MFN obligation under the GATS suggests that export restrictions on services fall outside the scope of this commitment. More specifically, Article II:1 of the GATS stipulates that "each Member shall accord immediately and unconditionally to services and service suppliers of any other Member treatment no less favourable than that it accords to like services and service suppliers of any other country." A textual interpretation favoured by WTO adjudicators[843] entails that the MFN obligation applies only to foreign services or service suppliers, and not to foreign service recipients. Hence, prohibitions on the export of services do not breach the MFN obligation under the GATS.

However, export restrictions on services may be inconsistent with WTO commitments. More specifically, an analysis of WTO jurisprudence demonstrates that GATS commitments under mode 3 (commercial presence) also include the ability to export services from the territory of a WTO Member that has inscribed such commitments into its schedule. The WTO panel in *Mexico – Telecoms* had to decide whether Mexico's commitments under the GATS mode 3 (commercial presence) extend "to international services from Mexico to the United States supplied through commercial agencies commercially present in Mexico."[844] Following an examination of the definition of mode 3 and the term "commercial presence," the panel concluded as follows: "The definition of services supplied through a commercial presence makes explicit the location of the service supplier. It provides that a service supplier has a commercial presence – any type of business or professional establishment – in the territory of any other Member. The definition is silent with respect to any other territorial requirement (as in cross-border supply under mode 1) or nationality of the service consumer (as in consumption abroad under mode 2). Supply of a service through commercial presence would therefore not exclude a service that originates in the territory in which a commercial presence is established

843 In its early case law, the AB reiterated the approach established by the ICJ and declared its preference for the textual interpretation, stating: "Article 31 of the VCLT provides that the words of the treaty form the foundation for the interpretive process: 'interpretation must be based above all upon the text of the treaty.'" *Appellate Body Report, Japan – Taxes on Alcoholic Beverages, WT/DS8/AB/R, WT/DS10/AB/R, WT/DS11/AB/R, adopted 1 November 1996, DSR 1996:I, p 97* 11. In subsequent disputes both the panels and the AB followed this approach.

844 *Panel Report, Mexico – Measures Affecting Telecommunications Services, WT/DS204/R, adopted 1 June 2004, DSR 2004:IV, p 1537* [7.352].

(such as Mexico), but is delivered into the territory of any other Member (such as the United States)."[845]

In *China – Electronic Payment Services*, the panel concluded that if a WTO Member had undertaken market access commitments under mode 3 (commercial presence), these commitments imply the export of services from that Member's territory. In particular, the panel observed: "The definition of services supplied through commercial presence addresses only the location of the foreign service supplier, not that of the recipient of the relevant service, nor the nationality of the recipient. It indicates that for purposes of the GATS a service is supplied through mode 3 if a service supplier of a Member supplies its service through commercial presence in the territory of another Member. The definition does not state that a foreign service supplier may supply its services only to recipients that are in the territory of the Member in which the service supplier has established a commercial presence and are nationals of that Member. Nor does the definition state that a foreign service supplier may not supply its services to recipients that are outside the territory of the Member in which the service supplier has established a commercial presence."[846]

These observations are particularly important when it comes to determining the legality of export restrictions on services under the GATS. Indeed, they entail that if a WTO Member imposes an export ban on services, any other Member can challenge this measure if the former Member undertook market access commitments for a particular services sector in mode 3 (commercial presence). Yet this proposition must be qualified in several ways. In this regard, Adlung emphasises that: "Members remain free to impose export restrictions (a) on their own services or service suppliers – even in the event of full commitments under Article XVI – as well as (b) on any services or service suppliers, whether foreign or national, in sectors not subject to specific commitments."[847]

Our analysis reveals that export restrictions on services might be WTO consistent, with the exception of restrictions that apply to liberalised services sectors and that impede the right of service suppliers to export their services through a commercial presence to other WTO Members.

7.3 *Restrictions on Traffic in Transit and Goods in Transit*

In their efforts to inflict economic pain on sanctioned states and their entities, states can impose restrictions on traffic and goods in transit, in addition

845 ibid [7.375].

846 *Panel Report, China – Certain Measures Affecting Electronic Payment Services, WT/DS413/R and Add1, adopted 31 August 2012, DSR 2012:X, p 5305* [7.617].

847 Adlung (n 841) 498.

to more conventional import and export restrictions. To take one example, US economic sanctions against Cuba prohibit ships trading with Cuba from docking at US ports for six months after the ship has left a Cuban port.[848] Furthermore, the sanctions prohibit entry onto US territory of goods that were transported from or through Cuba.[849] These ambiguously formulated restrictions may violate Article V of the GATT 1994 that protects the freedom of transit. More specifically, there may be a breach of obligations prescribed by Article V:2[850] and Article V:6.[851]

Freedom of transit entails that "goods in international transit from any Member must be allowed entry whenever destined for the territory of a third country."[852] WTO adjudicators distinguish obligations under the first and the second sentences of Article V:2. In particular, the following observation describes their scope and their interrelations: "the first sentence in Article V:2 addresses freedom of transit for goods in international transit. As a complement to this protection, the panel considers that Article V:2, second sentence further prohibits Members from making distinctions in the treatment of goods, based on their origin or trajectory prior to arriving in their territory, based on their ownership, or based on the transport or vessel of the goods. Accordingly, the panel concludes that Article V:2, second sentence requires that goods from all Members must be ensured an identical level of access and equal conditions when proceeding in international transit."[853]

---

848 Cuban Assets Control Regulations 31 CFR § 515.207 Entry of vessels engaged in trade with Cuba. With the enactment of Cuban Liberty and Democratic Solidarity (LIBERTAD) Act of 1996 these restrictions were codified. Cuban Liberty and Democratic Solidarity (LIBERTAD) Act of 1996, Pub. L. No. 104–114, 110 Stat. 785 (1996) (codified at 22 U.S.C. §§ 6021–6091).

849 ibid § 6040.

850 Article V:2 reads as follows: "There shall be freedom of transit through the territory of each contracting party, via the routes most convenient for international transit, for traffic in transit to or from the territory of other contracting parties. No distinction shall be made which is based on the flag of vessels, the place of origin, departure, entry, exit or destination, or on any circumstances relating to the ownership of goods, of vessels or of other means of transport."

851 The relevant part of Article V:6 reads as follows: "Each contracting party shall accord to products which have been in transit through the territory of any other contracting party treatment no less favourable than that which would have been accorded to such products had they been transported from their place of origin to their destination without going through the territory of such other contracting party."

852 *Panel Report, Colombia – Indicative Prices and Restrictions on Ports of Entry, WT/DS366/R and Corr.1, adopted 20 May 2009, DSR 2009:VI, p. 2535* [7.401].

853 ibid [7.402].

The scope of the obligation stipulated in Article V:2 first sentence was further clarified by the panel in *Russia – Traffic in Transit* as follows: "under the first sentence of Article V:2: a. Each Member is required to guarantee freedom of transit through its territory for any traffic in transit entering from any other Member, and b. Each Member is required to guarantee freedom of transit through its territory for traffic in transit to exit to any other Member."[854] For this reason, in order to conclude that a particular regulation is inconsistent with the first sentence of Article V:2 of the GATT 1994, it is sufficient to establish "that a Member has precluded transit through its territory for traffic in transit entering its territory from any other Member."[855]

Regarding the obligation under Article V:6 of the GATT 1994, the panel in *Colombia – Ports of Entry* noted that "Article V:6 generally extends MFN protection to Members' goods which 'have been in transit.'"[856] Furthermore, the panel concluded that this obligation applies to foreign goods whose final destination is a concerned WTO Member.[857] In particular, the panel observed: "Article V:2 extends MFN protection to goods in transit through Member countries, while Article V:6 extends MFN protection from discrimination based on the geographic course of goods in transit upon reaching their final destination."[858] In other words, "products that are transported from their place of origin which pass through any other Member country on the route to their final destination must be treated no less favourably than had those same products been transported from their place of origin to their final destination without ever passing through that other Member's territory."[859]

The aforementioned US sanctions that prohibit vessels leaving a Cuban port from using a US port as a transit stop violate US commitments under Article V:2 of the GATT 1994. As has been pointed out, the first sentence of Article V:2 guarantees freedom of transit for traffic in transit from the territory of other WTO Members. In other words, this commitment entitles any vessel from other WTO Members to enter any US port, if the vessel is "in transit" in the meaning of Article V:1 of the GATT 1994[860] and irrespective of the previous route taken by the vessel. The second sentence of Article V:2 forbids any

854 *Panel Report, Russia – Measures Concerning Traffic in Transit,* (n 7) [7.172].
855 ibid [7.173].
856 *Panel Report, Colombia – Indicative Prices and Restrictions on Ports of Entry,* (n 852) [7.443].
857 ibid [7.466].
858 ibid [7.467].
859 ibid [7.478].
860 Article V:1, in the relevant part, reads as follows: "[...] vessels [...] shall be deemed to be in transit across the territory of a contracting party when the passage across such territory, with or without trans-shipment, warehousing, breaking bulk, or change in the mode of

distinction between vessels in international transit based on different criteria, including place of departure. The US prohibition against vessels departing from Cuban ports represents a straightforward violation of the second sentence of Article V:2 of the GATT 1994.

Similarly, the US sanctions that prohibit entry onto US territory of goods that have been transported from or through Cuba infringe Article V:6 of the GATT 1994, which according to the established case law "extends MFN protection from discrimination based on the geographic course of goods in transit upon reaching their final destination."[861] Indeed, such a blatant prohibition on all goods that were not only transported, but also transited through Cuba would represent a violation of the WTO commitment embedded in Article V:6 of the GATT 1994. Both scholarly analysis[862] and the EU's attempt to challenge the WTO consistency of unilateral US sanctions against Cuba[863] attest to the correctness of this conclusion.

Another example relevant for our discussion are the restrictions enacted by the Russian Federation against the traffic in transit entering into its territory from Ukraine. These additional prohibitions, which were enacted against the backdrop of deteriorating trade relations between the countries and were fuelled by Ukraine's closer economic integration with the European Union,[864] became the subject matter of a dispute before the WTO.[865] In this dispute, the Russian Federation invoked the national security exception enshrined in the GATT 1994, and thus the panel started its analysis from an examination of whether the preconditions stipulated by the national security clause were met.[866] After arriving at an affirmative conclusion, the panel proceeded on the

---

transport, is only a portion of a complete journey beginning and terminating beyond the frontier of the contracting party across whose territory the traffic passes."

861 *Panel Report, Colombia – Indicative Prices and Restrictions on Ports of Entry,* (n 852) [7.467].

862 John Spanogle, 'Can Helms-Burton be challenged under WTO?' (1998) XXVII Stetson Law Review 1313.

863 The European Union (back then the European Communities) in its request to establish a panel contended that US sanctions against Cuba that prohibit "vessels which have entered a Cuban port for trade in goods or services from loading or unloading freight in US ports within 180 days after having departed from the Cuban port" are inconsistent with Article V of GATT 1994. WTO, 'United States – The Cuban Liberty and Democratic Solidarity Act. Request for the Establishment of a Panel by the European Communities. WTO Doc WT/DS38/2, 8 October 1996.'

864 Iryna Bogdanova, 'Turning Crisis into Opportunity: Unfolding Ukraine's Trade Potential with the Canada-Ukraine Free Trade Agreement' (2021) VIII (2) East/West Journal of Ukrainian Studies 151. doi.org/10.21226/ewjus561.

865 *Panel Report, Russia – Measures Concerning Traffic in Transit,* (n 7) [7.3 Factual background].

866 ibid.

arguendo basis and examined Ukraine's claims that the restrictions on the traffic in transit coming from Ukraine were inconsistent with various obligations under Article V of the GATT 1994.[867] After scrutinising obligations under different parts of Article V, the panel determined that restrictions on the traffic in transit were inconsistent with the first sentence of Article V:2[868] and the second sentence of Article V:2 of the GATT 1994.[869]

In light of earlier WTO jurisprudence, it is evident that unilateral economic sanctions that restrain the WTO Members' freedom of transit, covering both traffic and shipments of goods in transit, would breach the WTO obligations of the state enacting them.

7.4 *The Freezing of Assets and Restrictions on Financial Transactions*

States habitually freeze assets or prohibit financial transactions with targeted states, entities and individuals.[870] For example, the unilateral US sanctions that target perpetrators of cyberattacks prohibit any payments to the blacklisted individuals, entities and government bodies.[871] Unilateral EU sanctions punish actors responsible for cyberattacks that threaten the EU or its Member States and lay out prohibitions similar to the US cyber sanctions: "All funds and economic resources belonging to, owned, held or controlled by any natural or legal person, entity or body listed in Annex I shall be frozen."[872] In addition to the freezing of funds and economic resources, the EU sanctions stipulate that: "No funds or economic resources shall be made available, directly or indirectly, to or for the benefit of natural or legal persons, entities or bodies listed in Annex I."[873] Annex I contains a list of sanctioned natural and legal persons, entities and bodies.

867 "[…] the Panel is mindful that, should its findings on Russia's invocation of Article XXI(b)(iii) be reversed in the event of an appeal, it may be necessary for the Appellate Body to complete the analysis. Accordingly, in Section 7.6.2, the Panel proceeds to analyse those aspects of Ukraine's claims which, were it not for the fact that the measures were taken in time of an 'emergency in international relations' (and met the other conditions of Article XXI(b)), would enable the Appellate Body to complete the legal analysis." ibid [7.154].

868 ibid [7.183].

869 ibid [7.196].

870 "Travel bans and assets freezes are the two most common types of sanctions imposed by the EU, making up 75 per cent and 62 per cent of the episodes respectively." Francesco Giumelli, Fabian Hoffmann and Anna Książczaková, 'The when, what, where and why of European Union sanctions' (2021) 30(1) European Security 1, 10.

871 President of the United States of America. Executive Order 13694 of April 1, 2015 (n 203); President of the United States of America. Executive Order 13757 of December 28, 2016 (n 204).

872 Council Regulation (EU) 2019/796 of 17 May 2019, Art. 3(1) (n 205).

873 Art. 3(2), ibid.

The EU prohibition on making funds available is interpreted broadly. In particular, it has been explained that "[m]aking funds available to a designated person or entity, be it by way of payment for goods and services, [...] is generally prohibited."[874] Although the EU cyber sanctions allow exceptions to these prohibitions, these exceptions do not cover regular business transactions and are, to a large extent, established on humanitarian grounds.[875]

The above-mentioned examples of unilateral sanctions imposed by the European Union and the United States would at least be incompatible with the obligation under Article XI:1 of the GATT 1994. As demonstrated in the previous sections, where conventional import and export restrictions on trade in goods were analysed against the background of the WTO obligations, the scope of Article XI:1 of the GATT 1994 is comprehensive.[876] More precisely, obligations under this article are invoked when prohibitions or restrictions "have a limiting effect on the quantity or amount of a product being imported or exported."[877] All-encompassing restrictions on financial transactions with the targeted individuals and entities result in indirect restrictions on imports from and exports to the targeted states. This conjecture is borne out by the *de facto* impossibility of engaging in import and export transactions with sanctioned persons without violating the restriction on "making funds available." Thus, unilateral sanctions that prevent anyone under the jurisdiction of a sanctioning state from providing funds and making any other payments to the sanctioned persons may violate Article XI:1 of the GATT 1994.

Apart from this, asset freezes and prohibitions on financial transactions could potentially breach commitments under Article X:2 of the GATT 1994. This article requires that any measure of general application that imposes restriction or prohibition "on imports, or on the transfer of payments therefor" shall not be enforced before it has been officially published. In previous WTO disputes, adjudicators explained the meaning of the term "measure of general application," such that a measure "affects an unidentified number of economic operators, including domestic and foreign producers" and does not exclusively

874 Council of the European Union, EU Best Practices for the Effective Implementation of Restrictive Measures, Doc. 8519/18 (4 May 2018), para. 49.

875 For example, Article 4 provides a list of circumstances that entitle the competent authorities of the EU Member States to make funds or economic resources available. Council Regulation (EU) 2019/796 of 17 May 2019 (n 205).

876 See chapter 2, subsections 7.1 Import restrictions and 7.2 Export restrictions.

877 *Appellate Body Reports, China – Measures Related to the Exportation of Various Raw Materials* (n 838) [320].

apply to "a specific company" or "a specific shipment."[878] Unilateral economic sanctions discussed above fall under this definition. Despite being targeted, they usually concern a number of entities and individuals in a particular state, including entities owned by the targeted individuals,[879] as well as their family members.[880] Furthermore, they forbid domestic entities in a sanctioning state from dealing with the sanctioned persons. In other words, they prohibit domestic constituencies from engaging in transactions with the targeted entities.

One more clarification is warranted in this regard. The panel in *US – Countervailing and Anti-Dumping Measures (China)* distinguished "measure of general application" from other measures in the following way: "The fact that a relevant measure has a narrow regulatory scope does not demonstrate that this measure is not generally applicable. [...] a relevant measure that applies to a class or category of people, entities, situations, or cases, that have some attribute in common would, in principle, constitute a measure of general application. In contrast, a relevant measure that applies to named or otherwise specifically identified persons, entities, situations, or cases would not be a measure of general application, but one of particular application." The majority of regulations on the basis of which unilateral sanctions are introduced prescribe reasons for the sanctions, the scope of the established prohibitions, listing criteria and other relevant details. The list of the sanctioned states, bodies, legal entities and individuals is either attached as an annex to a general sanctions regulation or mentioned at the end of the regulation. Thus, it can be argued that unilateral

878 *Panel Report, United States – Restrictions on Imports of Cotton and Man-made Fibre Underwear, WT/DS24/R, adopted 25 February 1997, as modified by Appellate Body Report WT/DS24/AB/R, DSR 1997:I, p. 31,* [7.65].

879 For example, unilateral US sanctions imposed on human rights grounds, as well as sanctions against perpetrators of cyber-enabled malicious activities, prohibit not only dealing with sanctioned persons, but also with the legal entities owned by them. For more, see Bogdanova, 'Targeted Economic Sanctions and WTO Law' (n 230).

880 For example, one of the sisters of Syria's president Bashar al Assad, along with the other family members, has been added to the sanctioned persons' list for the following reasons: "Bushra was one of 12 Assad family members added to an EU sanctions list in 2012 on the grounds that she was 'benefiting from and associated with' her brother's dictatorship because of her 'close personal relationship and intrinsic financial relationship' to him and 'other core Syrian regime figures.' A travel ban and asset-freezing were imposed as a result." Martin Bentham and Benedict Moore-Bridger, 'Assad family cash frozen after dictator's niece found living in London,' *Evening Standard* (18 April 2019) https://www.standard.co.uk/news/crime/assad-family-cash-frozen-after-dictator-s-niece-found-living-in-london-a4121211.html.

economic sanctions, even when they are targeted, constitute a "measure of general application" and hence are subject to the obligation under Article X:2.

A complaining party may argue that unilateral economic sanctions of a responding party are in breach of Article X:2 of the GATT 1994 in virtue of the fact that there was no reasonable period of time between the publication of regulations imposing sanctions and its effective date, i.e. implementation. Indeed, as the practice demonstrates, sanctioning states announce restrictions such as asset freezes and prohibitions on financial transactions and then immediately implement them.[881] The WTO Members' attempts to question the WTO-consistency of other Members' unilateral sanctions bolster the viability of this argument.[882]

This brings us to potential breaches of trade in services rules. Since restrictions on financial transactions, including restrictions on payments and other money transfers, may have negative repercussions for the supply of services by foreign service suppliers, the transparency obligation under Article III:1 of the GATS, which stipulates a duty comparable to Article X:2 of the GATT 1994, may also be infringed.[883]

Furthermore, prohibitions on financial transactions with sanctioned persons inevitably entail restrictions on international transfers and payments for

---

881 "I therefore determine that for these measures to be effective in addressing the national emergency declared in Executive Order 13692, there need be no prior notice of a listing or determination made pursuant to section 1 of this order." President of the United States. Executive Order 13850 of November 1, 2018. Blocking Property of Additional Persons Contributing to the Situation in Venezuela. In one of the recent disputes before the US domestic court, the plaintiffs even argued that the practice of designating an entity under US sanctions regulations without providing prior notice or an opportunity to be heard prior to the designation breach the due process rights guaranteed under the US Constitution. *Fulmen Company v. Office of Foreign Assets Control*, 'United States District Court for the District of Columbia, Case No. 18–2949, Memorandum Opinion, Mar. 31, 2020.'

882 In several requests for consultations filed before the WTO to challenge unilateral sanctions, complaining parties contended that such measures violate obligations under Article X:2 of the GATT 1994. WTO, 'Ukraine – Measures Relating to Trade in Goods and Services, Request for Consultations by the Russian Federation, WTO Doc WT/DS525/1, G/L/1179 S/L/414, G/TBT/D/50 G/LIC/D/52, G/SPS/GEN/1549, 1 June 2017'; WTO, 'Russia – Measures Concerning the Importation and Transit of Certain Ukrainian Products. Request for Consultations by Ukraine, WTO Doc WT/DS532/1, G/L/1189 G/TFA/D1/1, G/SPS/GEN/1582, 19 October 2017.'

883 Article III:1 of the GATS reads as follows: "Each Member shall publish promptly and, except in emergency situations, at the latest by the time of their entry into force, all relevant measures of general application which pertain to or affect the operation of this Agreement. International agreements pertaining to or affecting trade in services to which a Member is a signatory shall also be published."

various transactions, involving transactions that could be related to trade in services. This outcome contradicts Article XI:1 of the GATS, which stipulates that: "Except under the circumstances envisaged in Article XII, a Member shall not apply restrictions on international transfers and payments for current transactions relating to its specific commitments."

Scholars who have examined the compatibility of asset freezes and prohibitions on financial transactions with WTO commitments, also concur that such restrictions may conflict with the WTO Members' commitments under the GATS. Peter-Tobias Stoll and others contend that "under Art. XI GATS, a Member shall not apply restrictions on international transfers and payments for current transactions relating to its specific commitments in the areas of trade in services. The freezing of assets and the blocking of financial transactions are likely to be in conflict with this obligation."[884] Tom Ruys and Cedric Ryngaert have observed that secondary sanctions implying restrictions on international transfers and payments and impeding trade in services thereby, face a significant risk of being inconsistent with Article XI:1 of the GATS.[885] However, they point out that the reference to the rights and obligations of the members of the International Monetary Fund under the Articles of Agreement of the Fund in Article XI:2 of the GATS may prevent some secondary sanctions from being incompatible with Article XI:1 of the GATS.[886]

7.5 *Visa Restrictions*

Visa restrictions, i.e. restrictions on the issuance of new visas and revocation of the already-issued visas, are frequently used. These bans can apply to specific individuals, to employees of the targeted legal entities and even to all nationals of a sanctioned state. For example, in summer 2020, the United States introduced visa restrictions against employees of the Chinese technology company Huawei for their alleged involvement in human rights abuses.[887]

Visa restrictions may infringe obligations under the GATS, as well as the GATS Annex on Movement of Natural Persons. In support of this claim, we can cite the following example. In 1996, the EU (at that time the EC), in its attempt to question the legality of the US unilateral sanctions against Cuba,

---

884 Stoll and others (n 232) 56.

885 Ruys and Ryngaert (n 555).

886 ibid.

887 *Press Statement*, U.S. Imposes Visa Restrictions on Certain Employees of Chinese Technology Companies that Abuse Human Rights (15 July 2020) https://2017-2021.state.gov/u-s-imposes-visa-restrictions-on-certain-employees-of-chinese-technology-companies-that-abuse-human-rights/index.html.

argued that visa denials and exclusions on the part of the United States, prescribed under the relevant laws and regulations, are inconsistent with Articles II, III, VI, XVI and XVII of GATS, as well as with paragraphs 3 and 4 of the GATS Annex on the Movement of Natural Persons.[888] Similarly, Qatar – in its 2017 request for consultations with the UAE – maintained that "prohibiting Qatari persons [...] from crossing maritime borders with the UAE, or entering the UAE via airspace, to supply services" is a violation of Article II:1 of the GATS.[889] Furthermore, Qatar submitted that transparency obligations under Article III of the GATS were infringed and market access was unduly restricted in violation of Article XVI of the GATS by various sanctions, which *inter alia* include travel bans.[890]

The following obligations under the GATS might be breached by a WTO Member that implements visa restrictions:

- Most-Favoured-Nation treatment of Article II:1 – if a WTO Member has undertaken commitment to allow movement of natural persons in a specific service sector and visa restrictions undermine that commitment with respect to only some service suppliers
- Transparency obligations under Article III – if sanctions entailing visa restrictions were implemented before they were published or if there was no reasonable grace period between the publication of regulations imposing the sanctions and their effective date, i.e. implementation
- The obligation to administer measures of general application affecting trade in services "in a reasonable, objective and impartial manner" embedded in Article VI:1 – if a WTO Member imposes economic sanctions in the form of visa restrictions against designated actors from some WTO Members but not against others, even if the latter formally meet the criteria for being designated
- Market access obligations stipulated in Article XVI and the Members' schedules of commitments – if particular obligations were inscribed in the schedule of commitments and then breached by the Member enacting sanctions
- National treatment obligations under Article XVII – if the relevant commitments were undertaken and no qualifications were set, which could allow visa restrictions to be enacted

888 WTO, 'United States – The Cuban Liberty and Democratic Solidarity Act,' (n 863).

889 WTO, 'United Arab Emirates – Measures Relating to Trade in Goods and Services, and Trade-Related Aspects of Intellectual Property Rights. Request for Consultations by Qatar. WTO Doc WT/DS526/1, G/L/1180 S/L/415, IP/D/35, 4 August 2017.'

890 ibid.

– Annex on Movement of Natural Persons Supplying Services under the Agreement, in particular the obligation under paragraph 4 of this Annex[891]

7.6 *Secondary Sanctions and Their Compatibility with WTO Law*

In the previous section of the book, secondary sanctions and their compatibility with the principles for ascertaining jurisdiction in international law were discussed.[892] However, secondary sanctions, i.e. sanctions that regulate the conduct of third states and their legal entities and prevent them from engaging in business transactions with the sanctioned states, their nationals and entities, may be incompatible not only with the principles establishing jurisdiction, but also with WTO commitments.[893] The analysis below provides examples of secondary sanctions that are at risk of being found inconsistent with the obligations under WTO law, and it discusses the WTO compatibility of secondary sanctions.

The unilateral US economic sanctions against Cuba include a prohibition on ships trading with Cuba docking at US ports for six months ("for a period of 180 days") after leaving a Cuban port.[894] The potential of this prohibition to violate the relevant WTO commitments can be easily illustrated by the following example. Let us imagine a situation in which goods originating in the European Union are to be transported to Cuba, yet the vessel that is to transport them is traveling to the United States. After making a stop in Cuba, the vessel would be prohibited from entering US ports for 180 days. As a result, a shipping company may refuse to transport the EU goods, and hence this restriction may entail financial losses for the European Union's exporters if their good are destined for the Cuban market.

---

891 Para. 4 of the Annex on Movement of Natural Persons Supplying Services under the Agreement reads as follows: "The Agreement shall not prevent a Member from applying measures to regulate the entry of natural persons into, or their temporary stay in, its territory, including those measures necessary to protect the integrity of, and to ensure the orderly movement of natural persons across, its borders, provided that such measures are not applied in such a manner as to nullify or impair the benefits accruing to any Member under the terms of a specific commitment."

892 See chapter 2, section 4. Unilateral economic sanctions and established principles of jurisdiction in international law.

893 "The secondary boycott seeks to halt third-party nations from trading with the target country. This essentially amounts to an infringement on foreign policy making in third-party countries where trading with the target nation is not prohibited." Timothy S Dunning, 'D'Amato in a China Shop: Problems of Extraterritoriality with the Iran and Libya Sanctions Act of 1996' (1998) 19 U. Pa. J. Int'l L. 169, 184.

894 Cuban Assets Control Regulations 31 CFR § 515.207 Entry of vessels engaged in trade with Cuba (n 848).

Another example of secondary sanctions are the recently announced restrictions on certain sectors of the Iranian economy introduced unilaterally by the United States.[895] These sanctions target not only US-incorporated entities and individuals for their involvement in business transactions in the identified sectors of the Iranian economy – the construction, mining, manufacturing or textiles sectors and other sectors as may be determined by the Secretary of the Treasury – but also any non-US person engaged in the same conduct.[896] The precondition for the application of these sanctions is that a non-US entity or a foreign national have "knowingly engaged" in the prohibited conduct.[897] The all-encompassing formulation and the severe penalties employed to enforce the prescribed restrictions make the reach of these sanctions extremely broad.[898] In other words, legal entities incorporated anywhere in the world are obligated to comply with the sanctions or risk having their assets in the United States frozen and being deprived of access to the US market.[899]

Given this, the question that should be considered is whether US secondary sanctions intended to compel US trading partners to comply with them breach WTO obligations? If yes, then what obligations?

There is no unanimity among legal scholars about whether secondary sanctions are *ipso facto* inconsistent with WTO law. For example, there is certain scepticism in academic literature concerning the possibility of declaring secondary sanctions to be inconsistent with MFN and national treatment obligations.[900] In particular, Tom Ruys and Cedric Ryngaert have examined the

895 President of the United States. Executive Order 13902 of January 10, 2020. Imposing Sanctions With Respect to Additional Sectors of Iran.

896 ibid, Section 1. (a)(i) and Section 1. (a)(ii).

897 ibid, Section 1. (a)(ii).

898 The following penalties apply to non-US persons who have "knowingly engaged" in transactions with Iran and Iranian entities in the construction, mining, manufacturing, or textiles sectors and other sectors, as may be determined by the Secretary of the Treasury: all property and interests in property should be blocked and "may not be transferred, paid, exported, withdrawn, or otherwise dealt in." Furthermore, the following prohibitions apply to the non-US persons who do not comply with the sanctions: "(a) the making of any contribution or provision of funds, goods, or services by, to, or for the benefit of any person whose property and interests in property are blocked pursuant to this order; and (b) the receipt of any contribution or provision of funds, goods, or services from any such person." ibid.

899 ibid.

900 "Overall, it seems unlikely that secondary sanctions seeking to restrict trade between the country that is the primary sanctions target and third states would contravene the national treatment or MFN principles." However, it should be noted that the authors have also provided examples of academic studies arguing for the opposite point of view. Ruys and Ryngaert (n 555) 42.

consistency of secondary sanctions with the various obligations under WTO law.[901] According to their analysis, the third states that might be *de facto* prohibited from trading with the targeted state and/or its entities cannot argue, with few exceptions, that their entitlements under the MFN and national treatment provisions have been breached.[902] However, in their view, the violation of the obligation under Article XI:1 of the GATT 1994,[903] as well as potential violations of other obligations, such as commitments under the Government Procurement Agreement could be established.[904] By contrast, Andrew Mitchell, discussing the EU's efforts to question the WTO-compatibility of the US secondary sanctions targeting Cuba, observes that "[t]he 'consensus' among commentators was that the panel would likely have struck down the secondary sanctions."[905]

It is hard to agree with the view that the MFN obligation under the GATT 1994 is not breached by secondary sanctions, which discriminate against goods based not on their characteristics, but on the basis of compliance with the foreign policy preferences of a particular state. It should be recalled that in order to find a violation under the MFN clause of the GATT 1994, the following prerequisites should be met: "(i) that the measure at issue falls within the scope of application of Article I:1; (ii) that the imported products at issue are 'like' products within the meaning of Article I:1; (iii) that the measure at issue confers an 'advantage, favour, privilege, or immunity' on a product originating in the territory of any country; and (iv) that the advantage so accorded is not extended 'immediately' and 'unconditionally' to 'like' products originating in the territory of all Members. Thus, if a Member grants any advantage to any product originating in the territory of any other country, such advantage must be accorded 'immediately and unconditionally' to like products originating from all other Members."[906] If, as a result of secondary sanctions, import or export restrictions are imposed on a third state or its legal entities solely for the reason of non-compliance with these secondary sanctions, these restrictions may be challenged before the WTO. A complaining state may argue that the goods thus targeted are "like" the goods imported from any other WTO Member

901 ibid.

902 ibid 39–43.

903 ibid 43–46.

904 ibid 46–51.

905 Andrew D Mitchell, 'Sanctions and the World Trade Organization' §13 in Larissa van den Herik (ed), *Research Handbook on UN Sanctions and International Law*, (Cheltenham, Edward Elgar Publishing 2017), 301.

906 *Appellate Body Reports, European Communities – Measures Prohibiting the Importation and Marketing of Seal Products,* (n 822) [5.86].

and thus, an "advantage, favour, privilege, or immunity" in the form of market access, if it is a question of import prohibitions, or an "advantage, favour, privilege, or immunity" in the form of access to exported goods, if it is a question of export prohibitions, was not granted to the goods originating in a state that is targeted for its non-adherence to secondary sanctions. Furthermore, bearing in mind the comprehensive nature of the obligation not to introduce quantitative restrictions, which is enshrined in Article XI:1 of the GATT 1994, this obligation would be breached by the secondary sanctions that punish third states and their entities for non-compliance.

8 Conclusion

A detailed analysis of the legality of unilateral economic sanctions has demonstrated the lack of any certainty in this area. The discussion of whether unilateral economic sanctions encroach on the principles embedded in the UN Charter started in the 1960s and is still ongoing. The ILC codification of the customary international law on state responsibility also sheds little light on the legal status of third-party countermeasures. To further complicate the matter, states design their sanctioning programmes in such a way as to give them extraterritorial effect, thus sowing the seeds of the subsequent deliberations on the consistency of their sanctions with the principles on ascertaining jurisdiction in international law. Moreover, the recent trend towards the imposition of targeted sanctions against central banks, heads of state and senior government officials raises the question of their relations with state immunity and immunities guaranteed to senior government officials.

WTO law stands as an exception. More specifically, various forms of unilateral economic sanctions face a significant risk of being found inconsistent with the relevant disciplines of the WTO Agreements. Moreover, the obligations under WTO law are protected by the dispute settlement system. Thus, it is no coincidence that when states are willing to question the legality of unilateral economic sanctions, they are most likely to initiate a dispute before the WTO.

Despite recent developments, both in law and in practice, two main deficiencies inherent in economic coercion have still not been resolved, namely that reliance on economic pressure can be politically motivated on some occasions, while on other occasions states might be reluctant to employ economic sanctions, even if there is a pressing need for such measures.

PART 2

The International Enforcement of Human Rights and the Legality of Unilateral Human Rights Sanctions

CHAPTER 3

The International Enforcement of Human Rights

In Part 2, I analyse the international enforcement of human rights and to what extent unilateral economic sanctions can be deployed to this effect. In the first section of this chapter, the enforcement mechanisms prescribed by the core international human rights treaties are examined. Before we proceed with this analysis, there will be a brief description of these treaties. The following section focuses on the protection of human rights that have gained special status, namely jus cogens and obligations erga omnes. The chapter then concludes with an assessment of the role played by the UN in human rights protection, and in particular of the contribution made by the Human Rights Council and the Security Council to human rights protection.

This chapter argues that the international enforcement of human rights is hindered by a number of deficiencies in the system. First and foremost, the efficiency of the treaty-based instruments of enforcement is undermined by the predominant role played by consent in international law, as well as by the non-reciprocal nature of human rights obligations. Second, definitional ambiguity and a lack of well-defined normative implications hamper the protection of those human rights that have gained special status, such as jus cogens and obligations erga omnes. Finally, the political nature of the Human Rights Council and the Security Council impacts the effectiveness of these bodies and their efforts to promote human rights.

Given the voluminous literature on the subject, this chapter does not intend to provide thorough and all-encompassing analysis of international human rights enforcement.[907] Its aim is narrower, namely to outline the principal shortcomings of the existing regime and set the stage for the subsequent discussion of the contribution made by unilateral economic sanctions and the doctrine of Common Concern of Humankind to the enhanced protection of human rights.

Furthermore, I intentionally avoid discussing the enforcement of human rights by regional human rights courts. There are two reasons for this: First,

907 The following recent books are devoted to the subject: Walter Kälin and Jörg Künzli, *The Law of International Human Rights Protection* (2nd ed, Oxford University Press 2019); Surya P Subedi, *The Effectiveness of the UN Human Rights System: Reform and the Judicialisation of Human Rights* (Routledge 2017); Christian Tomuschat, *Human Rights: Between Idealism and Realism* (3rd ed, Oxford University Press 2014).

DOI:10.1163/9789004507890_005

regional courts enforce regional human rights standards, which are embedded in regional conventions. The European Court of Human Rights, the Inter-American Court of Human Rights and the African Court on Human and Peoples' Rights are prominent regional courts that are actively engaged in the resolution of disputes involving alleged violations of the states' human rights obligations as enshrined in the European Convention on Human Rights, the American Convention on Human Rights and African Charter on Human and Peoples' Rights respectively. Second, the practice of these regional courts is so diverse and voluminous that any in-depth analysis of it would go beyond the scope of this study.

1 Human Rights Treaties and Enforcement Mechanisms

The concept of human rights is grounded in the idea of the intrinsic value of each individual. The philosopher James Griffin explains this idea as follows: "a human right is one that a person has, not in virtue of any special status or relation to others, but simply in virtue of being human."[908] The foundations of this view can be traced back to the works of ancient philosophers, although back then the idea of human rights was hardly distinguished from the broader concepts of justice and natural law.[909] Later on, the doctrine of human rights was closely intertwined with the concept of natural law. Griffin illustrates the beliefs behind the natural law idea of human rights as follows: "God has placed in us certain dispositions towards the good; that these dispositions give rise to precepts of action; that natural laws are expressions of these precepts; and that natural rights are derivable from natural laws."[910] Although such beliefs

908 James Griffin, 'Discrepancies Between the Best Philosophical Account of Human Rights and the International Law of Human Rights' (2001) 101 Proceedings of the Aristotelian Society 1, 2.

909 The history of the concept of human rights is full of controversies, and it remains highly contested. Therefore, any detailed discussion of the matter would be beyond the scope of this research. The only clarification that should be made is that the roots of the modern idea of human rights are neither exclusively European nor exclusively secular. Ancient philosophers, such as Plato and Aristotle, elaborated in their writings on natural law, justice and the role of the individual. For more, see Micheline R Ishay, *The Human Rights Reader: Major Political Essays, Speeches and Documents from Ancient Times to the Present* (2nd edition, Routledge 2007).

910 James Griffin, 'Human Rights and the Autonomy of International Law' in Samantha Besson and John Tasioulas (eds.), *The Philosophy of International Law* (Oxford University Press 2010) 339. James Griffin acknowledged that human rights were engraved in natural

were later abandoned, the ethical content of the term "human rights" was not.[911]

Despite the early recognition accorded to the concept, it was not until the end of World War II – and not before the war's atrocities were documented and publicised – that the idea of human rights found widespread support among states and non-state actors. Prior to World War II, international human rights law was almost non-existent. As Sarah Joseph accurately observes: "a State's treatment of its own citizens was generally recognized as a sovereign matter of no international concern."[912]

The atrocities that occurred during World War II revealed the need for significant changes in this area. The adoption of the UN Charter and the Universal Declaration of Human Rights paved the way for the subsequent development of international human rights law. As Eric Posner acknowledges: "Legally, the modern era of human rights began with the Universal Declaration and the recognition that individuals, rather than merely states, possess rights under international law, and thus are entitled to legal protection from abuses by their own governments. Before then, abused populations could appeal to a foreign government for aid, but no one would have said that their appeal was grounded in violation of individual rights."[913]

Indeed, although the historical record bears witness to early attempts to establish basic human rights standards, international human rights law emerged only after World War II.[914] The subsequent increase in the awareness of human rights and their protection globally is accurately reflected in the following statement: "in this modern age a state's treatment of its own citizens is a matter of international concern."[915]

---

law, which was later abandoned. In his view, the subsequent proliferation of international human rights law did not bring satisfactory determinateness to the term "human rights." In his search for their ethical underpinnings, Griffin has explored various accounts of human rights, such as functional (Dworkin, Rawls), political (Raz) and traditional (Griffin). In Griffin's view, human rights are "protections of our normative agency, of what I call our 'personhood'."

911 ibid 345.

912 Sarah Joseph, *Blame It on the WTO?: A Human Rights Critique* (Oxford University Press 2011) 13.

913 Eric A Posner, *The Twilight of Human Rights Law* (Oxford University Press 2014) 19.

914 Charles R Beitz, *The Idea of Human Rights* (Oxford University Press 2009) 14–27.

915 *Filartiga v. Pena-Irala, 630 F2d 876 (2d Cir 1980)* (United States Court of Appeals, Second Circuit): This was one of the landmark decisions. Unfortunately, in the subsequent cases, in particular, Kadic v. Karadžić and Kiobel v. Royal Dutch Petroleum Co, the court substantially narrowed down the application of the rule that allowed perpetrators of human rights violations to be punished for the actions committed abroad.

The number of international human rights treaties, as well as the number of states participating in these treaties, has increased drastically in the past seventy years.[916] Eric Posner has observed that the number of declared human rights has been increasing exponentially – as of today, there are more than three hundred of them.[917] Despite such developments, weak and inefficient enforcement mechanisms are the Achilles heel of international human rights law. Suffice it to say: "Enforcement machinery has not kept pace with standard-setting."[918] As the former judge of the ICJ Thomas Buergenthal has emphasised: "Probably no other branch of international law has grown as rapidly as contemporary international human rights law. It is nevertheless true that this normative growth and evolution of international human rights has not resulted in comparable compliance by states with their international human rights obligations."[919] This view is confirmed by human rights organisations and advocates, who report numerous examples of grave human rights violations.[920]

1.1 *The Core Human Rights Treaties: A Short Review*

1.1.1 Convention on the Prevention and Punishment of the Crime of Genocide (Genocide Convention)

The historical record provides ample evidence of numerous occurrences of genocide. Yet, it is worth recalling that the term "genocide" is a creation of the twentieth century. It was Raphael Lemkin who coined the term and laid the foundation for the future convention.[921] His thorny life path and a worldwide

---

916 'Status of Ratification Interactive Dashboard' <https://indicators.ohchr.org/>.

917 Posner (n 913).

918 Sarah Joseph and Joanna Kyriakakis, 'The United Nations and Human Rights' in Sarah Joseph (ed), *Research handbook on international human rights law* (Edward Elgar 2010) 2.

919 Thomas Buergenthal, 'International Human Rights: Need for Further Institutional Development' (2018) 50 Case Western Reserve Journal of International Law 9, 15.

920 For instance, annual reports issued by such international non-governmental organisations as Human Rights Watch and Amnesty International provide little reason to believe that respect for human rights is blossoming around the globe. Kenneth Roth, the executive director of Human Rights Watch, has acknowledged that "Mass atrocities have proliferated with near impunity in countries such as Yemen, Syria, Burma, and South Sudan." *World Report 2018: Events of 2017* (2018) <https://www.hrw.org/sites/default/files/world_report_download/201801world_report_web.pdf>. In describing Myanmar's discrimination against the Rohingya people, Amnesty International's report warns: "This episode will stand in history as yet another testament to the world's catastrophic failure to address conditions that provide fertile ground for mass atrocity crimes." Amnesty International, *Amnesty International Report 2017/2018: The State of the World's Human Rights.* (Amnesty International UK 2018).

921 Raphaël Lemkin, *Axis Rule in Occupied Europe: Laws of Occupation, Analysis of Government, Proposals for Redress* (Carnegie Endowment for International Peace 1944);

campaign for the genocide convention are described as "the one-man campaign against genocide."[922] While the exact contours of the crime of genocide have been fixed in the Genocide Convention, Raphael Lemkin's valuable contribution can be described as "the inspiration for the concept."[923]

The Convention on the Prevention and Punishment of the Crime of Genocide entered into force in 1951. The Genocide Convention confirmed that genocide is a crime under international law irrespective of whether it was committed in times of peace or in times of war.[924] Parties to the convention are under an obligation to prevent genocide, as well as to punish it.[925] The scope of these obligations was later clarified by the ICJ in two disputes that were sparked by the dissolution of the former Yugoslavia.[926] The policies of Myanmar's government against the Rohingya ethnic group gave rise to a new dispute before the ICJ, in which the Gambia invoked the Genocide Convention as a ground for its legal claims.[927]

1.1.2 International Convention on the Elimination of All Forms of Racial Discrimination (ICERD)

This convention reflects the prevailing international sentiment regarding racial discrimination in the 1960s, and thus its adoption should be evaluated against the historical background. The discussion of racial discrimination under the auspices of the UN began in 1949, with the Secretary-General's

---

Raphael Lemkin, 'Genocide as a Crime under International Law' (1947) 41 The American Journal of International Law 145.

922 John Cooper, *Raphael Lemkin and the Struggle for the Genocide Convention* (Palgrave Macmillan 2008).

923 John Quigley, *The Genocide Convention: An International Law Analysis* (Ashgate 2006) 5.

924 Article I reads as follows: "The Contracting Parties confirm that genocide, whether committed in time of peace or in time of war, is a crime under international law which they undertake to prevent and to punish." Convention on the Prevention and Punishment of the Crime of Genocide (adopted 9 December 1948, entered into force 12 January 1951) UNTS vol. 78 p. 277 (Genocide Convention).

925 Article I and Article IV of the Genocide Convention – the scope of the obligations to prevent and punish genocide was further elaborated in the ICJ judgements. ibid.

926 *Application of the Convention on the Prevention and Punishment of the Crime of Genocide (Bosnia and Herzegovina v. Serbia and Montenegro), Judgment, ICJ Reports 2007, p 43*; *Application of the Convention on the Prevention and Punishment of the Crime of Genocide (Croatia v. Serbia), Judgment, ICJ Reports 2015, p 3*.

927 'International Court of Justice. Application of the Convention on the Prevention and Punishment of the Crime of Genocide (The Gambia v. Myanmar). Application Instituting Proceedings and Request for the Indication of Provisional Measures, November 11, 2019' <https://www.icj-cij.org/en/case/178/institution-proceedings>.

memorandum *The Main Types and Causes of Discrimination*.[928] The subsequent discussion was instigated by a number of events, which set the process in motion. Michael Banton succinctly boiled down the historical scene to the following statement: "At the end of the 1950s, alarmed by reports of attacks on synagogues and Jewish burial grounds in what was then colloquially known as 'West Germany,' by Arab anxieties about policies in Israel and by the priorities of newly emerging states in sub-Saharan Africa, some states pushed for a legal prohibition of racial and religious discrimination."[929] Against this backdrop, the Declaration on the Elimination of All Forms of Racial Discrimination was adopted in 1963.[930] This Declaration laid the foundation for the future convention opened for signature by the General Assembly in December 1965.[931]

The convention defines the term "racial discrimination" as "any distinction, exclusion, restriction or preference based on race, colour, descent, or national or ethnic origin which has the purpose or effect of nullifying or impairing the recognition, enjoyment or exercise, on an equal footing, of human rights and fundamental freedoms in the political, economic, social, cultural or any other field of public life."[932] The substantive obligations include the duty to pursue the policies of eliminating racial discrimination[933] and the obligation to condemn propaganda and organisations that promote or incite racial discrimination,[934] as well as to guarantee equality before the law in the enjoyment of a number of rights.[935] The final text of the convention not only stipulates the substantive obligations, but also prescribes the reporting obligation as well as interstate and individual complaints mechanisms.[936] The aforesaid provisions enabled advanced monitoring and scrutiny of the states' compliance with the obligations undertaken.

The obligations under this convention inspired several disputes before the ICJ, which will be discussed later in this chapter. For instance, the UAE's

928 Michael Banton, *International Action against Racial Discrimination* (Clarendon Press 1996) 51–52.

929 Michael Banton, *What We Now Know About Race and Ethnicity* (1st ed., Berghahn Books 2018) 51.

930 United Nations Declaration on the Elimination of All Forms of Racial Discrimination, UNGA Res 1904 (20 November 1963) A/RES/1904.

931 International Convention on the Elimination of All Forms of Racial Discrimination (adopted 21 December 1965, entered into force 4 January 1969) UNTS vol. 660 p. 195 (ICERD).

932 Article 1 ibid.

933 Article 2 ibid.

934 Article 4 ibid.

935 Article 5 ibid.

936 Part 2 ibid.

restrictive measures against Qatari nationals imposed in summer 2017 led to a dispute before the ICJ.[937] Qatar initiated proceedings not only before the court, but also before the Committee on the Elimination of Racial Discrimination that was established according to the convention.[938] The UAE argued before the court that these parallel proceedings although allowed under the relevant provisions of the convention constitute abuse of rights on behalf of Qatar.[939] The court disagreed with this view.[940] Its arguments are discussed in the subsequent section.[941]

1.1.3 International Covenant on Civil and Political Rights (ICCPR)

The International Covenant on Civil and Political Rights is one of the core international human rights treaties, which was adopted along with the International Covenant on Economic, Social and Cultural Rights in 1966.[942] These covenants were a sequel to the Universal Declaration of Human Rights, the adoption of which represented a starting point for the human rights movement.

The adoption of two covenants instead of one became a symbol of lingering tensions between Western ideology that glorified individual and political freedoms and the philosophy of the communist-bloc states, which praised economic and social benefits over political freedoms.[943] Sarah Joseph describes the decision to adopt two independent covenants as follows: "Cold War politics, as well as perceptions over fundamental differences between civil and political rights on the one hand, and economic, social and cultural rights on the other, led to a decision to split the rights into two Covenants."[944]

937 'International Court of Justice. Application of the International Convention on the Elimination of All Forms of Racial Discrimination (Qatar v. United Arab Emirates). Application Instituting Proceedings, June 11, 2018.'

938 ibid.; Qatar, 'An Inter-State Communication against the United Arab Emirates' <https://www.ohchr.org/EN/NewsEvents/Pages/DisplayNews.aspx?NewsID=23566&LangID=E>.

939 'International Court of Justice. Application of the International Convention on the Elimination of All Forms of Racial Discrimination (Qatar v. United Arab Emirates). Request for the Indication of Provisional Measures of the United Arab Emirates, March 22, 2019.'

940 *Application of the International Convention on the Elimination of All Forms of Racial Discrimination (Qatar v. United Arab Emirates) Request for the Indication of Provisional Measures Order, June 14, 2019*.

941 For more details, see chapter 3, subsection 1.6 Dispute settlement provisions and the role of the International Court of Justice.

942 International Covenant on Civil and Political Rights (adopted 16 December 1966, entered into force 23 March 1976) UNTS vol. 999 p. 171 (ICCPR).

943 Sarah Joseph, *Blame It on the WTO?: A Human Rights Critique* (Oxford University Press 2013) 17.

944 ibid.

The International Covenant on Civil and Political Rights was opened for signature in 1966 and entered into force in 1976. A similar fate befell the International Covenant on Economic, Social and Cultural Rights.

International Covenant on Civil and Political Rights guarantees protection to diverse human rights, ranging from the right to life[945] to the prohibition of torture[946] and slavery (servitude, forced or compulsory labour),[947] along with such rights as the right to liberty and security of one's person,[948] the right to liberty of movement[949] and equality before courts and tribunals,[950] along with many others. The Covenant enables the state parties to derogate from their obligations "in time of public emergency which threatens the life of the nation and the existence of which is officially proclaimed."[951] It should be noted that such derogation is not possible for a number of protected rights.[952]

1.1.4 International Covenant on Economic, Social and Cultural Rights (ICESCR)

The International Covenant on Economic, Social and Cultural Rights was adopted in 1966 and entered into force a decade later.[953] At the time of its adoption, the exact contours of economic, social and cultural rights had not been determined with great precision.[954] Indeed, even today, the distinction between the various groups of rights is not entirely clear. In this vein, Manisuli Ssenyonjo observes: "the distinction between 'social,' 'economic' and 'cultural' rights does not hold both in theory and practice, and it is unproductive to seek to distinguish rights that are so closely intertwined."[955]

The ambit of the substantive obligations under the Covenant hinges on the party's capacity to fulfil its obligations.[956] It by no means implies that the

945 Article 6 ICCPR.

946 Article 7 ibid.

947 Article 8 ibid.

948 Article 9 ibid.

949 Article 11 ibid.

950 Article 14 ibid.

951 Article 4 ibid.

952 The relevant part of Article 4 reads as follows: "No derogation from articles 6, 7, 8 (paragraphs 1 and 2), 11, 15, 16 and 18 may be made under this provision." ibid.

953 International Covenant on Economic, Social and Cultural Rights (adopted 16 December 1966, entered into force 3 January 1976) UNTS vol. 993 p. 3 (ICESCR).

954 Joseph (n 943) 19.

955 Manisuli Ssenyonjo, *Economic, Social and Cultural Rights in International Law* (Hart Publishing 2009) 39.

956 The relevant part of Article 2 reads as follows: "Each State Party to the present Covenant undertakes to take steps, individually and through international assistance and co-operation, especially economic and technical, to the maximum of its available resources,

drafters intended to promote a standstill and hamper any further developments. To the contrary, the progressive realisation of the enumerated rights constitutes the core principle of the Covenant.[957]

This Covenant guarantees the right to work,[958] the right to just and favourable conditions of work,[959] the right to form trade unions and the right to strike,[960] the right to social security[961] and the right to an adequate standard of living, including adequate food, clothing and housing.[962]

1.1.5 Convention on the Elimination of All Forms of Discrimination against Women (CEDAW)

The Convention on the Elimination of All Forms of Discrimination against Women was adopted in 1979 and entered into force two years later.[963] The promotion of women's rights was debated at length in the 1970s and 1980s.[964] Several international conferences devoted to gender equality, women's rights and their promotion preceded the convention's adoption.[965] The rationale that underlines the need for such a convention has been well captured by Susanne Zwingel: "we have seen that CEDAW is created within a broader, in itself evolving, global discourse on gender equality and that a variety of women's rights proponents have used it to influence domestic practices."[966]

---

with a view to achieving progressively the full realization of the rights recognized in the present Covenant by all appropriate means, including particularly the adoption of legislative measures."

957 Article 2 ibid.

958 Article 6 ibid.

959 Article 7 ibid.

960 Article 8 ibid.

961 Article 9 ibid.

962 Article 11 ibid.

963 Convention on the Elimination of All Forms of Discrimination Against Women (adopted 18 December 1979, entered into force 3 September 1981) UNTS vol. 1249 p. 13 (CEDAW).

964 Susanne Zwingel, *Translating International Women's Rights: The CEDAW Convention in Context* (Palgrave Macmillan 2016) 40–41.

965 "On the initiative of the women's organization WIDF (Women's International Democratic Federation) and after overcoming some governmental resistance, the UN General Assembly declared the year 1975 International Women's Year of the United Nations. The same year, the first World Conference on Women was held in Mexico. It had 'repercussions such as the initiators had hardly dared to dream of.' Following the conference's World Plan of Action, the UN General Assembly proclaimed the years 1976–1985 the UN Decade for Women with a focus on equality, development, and peace. This Decade contained two more conferences, one in Copenhagen (1980) and one in Nairobi (1985). It became a watershed for placing women's concerns on the international agenda." ibid.

966 ibid 7.

The convention provides a broad definition of the term "discrimination against women."[967] It prescribes a number of obligations to promote gender equality, such as the obligation to adopt appropriate legislation to prohibit discrimination against women,[968] to guarantee the right to vote and participate in the formulation of government policy[969] and to ensure to women equal rights with men in the field of education,[970] as well as other obligations.

1.1.6 Convention against Torture and Other Cruel, Inhuman or Degrading Treatment or Punishment (CAT)

The Convention against Torture and Other Cruel, Inhuman or Degrading Treatment or Punishment was adopted in 1984 and entered into force three years later.[971] The convention prescribes the absolute prohibition of torture and other forms of ill-treatment.[972] The convention obligates parties to take effective measures to prohibit and prevent torture, and it imposes an obligation of non-refoulement if there are reasonable grounds to believe that a person would be subjected to torture.[973] As Nora Sveaass points out: "State involvement and responsibility relate both to acts of violations actually committed and acts of omission, that is, where state or state agents have failed to protect and prevent."[974]

Article 7 of the convention contains the follow prescription: "The State Party in the territory under whose jurisdiction a person alleged to have committed

967 Article 1 stipulates: "the term 'discrimination against women' shall mean any distinction, exclusion or restriction made on the basis of sex which has the effect or purpose of impairing or nullifying the recognition, enjoyment or exercise by women, irrespective of their marital status, on a basis of equality of men and women, of human rights and fundamental freedoms in the political, economic, social, cultural, civil or any other field."

968 Article 2 ibid.

969 Article 7 ibid.

970 Article 10 ibid.

971 Convention Against Torture and Other Cruel, Inhuman or Degrading Treatment or Punishment (adopted 10 December 1984, entered into force 26 June 1987) UNTS vol. 1465 p. 85 (CAT).

972 The relevant part of Article 2 reads as follows: "No exceptional circumstances whatsoever, whether a state of war or a threat of war, internal political instability or any other public emergency, may be invoked as a justification of torture." ibid.

973 Article 1, 2 and 3 ibid.

974 Nora Sveaass, 'The United Nations Convention Against Torture and Other Cruel, Inhuman or Degrading Treatment or Punishment: The Absolute Prohibition and the Obligation to Prevent' in Metin Başoğlu (ed), *Torture and Its Definition In International Law: An Interdisciplinary Approach* (Oxford University Press 2017).

any offence referred to in article 4 is found shall in the cases contemplated in article 5, if it does not extradite him, submit the case to its competent authorities for the purpose of prosecution." This obligation became the subject matter of the ICJ dispute between Belgium and Senegal, in which Belgium argued that Mr Hissène Habré, the former president of Chad, should be either prosecuted by Senegal or extradited to Belgium.[975] In its judgement, the court upheld Belgium's legal claims.[976] The argumentation of the court is discussed in the subsequent section.[977]

1.1.7 Convention on the Rights of the Child (CRC)

The Convention on the Rights of the Child was adopted in 1989 and entered into force a year later.[978] Mhairi Cowden describes the adoption of the convention as: "perhaps the biggest real step forward in the children's rights movement."[979] Numerous declarations on children's rights paved the way for the convention. For example, the fifth assembly of the League of Nations adopted the Declaration of the Rights of the Child in 1924.[980] The more comprehensive Declaration of the Rights of the Child was adopted by the General Assembly.[981] In spite of the valuable role played by these declarations, they included overly general principles.

Given the number of the convention's ratifications, as well as considerable support for its three optional protocols, it might be considered one of the most influential international human rights treaties.[982] Yet this hypothesis appears rather optimistic: the parties to the convention have not made extensive use of it. Writing on the occasion of the 25th anniversary of the

975 *Questions relating to the Obligation to Prosecute or Extradite (Belgium v. Senegal), Judgment, ICJ Reports 2012, p 422.*

976 ibid.

977 For more details, see chapter 3, subsection 1.6 Dispute settlement provisions and the role of the International Court of Justice.

978 Convention on the Rights of the Child (adopted 20 November1989, entered into force 2 September 1990) UNTS vol. 1577 p. 3 (CRC).

979 Mhairi Cowden, *Children's Rights: From Philosophy to Public Policy* (Palgrave Macmillan 2016) 8.

980 Geneva Declaration of the Rights of the Child of 1924, adopted 26 September 1924, League of Nations O.J. Spec. Supp. 21.

981 Declaration of the Rights of the Child UNGA (20 November 1959) UN Doc A/RES/1386(XIV).

982 One hundred ninety-six countries became state parties to the Convention, with only one notable exception – the United States. 'Status of Ratification Interactive Dashboard' (n 916).

convention's adoption, Brian Milne gloomily observes: "There is a veneer of concern about children's rights. On the ground little has changed except that poverty appears to be hurting more children than ever before, and it would be callous to overlook the effect of, for example, HIV and AIDS on them. In many western countries, an almost obsessive fear of 'stranger danger' has consigned children to a life indoors where, ironically, most abuse and neglect occur anyway. That angst is gradually permeating other parts of our small world. Children's rights are becoming less and less realisable as children become less visible."[983]

1.1.8 International Convention on the Protection of the Rights of All Migrant Workers and Members of Their Families (ICMW)

The International Convention on the Protection of the Rights of All Migrant Workers and Members of Their Families was adopted in 1990 and came into force thirteen years later.[984] Notwithstanding its significance, the number of states that have ratified this convention remains insufficient.[985] The reasons behind the states' reluctance to ratify the convention are described as follows: "Even though migrants' labour is increasingly essential in the world economy, the noneconomic aspect of migration – and especially the human and labour rights of migrants – remains a neglected dimension of globalization."[986]

The convention ensures a broad range of rights, the majority of which have been formulated in other human rights treaties. Yet the essential contribution of the convention is that it expands these rights to migrant workers and members of their families.[987]

---

983 Brian Milne, *Rights of the Child: 25 Years After the Adoption of the UN Convention* (Springer International Publishing 2015) 4.

984 International Convention on the Protection of the Rights of All Migrant Workers and Members of Their Families (adopted 18 December 1990, entered into force 1 July 2003) UNTS vol. 2220 p. 3 (ICMW).

985 As of November 2018, 131 countries have not taken any actions in respect of the convention. 'Status of Ratification Interactive Dashboard' (n 916).

986 Paul de Guchteneire and Antoine Pécoud, 'Introduction: The UN Convention on Migrant Workers' Rights' in Ryszard Cholewinski, Paul de Guchteneire and Antoine Pecoud (eds.), *Migration and Human Rights: The United Nations Convention on Migrant Workers' Rights* (Cambridge University Press 2009) 2.

987 Article 1 prescribes that the convention applies to "to all migrant workers and members of their families" and it applies "during the entire migration process of migrant workers and members of their families."

1.1.9 International Convention for the Protection of All Persons from Enforced Disappearance (CPED)

International Convention for the Protection of All Persons from Enforced Disappearance was adopted in 2006 and entered into force in 2010.[988] Yet, the number of states that have ratified the convention remains low.[989]

Before the work on the draft of the convention was initiated, several states expressed their concerns as to the necessity of a new international instrument.[990] A solid argument that deserves consideration is that a new convention might overlap with existing rights under the International Covenant on Civil and Political Rights. Tullio Scovazzi and Gabriella Citroni dismiss this concern in the following way: "Indeed, it is true that the International Covenant on Civil and Political Rights protects the majority of the rights violated by an enforced disappearance. However, the Covenant does not establish specific obligations with regard to prevention, investigation, repression and international cooperation in cases of enforced disappearances. Nor does the Covenant stipulate any obligation to codify enforced disappearance as an autonomous offence under domestic criminal law, to exercise territorial and extra-territorial criminal jurisdiction with respect to the presumed perpetrators of the offence, to maintain registers of detained persons, or to prevent and suppress the abduction of children born during the captivity of their disappeared mothers."[991] These arguments demonstrate that the convention is a viable instrument for preventing and remedying instances of enforced disappearances.

1.1.10 Convention on the Rights of Persons with Disabilities (CRPD)

The Convention on the Rights of Persons with Disabilities and its Optional Protocol were adopted in 2006 and entered into force in 2008.[992] Since its opening for signature, 177 states have ratified the convention, and 92 have ratified the optional protocol.[993]

---

988 International Convention for the Protection of All Persons from Enforced Disappearance (adopted 20 December 2006, entered into force 23 December 2010) UNTS vol. 2716 p. 3 (CPED).

989 As of November 2018, 89 countries have not taken any actions in respect of the convention. 'Status of Ratification Interactive Dashboard' (n 916).

990 Tullio Scovazzi and Gabriella Citroni, *The Struggle against Enforced Disappearance and the 2007 United Nations Convention* (Brill Nijhoff 2007).

991 ibid 259.

992 Convention on the Rights of Persons with Disabilities (adopted 13 December 2006, entered into force 3 May 2008) UNTS vol. 2515 p. 3 (CRPD).

993 'Convention on the Rights of Persons with Disabilities (CRPD)' (*un.org*) <https://www.un.org/development/desa/disabilities/convention-on-the-rights-of-persons-with-disabilities.html>.

The authors of the commentary to the convention distinguish four different phases in the treatment of disabled persons within the UN system. These phases are: disabled persons as invisible citizens[994] (1945–1970), disabled persons as subjects of rehabilitation[995] (1970–1980), disabled persons as objects of human rights[996] (1980–2000) and disabled persons as agents of human rights. The fourth phase culminated in the adoption of a new convention and its subsequent ratification. The adoption of the convention reflects a drastic change in the attitude towards disabled persons, which can be described as follows: "The result is a convention that differs considerably from earlier disability instruments. Unlike the declarations of the 1970s, the Convention contains no caveats relating to the possibility of enjoying human rights under impairment conditions."[997]

1.2 *Reporting Obligation*

The core human rights treaties discussed in this chapter impose an obligation to report measures undertaken for their implementation. The only exception is the Genocide Convention. In essence, the reporting obligation is comprised of two pillars of self-reporting. After becoming a party to a human rights convention, a state is obliged to submit an initial report, which must contain information on the measures introduced to give effect to the rights guaranteed. Subsequently, a state party is under an obligation either to prepare regular reports or to report upon request.

Human rights conventions establish specialised committees that are authorised to consider submitted reports, as well as to produce their own reports. Several human rights treaties entitle the respective committees to make suggestions or general recommendations with respect to submitted reports.

---

994 "[…] disabled persons in general were regarded as objects of rehabilitation, while as citizens and rights holders, they remained invisible." Theresia Degener and Andrew Begg, 'From Invisible Citizens to Agents of Change: A Short History of the Struggle for the Recognition of the Rights of Persons with Disabilities at the United Nations' in Valentina Della Fina, Rachele Cera and Giuseppe Palmisano (eds.), *The United Nations Convention on the Rights of Persons with Disabilities: A Commentary* (Springer International Publishing 2017) 3.

995 "Disabled persons in this second phase were increasingly seen as agents in their own affairs. But these affairs were mainly rehabilitation affairs, with the focus on fixing the impaired individual." ibid 6.

996 "During this third phase, however, the disability rights movement was gaining strength and experience in political advocacy, and by the dawn of the new millennium, disabled persons' organisations had become articulate policy advocates, no longer prepared to allow others to speak on their behalf." ibid 11.

997 ibid 37.

Table 3 below summarises the scope of the reporting obligation embedded in the core international human rights conventions.

The state reporting obligation has multiple objectives. The Harmonized Guidelines on Reporting under the International Human Rights Treaties enumerates the principal objectives of state reporting as a commitment to treaties, review of the implementation of human rights at the national level and basis for constructive dialogue at the international level.[998]

1.3 *Mechanisms for Interstate Complaints*

The majority of human rights conventions prescribe a mechanism of interstate complaints that comprises three distinct stages. These stages are:

- Written explanations: the state party against which the claim of an alleged violation is submitted provides written explanations within three months.
- Filing a complaint: if the matter is not resolved within six months of the submission of the initial communication, each of the state parties involved in the previous stage can notify the committee established under the relevant treaty to consider the matter.
- Consideration of the complaint: a committee considers a complaint if all the available domestic remedies have been exhausted or such remedies are unreasonably prolonged. The primary objective of the committee is to facilitate a friendly solution between the parties involved. The committee gathers relevant information by requesting the parties to supply such information and by allowing the parties to present information either orally or in writing. Within twelve months, the committee examines the matter before it and prepares a report. If the parties have reached a solution, the committee confines its report to a brief statement of the facts and of the solution reached; if not, the committee confines its report to a brief statement of the facts and the parties' written submissions and record of the oral submissions. The report is communicated to the parties concerned.

Table 4 summarises the mechanisms of interstate complaints prescribed by the core human rights conventions.

1.4 *Mechanisms for Individual Complaints*

A number of human rights treaties introduce a mechanism for individual complaints. In some instances, a mechanism of this type is prescribed by optional protocols. As a rule, complaints can be lodged by individuals or groups of

998 Secretary-General, 'Compilation of Guidelines on the Form and Content of Reports to Be Submitted by States Parties to the International Human Rights Treaties UN Doc HRI/GEN/2/REV.6' (2009).

TABLE 3 Reporting obligation in the core human rights conventions

Human rights treaty	Duty to report	Body authorised to review reports	Outcome of the report's examination
ICERD	Every two years or upon the committee's request	Committee on the Elimination of Racial Discrimination, eighteen experts	The committee examines reports and prepares its own report to submit to the General Assembly.
ICCPR	Upon the committee's request; additional reporting duty applies under the Second Optional Protocol	Human Rights Committee (CCPR), eighteen members	The committee reviews reports and prepares its report to the state parties.
ICESCR	Every five years	Committee on Economic, Social and Cultural Rights (CESCR), eighteen experts	The committee examines reports and makes suggestions or general recommendations.
CEDAW	Every four years or upon the committee's request	Committee on the Elimination of Discrimination against Women, twenty-three experts	The committee considers reports and makes suggestions or general recommendations.
CAT	Every four years or upon the committee's request	Committee against Torture, ten experts	The committee examines reports and may prepare general recommendations if it considers them appropriate.
CRC	Every five years; additionally, the optional protocols prescribe reporting obligations	Committee on the Rights of the Child, ten experts	The committee considers reports and makes suggestions or general recommendations.

TABLE 3 Reporting obligation in the core human rights conventions (*cont.*)

Human rights treaty	Duty to report	Body authorised to review reports	Outcome of the report's examination
ICMW	Every five years or upon the committee's request	Committee on the Protection of the Rights of All Migrant Workers and Members of Their Families, fourteen experts	The committee considers reports and prepares country-specific comments.
CPED	Parties are not obligated to submit regular reports	Committee on Enforced Disappearances, ten members	The committee considers reports.
CRPD	Every four years	Committee on the Rights of Persons with Disabilities, eighteen experts	The committee considers reports.

individuals subject to the jurisdiction of the state that recognised the competence of the committee to consider them. The committees review submitted complaints in two stages:

- Written explanations: a state party concerned is informed about a complaint and prepares written explanations within six months.
- Consideration: a committee examines the complaint in light of all the available information provided by the petitioner and the state party concerned and prepares its views on the matter. The committee forwards its views to all the parties concerned. The follow-up procedures are laid down by certain human rights treaties.

Table 5 summarises the individual complaints mechanisms prescribed by the core human rights conventions.

1.5 *Inquiry Procedure*

Several human rights treaties or their optional protocols authorise a committee to initiate an inquiry procedure if the following preconditions are met:

TABLE 4 Mechanisms of interstate complaints in the core human rights conventions

Human rights treaty	Stages of the complaint mechanism	Body authorised to hear complaints	Outcome of the examination of a complaint
ICERD	Three stages: written explanations, filing a complaint and consideration of a complaint.	Ad hoc Conciliation Commission, which comprises five members	Commission's findings are restricted to the questions of facts. The commission also prepares recommendations "proper for the amicable solution of the dispute." Parties may accept or reject these recommendations. The commission's report, along with the parties' acceptance or rejection, declarations are communicated to the other parties.
ICCPR	Three stages: written explanations, filing a complaint and consideration of a complaint.	Human Rights Committee (CCPR) or the committee may appoint an ad hoc Conciliation Commission	Within twelve months the committee prepares a report. There are two possible types of report: - if the parties have reached a solution, the report is a brief statement of facts and of a solution reached - if not, the report is a brief statement of facts, parties' written submissions and record of the oral submissions The report is communicated to the parties concerned.
ICESCR	A mechanism is prescribed by the Optional Protocol.	Committee on Economic, Social and Cultural Rights	Within twelve months the committee prepares a report. There are two possible types of report:

TABLE 4 Mechanisms of interstate complaints in the core human rights conventions (*cont.*)

Human rights treaty	Stages of the complaint mechanism	Body authorised to hear complaints	Outcome of the examination of a complaint
	Three stages: written explanations, filing a complaint and complaint's consideration.		- if the parties have reached a solution, the report is a brief statement of facts and of a solution reached - if not, the report is a brief statement of facts, parties' written submissions and a record of the oral submissions The committee also may communicate any views that it considers relevant to the issue discussed. The report is communicated to the parties concerned.
CEDAW	The Convention does not prescribe any mechanism for interstate complaints. The Optional Protocol to the convention does not fill this gap either.		
CAT	Three stages: written explanations, filing a complaint and consideration of a complaint.	Committee against Torture or it can set up an ad hoc conciliation commission	Within twelve months the committee prepares a report. There are two possible types of report: - if the parties have reached a solution, the report is a brief statement of facts and of a solution reached - if not, the report is a brief statement of facts, parties' written submissions and record of the oral submissions The report is communicated to the parties concerned.

TABLE 4 Mechanisms of interstate complaints in the core human rights conventions (*cont.*)

Human rights treaty	Stages of the complaint mechanism	Body authorised to hear complaints	Outcome of the examination of a complaint
CRC	A mechanism is introduced in the Optional Protocol	Committee on the Rights of the Child	The role of the committee in examining such complaints is significantly restricted: the committee must make available its good offices for the parties concerned.
ICMW	Three stages: written explanations, filing a complaint and consideration of a complaint.	Committee on the Protection of the Rights of All Migrant Workers and Members of Their Families	Within twelve months the committee prepares a report. There are two possible types of report: - if the parties have reached a solution, the report is a brief statement of facts and of a solution reached - if not, the report is a brief statement of facts, parties' written submissions and record of the oral submissions The report is communicated to the parties concerned.
CPED	The convention allows parties to lodge a complaint that the other party is not fulfilling its obligations under the convention, if both parties have accepted the competence of the committee. Yet the convention does not prescribe an exact procedure for review.		
CRPD	Neither the convention nor the optional protocol to the convention prescribes interstate complaints mechanism.		

– Reliable information that grave or systematic violations of guaranteed rights have taken place
– Recognition by a concerned state party of the committee's competence to exercise this right

TABLE 5 Individual complaints mechanisms in the core human rights conventions

Human rights treaty	Stages of the complaint mechanism	Body authorised to hear complaints	Outcome of the examination of a complaint
ICERD	Two stages: examination by a specially appointed national body and examination by the committee.	Committee on the Elimination of Racial Discrimination	The committee may prepare suggestions or recommendation, if it considers them necessary, and forward them to the parties.
ICCPR	The optional protocol introduces the procedure. Two stages: stage of written explanations and stage of consideration.	Human Rights Committee (CCPR)	The committee considers the initial communication from a petitioner and the state's written explanations and forwards its views to the parties.
ICESCR	The optional protocol prescribes the procedure. Two stages: stage of written explanations and stage of consideration.	Committee on Economic, Social and Cultural Rights	The committee examines submitted documents and may prepare recommendations to the parties. As a part of the follow-up procedure, a state has to provide information on the actions undertaken.
CEDAW	The optional protocol introduces the procedure. Two stages: stage of written explanations and stage of consideration.	Committee on the Elimination of Discrimination against Women	The committee reviews complaints and submits its views, along with recommendations to the parties. A state party concerned has to respond to any recommendation made within six months.

TABLE 5 Individual complaints mechanisms in the core human rights conventions (*cont.*)

Human rights treaty	**Stages of the complaint mechanism**	**Body authorised to hear complaints**	**Outcome of the examination of a complaint**
CAT	Two stages: stage of written explanations and stage of consideration.	Committee against Torture	The committee examines the complaint in light of all the available information provided by the petitioner and the state party, and lays down its views on the matter. The committee's views are forwarded to the parties.
CRC	The optional protocol introduces the procedure. Two stages: stage of written explanations and stage of consideration.	Committee on the Rights of the Child	The committee examines the complaint in light of all the available information provided by the petitioner and the state party, and lays down its views. The committee's views are forwarded to the parties. A state party has to respond to any recommendation made within six months.
ICMW	Two stages: stage of written explanations and stage of consideration.	Committee on the Protection of the Rights of All Migrant Workers and Members of Their Families	The committee examines the complaint in light of all the available information provided by the petitioner and the state party, and lays down its views. The committee's views are forwarded to the parties.

TABLE 5 Individual complaints mechanisms in the core human rights conventions (*cont.*)

Human rights treaty	Stages of the complaint mechanism	Body authorised to hear complaints	Outcome of the examination of a complaint
CPED	Two stages: stage of written explanations and stage of consideration.	Committee on Enforced Disappearances	The committee examines the complaint in light of all the available information provided by the petitioner and the state party, and lays down its views. These views are forwarded to the parties.
CRPD	The optional protocol introduces the procedure. Two stages: stage of written explanations and stage of consideration.	Committee on the Rights of Persons with Disabilities	The committee examines the complaint and prepares suggestions and recommendations. The committee's views are forwarded to the parties.

With respect of any such inquiry, a committee can exercise the following functions: 1) designate one of its members to conduct an inquiry and report the results or 2) authorise a member to visit the territory of a state party and inform the state party of any findings on the matter, as well as providing comments and recommendations. A state party that has received such recommendations is obligated to transmit its observations to a committee within six months. A committee might request that a state party inform it about the measures undertaken after the period of six months has passed.

1.6 *Dispute Settlement Provisions and the Role of the International Court of Justice*

The core human rights conventions incorporate dispute-settlement provisions that grant jurisdiction to the ICJ.[999] As of today, the parties have invoked

999 Article IX Genocide Convention; Article 22 ICERD; Article 29 CEDAW; Article 30 CAT; Article 92 ICMW; Article 42 CPED.

TABLE 6 Inquiry procedures in the core human rights conventions

Human rights treaty	Prerequisites for initiating an inquiry procedure	Outcome of the inquiry
ICERD	Inquiry procedure does not exist.	
ICCPR	Inquiry procedure does not exist.	
ICESCR (Optional protocol)	Two preconditions: reliable information about the grave and systematic violations and consent of a state party to recognise the committee's competence.	The committee can exercise the following functions: designate a member to conduct an inquiry and report the results, authorise a member to visit the territory of a state party and inform the state party of any findings on the matter, as well as comments and recommendations. A state party that has received such recommendations shall transmit its observations to the committee within six months; the committee might request a state party to inform it about the measures undertaken after six months have passed.
CEDAW (Optional protocol)	Two preconditions: reliable information about the grave and systematic violations and consent of a state party to recognise the committee's competence.	The committee can exercise the following functions: designate a member to conduct an inquiry and report the results, authorise a member to visit the territory of a state party if necessary and inform the state party of any findings, as well as comments and recommendations. The committee informs a state party, and it must respond within six months and inform the committee about measures undertaken. The committee may request a state party to inform it about the undertaken measures after six months have passed.
CAT	Precondition: if there is reliable information that torture is being systematically practised in a state party.	The committee can appoint a member to conduct an inquiry and report its conclusions. Such an inquiry may include a visit to the territory of a state party, if that state party agrees. The findings of an inquiry along with the committee's comments or suggestions are sent to the party.

TABLE 6 Inquiry procedures in the core human rights conventions (*cont.*)

Human rights treaty	Prerequisites for initiating an inquiry procedure	Outcome of the inquiry
CRC (Optional protocol)	Two preconditions: reliable information about the grave and systematic violations and consent of a state party to recognise the committee's competence.	The committee can appoint a member to conduct an inquiry and report its conclusions. Such an inquiry may include a visit to the territory of a state party if a state party agrees. After examining the findings of such an inquiry, the committee transmits them to the state party, as well as its comments and recommendations. The state party has six months to respond and submit its observations. The committee may request a state party to inform it about the measures undertaken after six months have passed.
ICMW	Inquiry procedure does not exist.	
CPED	If the committee receives information that enforced disappearance is being practised on a widespread or systematic basis in the territory of a state party, it may urgently bring the matter to the attention of the General Assembly.	The committee may organise a visit to a state party if there is reliable information that that state party is seriously violating the convention. A member of the committee may organise such a visit only if the state party agrees and the further modalities of this visit are determined by the state party and the committee in consultation. After the visit, the committee member reports to the committee, and the committee communicates its observations and recommendations to the state party.
CRPD (Optional protocol)	Two preconditions: reliable information about the grave and systematic violations and consent of a state party to recognise the committee's competence.	A member of the committee can be designated to examine this information and if necessary, to visit the state party. Such a visit is possible only if the state party agrees. The committee communicates its findings along with comments and recommendation to the state party. Within six months, the state party can submit its observations. After six months have passed, the committee may require the state party to inform it about the measures undertaken.

provisions from five international human rights conventions in disputes before the court. The pertinent court practice is analysed below. Before proceeding with the analysis of the court practice, I will briefly discuss whether parallel proceedings before a specialised human rights committee and the ICJ are allowed.

The recent dispute between Qatar and the UAE has raised a question regarding the legal nature of the proceedings before the Committee on the Elimination of Racial Discrimination and the ICJ. In its submission before the court, the UAE argued that Qatar should not be permitted to go ahead with the parallel proceedings before the committee and the court.[1000] The UAE justified this legal position by invoking the principle of lis pendens, which is known in domestic legal systems, and by arguing that the parallel proceedings would constitute abuse of rights by Qatar.[1001] Furthermore, it was contended that the ICERD prescribes the sequential framework for the settlement of disputes, thus requiring a complaining state to initiate an interstate complaints procedure first, and only then proceed with a dispute before the ICJ.[1002] The court emphasised that, at this stage of the proceedings, there is no need to make any pronouncements on the matter.[1003]

1000 On 22 March 2019, the UAE filed a request for an indication of provisional measures before the ICJ. Among the other provisional measures, the UAE requested "(i) Qatar immediately withdraw its Communication submitted to the CERD Committee pursuant to Article 11 of the CERD on 8 March 2018 against the UAE and take all necessary measures to terminate consideration thereof by the CERD Committee." 'International Court of Justice. Application of the International Convention on the Elimination of All Forms of Racial Discrimination (Qatar v. United Arab Emirates). Request for the Indication of Provisional Measures of the United Arab Emirates, March 22, 2019' (n 939).

1001 The UAE argued: "Qatar has thus created a lis pendens that constitutes an abuse of the CERD dispute resolution mechanism. Through its conduct, Qatar has deliberately manipulated and distorted that dispute resolution mechanism so as to force the UAE to defend itself in two overlapping proceedings – between the same Parties, commenced under the same instrument and involving the same allegations of fact and law." ibid para. 41.

1002 ibid.

1003 "The Court has already examined this issue in its Order of 23 July 2018 on the Request for the indication of provisional measures submitted by Qatar. In that context, the Court noted that: Although the Parties disagree as to whether negotiations and recourse to the procedures referred to in Article 22 of CERD constitute alternative or cumulative preconditions to be fulfilled before the seisin of the Court, the Court is of the view that it need not make a pronouncement on the issue at this stage of the proceedings … Nor does it consider it necessary, for the present purposes, to decide whether any electa una via principle or lis pendens exception are applicable in the present situation." *Application of the International Convention on the Elimination of All Forms of Racial Discrimination, Order, June 14, 2019* (n 940).

1.6.1 Disputes in Which the Convention on the Prevention and Punishment of the Crime of Genocide Was Invoked

On two occasions, the ICJ discussed the crime of genocide under the Genocide Convention,[1004] while a third dispute was initiated against Myanmar in 2019.[1005] The earlier disputes had been triggered by the dissolution of the former Socialist Federal Republic of Yugoslavia in the 1990s, which provoked dreadful military conflicts between the different ethnic groups.

The first dispute was initiated by the Republic of Bosnia and Herzegovina in 1993. Bosnia and Herzegovina relied upon Article IX of the Genocide Convention as the basis for the court's jurisdiction. In its judgement of 11 July 1996, the court dismissed the preliminary objections and found that it had jurisdiction to adjudicate the dispute and that the application was admissible.[1006] The proceedings in this particular dispute raised many intricate procedural questions. In spite of their significance, I will focus on discussing the merits of the present case.

At the outset, the court pronounced that the crime of genocide comprises two elements: actions directed against the members of the protected group and specific intent, i.e. "intent to destroy, in whole or in part, a national, ethnical, racial or religious group, as such."[1007] The categories of actions that constitute the first element of the crime are enumerated in Article II of the Genocide Convention.[1008] The specific intent (*dolus specialis*) ought, in the court's view, to be characterised as follows: "It is not enough that the members of the group are targeted because they belong to that group, that is because the perpetrator has a discriminatory intent. Something more is required. The acts listed in Article II

1004 *Application of the Convention on the Prevention and Punishment of the Crime of Genocide (Bosnia and Herzegovina v. Serbia and Montenegro), Judgment* (n 926); *Application of the Convention on the Prevention and Punishment of the Crime of Genocide (Croatia v. Serbia), Judgment* (n 926).

1005 'International Court of Justice. Application of the Convention on the Prevention and Punishment of the Crime of Genocide (The Gambia v. Myanmar). Application Instituting Proceedings and Request for the Indication of Provisional Measures, November 11, 2019' (n 927).

1006 *Application of the Convention on the Prevention and Punishment of the Crime of Genocide, Preliminary Objections, Judgment, ICJ Reports 1996, p 595.*

1007 *Application of the Convention on the Prevention and Punishment of the Crime of Genocide (Bosnia and Herzegovina v. Serbia and Montenegro), Judgment* (n 926).

1008 Article II reads as follows: "In the present Convention, genocide means any of the following acts committed with intent to destroy, in whole or in part, a national, ethnical, racial or religious group, as such: (a) Killing members of the group; (b) Causing serious bodily or mental harm to members of the group; (c) Deliberately inflicting on the group conditions of life calculated to bring about its physical destruction in whole or in part; (d) Imposing

must be done with intent to destroy the group as such in whole or in part. The words 'as such' emphasize that intent to destroy the protected group."[1009]

Despite confirming that the massacre at Srebrenica constituted genocide, in the sense outlined in the Genocide Convention, the court found that the acts of genocide at Srebrenica could not be attributed to the respondent and thus did not entail the respondent's international responsibility.[1010] Notwithstanding these findings, the court upheld that the respondent had violated the obligation to prevent genocide prescribed by Article I[1011] and the obligation to punish genocide embedded in Article IV of the Genocide Convention.[1012]

The second dispute was initiated by the Republic of Croatia in 1999.[1013] In 2008, the court found that it had jurisdiction to entertain the application.[1014] Serbia filed counterclaims and argued that the Republic of Croatia had violated its obligations under the Genocide Convention during and after Operation Storm in August 1995.[1015]

The court confirmed that mass atrocities had taken place during the conflict and that some of these atrocities constituted actions (*actus reus*) of genocide – in other words, they fell under the actions enumerated in Article II of the convention.[1016] In spite of this determination, the court questioned the presence of specific intent, concluding as follows: "in the opinion of the Court, Croatia has not established that the only reasonable inference that can be drawn from the pattern of conduct it relied upon was the intent to destroy, in whole or in

---

measures intended to prevent births within the group; (e) Forcibly transferring children of the group to another group."

1009 *Application of the Convention on the Prevention and Punishment of the Crime of Genocide (Bosnia and Herzegovina v. Serbia and Montenegro), Judgment* (n 926) [187].

1010 ibid [395] and [412].

1011 Article I reads as follows: "The Contracting Parties confirm that genocide, whether committed in time of peace or in time of war, is a crime under international law which they undertake to prevent and to punish."

1012 Article IV stipulates: "Persons committing genocide or any of the other acts enumerated in article III shall be punished, whether they are constitutionally responsible rulers, public officials or private individuals."

1013 'International Court of Justice. Application of the Convention on the Prevention and Punishment of the Crime of Genocide (Croatia v. Serbia). Application Instituting Proceedings, July 2, 1999.'

1014 *Application of the Convention on the Prevention and Punishment of the Crime of Genocide (Croatia v. Serbia), Preliminary Objections, Judgment, ICJ Reports 2008, p 412.*

1015 'International Court of Justice. Application of the Convention on the Prevention and Punishment of the Crime of Genocide (Croatia v. Serbia). Counter-Memorial of Serbia, December 1, 2009.'

1016 *Application of the Convention on the Prevention and Punishment of the Crime of Genocide (Croatia v. Serbia), Judgment* (n 926).

part, the Croat group. The acts constituting the actus reus of genocide within the meaning of Article II (a) and (b) of the Convention were not committed with the specific intent required for them to be characterized as acts of genocide."[1017] Consequently, Croatia's claims were dismissed in their entirety.[1018] A similar fate befell the Serbian counterclaims.[1019]

In November 2019, the Gambia initiated a dispute against Myanmar for an alleged violation of the Genocide Convention.[1020] In its application, the Gambia argues that "acts adopted, taken and condoned by the Government of Myanmar against members of the Rohingya group, [...] are genocidal in character [...]. They have been perpetrated in manifest violation of the 1948 Convention on the Prevention and Punishment of the Crime of Genocide."[1021] The Gambia requested that the court indicate provisional measures.[1022] In January 2020, the ICJ recognised its prima facie jurisdiction, as well as the Gambia's prima facie standing to submit the dispute against Myanmar before the court.[1023] Furthermore, the court unanimously adopted a number of provisional measures, which are compulsory for Myanmar.[1024]

1.6.2 Disputes in Which the International Convention on the Elimination of All Forms of Racial Discrimination Was Invoked

A number of politically tainted disputes between neighbouring countries have been brought before the court, invoking the provisions of the ICERD.

The five-day-long military conflict between Georgia and the Russian Federation sowed the seeds of a future dispute before the ICJ.[1025] On 12 August

1017 ibid [440].

1018 ibid [524].

1019 ibid.

1020 'International Court of Justice. Application of the Convention on the Prevention and Punishment of the Crime of Genocide (The Gambia v. Myanmar). Application Instituting Proceedings and Request for the Indication of Provisional Measures, November 11, 2019' (n 927).

1021 ibid.

1022 ibid.

1023 *International Court of Justice, Application of the Convention on the Prevention and Punishment of the Crime of Genocide (The Gambia v. Myanmar), Request for the indication of provisional measures, Order, January 23, 2020.*

1024 ibid.

1025 The tension between the two border regions of Georgia – South Ossetia and Abkhazia and Georgia started in the early 1990s. So far as South Ossetia is concerned, on 24 June 1992, Georgia and the Russian Federation concluded an agreement on principles of settlement of the Georgian Ossetian conflict (the Sochi Agreement). So far as Abkhazia is concerned, on 3 September 1992, the president of the Russian Federation and the chairman of

2008, the government of Georgia filed an application instituting proceedings against the Russian Federation in respect of a dispute concerning "actions on and around the territory of Georgia" in breach of the ICERD.[1026] Both states are parties to the convention, of which Article 22 grants jurisdiction to the court.[1027]

The Russian Federation raised four preliminary objections to the court's jurisdiction.[1028] The court dismissed the first preliminary objection, to the effect that there was no "dispute" between the parties in the meaning of Article 22.[1029] Yet, after observing that Georgia had not genuinely attempted to engage in negotiations with the Russian Federation to resolve the dispute, the court

---

the state council of the Republic of Georgia signed the Moscow Agreement. In September 1993, the military confrontation between the parties resumed. After the UN Security Council and the Russian Federation expressed their grave concerns about the outbreak of violence and the subsequent humanitarian crisis, which was characterised by gross human rights violations, the parties agreed to participate in the peace negotiations. The first round of negotiations between the Georgian and Abkhaz sides was held in Geneva from 30 November to 1 December 1993. After the peace negotiations, both regions were considered parts of Georgia, with a Russian peacekeeping mission deployed there. The tension between the central government and the two border regions resulted in a five-day war in early August 2008, in which the Russian Federation was also involved. *Application of the International Convention on the Elimination of All Forms of Racial Discrimination (Georgia v. Russian Federation), Preliminary Objections, Judgment, ICJ Reports 2011, p 70.*

1026 ibid 75–76.

1027 Article 22 reads as follows: "Any dispute between two or more States Parties with respect to the interpretation or application of this Convention, which is not settled by negotiation or by the procedures expressly provided for in this Convention, shall, at the request of any of the parties to the dispute, be referred to the International Court of Justice for decision, unless the disputants agree to another mode of settlement."

1028 "The Russian Federation has raised four preliminary objections to the Court's jurisdiction under Article 22 of CERD. According to the first preliminary objection put forward by the Russian Federation, there was no dispute between the Parties regarding the interpretation or application of CERD at the date Georgia filed its Application. In its second preliminary objection, the Russian Federation argues that the procedural requirements of Article 22 of CERD for recourse to the Court have not been fulfilled. The Russian Federation contends in its third objection that the alleged wrongful conduct took place outside its territory and therefore the Court lacks jurisdiction ratione loci to entertain the case. During the oral proceedings, the Russian Federation stated that this objection did not possess an exclusively preliminary character. Finally, according to the Russian Federation's fourth objection, any jurisdiction the Court might have is limited ratione temporis to the events which occurred after the entry into force of CERD as between the Parties, that is, 2 July 1999." *Application of the International Convention on the Elimination of All Forms of Racial Discrimination* (*Georgia v. Russian Federation*), *Preliminary Objections, Judgment* (n 1025) [22].

1029 ibid [114].

concluded that the prerequisites of Article 22 were not fulfilled.[1030] The court upheld the second preliminary objection, and thus the dispute did not proceed to the merits phase.[1031]

In January 2017, Ukraine initiated proceedings against the Russian Federation.[1032] Among other allegations, Ukraine claimed that the Russian Federation violated the ICERD, due to its treatment of the non-Russian ethnic communities of the Crimean peninsula.[1033] In order to establish the jurisdiction of the court, Ukraine has relied upon Article 22 and demonstrated that Ukraine made numerous attempts to negotiate a satisfactory solution.[1034] Ukraine contends that despite its numerous efforts, the Russian Federation "largely failed to respond to Ukraine's correspondence, declined to engage on the substance of the dispute, and consistently failed to negotiate in a constructive manner."[1035] Ukraine thus argues that the court is authorised to entertain the dispute between the parties.[1036]

The claims on the merits include allegations that the Russian Federation conducted a campaign of discrimination against the non-Russian ethnic communities of the Crimean peninsula – i.e. ethnic Ukrainians and Crimean Tatars.[1037] Ukraine describes the policy pursued by the Russian Federation in the following terms: "Russian authorities are pursuing on the Crimean peninsula a policy of cultural erasure through a pattern of discriminatory actions, treating groups that are not ethnic Russian as threats to the regime whose identity and culture must be suppressed."[1038]

In September 2018, the Russian Federation raised certain preliminary objections to the court's jurisdiction and the admissibility of the aforesaid application.[1039] Ukraine then presented its observations and submissions on the

1030 ibid [169]–[184].

1031 ibid [187].

1032 'International Court of Justice. Application of the International Convention for the Suppression of the Financing of Terrorism and of the International Convention on the Elimination of All Forms of Racial Discrimination (Ukraine v. Russian Federation). Application Instituting Proceedings, January 16, 2017.'

1033 ibid.

1034 ibid.

1035 ibid 18.

1036 ibid 20.

1037 ibid 56–82.

1038 ibid 86–88.

1039 'International Court of Justice. Application of the International Convention for the Suppression of the Financing of Terrorism and of the International Convention on the Elimination of All Forms of Racial Discrimination (Ukraine v. Russian Federation). Preliminary Objections Submitted by the Russian Federation, September 12, 2018.'

preliminary objections.[1040] In November 2019, the court announced its decision, dismissing the preliminary objections to its jurisdiction and acknowledging the admissibility of the legal claims.[1041]

In June 2018, Qatar initiated a dispute against the UAE.[1042] Qatar argued that the restrictive measures recently imposed by the UAE constituted a flagrant violation of the ICERD.[1043] Qatar contended that the discriminatory measures have interfered with basic human rights protected by the ICERD, including the right to marriage and choice of spouse, freedom of expression, the right to education, the right to medical treatment, the right to work, the right to property and other rights.[1044]

Qatar submitted that the court was granted jurisdiction under Article 22 of the aforesaid convention. Furthermore, in Qatar's view, the prerequisites prescribed by Article 22 had been fulfilled.[1045] That is to say, Qatar made countless efforts to engage in negotiations to resolve the ongoing political crisis.[1046] Yet, these efforts did not bring the desired results.[1047]

In July 2018, the court issued an order indicating provisional measures.[1048] In April 2019, the UAE filed preliminary objections to the court's jurisdiction and admissibility of the application,[1049] and in 2021, the court upheld the first preliminary objection and agreed that it did not have jurisdiction.

1040 'International Court of Justice. Application of the International Convention for the Suppression of the Financing of Terrorism and of the International Convention on the Elimination of All Forms of Racial Discrimination (Ukraine v. Russian Federation). Written Statement of Observations and Submissions on the Preliminary Objections of the Russian Federation Submitted by Ukraine, January 14, 2019.'

1041 *Application of the International Convention for the Suppression of the Financing of Terrorism and of the International Convention on the Elimination of All Forms of Racial Discrimination (Ukraine v. Russian Federation) Preliminary objections, Judgment, ICJ, 2019.*

1042 'International Court of Justice. Application of the International Convention on the Elimination of All Forms of Racial Discrimination (Qatar v. United Arab Emirates). Application Instituting Proceedings, June 11, 2018' (n 937).

1043 ibid.

1044 ibid 32–44.

1045 ibid 10–20.

1046 ibid.

1047 ibid.

1048 *Application of the International Convention on the Elimination of All Forms of Racial Discrimination, Order, June 14, 2019* (n 940).

1049 'International Court of Justice. Application of the International Convention on the Elimination of All Forms of Racial Discrimination (Qatar v. United Arab Emirates). Order, May 2, 2019.'

1.6.3 Disputes in Which the International Covenant on Civil and Political Rights Was Invoked

In December 1998, the Republic of Guinea initiated a dispute against the Democratic Republic of the Congo concerning "serious violations of international law" alleged to have been committed "upon the person of a Guinean national."[1050] The respondent submitted preliminary objections. In its judgment on the preliminary objections, the court declared the application admissible "in so far as it concerns protection of Mr Diallo's rights as an individual" and "in so far as it concerns protection of [his] direct rights as associé in Africom-Zaire and Africontainers-Zaire."[1051]

On the merits, Guinea maintained that Mr Diallo was the victim of the arrest and detention measures in 1988–1989 and of the arrest, detention and expulsion measures in 1995–1996.[1052] The claims related to 1988–1989 arrest were deemed inadmissible.[1053] Regarding other claims, the court concluded that Mr Diallo had remained in continuous detention for 66 days[1054] and that he had been in detention before his expulsion between 25 and 31 January 1996.[1055]

The court concluded that the expulsion of Mr Diallo was not decided "in accordance with law"[1056] and therefore the disputed actions violated Article 13 of the ICCPR.[1057] The court further found that Mr Diallo's arrest and detention

1050 'International Court of Justice. Ahmadou Sadio Diallo (Republic of Guinea v. Democratic Republic of the Congo). Application Instituting Proceedings. December 28, 1998.'

1051 *Ahmadou Sadio Diallo (Republic of Guinea v. Democratic Republic of the Congo), Preliminary Objections, Judgment, ICJ Reports 2007, p 582.*

1052 *Ahmadou Sadio Diallo (Republic of Guinea v. Democratic Republic of the Congo), Merits, Judgment, ICJ Reports 2010, p 639* 652–659.

1053 ibid.

1054 ibid 662.

1055 ibid.

1056 The court interpreted the requirements of Article 13 as follows: "the expulsion of an alien lawfully in the territory of a State which is a party to these instruments can only be compatible with the international obligations of that State if it is decided in accordance with 'the law,' in other words, the domestic law applicable in that respect. Compliance with international law is to some extent dependent here on compliance with internal law. However, it is clear that while 'accordance with law' as thus defined is a necessary condition for compliance with the above-mentioned provisions, it is not the sufficient condition. First, the applicable domestic law must itself be compatible with the other requirements of the Covenant and the African Charter; second, an expulsion must not be arbitrary, since protection against arbitrary treatment lies at the heart of the rights guaranteed by the international norms protecting human rights, in particular, those set out in the two treaties applicable in this case." ibid 663.

1057 ibid 666.

were arbitrary within the meaning of Article 9, paragraph 1 of the ICCPR.[1058] Additionally, Mr Diallo's right to be "informed, at the time of arrest, of the reasons for his arrest" – a right guaranteed in all cases, irrespective of the grounds for the arrest, was breached.[1059] The court rejected other legal claims.[1060]

Another dispute in which the court asserted that there had been violations of the ICCPR was the dispute between the Democratic Republic of the Congo and Uganda.[1061] The dispute was triggered by the military occupation of the territory of the Democratic Republic of the Congo.[1062] In its judgement, the court made several significant findings with far-reaching implications. For example, the court declared that the state that occupies a territory belonging to another state is bound by international human rights law.[1063] The court went further and declared: "The Court, having concluded that Uganda was an occupying Power in Ituri at the relevant time, finds that Uganda's responsibility is engaged both for any acts of its military that violated its international obligations and for any lack of vigilance in preventing violations of human rights and international humanitarian law by other actors present in the occupied territory, including rebel groups acting on their own account."[1064]

The court concluded that Uganda had violated a number of human rights conventions, more specifically ICCPR Articles 6, paragraph 1, and 7; CRC Article 38, paragraphs 2 and 3, as well as Optional Protocol to the CRC Articles 1, 2, 3, paragraph 3, 4, 5 and 6.[1065] The court concluded that Uganda was under an obligation to make reparation for its internationally wrongful acts, including violations of international human rights law.[1066]

1058 ibid 669.

1059 ibid 670.

1060 ibid 682, 686 and 690–691.

1061 *Armed Activities on the Territory of the Congo (Democratic Republic of the Congo v. Uganda), Judgment* (n 417).

1062 ibid.

1063 "The Court thus concludes that Uganda was the occupying Power in Ituri at the relevant time. As such it was under an obligation, according to Article 43 of the Hague Regulations of 1907, to take all the measures in its power to restore, and ensure, as far as possible, public order and safety in the occupied area, while respecting, unless absolutely prevented, the laws in force in the DRC. This obligation comprised the duty to secure respect for the applicable rules of international human rights law and international humanitarian law, to protect the inhabitants of the occupied territory against acts of violence, and not to tolerate such violence by any third party." ibid 231.

1064 ibid.

1065 ibid 244.

1066 ibid 257.

1.6.4 Disputes in Which the Convention against Torture and Other Cruel, Inhuman or Degrading Treatment or Punishment Was Invoked

In 1999, the Democratic Republic of the Congo instituted proceedings against Burundi, Uganda and Rwanda before the ICJ, relying upon the CAT as one of the grounds for the court's jurisdiction.[1067] In 2001, proceedings against Burundi and Rwanda were discontinued at the applicant's request. The proceedings against Uganda continued, and the court found that Uganda had violated its international obligations, including flagrant violations of the ICCPR and CRC.[1068] This dispute and the court's conclusions were discussed earlier.

In May 2002, the Democratic Republic of the Congo filed an application instituting proceedings against Rwanda for "massive, serious and flagrant violations of human rights and international humanitarian law."[1069] The Democratic Republic of the Congo relied upon the numerous provisions of the human rights treaties to assert the court's jurisdiction, including the CAT.[1070] In its judgement, the court denied having jurisdiction.[1071]

In the dispute between Belgium and Senegal, the ICJ was faced with a request to interpret the ambit of the obligation *aut dedere aut judicare* (that is to say, "to prosecute or extradite") enshrined in Article 7 of the CAT.[1072] The dispute was initiated by Belgium in relation to Senegal's compliance with its obligation to prosecute Mr Hissène Habré, former president of the Republic of Chad, or to extradite him to Belgium for the purposes of criminal proceedings.[1073] The court confirmed its jurisdiction to entertain the dispute, as well as the admissibility of the legal claims.[1074] The subsequent discussion of the

1067 'International Court of Justice. Armed Activities on the Territory of the Congo (Democratic Republic of the Congo v. Burundi). Application Instituting Proceedings, June 23, 1999'; 'International Court of Justice, Armed Activities on the Territory of the Congo (Democratic Republic of the Congo v. Rwanda), Application Instituting Proceedings, June 23, 1999.'

1068 *Armed Activities on the Territory of the Congo (Democratic Republic of the Congo v. Uganda), Judgment* (n 417).

1069 *Armed Activities on the Territory of the Congo (New Application: 2002) (Democratic Republic of the Congo v. Rwanda), Jurisdiction and Admissibility, Judgment, ICJ Reports 2006, p 6.*

1070 ibid.

1071 ibid.

1072 *Questions relating to the Obligation to Prosecute or Extradite (Belgium v. Senegal), Judgment* (n 975).

1073 ibid 426–427.

1074 ibid.

merits focused on two pertinent provisions of the convention: Article 6, paragraph 2[1075] and Article 7, paragraph 1.[1076]

Concerning the obligation incumbent on states under Article 6, paragraph 2, the ICJ pronounced: "In the opinion of the Court, the preliminary inquiry provided for in Article 6, paragraph 2, is intended, like any inquiry carried out by the competent authorities, to corroborate or not the suspicions regarding the person in question. That inquiry is conducted by those authorities which have the task of drawing up a case file and collecting facts and evidence; this may consist of documents or witness statements relating to the events at issue and to the suspect's possible involvement in the matter concerned."[1077] After examining the factual circumstances in light of the foregoing statement, the court concluded that Senegal breached its obligation under Article 6, paragraph 2.[1078]

Regarding the obligation "to prosecute or extradite," the ICJ observed: "It follows that the choice between extradition or submission for prosecution, pursuant to the Convention, does not mean that the two alternatives are to be given the same weight. Extradition is an option offered to the State by the Convention, whereas prosecution is an international obligation under the Convention, the violation of which is a wrongful act engaging the responsibility of the State."[1079]

The court decided that Senegal had violated its international obligations under the convention and declared that Senegal was required to submit the case to competent Senegalese authorities for the purposes of prosecuting Mr Habré, if it decided not to extradite him.[1080]

1075 "Under the terms of Article 6, paragraph 2, of the Convention, the State in whose territory a person alleged to have committed acts of torture is present 'shall immediately make a preliminary inquiry into the facts.'" ibid 452.

1076 Article 7, paragraph 1, of the convention provides: "The State Party in the territory under whose jurisdiction a person alleged to have committed any offence referred to in Article 4 is found shall in the cases contemplated in Article 5, if it does not extradite him, submit the case to its competent authorities for the purpose of prosecution." ibid 454.

1077 ibid 453.

1078 ibid 454.

1079 ibid 456.

1080 *Questions relating to the Obligation to Prosecute or Extradite (Belgium v. Senegal), Judgment* (n 975).

1.6.5 Disputes in Which the Convention on the Rights of the Child Was Invoked

The court discussed the obligations under the convention in *Armed Activities on the Territory of the Congo*.[1081] The alleged violations of the convention occurred in the course of the military occupation of the parts of the Democratic Republic of the Congo by Uganda. The court confirmed that such an occupation had, in fact, occurred.[1082] The fact of the exercising power over the territory of another state, in the court's view, established a presumption for the occupying state to be bounded by international humanitarian law and human rights law.[1083]

With respect to the violations of the CRC, the court made the following observation: "The Court finds that there is convincing evidence of the training in UPDF training camps of child soldiers and of the UPDF's failure to prevent the recruitment of child soldiers in areas under its control. The Fifth Report of the Secretary-General on MONUC [...] refers to the confirmed 'cross-border deportation of recruited Congolese children from the Bunia, Beni and Butembo region to Uganda.' The Eleventh Report of the Secretary-General on MONUC [...] points out that the local UPDF authorities in and around Bunia in Ituri district 'have failed to prevent the fresh recruitment or re-recruitment of children' as child soldiers. MONUC's special report on the events in Ituri, January 2002 – December 2003 [...] refers to several incidents where Congolese children were transferred to UPDF training camps for military training."[1084] Thus, the court concluded that Uganda had violated the CRC Article 38, paragraphs 2 and 3, as well as Optional Protocol to the CRC Articles 1, 2, 3 paragraphs 3, 4, 5 and 6.[1085]

1.7 *The Deficiencies of Treaty-Based Enforcement Mechanisms*

Enforcement mechanisms in the field of human rights suffer from a number of deficiencies, which significantly impair the protection of guaranteed rights. It has already become obvious to scholars and practitioners that the effective protection of human rights requires not only the ratification of human rights conventions and their optional protocols, but also the implementation of commitments that have been undertaken. Indeed, research conducted by political scientists and international relations scholars demonstrates that, in itself, the ratification of human rights treaties improves human rights protection only marginally.

1081 *Armed Activities on the Territory of the Congo (Democratic Republic of the Congo v. Uganda), Judgment* (n 417).

1082 ibid.

1083 ibid.

1084 ibid 241.

1085 ibid 244.

In the last two decades, numerous attempts have been undertaken to explain the paradox that an increased number of human rights commitments[1086] does not translate into the improved compliance with human rights obligations. In order to explain this paradox, scholars have relied on statistical methods to explain the relationship between human rights treaties and the effective protection of human rights.

The outcomes of these analyses vary, with some being more optimistic than others. Early studies have demonstrated the lack of clear causal connection between the ratification of human rights treaties and enhanced respect for human rights.[1087] Some scholars suggest that the ratification of human rights treaties brings positive results only in countries with strong democratic traditions and an active civil society.[1088]

1086 According to Eric Posner "the number of human rights increased from 20 in 1975 to 100 in 1980, to 175 in 1990, to 300 today." Posner (n 913) 92.

1087 The article tests empirically whether becoming a party to the International Covenant on Civil and Political Rights and its optional protocol has an observable impact on a state's actual behaviour. The conclusion is that "perhaps it may be overly optimistic to expect that being a party to this international covenant will produce an observable impact." Linda Camp Keith, 'The United Nations International Covenant on Civil and Political Rights: Does It Make a Difference in Human Rights Behavior?' (1999) 36 Journal of Peace Research 95; Hathaway notes that "the analysis relies on a database encompassing the experiences of 166 nations over a nearly forty-year period in five areas of human rights law: genocide, torture, fair and public trials, civil liberties, and political representation of women." She concludes: "The results suggest that not only is treaty ratification not associated with better human rights practices than otherwise expected, but it is often associated with worse practices. Countries that ratify human rights treaties often appear less likely, rather than more likely, to conform to the requirements of the treaties than countries that do not ratify these treaties." In her view, on many occasions states are rewarded for ratifying human rights treaties, yet the weak enforcement mechanisms do not enhance respect for human rights. Oona A Hathaway, 'Do Human Rights Treaties Make a Difference?' (2002) 111 The Yale Law Journal 1935. The general conclusion is that "the legal regime has no effect or a negative effect on practice, but that global civil society has a positive impact on practice." Emilie M Hafner-Burton and Kiyoteru Tsutsui, 'Human Rights in a Globalizing World: The Paradox of Empty Promises' (2005) 110 The American Journal of Sociology 1373; In his article, Eric Neumayer provides a detailed summary of the theoretical expectations on the impact of ratification of the human rights treaties. His quantitative analysis confirmed that "We found only few cases in which treaty ratification has unconditional beneficial effects on human rights. In most cases, for treaty ratification to work, there must be conditions for domestic groups, parties, and individuals and for civil society to persuade, convince, and perhaps pressure governments into translating the formal promise of better human rights protection into actual reality." Eric Neumayer, 'Do International Human Rights Treaties Improve Respect for Human Rights?' (2005) 49 The Journal of Conflict Resolution 925.

1088 Emilie M Hafner-Burton and Kiyoteru Tsutsui, 'Justice Lost! The Failure of International Human Rights Law to Matter Where Needed Most' (2007) 44 Journal of Peace Research 407.

Subsequent research has found, to the contrary, that there exists a causal relationship between treaty ratification and improved respect for human rights.[1089] However, these effects are conditional and are observed either among democracies or only with respect to specific human rights. For instance, Daniel Hill reported the beneficial effect of the CEDAW on women's political rights. At the same time, Hill argues that the ratification of the CAT is associated with worse torture practices.[1090] Conversely, Christopher Fariss finds a positive relationship between the ratification of the CAT and enhanced respect for human rights.[1091]

Not everyone shares this optimistic view on compliance with international human rights treaties. Emilie Hafner-Burton and Kiyoteru Tsutsui argue that the primary targets of the international human rights regime were repressive, autocratic states and that the research on the positive impact of treaties explicitly acknowledges that human rights treaties are incapable of constraining such states.[1092] Eric Posner and Adam Chilton suggest that improved compliance with human rights treaties can be caused by observable, long-term historical trends and claim that the causal relationship between treaty ratification and enhanced respect for human rights is not as strong as is argued.[1093]

1089 Beth Simmons has also provided examples of compliance with human rights treaties that improved respect for human rights. Beth A Simmons, *Mobilizing for Human Rights: International Law in Domestic Politics* (Cambridge University Press 2009).

1090 "I examine human rights behaviour in the context of three of the core UN human rights treaties: the International Covenant on Civil and Political Rights (ICCPR), the Convention against Torture and other Cruel, Inhuman or Degrading Treatment or Punishment (CAT), and the Convention on the Elimination of All Forms of Discrimination against Women (CEDAW). The analysis is conducted using pooled time-series data on 165 states from 1976 to 2006." Daniel Hill concludes that "while the CEDAW shows promise for improving state behaviour the CAT and, to a lesser extent, the ICCPR seem to actually be associated with worse practices." Daniel W Hill, 'Estimating the Effects of Human Rights Treaties on State Behavior' (2010) 72 The Journal of Politics 1161.

1091 Christopher J Fariss, 'Respect for Human Rights Has Improved Over Time: Modeling the Changing Standard of Accountability' (2014) 108 The American Political Science Review 297.

1092 "The optimism, however, is narrow in scope, as current scholarship implies that human rights laws matter least among governments that were the primary targets of the legal regime – terribly repressive, autocratic states without internal advocates for reform." Hafner-Burton and Tsutsui (n 1088) 408.

1093 The effectiveness of two human rights treaties the Convention on the Elimination of Discrimination Against Women and the Convention Against Torture was evaluated. Adam S Chilton and Eric A Posner, 'Respect for Human Rights: Law and History' (2016) SSRN Electronic Journal <https://www.ssrn.com/abstract=2815272>.

The overall conclusion is that the ratification of human rights treaties does not guarantee inevitable improvements in human rights protection. Furthermore, as becomes clear, the enforcement mechanisms prescribed by the core human rights treaties are not conducive to better compliance. While this hypothesis appears rather tragic, it gives new impetus to the human rights debate.

Below I analyse the shortcomings of the enforcement mechanisms established by the core human rights conventions.

1.7.1 Reporting Obligation

Walter Kälin and Jörg Künzli describe the state reporting obligation as: "the weakest monitoring instrument."[1094] Indeed, states parties to the international human rights treaties frequently neglect their reporting obligations or submit their reports with significant delays. Notably, this tendency is observed predominantly among developing states and emerging economies. – i.e. precisely the states in which these treaties aim to implement international human rights standards.

The analysis of the most recent reports prepared by the various committees buttresses this conclusion. More specifically, the Committee against Torture reported that "there were 26 States parties with overdue initial reports and 39 States parties with overdue periodic reports."[1095] By the same token, the Committee on the Elimination of Racial Discrimination incorporated into its recent report a three-page list of state parties whose reports are overdue by at least five years.[1096] What is remarkable is that several parties delayed their reports for decades: Sierra Leone has done so since 1976, Liberia since 1977, the Gambia since 1982, the Central African Republic since 1986 and Hungary since 2004.[1097]

The Human Rights Committee's 2018 report voiced a deep concern in this regard: "The Committee draws particular attention to the fact that 16 initial reports are overdue, of which 7 are overdue by between 5 and 10 years and 8 are overdue by 10 years or more. The result is the frustration of a crucial objective

1094 Walter Kälin and Jörg Künzli, *The Law of International Human Rights Protection* (1st publ., Oxford University Press 2009) 211.

1095 UN Committee against Torture, 'Report of the Committee against Torture. UN Doc A/73/44' (2018) General Assembly Official Records Seventy-third Session Supplement No. 44 5.

1096 UN Committee on the Elimination of Racial Discrimination, 'Report of the Committee on the Elimination of Racial Discrimination, UN Doc A/73/18' (2018) General Assembly Official Records Seventy-third Session Supplement No. 18.

1097 ibid 18–20.

of the Covenant, namely, to enable the Committee to monitor compliance by States parties with their obligations under the Covenant on the basis of periodic reports. The Committee addresses reminders at regular intervals to all those States parties whose reports are significantly overdue."[1098]

The competence of the specialised committees to enforce reporting obligations is constrained. For example, the Committee against Torture sends reminders to the states, whose reports are overdue by four or more years.[1099] Additionally, the committee decided that if Cabo Verde and Seychelles did not submit their respective reports, which have been overdue since 1993, the committee would examine the measures undertaken to implement the convention in the absence of these reports.[1100] In this vein, the Committee on Enforced Disappearances announced its decision to examine compliance with the obligations in the absence of a report, when the latter is more than five years overdue.[1101]

The Committee on Economic, Social and Cultural Rights has adopted a special procedure in response to non-reporting state parties and long overdue reports and devoted one of its sessions to discussing the matter.[1102] Regarding non-reporting states, the committee receives information from international and national non-governmental organisations on the status of the implementation of economic, social and cultural rights.[1103]

The final outcome of state reporting is the preparation and adoption of legally non-binding recommendations (concluding observations). In order to assess the effectiveness of such concluding observations, Jasper Krommendijk examined the implementation of the recommendations of the UN human rights treaty bodies in the Netherlands, New Zealand and Finland.[1104] Krommendijk concludes: "The large majority of COs [concluding observations] has largely remained ineffective in the Netherlands, New Zealand and

---

1098 UN Human Rights Committee, 'Report of the Human Rights Committee, UN Doc A/73/40' (2018) General Assembly Official Records Seventy-third Session Supplement No. 40 10.

1099 UN Committee against Torture (n 1095) 6.

1100 ibid.

1101 UN Committee on Enforced Disappearances, 'Report of the Committee on Enforced Disappearances, UN Doc A/73/56' (2018) General Assembly Official Records Seventy-third Session Supplement No. 56 12.

1102 UN Committee on Economic, Social and Cultural Rights, 'Committee on Economic, Social and Cultural Rights, UN Doc E/2018/22, E/C.12/2017/3' (2018) Economic and Social Council Official Records Supplement No. 2 8.

1103 ibid 9.

1104 Jasper Krommendijk, 'The (In)Effectiveness of UN Human Rights Treaty Body Recommendations' (2015) 33 Netherlands Quarterly of Human Rights 194.

Finland. COs have either been rejected by governments or they have been so vague and broad that they simply did not elicit any follow-up measures. This general propensity for COs to remain ineffective stems from and is exacerbated by the limited overall legitimacy of the treaty bodies, the reporting process and the constructive dialogue in the eyes of government officials."[1105]

1.7.2 Mechanisms of Interstate and Individual Complaints

First and foremost, states parties to the core international human rights conventions do not rely frequently upon the interstate complaints mechanisms. We can illustrate this trend with the following example. The ICERD entered into force in 1969 and prescribes an interstate complaints mechanism. The first two complaints under this mechanism were the communications from Qatar against Saudi Arabia and the UAE submitted in March 2018.[1106] These communications were followed by Palestine's communication against Israel.[1107] More importantly, the Committee on the Elimination of Racial Discrimination has pointed out the following: "It is the first time that a human rights treaty body receives an inter-state communication."[1108]

Second, the prescribed mechanisms for addressing interstate complaints suffer from a severe defect, namely a lack of effective remedies. If there is a disagreement between the parties, the role of a specialised committee is significantly constrained. As a rule, a committee prepares a communication on the matter and informs the parties concerned about its findings.[1109] Suffice it to say that this mechanism has proved to be ineffective.[1110]

The ineffectiveness of mechanisms of interstate complaints has had far-reaching implications. It paved the way for a new avenue for recourse, namely individual complaints mechanisms. Notwithstanding the existing procedural hurdles,[1111] the individual complaints procedure has been frequently

1105 ibid 221.

1106 Qatar (n 938); Qatar, 'An Inter-State Communication against the Kingdom of Saudi Arabia' <https://www.ohchr.org/EN/NewsEvents/Pages/DisplayNews.aspx?NewsID=23566&LangID=E>.

1107 'CERD Information Note on Inter-State Communications' <https://www.ohchr.org/EN/NewsEvents/Pages/DisplayNews.aspx?NewsID=23566&LangID=E>.

1108 ibid.

1109 For more details, see Table 4.

1110 "A fourth modality is that of dealing with inter-state complaints. This has remained a dead letter." John Morijn, 'Reforming United Nations Human Rights Treaty Monitoring Reform' (2011) 58 Netherlands International Law Review 295, 302.

1111 By procedural hurdles, I mean that the majority of the core human rights treaties allow recourse to this procedure only if the state party concerned accepted the competence of the relevant committee. The other prerequisites include exhaustion of national remedies

relied upon, a development that has caused delays in examining individual communications.[1112]

The recent study has identified the following shortcomings of the individual complaints procedure: states parties to human rights conventions are hesitant to recognise the competence of the committees to review communications from individuals,[1113] the number of received communications is small compared to the number of cases received by regional human rights courts[1114] and the implementation rate of treaty body decisions and recommendations is very low.[1115]

1.7.3 Inquiry Procedure

The inquiry procedure entitles a committee to investigate systemic and grave violations of guaranteed rights. However, this subsidiary competence of the specialised committees ought to be taken with a grain of salt. More specifically, the committees cannot proceed with their inquiries without the consent of a concerned state party. Furthermore, even if a committee receives such consent and is able to conduct an independent investigation into the matter, it is not authorised to impose any form of obligation on a non-compliant state. The outcome of such an investigation is to bring the matter to the attention of a state party and request that party to provide further explanation.

1.7.4 Dispute Settlement and the Practice of the International Court of Justice

Our analysis has revealed that only a small number of disputes before the ICJ pertain to violations of international human rights conventions. Furthermore, some disputes are politically motivated. This outcome can be explained by the fact that such proceedings are time-consuming and require substantial

---

and lis pendens rule (the precondition that the same matter cannot be examined under another procedure of international investigation or settlement).

1112 "Furthermore, the backlog and delays in the examination of individual communications became visible as more and more States recognized the competence of the committees to consider communications." Aslan Abashidze and Aleksandra Koneva, 'The Process of Strengthening the Human Rights Treaty Body System: The Road towards Effectiveness or Inefficiency?' (2019) 66 Netherlands International Law Review 357, 362.

1113 Claire Callejón, Kamelia Kemileva and Felix Kirchmeier, *Treaty Bodies' Individual Communication Procedures: Providing Redress and Reparation to Victims of Human Rights Violations* (2019) Académie de droit international humanitaire et de droits humains à Genève 9.

1114 ibid.

1115 Various studies have demonstrated that the implementation rate ranges from 22% to 42% depending on the committee. ibid 39.

financial investments. In addition, a decision to initiate a dispute before the ICJ is a move that demands political will.

Another distinctive feature of these disputes is that the vast majority of them represent instances of diplomatic protection – in other words, states protect their citizens. Remarkably, the only dispute that has ever been initiated against a state that violated the human rights of its own citizens is the dispute recently lodged by the Gambia against Myanmar.

2 Enforcement of Human Rights That Have Acquired a Special Status

2.1 *Jus Cogens*

The concept of jus cogens was recognised in positive international law through Article 53 of the VCLT.[1116] According to the ILC, the most frequently cited candidates for the status of jus cogens include: (a) the prohibition of aggressive use of force; (b) the right to self-defence; (c) the prohibition of genocide; (d) the prohibition of torture; (e) crimes against humanity; (f) the prohibition of slavery and slave trade; (g) the prohibition of piracy; (h) the prohibition of racial discrimination and apartheid; and (i) the prohibition of hostilities directed at the civilian population ("basic rules of international humanitarian law").[1117] In 2019, the Drafting Committee of the ILC provisionally adopted draft conclusions on the topic peremptory norms of general international law (jus cogens).[1118] The annex to the draft conclusions lays out a non-exhaustive list of jus cogens norms.[1119] This list is almost identical to the abovementioned examples of jus cogens, although the prohibition of piracy is not included, while the right to self-defence is replaced by the right to self-determination.[1120]

1116 Article 53 reads as follows: "A treaty is void if, at the time of its conclusion, it conflicts with a peremptory norm of general international law. For the purposes of the present Convention, a peremptory norm of general international law is a norm accepted and recognized by the international community of States as a whole as a norm from which no derogation is permitted and which can be modified only by a subsequent norm of general international law having the same character." Vienna Convention on the Law of Treaties (adopted 23 May 1969, entered into force 27 January 1980) 1155 UNTS 331.

1117 Martti Koskenniemi, 'Fragmentation of International Law: Difficulties Arising from the Diversification and Expansion of International Law: Report of the Study Group of the International Law Commission.' (2006) para 374.

1118 ILC, 'Peremptory Norms of General International Law (Jus Cogens). Text of the Draft Conclusions and Draft Annex Provisionally Adopted by the Drafting Committee on First Reading. UN Doc A/CN.4/L.936' (2019). (ILC, 'Peremptory Norms of General International Law (Jus Cogens)').

1119 ibid.

1120 ibid.

While there is much to quibble about when it comes to jus cogens, one cannot help noticing an intrinsic relationship between jus cogens and human rights.[1121] It appears that the overwhelming majority of the jus cogens norms enumerated above are tantamount to recognised human rights. Furthermore, the protection of these human rights is guaranteed under the various human rights treaties.[1122] Thus, these norms can benefit from the protection guaranteed under the special treaty regime, as well as from the protection guaranteed by their special status as jus cogens.[1123] Notwithstanding their universal recognition in theory, enforcement of jus cogens norms faces a number of difficulties, which are discussed below.

2.1.1 Definitional Ambiguity

To begin with, the definition of what norms constitute jus cogens evades precise formulation. The negotiating history of the VCLT suggests that the drafters deliberately preserved this ambiguity. The ILC contended that "the prudent course seems to be to … leave the full content of this rule to be worked out in State practice and in the jurisprudence of international tribunals."[1124]

While the exact contours of jus cogens have not been determined, the scope of the concept was debated at length within the international community.[1125] Despite this, the concept remains obscure. As Thomas Cottier accurately points out: "The scope and boundaries of jus cogens, however, remain controversial and contested in a decentralized legal order, in particular in relation to core labour standards and humanitarian law."[1126] As a result, many human rights are heralded as jus cogens, and in some cases these claims are not well founded.[1127]

1121 Andrea Bianchi accurately points out: "There is an almost intrinsic relationship between peremptory norms and human rights." Andrea Bianchi, 'Human Rights and the Magic of Jus Cogens' (2008) 19 European Journal of International Law 491, 491.

1122 For example, the prohibition of genocide and the prohibition of torture.

1123 In this regard, some scholars, such as Dinah Shelton, contend that the norms that are embedded in a treaty or gained a status of international customary law are not likely to benefit much from being recognised as jus cogens. Dinah Shelton, 'Normative Hierarchy in International Law' (2006) 100 The American Journal of International Law 291.

1124 Special Rapporteur Sir Humphrey Waldock, 'Second Report on the Law of Treaties, Doc A/CN.4/156 and Add.1-3' (Yearbook of the International Law Commission, Volume II 1963) 53.

1125 Karl Zemanek, 'The Metamorphosis of Jus Cogens: From an Institution of Treaty Law to the Bedrock of the International Legal Order?' in Enzo Cannizzaro (ed), *The Law of Treaties Beyond the Vienna Convention* (Oxford University Press 2011).

1126 Thomas Cottier, 'Improving Compliance: Jus Cogens and International Economic Law' in den Maarten Heijer and Harmen van der Wilt (eds.), *Netherlands Yearbook of International Law 2015: Jus Cogens: Quo Vadis?* (TMC Asser Press 2016).

1127 Dinah Shelton provides an extensive list of examples of jus cogens norms, which range from all humanitarian norms to the right to development and even free trade. Shelton (n 1123) 303. For more, see Bianchi (n 1121).

Further complicating matters, the theoretical underpinnings of jus cogens are not clearly defined. Legal scholars have extensively debated what theory should form a theoretical foundation of jus cogens.[1128] The debate has focused on the discussion of three justificatory theories: natural law, public order theory and customary international law.[1129] Each of these theories defines the content of the concept differently.[1130] Yet despite having been extensively developed by scholars, none of these theories "provides a self-evidently coherent account for jus cogens status or the process for determining whether or not a norm has the status."[1131] Writing on the subject in 2015, Matthew Saul concluded: "it is apparent that after over forty years of scholarly and judicial attention, the source and method question for jus cogens identification has hardly progressed."[1132]

In 2015, the ILC included the discussion of the peremptory norms of general international law (jus cogens) in its programme of work. The draft conclusions provisionally adopted by the Drafting Committee in 2019 suggest that: "Customary international law is the most common basis for peremptory norms of general international law (jus cogens)."[1133] Furthermore, the criteria for the identification of a peremptory norm of general international law (jus cogens) were put forward.[1134] Hopefully, the subsequent work of the ILC will provide a roadmap through the thicket that has grown up around this area.

Notably, the ICJ has only infrequently resorted to the concept of jus cogens. In this regard, Karl Zemanek observes that the ICJ "has over decades only vaguely hinted at the possible existence of peremptory norms in international law."[1135] Instead, the court established two other concepts of uncertain scope and character: "intransgressible principles of international customary law" and "obligations *erga omnes*."[1136] Only in 2006 did the ICJ issue a reassurance that the prohibition of genocide is a peremptory norm of general international law.[1137] However, the court did not offer any criterion that would apply to the

---

1128 Zemanek (n 1125) 381–411.

1129 Zemanek (n 1125); Matthew Saul, 'Identifying Jus Cogens Norms: The Interaction of Scholars and International Judges' (2015) 5 Asian Journal of International Law 26.

1130 Shelton (n 1123) 303.

1131 Saul (n 1129) 31.

1132 ibid 33.

1133 ILC, 'Peremptory Norms of General International Law (Jus Cogens)' (n 1118).

1134 ibid.

1135 Zemanek (n 1125) 387.

1136 Andreas Paulus, 'Jus Cogens in a Time of Hegemony and Fragmentation – An Attempt at a Re-Appraisal' (2005) 74 Nordic Journal of International Law 297.

1137 *Armed Activities on the Territory of the Congo (New Application: 2002) (Democratic Republic of the Congo v. Rwanda), Jurisdiction and Admissibility, Judgment* (n 1069).

identification of other peremptory norms.[1138] In the subsequent dispute, the court pronounced: "There is no doubt, moreover, that the prohibition of inhuman and degrading treatment is among the rules of general international law which are binding on States in all circumstances, even apart from any treaty commitments."[1139]

2.1.2 Normative Implications of Jus Cogens

The second difficulty that impairs the enforcement of jus cogens is the scope of its normative implications outside of the law of treaties.[1140] In this regard, Jutta Brunnée notes: "aside from the fact that peremptory norms are non-derogable, the legal effects that flow from the jus cogens status of a norm are far from settled."[1141] Dinah Shelton has analysed the practice of the ICJ and other international tribunals only to buttress the foregoing conclusion.[1142]

In order to illustrate this deficiency, I will examine whether norms of jus cogens could be invoked as a basis for the ICJ jurisdiction and whether such norms could establish an exception to state immunity and to the immunity of high-ranking government officials.

2.1.2.1 *Norms of Jus Cogens and the Jurisdiction of the International Court of Justice*

In several disputes, the court has asserted that the mere fact that the jus cogens norm may be at issue in a dispute could not in itself provide a basis for the

1138 Shelton (n 1123) 306.

1139 *Ahmadou Sadio Diallo (Republic of Guinea v. Democratic Republic of the Congo), Merits, Judgment* (n 1052) 671.

1140 Jure Vidmar provides an excellent analysis of the instances when some treaty obligations, including an obligation to implement the decisions of the United Nations Security Council, might potentially violate the jus cogens norms. Vidmar further examines whether such treaties can be recognised as void or whether some other conflict-resolution techniques might be used. His analysis demonstrates that the role of jus cogens might be questioned even in its main domain, which is treaty law. Jure Vidmar, 'Rethinking Jus Cogens After Germany v. Italy: Back to Article 53?' (2013) 60 Netherlands International Law Review 1.

1141 Jutta Brunnée, 'The Prohibition on Torture: Driving Jus Cogens Home?' (2010) 104 Proceedings of the ASIL Annual Meeting 454.

1142 "In any event, the Court was unwilling in any of the cases to recognize specific consequences from the invocation of a peremptory norm. Other international and national courts have shown similar hesitancy." Later in the article, Shelton provides two examples in which the courts were willing to admit that jus cogens norms carry some normative implications. Shelton (n 1123) 309.

court's jurisdiction,[1143] emphasising that "the fact that a dispute relates to compliance with a norm having such a character, which is assuredly the case with regard to the prohibition of genocide, cannot of itself provide a basis for the jurisdiction of the Court to entertain that dispute. Under the Court's Statute, that jurisdiction is always based on the consent of the parties."[1144]

On another occasion, discussing the court's jurisdiction under the Genocide Convention, the court concluded: "Article IX does not afford a basis on which the Court can exercise jurisdiction over a dispute concerning an alleged violation of the customary international law obligations regarding genocide."[1145] Furthermore, in discussing the ambit of jurisdiction granted under Article IX of the Genocide Convention, it observed: "It [the court] has no power to rule on alleged breaches of other obligations under international law, not amounting to genocide, particularly those protecting human rights in armed conflict. That is so even if the alleged breaches are of obligations under peremptory norms, or of obligations which protect essential humanitarian values, and which may be owed erga omnes."[1146]

A similar fate has befallen the prohibition of racial discrimination. In the dispute between Georgia and the Russian Federation, the court observed at the stage of preliminary objections that Article 22 of the ICERD authorises it to decide disputes about racial discrimination only after the involved parties had ratified the relevant convention.[1147] Thus, the court was deprived of the

---

1143 *Armed Activities on the Territory of the Congo (New Application: 2002) (Democratic Republic of the Congo v. Rwanda), Jurisdiction and Admissibility, Judgment* (n 1069); Another observation on the court's jurisdiction: "Furthermore, since Article IX provides for jurisdiction only with regard to 'the interpretation, application or fulfilment of the Convention, including … the responsibility of a State for genocide or for any of the other acts enumerated in Article III,' the jurisdiction of the Court does not extend to allegations of violation of the customary international law on genocide. It is, of course, well established that the Convention enshrines principles that also form part of customary international law. Article I provides that '[t]he Contracting Parties confirm that genocide, whether committed in time of peace or in time of war, is a crime under international law.' The Court has also repeatedly stated that the Convention embodies principles that are part of customary international law." *Application of the Convention on the Prevention and Punishment of the Crime of Genocide (Croatia v. Serbia), Judgment* (n 926).

1144 *Armed Activities on the Territory of the Congo (New Application: 2002) (Democratic Republic of the Congo v. Rwanda), Jurisdiction and Admissibility, Judgment* (n 1069) 32.

1145 *Application of the Convention on the Prevention and Punishment of the Crime of Genocide (Croatia v. Serbia), Judgment* (n 926) 48.

1146 *Application of the Convention on the Prevention and Punishment of the Crime of Genocide (Bosnia and Herzegovina v. Serbia and Montenegro), Judgment* (n 926) 104.

1147 *Application of the International Convention on the Elimination of All Forms of Racial Discrimination (Georgia v. Russian Federation), Preliminary Objections, Judgment* (n 1025).

jurisdiction necessary to adjudicate the incidents of racial discrimination that occurred before the concerned party ratified the convention.[1148]

2.1.2.2 *Norms of Jus Cogens and State Immunity*

In the early 2000s, several national courts were confronted with a need to adjudicate whether violations of jus cogens override state immunity accorded under international law. Any solution to this conundrum would have had far-reaching implications. As one could reasonably expect, court practice was inconsistent. For example, Italian and Greek courts favoured the view that crimes committed during World War II could not benefit from the protection guaranteed by the principle of sovereign immunity.[1149] By contrast, Canadian and British courts supported the opposite view.[1150]

In *Jurisdictional Immunities of the State*, the ICJ ruled that the peremptory norms cannot automatically displace state immunity entitlements.[1151] In essence, the court's decision is based on the "substantive-procedural" distinction, implying that jus cogens norms are substantive and customary law of state immunity is procedural in nature.[1152]

1148 "It follows from this general finding of the Court and the specific findings made in earlier paragraphs that Georgia has not, in the Court's opinion, cited any document or statement made before it became a party to CERD in July 1999 which provides support for its contention that 'the dispute with Russia over ethnic cleansing is long-standing and legitimate and not of recent invention' (paragraph 34 above). The Court adds that even if this were the case, such dispute, though about racial discrimination, could not have been a dispute with respect to the interpretation or application of CERD, the only kind of dispute in respect of which the Court is given jurisdiction by Article 22 of that Convention." ibid 100.

1149 *Prefecture of Voiotia v. Federal Republic of Germany Case No 11/2000* (Areios Pagos (Hellenic Supreme Court)); *Ferrini v. Federal Republic of Germany, judgment No 5044/2044* [2003] 87 Riv Dirit Internazionale 539 (Italian Supreme Court (Corte di Cassazione)).

1150 *Bouzari v. Islamic Republic of Iran, OJ No 2800* [2004] Ontario Court of Appeal Toronto, Ontario Docket No. C38295; *Jones v. Ministry of the Interior of the Kingdom of Saudi Arabia* (EWCA Civ 1394).

1151 *Jurisdictional Immunities of the State (Germany v. Italy: Greece intervening), Judgment* (n 786). This decision was preceded by the decision in another controversial dispute, in which the court ruled that the immunity of the government officials under customary international law shall be respected even when these officials are charged with the grave violations of international humanitarian law. *Arrest Warrant of 11 April 2000 (Democratic Republic of the Congo v. Belgium), Judgment* (n 804).

1152 *Jurisdictional Immunities of the State (Germany v. Italy: Greece intervening), Judgment* (n 786) 140–142.

The literature abounds in claims that this is not a tenable intellectual position.[1153] By contrast, some scholars argue that the "substantive-procedural" distinction is well established in international law.[1154]

2.1.2.3 *Norms of Jus Cogens and the Immunity of High-Ranking Government Officials*

Despite the special status of jus cogens, national and international adjudicators have shown little sympathy for the argument that the peremptory norms grant an exception to the immunities guaranteed under international law.[1155] After a thorough examination of the pertinent court practice, Andrea Bianchi draws the following conclusion: "the difficulty of relying on the inderogable character of peremptory norms to sweep away lower ranking rules of international law has turned into an overall failure, where the primacy of jus cogens risks being identified with a rhetorical tool of dubious utility and little practical impact."[1156]

Erika De Wet contends that the main shortcoming of the concept of jus cogens is its narrowly defined normative implications.[1157] De Wet illustrates this shortcoming with reference to the conflict that exists between a torture victim's right to trial and the obligation under customary international law to provide immunity to foreign states and their officials.[1158] De Wet reaches the following conclusion: "Closer scrutiny reveals that there is no direct conflict between the law of immunity and *jus cogens*, as the normative scope of the peremptory obligation only encompasses the prohibition of torture as such (a negative obligation not to engage in torture). It does not yet encompass an ancillary obligation to deny immunity. Put another way, access to court is not seen as a peremptory norm."[1159]

It is also useful to mention ICJ practice in interpreting and applying the international customary law of immunity. In *Arrest Warrant of 11 April 2000*, the

---

1153 In the introduction to his article, Stefan Talmon provides numerous examples of such claims. Stefan Talmon, 'Jus Cogens after Germany v. Italy: Substantive and Procedural Rules Distinguished' (2012) 25 Leiden Journal of International Law 979.

1154 ibid.

1155 For a review of the relevant court practice, see Daniel Costelloe, *Legal Consequences of Peremptory Norms in International Law* (Cambridge University Press 2017); Bianchi (n 1121); Talmon (n 1153).

1156 Bianchi (n 1121) 501.

1157 Erika de Wet, 'Jus Cogens and Obligations Erga Omnes' in Dinah Shelton (ed), *The Oxford Handbook of International Human Rights Law* (2013).

1158 ibid.

1159 ibid 549.

ICJ confirmed that senior government officials enjoy immunity under international law for their time in office, even if they are charged with serious violations of human rights.[1160]

2.2 *Obligations Erga Omnes*

The concept of obligations erga omnes came into being in the ICJ judgement in *Barcelona Traction*.[1161] Maurizio Ragazzi traces the history of the concept back to the earlier writings of the two ICJ judges, who were members of the court at that time – Manfred Lachs and Philip Jessup.[1162] Ragazzi also notes that the contributions of the other scholars nourished the concept as well.[1163]

Christian Tams observes that the ICJ took the concept of obligations erga omnes out of its original context and altered the meaning given to it by international law scholars.[1164] Furthermore, Tams argues that the court did not succeed in developing a fully articulated concept, and as a result it is still hidden by the veil of obscurity.[1165] An analysis of the court's practice buttresses this conclusion: "the term 'erga omnes' has become a legal vademecum prescribed to produce a wide array of legal effects."[1166] We proceed with the discussion of the problems related to the enforcement of obligations erga omnes.

2.2.1 Definitional Ambiguity

The definition of obligations erga omnes has been extensively debated. To simplify a lengthy discussion, we can quote Maurizio Ragazzi: "there is a tendency, in the international literature, to dilute the examination of obligations erga omnes by referring to other concepts and, when specifically discussing obligations erga omnes, to concentrate on their corresponding rights and remedies.

1160 *Arrest Warrant of 11 April 2000 (Democratic Republic of the Congo v. Belgium), Judgment* (n 804).

1161 *Barcelona Traction, Light and Power Company, Limited, Judgment, ICJ Reports 1970, p 3.*

1162 Maurizio Ragazzi, *The Concept of International Obligations Erga Omnes* (Clarendon Press 1997) 7–9.

1163 ibid.

1164 "Traditionally, those claiming that treaty obligations qualified as obligations erga omnes intended to broaden the circle of States bound by the rule. Recognition of erga omnes effects thus modified the scope (ratione personae) of a primary rule of international law. Of course, this traditional erga omnes effect could eventually affect the secondary rules governing responses to breaches." Tams (n 505) 105–106.

1165 "However, by taking a well-established concept out of its traditional context and by failing to set out the reasons for doing so, the Court significantly increased the risk of terminological confusion." ibid 106.

1166 ibid 115.

As a result of this attitude, almost thirty years after the International Court's dictum in the Barcelona Tractions case the very concept of obligations erga omnes still lacks a precise definition."[1167] This conclusion was drawn more than two decades ago, yet it is still relevant.

Further complicating matters, the very passage of the ICJ judgement from which the lofty concept of erga omnes emerged sows the seeds of misunderstanding. More specifically, the examples of the obligations erga omnes provided by the ICJ – the prohibition of aggression, genocide, slavery and racial discrimination – fall squarely within the norms of jus cogens. While the exact contours of the overlap have not been determined by the ICJ, the distinguishing traits of both concepts have been moulded by international lawyers. Ragazzi contends that the starting point for comparing the two concepts is the following: "when referring to jus cogens, one invariably refers to norms, whereas, when referring to erga omnes, one invariably refers to obligations."[1168] However, Ragazzi has carefully eschewed any further comparison, concluding: "One can compare entities or concepts belonging to the same category, such as a rule with another rule or an obligation with another obligation, but not a rule with an obligation."[1169] Discussing the relationship between obligations erga omnes and jus cogens, Christian Tams observes: "views expressed range from mere overlap, to partial identity (all peremptory norms imposing obligations erga omnes), or complete identity."[1170] Michael Byers argues that "jus cogens rules necessarily apply erga omnes,"[1171] yet the erga omnes rules are not necessarily jus cogens.[1172] Erika de Wet, for her part, echoes the view expressed by Byers.[1173]

The draft conclusions provisionally adopted by the Drafting Committee of the ILC contain the following stipulation: "Peremptory norms of general international law (jus cogens) give rise to obligations owed to the international community as a whole (obligations erga omnes), in which all States have a legal interest."[1174]

The pertinent court practice provides a number of examples of international obligations which, in the ICJ's view, constitute obligations erga omnes. Among

1167 Ragazzi (n 1162) 15–16.

1168 ibid 190.

1169 ibid 193.

1170 Tams (n 505) 146.

1171 Michael Byers, 'Conceptualising the Relationship between Jus Cogens and Erga Omnes Rules' (1997) 66 Nordic Journal of International Law 211, 236.

1172 ibid 237.

1173 de Wet (n 1157) 555.

1174 ILC, 'Peremptory Norms of General International Law (Jus Cogens)' (n 1118).

these examples are the right to self-determination,[1175] the rights and obligations enshrined in the genocide convention[1176] and the rules of humanitarian law applicable in armed conflict.[1177] Nonetheless, court practice does not shed much light on the definitional ambiguity or on the distinction between obligations erga omnes and jus cogens.

2.2.2 The Normative Implications Attributable to the Concept of Obligations Erga Omnes

The theoretical debates on the normative implications of the concept frequently include a discussion of a right of standing to institute ICJ proceedings.[1178] It appears that the two opposing views dominate the debate.[1179] Despite the apparent value of this theoretical debate, the obvious stumbling block for erga omnes enforcement are the rules governing the court's jurisdiction. The court's practice is conclusive in this regard: the mere fact that obligations erga omnes may be at issue in a dispute would not give the court jurisdiction to entertain the dispute.[1180]

The right to take countermeasures is another avenue of recourse if a state violates obligations erga omnes. The Draft articles paved the way for the argument that a non-injured state is entitled to invoke state responsibility if obligations erga omnes are violated.[1181] Yet, the ILC was reluctant to depart from

---

1175 *East Timor (Portugal v. Australia), Judgment, ICJ Reports 1995, p 90* 102; *Legal Consequences of the Construction of a Wall in the Occupied Palestinian Territory, Advisory Opinion, ICJ Reports 2004, p 136* 199.

1176 *Application of the Convention on the Prevention and Punishment of the Crime of Genocide, Preliminary Objections, Judgment* (n 1006) 616.

1177 *Legal Consequences of the Construction of a Wall in the Occupied Palestinian Territory, Advisory Opinion* (n 1175) 199.

1178 Michael Byers asserts: "Generality of standing, rather than non-derogable character, is the essence of erga omnes rules." Byers (n 1171) 230.

1179 Tams (n 505) 158–197.

1180 "However, the Court considers that the erga omnes character of a norm and the rule of consent to jurisdiction are two different things. Whatever the nature of the obligations invoked, the Court could not rule on the lawfulness of the conduct of a State when its judgment would imply an evaluation of the lawfulness of the conduct of another State which is not a party to the case. Where this is so, the Court cannot act, even if the right in question is a right erga omnes." *East Timor (Portugal v. Australia), Judgment* (n 1175) 102. In this vein, "the mere fact that rights and obligations erga omnes may be at issue in a dispute would not give the court jurisdiction to entertain the dispute." *Armed Activities on the Territory of the Congo (New Application: 2002) (Democratic Republic of the Congo v. Rwanda), Jurisdiction and Admissibility, Judgment* (n 1069) [64].

1181 According to Article 48 of the Draft Articles, a non-injured state can invoke the responsibility of another state if "the obligation breached is owed to the international community as a whole." ILC, 'Draft Articles' (n 90).

the traditional tenets of international law, and thus the right of non-injured states to rely upon the countermeasures was recognised in an unduly cautious manner.[1182] It appears, though, that this unfortunate outcome sparked interest in the subject on the part of international legal scholars. A number of scholars contributed to the debate by demonstrating that the non-injured states habitually impose third-party countermeasures.[1183]

In view of the foregoing, the normative implications of the concept of obligations erga omnes are not well defined.

3 The Role of the Human Rights Council in the International Protection of Human Rights

The Human Rights Council was created by the General Assembly in 2006 to replace the former United Nations Commission on Human Rights.[1184] Walter Kälin and Jörg Künzli describe the rationale behind this decision as follows: "Over the years, the Commission on Human Rights came under increasing criticism because of declining credibility."[1185]

The Human Rights Council consists of forty-seven UN Member States, which are elected directly and based on the equitable geographical distribution.[1186] The contribution of the Human Rights Council to the international protection of human rights is channelled through three functions: it serves as an expert body on human rights issues, it conducts a universal periodic review and it administers the complaints procedure.[1187]

The Human Rights Council derives its expertise from the Advisory Committee and other mechanisms that were established by the Commission on Human Rights to address specific country situations and thematic issues (known as Special Procedures). The Advisory Committee is an expert

1182 Article 42 of the Draft articles entitles only injured states to rely upon the countermeasures, while the text of Article 48 does not refer to countermeasures. Furthermore, Article 54 of the Draft articles, which is entitled "Measures taken by States other than an injured State," does not refer to "countermeasures" but merely mentions "lawful measures." ibid.

1183 Tams (n 505); Dawidowicz, 'Public Law Enforcement without Public Law Safeguards?' (n 372); Dawidowicz, 'Third-Party Countermeasures' (n 372); Dawidowicz, *Third-Party Countermeasures in International Law* (n 372); Katselli Proukaki (n 372).

1184 UNGA Res 60/251 (3 April 2006) UN Doc A/RES/60/251.

1185 Kälin and Künzli (n 1094) 241.

1186 UNGA Res 60/251 (n 1184).

1187 UN Human Rights Council, 'Institution-Building of the United Nations Human Rights Council, UN Doc A/HRC/RES/5/1' (2007) 5.

think-tank comprising eighteen independent experts.[1188] The main focus of the Advisory Committee is to provide studies and research-based advice on the various aspects of human rights and their protection. The special procedures mechanism entrusts special rapporteurs, independent experts or working groups either with the thematic mandates or the country-specific mandates. In 2017, there were 44 thematic and 12 country mandates.[1189]

The Human Rights Council is entitled to conduct a review of the UN Member States' compliance with their human rights obligations, in particular with the four categories of human rights obligations: obligations under the UN Charter, obligations under the Universal Declaration of Human Rights, obligations under human rights instruments to which a state is a party and voluntary pledges and commitments made by states.[1190] Three main sources of information are taken into account in the course of such review: a report prepared by the state concerned, a compilation of the information contained in the reports of other treaty bodies and further credible information provided by other relevant stakeholders.[1191] The final outcome of the periodic review is a report containing a summary of the proceedings, conclusions or recommendations addressed to a member state and voluntary commitments that the state concerned might undertake.[1192]

Empirical research demonstrates that the universal periodic review mechanism is politically driven and states tend to align their broader political considerations with the recommendations expressed during such review. For example, Edward McMahon and Marta Ascherio conclude: "Clear regional patterns exist that continue to reflect the polarized nature of the contemporary international community. Embracing more fully the cultural relativity human rights argument, the Southern states in Asia and Africa tend to take a softer approach to addressing human rights issues among themselves."[1193]

Another deficiency of the universal periodic review was characterised as a "ritualism," which was described as an "acceptance of institutionalized means for securing regulatory goals while losing all focus in achieving the goals or

1188 ibid.

1189 'OHCHR | Special Procedures of the Human Rights Council' (*ohchr.org*) <https://www.ohchr.org/EN/HRBodies/SP/Pages/Welcomepage.aspx>.

1190 UN Human Rights Council (n 1187).

1191 ibid.

1192 ibid.

1193 Edward McMahon and Marta Ascherio, 'A Step Ahead in Promoting Human Rights? The Universal Periodic Review of the UN Human Rights Council' (2012) 18 Global Governance: A Review of Multilateralism and International Organizations 231, 245.

outcomes themselves."[1194] In particular, Walter Kälin observed that: "Elements of ritualism were already apparent during the first cycle, particularly when states [...] participated without the intention of accepting any recommendations; or accepted most or even all recommendations without being willing to implement them effectively. Ritualism was also apparent when peers made recommendations which were not based on an analysis of the human rights situation in the relevant state, or made recommendations that were too general, and largely devoid of content, or which served as a vehicle to praise friendly countries with problematic human rights records."[1195] Thus, despite explicitly acknowledging that the universal periodic review should be non-politicised,[1196] the reality looks very different.[1197]

The complaints procedure came into being "to address consistent patterns of gross and reliably attested violations of all human rights and all fundamental freedoms occurring in any part of the world and under any circumstances."[1198] Complaints of this type can be submitted by any individual, group of individuals or non-governmental organisation against any member of the UN.[1199] Admissibility criteria are enumerated in the Human Rights Council resolution.[1200]

4 The Role of the UN Security Council in Responding to Atrocities

The Security Council has no competence to enforce international law, not even the peremptory norms of international law (jus cogens) or obligations erga omnes.[1201] The competence of the Security Council is narrowed down to

1194 Hilary Charlesworth and Emma Larking, 'Introduction: The Regulatory Power of the Universal Periodic Review' in Hilary Charlesworth and Emma Larking (eds.), *Human Rights and the Universal Periodic Review: Rituals and Ritualism* (Cambridge University Press 2015).

1195 Walter Kälin, 'Ritual and Ritualism at the Universal Periodic Review: A Preliminary Appraisal' in Hilary Charlesworth and Emma Larking (eds.), *Human Rights and the Universal Periodic Review: Rituals and Ritualism* (Cambridge University Press 2015) 40.

1196 UN Human Rights Council (n 1187).

1197 Rosa Freedman, 'The United Nations Human Rights Council: More of the Same?' (2013) 31 Wisconsin International Law Journal 208; Mao Junxiang and Sheng Xi, 'Strength of Review and Scale of Response: A Quantitative Analysis of Human Rights Council Universal Periodic Review on China' (2017) 23 Buffalo Human Rights Law Review 1.

1198 UN Human Rights Council (n 1187).

1199 ibid.

1200 ibid.

1201 Hillgruber (n 503) 287.

imposing measures to preserve or restore the peace.[1202] Nonetheless, some human rights violations meet this high threshold of threatening peace and security. Thus, there were instances of grave human rights violations when the Security Council responded either by mandating humanitarian intervention or by approving collective economic sanctions.

4.1 *Humanitarian Intervention and Responsibility to Protect (R2P)*

The idea of humanitarian intervention dates back to the second half of the nineteenth century, and back then, interventions were justified by the "reason of humanity" – *raison d'humanité*.[1203] Humanitarian intervention was characterised as a "disinterested act," implying that an intervening state was not pursuing any of its interests, and the measure was grounded in the "laws of humanity."[1204] In the nineteenth century, there were at least three instances when England and France deployed or considered deploying humanitarian intervention: Greece in 1820, Syria in 1860 and Bulgaria in 1867.[1205]

The nineteenth-century paradigm of humanitarian intervention was framed as follows: "this intervention was made to rest on this Western conceit of a community of states committed to the principle of human solidarity, a principle that found its legal embodiment in human law."[1206] In this vein, Robert Pape argues that Kantian moral ethic – "the idea that human beings inherently have equal moral value and that the moral duties of one person to another arise from membership in the community of humankind" – is supported by various theories of humanitarian intervention and serves as a justification for such interventions.[1207]

1202 Article 39 of the UN Charter reads as follows: "The Security Council shall determine the existence of any threat to the peace, breach of the peace, or act of aggression and shall make recommendations, or decide what measures shall be taken in accordance with Articles 41 and 42, to maintain or restore international peace and security."

1203 "The idea of humanitarian intervention was developed in large part in dealing with the so-called Eastern question, for it was in reaction to the actions of the Ottoman Empire that international diplomacy first mobilized to put this doctrine into practice. Indeed, it was after the French deployment in Syria in 1860 that an explicit appeal was made to the 'reason of humanity' (raison d'humanite) as a basis on which to justify the intervention." Gustavo Gozzi, 'The "Discourse" of International Law and Humanitarian Intervention' (2017) 30 Ratio Juris 186, 188.

1204 ibid 189.

1205 Christopher J Coyne, *Doing Bad by Doing Good: Why Humanitarian Action Fails* (Stanford Economics and Finance 2013) 32.

1206 Gozzi (n 1203) 192.

1207 Robert Anthony Pape, 'When Duty Calls: A Pragmatic Standard of Humanitarian Intervention' (2012) 37 International Security 41, 45.

Since the creation of the UN, humanitarian intervention can only be authorised by the Security Council.[1208] Non-authorised unilateral humanitarian intervention allegedly violates Article 2(4) of the UN Charter, and therefore intervening states have invoked self-defence as a justification for their actions.[1209] The Kosovo crisis and the subsequent NATO intervention gave a new impetus to the debate on the consistency of unilateral humanitarian interventions with the provisions of the UN Charter.[1210]

The Security Council has not authorised humanitarian interventions as often as one might expect. Alex Bellamy and Paul Williams have summarised the Security Council's practice as follows: "The Council has long authorized peacekeepers to use 'all necessary means' to protect civilians, in contexts including Haiti, the Democratic Republic of Congo (DRC), Sudan, Liberia, Sierra Leone, Burundi and Cote d'Ivoire. But Resolution 1973 (17 March 2011) on the situation in Libya marked the first time the Council had authorized the use of force for human protection purposes against the wishes of a functioning state."[1211]

This new shift towards the protection of the civilian population against the ruling government was instigated by the doctrine of Responsibility to Protect (R2P), which emerged in 2001, following NATO's bombing of Yugoslavia and as a reaction to the subsequent debate on the legality of such humanitarian interventions.[1212] This doctrine posits that sovereignty is based on the ability and willingness of governments to accept the responsibility to protect their

1208 Article 2(4) of the UN Charter outlaws any unilateral recourse to military force. The Security Council can authorise the use of military force under Chapter VII.

1209 Peter Hilpold provides a few examples – India's backing of Bangladesh's independence war against Pakistan in 1971, Vietnam's intervention in Kampuchea in 1978 and 1979, and Tanzania's intervention against Idi Amin's regime in Uganda in 1979. Peter Hilpold, 'From Humanitarian Intervention to Responsibility to Protect: Making Utopia True?' in Ulrich Fastenrath and others (eds.), *From Bilateralism to Community Interest: Essays in Honour of Bruno Simma* (Oxford University Press 2011) 463.

1210 Louis Henkin, 'Kosovo and the Law of "Humanitarian Intervention"' (1999) 93 The American Journal of International Law 824; Michael Reisman, 'Kosovo's Antinomies' (1999) 93 The American Journal of International Law 860; Aidan Hehir, 'NATO's "Humanitarian Intervention" in Kosovo: Legal Precedent or Aberration?' (2009) 8 Journal of Human Rights 245.

1211 Alex J Bellamy and Paul D Williams, 'The New Politics of Protection? Côte d'Ivoire, Libya and the Responsibility to Protect' (2011) 87 International Affairs (Royal Institute of International Affairs 1944-) 825.

1212 International Commission on Intervention and State Sovereignty, 'The Responsibility to Protect: Report of the International Commission on Intervention and State Sovereignty' (2001).

citizens; failing that, the international community has a right to intervene.[1213] The R2P consists of the responsibility to prevent, the responsibility to react and the responsibility to rebuild.[1214] While the primary obligations under the R2P concern each individual state, secondary (subsidiary) obligations are attributed to the international community.[1215]

Peter Hilpold emphasises that R2P articulates a new interpretation of the concept of sovereignty[1216] and, as a consequence, a novel interpretation of the concept of responsibility as institutional responsibility.[1217] According to Peter Hilpold, unilateral military intervention, even as a part of the broader concept of the R2P, remains unacceptable to most states.[1218] He suggests that such an intervention should be an absolutely exceptional measure and should only be undertaken by the UN.[1219] The interrelation between the concept of R2P and the doctrine and emerging principle of Common Concern of Humankind are discussed in the next chapter of this book.[1220]

The most sensitive questions that are raised by the need to intervene are the following: when one should intervene (cost-benefit analysis) and who should intervene (duty allocation). While discussing the preconditions for humanitarian intervention, the idea of pragmatic humanitarian intervention suggested by Robert Pape deserves consideration.[1221] According to Pape, pragmatic humanitarian intervention is justified if the following preconditions are met: 1) Mass homicide occurs that is sponsored by the local government;[1222] 2) A viable

1213 Lloyd Axworthy, 'RtoP and the Evolution of State Sovereignty' in Jared Genser and Irwin Cotler (eds.), *The Responsibility to Protect: The Promise of Stopping Mass Atrocities in Our Time* (Oxford University Press 2012) 12.

1214 International Commission on Intervention and State Sovereignty (n 1212).

1215 William W Burke-White, 'Adoption of the Responsibility to Protect' in Jared Genser and Irwin Cotler (eds.), *The Responsibility to Protect: The Promise of Stopping Mass Atrocities in Our Time* (Oxford University Press 2012).

1216 "'Sovereignty' is no longer interpreted in the traditional Westphalian sense as the 'supreme authority within a territory' but as a concept based on human security and also implying, as a consequence, responsibilities." Hilpold (n 1209) 468.

1217 "It has been interpreted as 'institutional' responsibility, as a concept operating in two directions (externally, to respect the sovereignty of other states, and internally, to respect the dignity and basic rights of all the people within the state), and also as emphasizing that agents of State can be held accountable for their actions." ibid.

1218 Hilpold (n 1209).

1219 ibid 471.

1220 Chapter 5.

1221 Pape (n 1207).

1222 "A government can be assumed to have crossed the threshold for mass homicide when it has killed several thousand of its citizens (i.e., 2000 to 5000 unarmed protesters, bystanders, or those commonly called "civilians") in a concentrated period of time (i.e., one to two

plan for intervention with the estimates of casualties for the intervening forces is developed and the military costs are relatively low;[1223] 3) A strategy for lasting local security is developed and could be feasibly implemented.[1224]

Another question one might wonder about is: who should intervene? Or put differently: who has a legitimate right or even a duty to intervene? David Miller, in his article "Distributing Responsibilities," enumerates a number of principles for the responsibility allocation: causal responsibility, moral responsibility, the principle of capacity, the vulnerability principle and the communitarian principle.[1225] Another seminal work on the subject is James Pattison's book *Humanitarian Intervention and the Responsibility to Protect: Who Should Intervene?*[1226]

Despite the growing body of literature on the subject, a legally binding norm on the allocation of responsibility to intervene has not emerged yet, and the decision-making process of the Security Council is hampered by the vested interests of its permanent members.

4.2 *Collective Economic Sanctions*

Collective economic sanctions, coercive measures authorised by the Security Council that are compulsory for all UN Member States, gained momentum in the early 1990s.[1227] Their increasing deployment can be explained by

---

months), and it is likely to kill many times that number (i.e., 20000 to 50000) in the near future." ibid 53.

1223 "To resolve the clash of moral duties between prior obligations and those arising from the humanitarian emergency, states should engage in humanitarian intervention only when (1) the cost in lives according to reasonable estimates approaches the risks of complex peacetime and training operations and so is effectively near zero, or (2) when the individuals participating in the intervention volunteer." ibid 55.

1224 "For the pragmatic standard of humanitarian intervention, enduring security means the long-term cessation of mass homicide and the establishment of local stability without the need for an indefinite outside military commitment. There are two ways to achieve these objectives. The first requires de facto territorial and political separation of the perpetrator and the victims, either an autonomous zone within the context of the existing regime or a new state carved out from the territory of the old state. The second involves a political settlement where the government and the threatened population provide credible assurances to refrain from further violence. In practice, this requires significant demilitarization of both parties, a rare occurrence." ibid 59.

1225 David Miller, 'Distributing Responsibilities' (2001) 9 Journal of Political Philosophy 453.

1226 James Pattison, *Humanitarian Intervention and the Responsibility to Protect: Who Should Intervene?* (Oxford University Press 2010).

1227 Before 1990 the United Nations Security Council imposed sanctions in only two cases: against Rhodesia in 1966 and against South Africa in 1977. Between 1990 and 1994, nine sanctions regimes were established. For more details, see Mary Ellen O'Connell, 'Debating the Law of Sanctions' (2002) 13 European Journal of International Law 63.

humanitarian considerations: coercive economic measures are preferable to military intervention. Moreover, globalisation and economic interdependence have strengthened the role of economic coercion in international relations.[1228]

The negative impact of comprehensive economic sanctions on civilian populations has undermined their legitimacy.[1229] Thus, economic sanctions directed against named individuals, groups or entities, so-called "smart" or "targeted" sanctions, have replaced comprehensive coercive measures, which were directed against countries. The imposition of the Security Council's targeted economic sanctions is a two-step process. The existence of the special circumstances that justify coercive economic actions is the precondition for such measures and represents the first step. The second step is the identification of the potential "targets." Sanctions regimes authorised by the Security Council pursue different objectives and are administered autonomously.[1230] Collective economic sanctions commonly entail arms embargoes, travel restrictions, prohibitions targeting certain sectors of economy and assets freezes.

In the last decade, targeted economic sanctions authorised by the Security Council have come under fire for their alleged inconsistency with the human rights obligations of the UN Member States.[1231] National and regional judicial bodies, UN Member States and legal scholars have questioned the legitimacy of sanctions based on the lack of procedural due process rights guaranteed to the targeted individuals.[1232] This matter was partly resolved by the establishment of the Office of Ombudsperson.[1233] The Office of Ombudsperson accepts de-listing requests from the sanctioned individuals and entities included in

1228 "International battle lines are increasingly drawn in terms of markets and trade, rather than tanks and troops." Matthew Craven, 'Humanitarianism and the Quest for Smarter Sanctions' (2002) 13 European Journal of International Law 43, 44.

1229 An example that has been extensively discussed are the comprehensive economic sanctions against Iraq established under the Security Council Resolution 661 (1990). "No one knows with any precision how many Iraqi civilians have died as a result, but various agencies of the United Nations, which oversees the sanctions, have estimated that they have contributed to hundreds of thousands of deaths." Mueller and Mueller (n 149).

1230 "Since 1966, the Security Council has established 30 sanctions regimes, in Southern Rhodesia, South Africa, the former Yugoslavia (2), Haiti, Iraq (2), Angola, Rwanda, Sierra Leone, Somalia and Eritrea, Eritrea and Ethiopia, Liberia (3), DRC, Côte d'Ivoire, Sudan, Lebanon, DPRK, Iran, Libya (2), Guinea-Bissau, CAR, Yemen, South Sudan and Mali, as well as against ISIL (Da'esh) and Al-Qaida and the Taliban." 'Sanctions' (*United Nations Security Council*) <https://www.un.org/securitycouncil/sanctions/information>.

1231 Hovell (n 162); Sue E Eckert and Thomas J Biersteker, 'Due Process and Targeted Sanctions.' (Watson Institute for International Studies, Brown University 2012) An Update of the "Watson Report"; Halberstam and Stein (n 162); Fassbender (n 165).

1232 Hovell (n 162).

1233 UNSC Res 1904 (n 171)

the ISIL (Da'esh) and Al-Qaida Sanctions List.[1234] Other targeted individuals or entities may seek de-listing by means of the Focal Point de-listing procedure.[1235]

It must be noted that the Security Council adopts compulsory economic sanctions only if a resolution is not vetoed by its permanent members. The political nature of the Security Council's decision-making process undermined recent efforts to impose sanctions for grave human rights violations against Syria.[1236]

5 Conclusion

The international enforcement of human rights is multifaceted. First and foremost, international human rights conventions prescribe a number of obligations to improve human rights protection. Examples of such obligations include a reporting obligation, mechanisms for interstate complaints, mechanisms for individual complaints, inquiry procedures and an obligation to refer any dispute to the ICJ. The analysis in this chapter has revealed the deficiencies of these enforcement mechanisms that significantly impair the protection of guaranteed rights.

The additional protection that is guaranteed to human rights that have gained a special status of jus cogens or obligations erga omnes is undermined by the definitional ambiguity of both concepts. Furthermore, the normative implications of these concepts are not well defined.

These shortcomings are further exacerbated by the political nature of the Human Rights Council and the Security Council. In particular, international human rights scholars have described the universal periodic review of the Human Rights Council as a form of "ritualism," thus defeating the very purpose of this procedure. The Security Council protects human rights either by means of humanitarian intervention or collective economic sanctions. However, the practice of the Security Council lacks consistency, a weakness that flows logically from its political nature and the veto power exercised by its permanent members.

1234 ibid.

1235 UNSC Res 1730 (19 December 2006) UN Doc S/RES/1730. The mandate of the Focal Point was extended. UNSC Res 2253 (17 December 2015) UN Doc S/RES/2253; UNSC Res 2255 (22 December 2015) UN Doc S/RES/2255.

1236 'Security Council Fails to Adopt Draft Resolution Condemning Syria's Crackdown on Anti-Government Protestors, Owing to Veto by Russian Federation, China' (n 8); 'Security Council Fails to Adopt Draft Resolution on Syria as Russian Federation, China Veto Text Supporting Arab League's Proposed Peace Plan' (n 8).

CHAPTER 4

The Legality of Unilateral Economic Sanctions Imposed to Redress Human Rights Violations

The debate on the lawfulness of unilateral economic sanctions imposed to redress gross human rights violations has a political character. The European Union, the United States, Canada, Australia and a number of other states have traditionally been among the staunchest supporters of unilateral human rights sanctions,[1237] while the group of the developing countries supported by China and the Russian Federation lodge formal protests to such coercive measures on behalf of the international community.[1238] The tension between these two standards emerged vividly in the numerous declarations adopted under the auspices of the UN, in which developing countries insisted on the illegality of unilateral economic sanctions and other states opposed this view.[1239] Amidst this political debate, one strand of international law scholarship has recognised that the use of unilateral human rights sanctions has become an accepted customary international norm.[1240] Whereas this position might be tenable on the theoretical level, the consistent opposition expressed by states pours cold water on this idea in practice.[1241]

There is no well-established and precise definition of human rights sanctions. As Clara Portela points out, human rights sanctions are frequently conflated with sanctions aiming at goals such as democracy, good governance

1237 This trend is clearly reflected in the adoption of domestic laws that impose sanctions on foreign nationals involved in human right violations. For more details, see chapter 1, subsection 1.6 The increased use of unilateral economic sanctions and a new geo-economic world order.

1238 Hofer (n 22).

1239 Alexandra Hofer analyses numerous declarations adopted by the UN bodies that criticise unilateral sanctions. ibid.

1240 Cleveland (n 551); Buhm Suk Baek, 'Economic Sanctions Against Human Rights Violations' (2008) Cornell Law School Inter-University Graduate Student Conference Papers <https://scholarship.law.cornell.edu/lps_clacp/11>.

1241 Opposition to unilateral economic sanctions has also been expressed by the Special Rapporteur on the negative impact of unilateral coercive measures on the enjoyment of human rights Idriss Jazairy. UNHRC (n 407); Jazairy (n 407).

and the rule of law.[1242] That said, in the following discussion, human rights sanctions will be defined as economic restrictions – i.e. unilateral economic sanctions – imposed in order to promote human rights abroad and to punish grave human rights violations, as well as for other reasons related to an unsatisfactory human rights situation in other countries.[1243]

Starting from the 1970s, states occasionally levied unilateral economic sanctions to respond to grave and consistent patterns of human rights violations. Referring to US practice, scholars point out: "In the late 1970s, following a series of congressionally inspired initiatives and under the leadership of President Carter, human rights became a cause célèbre and priority goal of US sanctions policy."[1244] In this way human rights entered US foreign policy under the presidency of Jimmy Carter.[1245] This development resulted in an increased use of economic sanctions to promote human rights and punish regimes responsible for severe human rights violations.[1246] Describing US practice, Hufbauer and others observe: "Amendments both to the Foreign Assistance Act of 1962 and the Trade Act of 1974, passed in the 1970s and 1980s, mandated sanctions against countries that violated human rights, harbored international terrorists, or abetted drug production or distribution."[1247]

When it comes to the EU, the practice of using unilateral sanctions dates back to the early 1980s (when it was the European Economic Community),[1248] with the withdrawal of most-favourable-nation treatment in trade relations

---

1242 "[...] the imposition of sanctions in response to human rights breaches can hardly be dissociated from that addressing democratic backsliding. The same is true for sanctions imposed in pursuance of termination of violent conflict." Portela (n 24) 14.

1243 "Unilateral human rights sanctions are employed by countries for a variety of purposes. They may be used to punish a foreign state for its human rights practices, to deprive a rogue state of needed goods or foreign currency, to express the sending state's outrage at human rights atrocities, to prevent a state's own markets from contributing to human rights violations, to morally distance a state from human rights violators, and to generate pressure for the adoption of multilateral action." Cleveland (n 27) 135.

1244 Hufbauer and others (n 28) 13.

1245 "[...] Congress has, since the mid-1970s, pressured presidents to place more weight on human rights in modulating U.S. relations with foreign governments." David Skidmore and William Gates, 'After Tiananmen: The Struggle over U.S. Policy toward China in the Bush Administration' (1997) 27(3) Presidential Studies Quarterly 514, 518.

1246 Martin (n 98) 101–111.

1247 Hufbauer and others (n 28) 135.

1248 "No autonomous EU sanctions, as defined above, were observed in the time period before 1981 and the most important institutional factor at the start of sanctions policy was the European Political Co-operation (EPC) "London Report" in October 1981." Joakim Kreutz, 'Hard Measures by a Soft Power? Sanctions Policy of the European Union 1981–2004' (2005) Bonn International Center for Conversion, paper 45 1, 7.

with Poland in response to the arrests and detention of political opposition. This was one of the first instances in which EU sanctions were employed for the protection of human rights.[1249] Analysing the EU's practise of using human rights sanctions, Clara Portela, a distinguished scholar of economic sanctions, notes: "The EU has an established track-record in supporting human rights with the imposition of sanctions."[1250]

The most recent examples of widely discussed economic sanctions imposed on human rights grounds include sanctions imposed against China for its treatment of a Muslim minority – the Uyghurs – in the Xinjiang Uyghur Autonomous Region (XUAR), which spurred not only formal protests and allegations of genocide, but also resulted in economic sanctions being imposed by a number of states. The United States, for example, relied concurrently on several statutes to enact various types of economic restrictions targeting companies, as well as government officials who were involved in the mistreatment of Uyghurs and other ethnic minorities. In particular, in March 2021, several Chinese government officials were sanctioned in connection with serious human rights violations in the XUAR.[1251] In June 2021, the US Customs and Border Protection issued a withhold release order on silica-based products produced by Hoshine Silicon Industry Co. Ltd. and its subsidiaries.[1252] The withhold release order is not an outright ban on importation, but it does require importers either to demonstrate that the imported goods do not violate Section 307 of the Tariff Act of 1930 – which prohibits the importation of merchandise produced by convict, forced and/or indentured labor under penal sanctions – or to re-export their shipments.[1253] On the same day, the Department of Commerce's Bureau of Industry and Security added five Chinese entities to the so-called Entity List for "accepting or utilizing forced labor" in the XUAR, thus making the total number of sanctioned persons in relation to the human rights abuses of ethnic minorities in the XUAR equal to fifty three.[1254] Other restrictions were also put in place.

1249 ibid 21–22.

1250 Portela (n 24) 6.

1251 US Department of the Treasury. *Press Release.* Treasury Sanctions Chinese Government Officials in Connection with Serious Human Rights Abuse in Xinjiang. (22 March 2021) https://home.treasury.gov/news/press-releases/jy0070.

1252 US Customs and Border Protection. *Press Release.* The Department of Homeland Security Issues Withhold Release Order on Silica-Based Products Made by Forced Labor in Xinjiang. (24 June 2021) https://www.cbp.gov/newsroom/national-media-release/department-homeland-security-issues-withhold-release-order-silica.

1253 ibid.

1254 US Department of Commerce. *Press Release.* Commerce Department Adds Five Chinese Entities to the Entity List for Participating in China's Campaign of Forced Labor Against

In March 2021, the EU introduced economic sanctions against Chinese nationals and legal entities responsible for gross human rights violations in the XUAR.[1255] Among the targets sanctioned by the EU were the Xinjiang Production and Construction Corps (XPCC), which is defined in the relevant regulation as a "state-owned economic and paramilitary organisation."[1256] Among other things, this organisation is responsible for the use of forced labour: "the XPCC uses Uyghurs and people from other Muslim ethnic minorities as a forced workforce, in particular in cotton fields."[1257]

In response to the EU sanctions, China imposed unilateral sanctions on the EU policymakers, as well as on human rights activists.[1258] These tensions culminated in the adoption of a European Parliament resolution that declared that the ratification of the EU-China Comprehensive Agreement on Investment – which was the result of seven years of negotiations and had recently been finalised – "has justifiably been frozen because of the Chinese sanctions in place."[1259]

Canada also joined international efforts and imposed economic sanctions in response to human rights violations in the XUAR.[1260] In coordination with other states, the UK announced its sanctions against China on the same day as the United States, the European Union and Canada.[1261]

Muslims in Xinjiang. (24 June 2021) https://www.commerce.gov/news/press-releases/2021/06/commerce-department-adds-five-chinese-entities-entity-list.

1255 Council Implementing Regulation (EU) 2021/478 of 22 March 2021 implementing Regulation (EU) 2020/1998 concerning restrictive measures against serious human rights violations and abuses (OJ L); Council Decision (CFSP) 2021/481 of 22 March 2021 amending Decision (CFSP) 2020/1999 concerning restrictive measures against serious human rights violations and abuses (OJ L).

1256 ibid.

1257 ibid.

1258 Stuart Lau, 'China Slaps Retaliatory Sanctions on EU Officials' *POLITICO* (22 March 2021) https://www.politico.eu/article/china-slaps-retaliatory-sanctions-on-eu-officials/.

1259 European Parliament, Resolution of 20 May 2021 on Chinese countersanctions on EU entities and MEPs and MPs (2021/2644(RSP)). https://www.europarl.europa.eu/doceo/document/TA-9-2021-0255_EN.html.

1260 Global Affairs Canada. *News release*. Canada joins international partners in imposing new sanctions in response to human rights violations in Xinjiang. (22 March 2021) https://www.canada.ca/en/global-affairs/news/2021/03/canada-joins-international-partners-in-imposing-new-sanctions-in-response-to-human-rights-violations-in-xinjiang.html.

1261 Foreign, Commonwealth & Development Office. *Press release*. UK sanctions perpetrators of gross human rights violations in Xinjiang, alongside EU, Canada and US. (22 March 2021) https://www.gov.uk/government/news/uk-sanctions-perpetrators-of-gross-human-rights-violations-in-xinjiang-alongside-eu-canada-and-us.

Another recent example are the sanctions imposed in response to fraudulent presidential elections and the repression of political opposition in Belarus. A broad coalition of states joined the efforts to increase economic pressure on Alexander Lukashenko and his inner circle. The United States, the European Union, the United Kingdom and Canada imposed economic sanctions in August 2021 and then announced new sanctions against government officials, state-owned businesses and other organisations in December 2021.[1262]

The effectiveness of human rights sanctions cannot be determined with precision. While emphasising that opposition to human rights sanctions is partly grounded in allegations that they are inconsistent with human rights, Clara Portela has also highlighted that "the imposition of sanctions, which often responds to demands by the democratic opposition in the target country, can help to protect activists from prolonged imprisonment or mistreatment by the authorities."[1263] A distinguished human rights activist Aryeh Neier has given the following assessment of the effectiveness of human rights sanctions: "many examples could be cited to show that sanctions do not work and that, in some instances, they are counterproductive. Yet when used strictly for purposes of promoting human rights and applied steadily over sustained periods, with adjustments that reflect changes in human rights practices, the record for economic sanctions seems to be generally positive."[1264] In his in-depth analysis of the role of economic sanctions in ending the apartheid regime in South Africa, Lee Jones persuasively shows that different types of sanctions had different impacts on the regime and these impacts changed over the years.[1265] Yet, both Lee Jones and Aryeh Neier agree that economic sanctions played a role in ending apartheid and that this role was not marginal.[1266]

In 2012, the United States was the first country to pass a special law – the Sergei Magnitsky Rule of Law Accountability Act of 2012 (Magnitsky Act) – enabling economic sanctions to be imposed against perpetrators of certain categories of grave human rights violations that occurred in the Russian Federation.[1267] To be more specific, these sanctions targeted the individuals responsible for the mistreatment of Sergei Magnitsky – a Russian citizen who uncovered a major corruption scheme and was subsequently arrested, tortured

1262 Michael Volkov, 'United States, European Union, United Kingdom and Canada Coordinate Further Sanctions Against Belarus' *JD Supra* (21 December 2021). https://www.jdsupra.com/legalnews/united-states-european-union-united-2693437/.

1263 Portela (n 24) 6.

1264 Neier (n 140) 877.

1265 Jones (n 135) chapter 2.

1266 ibid.; Neier (n 140).

1267 Sergei Magnitsky Rule of Law Accountability Act of 2012 (n 186).

and denied sufficient medical assistance, ultimately resulting in his death in pretrial detention[1268] – as well as those individuals responsible for concealing the legal liability for this mistreatment or who financially benefitted from it.[1269] Furthermore, other individuals liable for extrajudicial killings, torture or other gross violations of internationally recognised human rights may be targeted by unilateral US economic sanctions.[1270]

In 2016, the application of the US Magnitsky-type sanctions was extended when Congress passed the Global Magnitsky Human Rights Accountability Act (Global Magnitsky Act).[1271] According to this act, any foreign national who is responsible for extrajudicial killings, torture or other gross violations of internationally recognised human rights or who is responsible for acts of significant corruption may be sanctioned.[1272]

These sanctions are dubbed Magnitsky-style or Magnitsky-type sanctions and they have also been introduced by other states. In 2017, Canada introduced legislation allowing it to sanction perpetrators of grave human rights violations abroad.[1273] Michael Nesbitt described Canada's decision to introduce the Magnitsky-style human rights sanctions as follows: "Including the power to sanctions for gross and systematic human rights abuses is a more honest explanation of what Canada has done in the past – and arguably for what it will want to do in the future."[1274]

In July 2020, the Global Human Rights Sanctions Regulations came into force in the United Kingdom.[1275] The first wave of UK human rights sanctions targeted 25 Russian nationals involved in the mistreatment and death of Sergei Magnitsky, 20 Saudi nationals involved in the death of journalist Jamal Khashoggi, two high-ranking Burmese military generals involved in the systematic and brutal violence against the Rohingya people and two organisations involved in the forced labour, torture and murder taking place in North Korea's gulags.[1276]

1268 *Magnitskiy and Others v. Russia App no 32631/09 and 53799/12* (n 185).

1269 Sergei Magnitsky Rule of Law Accountability Act of 2012 (n 186). Section 404. Para. (1).

1270 ibid Section 404.

1271 The Global Magnitsky Human Rights Accountability Act. (n 189).

1272 ibid.

1273 Justice for Victims of Corrupt Foreign Officials Act (n 194).

1274 Michael Nesbitt, 'Canada's Unilateral Sanctions Regime under Review: Extraterritoriality, Human Rights, Due Process, and Enforcement in Canada's Special Economic Measures Act' (2016) 48(2) Ottawa Law Review 507, 565–566.

1275 The Global Human Rights Sanctions Regulations 2020 (n 193).

1276 Foreign & Commonwealth Office. *Press Release.* UK announces first sanctions under new global human rights regime. (6 July 2020) https://www.gov.uk/government/news/uk-announces-first-sanctions-under-new-global-human-rights-regime.

After lengthy consultations, the EU announced the adoption of the Magnitsky-style sanctions in December 2020.[1277] This EU-level framework for human rights sanctions was preceded by the implementation of Magnitsky-type legislation in several EU Member States.[1278] According to the EU's Magnitsky-type sanctions, serious human rights violations and abuses encompass: (a) genocide; (b) crimes against humanity; and (c) the following serious human rights violations or abuses: (i) torture and other cruel, inhuman or degrading treatment or punishment, (ii) slavery, (iii) extrajudicial, summary or arbitrary executions and killings, (iv) the enforced disappearance of persons, (v) arbitrary arrests or detentions.[1279] Other types of widespread, systematic violations, as well as violations that are otherwise of serious concern in light of the objectives of the EU's common foreign and security policy, may trigger the imposition of human rights sanctions by the EU.[1280]

The Australian parliament voted in favour of Magnitsky-style sanctions, as well as other thematic sanctions on 2 December 2021.[1281] This enables Australia to impose sanctions to address serious violations and abuses of human rights, activities undermining good governance or the rule of law (including serious corruption), and serious violations of international humanitarian law.[1282]

While one group of states is enacting legislation to impose unilateral human rights sanctions, other states, like China, argue that these measures violate international law. Angela Poh, who conducted a comprehensive analysis of China's attitude towards economic sanctions and their use, observed: "The main themes of China's sanctions rhetoric suggest that 'Eurocentric values' that prioritise democracy and human rights over sovereignty cannot be used as a basis for sanctions. Sanctions also cannot be used to intervene in the domestic affairs of other states. In addition, China is opposed to the use of

---

1277 Council Decision (CFSP) 2020/1999 (n 199); Council Regulation (EU) 2020/1998 (n 199).

1278 Lithuania introduced Magnitsky sanctions by incorporating an "Magnitsky Amendment" to Article 133 of the Law on the Legal Status of Aliens, which was adopted in November 2017. Republic of Lithuania Law on the Legal Status of Aliens 29 April 2004 No. IX–2206. Estonia added to the existing "Law on Obligation to Leave and Prohibition of Entry," a provision to ban foreigners when there is a good reason to believe that they have participated in or contributed to a human rights violation abroad, involving death, serious injury or other criminal misconduct on political grounds. 'Amendments to the Law on Amending the Obligation to Leave and Prohibition on Entry Act 262 SE, Adopted 08.12.2016.'

1279 Article 1, 1(a)-1(c), Council Decision (CFSP) 2020/1999 (n 199).

1280 Article 1, 1(d) ibid.

1281 Autonomous Sanctions Amendment (Magnitsky-style and Other Thematic Sanctions) Bill 2021. https://parlinfo.aph.gov.au/parlInfo/download/legislation/bills/s1326_third-senate/toc_pdf/2116121.pdf;fileType=application%2Fpdf.

1282 ibid.

unilateral sanctions without the authorisation of the UN, such as those frequently imposed by the US and European states."[1283]

China, the Russian Federation and the majority of African states condemn the use of unilateral sanctions, arguing that these measures violate human rights. Since 1996, the UN General Assembly has regularly adopted resolutions entitled "Human rights and unilateral coercive measures" that condemn the use of unilateral sanctions and underline their incompatibility with the states' human rights obligations.[1284] The most recent of these resolutions was adopted in December 2020.[1285] Developing states that sponsor these resolutions and vote in their favour frequently contend that developed countries use human rights as a pretext for imposing economic sanctions.[1286]

Further complicating matters, the mandate of the special rapporteur on the negative effects of unilateral coercive measures on the enjoyment of human rights was established in 2014.[1287] The special rapporteur prepares annual reports on the negative impact of unilateral coercive measures on the enjoyment of human rights, with the first such report issued in 2015.[1288]

Thus, human rights sanctions have proved to be extremely controversial. In this regard, Jean-Marc Thouvenin observes that human rights may play a double role: on the one hand, economic sanctions are levied on human rights grounds; on the other hand, human rights obligations impose constraints on the right of states to use such measures.[1289] However, this statement is not substantiated by a comprehensive analysis of the legality of human rights sanctions or the identification of particular human rights that might be violated as the result of economic sanctions.[1290]

While there is much to quibble about when it comes to the legality of human rights sanctions, I tend to agree with the conclusion of a thematic study prepared by the Office of the United Nations High Commissioner for Human Rights: "Whether unilateral coercive measures are legal or illegal under public international law cannot be easily answered in general. Much depends upon

---

1283 Poh (n 401) 76.

1284 Hofer (n 22) 187.

1285 Human rights and unilateral coercive measures. UNGA Resolution 75/181. UN Doc A/RES/75/181 (28 December 2020).

1286 These statements have been made before the UN General Assembly's Third Committee. Hofer (22).

1287 Human Rights Council, Resolution 27/21, UN Doc A/HRC/RES/27/21 (3 October 2014).

1288 UNHRC (n 407).

1289 Jean-Marc Thouvenin, 'International Economic Sanctions and Fundamental Rights: Friend or Foe?' in Norman Weiß and Jean-Marc Thouvenin (eds.), *The Influence of Human Rights on International Law* (Springer 2015).

1290 ibid.

the specific form of coercive measures, on the applicable treaty law, if any, and on customary international law rules relevant to the assessment of coercive measures, as well as on potential grounds for precluding the wrongfulness of such measures."[1291]

In light of the above, the objective of this chapter is to unravel and connect the multiple threads in the complex issue of unilateral human rights sanctions and their legality under public international law.

1 Human Rights Sanctions and the Principle of Non-intervention

In chapter 2, we explored whether unilateral economic sanctions encroach on the principle of non-intervention embedded in the UN Charter.[1292] Now we will review the interrelations between the unilateral economic sanctions imposed to redress human rights violations and the principle of non-intervention.

As has been stated before, the ambit of the principle of non-intervention evades precise definition.[1293] Several UN declarations adopted to address the scope of the principle of non-intervention are so ambiguous that they undermine their very purpose. The adoption of the Declaration on the Inadmissibility of Intervention in the Domestic Affairs of States and the Protection of Their Independence and Sovereignty reveals that intervention is not confined to military intervention, yet it also entails other forms of intervention.[1294] In particular, the declaration reaffirms that: "No State may use or encourage the use of economic, political or any other type of measures to coerce another State in order to obtain from it the subordination of the exercise of its sovereign rights or to secure from it advantages of any kind."[1295] One cannot help noticing that this text is ambiguous, and it follows that the question of whether any form of economic coercion irrespective of its purpose meets the threshold for being an unlawful intervention remains unresolved. The Declaration on Principles of International Law concerning Friendly Relations has not provided any further

1291 Human Rights Council, Thematic study of the Office of the United Nations High Commissioner for Human Rights on the impact of unilateral coercive measures on the enjoyment of human rights, including recommendations on actions aimed at ending such measures. UN Doc A/HRC/19/33 (11 January 2012).

1292 For more details, see subsection 2.2 Unilateral economic sanctions as a violation of the principle of non-intervention.

1293 Maziar Jamnejad and Michael Wood describe the principle of non-intervention as: "One of the most potent and elusive of all international principles." Jamnejad and Wood (n 427).

1294 UNGA Res 2131.

1295 ibid.

clarity.[1296] In fact, even the text of this declaration resembles the one quoted above.[1297] The Charter of Economic Rights and Duties of States declares that relations among states shall be governed by a number of essential principles, including the principle of non-intervention and the principle of respect for human rights and international obligations.[1298] Bearing in mind these two principles, it should be stressed that the rationale behind the idea of internationalisation of human rights is not only to obligate an individual state to respect and protect the human rights of everyone under its jurisdiction, but also to make such commitments binding under international law. Thus, considering that the predominant majority of present-day states have taken on various obligations under the numerous human rights treaties,[1299] it might be untenable to argue that the use of economic pressure to coerce a state to fulfil its international human rights obligations would constitute a violation of the principle of non-intervention.

Mindful of the ongoing discussion on the legality of human rights sanctions, legal scholars take issue with the argument that coercive economic measures imposed to redress gross human rights violations are per se illegal. In her discussion of the prohibition on intervention and unilateral human rights sanctions, Sarah Cleveland concludes: "Customary international law traditionally has allowed states to use economic coercion for a wide range of purposes, and the relatively frequent use of economic sanctions by the United States and other developed nations since World War II makes it difficult to conclude that a customary international norm exists against the practice."[1300] Cleveland further buttresses her conclusion by declaring that human rights "are matters of international concern which justify intervention by the international community."[1301] In discussing non-forcible influence and the principle of non-intervention in light of the ICJ jurisprudence, Professor Lori Damrosch points out that "there is an increasing trend not only toward the use of economic sanctions to promote human rights objectives, but also

1296 UNGA Res 2625.

1297 The relevant part of the text reads: "No State may use or encourage the use of economic political or any other type of measures to coerce another State in order to obtain from it the subordination of the exercise of its sovereign rights and to secure from it advantages of any kind." ibid.

1298 Chapter 1 Fundamentals of international economic relations Charter of Economic Rights and Duties of States, UNGA Res 39/163 (17 December 1984) UN Doc A/RES/39/163.

1299 Information on the ratification of 18 international human rights treaties is available here: https://indicators.ohchr.org.

1300 Cleveland (n 551) 53.

1301 ibid 54.

toward acceptance of the legitimacy of such sanctions when employed for that purpose."[1302]

Yet not all scholars share this optimism. For instance, Alexandra Hofer contends that the sharp divide between developed and developing countries with respect to the lawfulness of unilateral economic sanctions still exists.[1303] Furthermore, the objectives underlying the imposition of these measures seem to be irrelevant for their opponents.

The overall conclusion is that the mere fact that unilateral economic sanctions are connected to an objective such as the protection of human rights does not in itself exempt them from being contested. Furthermore, it remains unclear whether the principle of non-intervention prevents states from imposing unilateral actions, such as economic sanctions, to target regimes that abuse human rights. The answer to the latter question depends on whether human rights violations are recognised as matters of domestic or of international concern. In this regard, Mortimer Sellers, discussing the interrelation between economic sanctions targeting human rights violations and the principle of non-intervention in the internal affairs of states, concludes: "Even if economic sanctions were in some very broad sense 'intervention' or 'interference,' economic sanctions against human rights violations would not invade the exclusively 'domestic' jurisdiction of any state, because human rights are a universal, and not a purely domestic or national concern."[1304] However, this view is not supported by all states. As Angela Poh posits, China's anti-sanctions rhetoric revolves around the idea that these measures cannot be used to intervene in the domestic affairs of other states and human rights should not be prioritised over sovereignty.[1305]

2 Economic Sanctions Targeting Human Rights Violations and the Draft Articles on Responsibility of States for Internationally Wrongful Acts

Countermeasures, including economic countermeasures, can be legal if certain preconditions are met, notably: if they are imposed as a response to a

1302 Lori Fisler Damrosch, 'Politics Across Borders: Nonintervention and Nonforcible Influence Over Domestic Affairs' (1989) 83 American Journal of International Law 1, 46.

1303 Hofer (n 22).

1304 Mortimer Newlin Stead Sellers, 'Economic Sanctions against Human Rights Violations' in Laura Picchio Forlati and Linos-Alexander Sicilianos (eds.), *Economic Sanctions in International Law* (Brill Academic Publishers 2004) 489.

1305 Poh (n 401).

previous violation of an international obligation and if they are relied upon by an injured state.[1306] These requirements were discussed in more detail in chapter 2.[1307]

Unilateral economic sanctions imposed on human rights grounds aim to remedy human rights violations abroad. Thus, the first precondition – the existence of a violation of an international obligation – can be ascertained. The establishment of the second precondition is problematic for human rights violations. In particular, it is debatable whether human rights violations whose victims are foreign nationals and that occur abroad may provide sufficient grounds for any other state to declare itself to be an injured state in the meaning of the Draft articles. It is worth recalling that the Draft articles define five categories of injured states for the purposes of invoking international responsibility:[1308] a) a state to which a breached obligation is owed individually; b) a state belonging to a group of states to which a breached obligation is owed, if the breach particularly affects that state; c) a state belonging to a group of states to which a breached obligation is owed, if the breach is of such a character as to radically change the position of all the other states to which the obligation is owed with respect to the further performance of the obligation; d) a state particularly affected by the breach, if a breached obligation is owed to the international community as a whole; e) any state when a breached obligation is owed to the international community as a whole and the breach is of such a character as to radically change the position of all the other states to which the obligation is owed with respect to the further performance of the obligation. In this regard, James Crawford states: "Human rights obligations are not, in the first instance at least, owed to particular states, and it is accordingly difficult to see how a human rights obligation could itself be the subject of legitimate countermeasures."[1309] This conclusion can be further buttressed by the ICJ's pronouncements in *Reservations to the Convention on Genocide*: "In such a convention the contracting States do not have any interests of their own; they merely have, one and all, a common interest, namely the accomplishment of those high purposes which are the raison d'être of the convention. Consequently, in a convention of this type, one cannot speak of individual advantages and disadvantages to States, or of the maintenance of a perfect contractual balance between rights and duties."[1310] From a legal standpoint,

1306 Article 49 ILC, 'Draft articles' (n 90).
1307 For more details, see subsection 3.1 Unilateral economic sanctions as countermeasures.
1308 Article 42 ILC, 'Draft articles' (n 90).
1309 Crawford (n 353) 692.
1310 *Reservations to the Convention on Genocide, Advisory Opinion: ICJ Reports 1951, p 15* 23.

this view may hold. However, it should be noted that both the historical record and empirical research affirm that grave human rights violations pose a threat to peace and long-term stability in individual countries, regions and even on a global scale.[1311] Hence, it can be argued that obligations under international human rights treaties are owed, at least partially, to the other states signatories to those treaties, at least to the extent to which such obligations are aimed at protecting peace and stability by providing human rights guarantees.

In light of the above, it should be stressed that economic sanctions for violations of human rights fall primarily into the category of third-party countermeasures or countermeasures imposed by non-injured states in the meaning of the Draft articles. Hence, the narrowly defined concept of direct injury prevents both states and individuals from invoking responsibility of the states responsible for human rights violations.[1312] This conclusion holds even for violations of human rights that have gained a special status, either jus cogens or erga omnes.[1313]

Views on the legality of third-party countermeasures vary significantly. Below, I outline the arguments advanced in favour of the legality of third-party countermeasures imposed on human rights grounds.

Martin Dawidowicz reiterates that the legal position of third-party countermeasures has been and remains uncertain.[1314] Nonetheless, Dawidowicz provides a number of the recent examples of such countermeasures imposed against Libya,[1315] Syria[1316] and Russia.[1317] The inferences drawn from these recent examples echo his previous conclusion that there is an abundance of state practice which is not Western-dominated and which is supported by the

1311 For more details, see chapter 5, subsection 3.4 Grave human rights violations as a threat to international peace and security.

1312 Dawidowicz, 'Public Law Enforcement without Public Law Safeguards?' (n 372) 336.

1313 This article was published before the Draft articles were adopted, yet the argument still holds. Byers (n 1171) 238.

1314 Dawidowicz, 'Third-Party Countermeasures' (n 372) 3.

1315 Restrictive measures against Libya included asset freezes as well as an expansion from the League of Arab States. Furthermore, as Dawidowicz points out: "these actions were taken prior to the enforcement measures adopted by the Security Council against Libya under Chapter VII UN Charter and therefore required independent justification." ibid 6.

1316 The European Union implemented numerous unilateral restrictive measures, which later were introduced by other states that aligned its unilateral restrictions with the European ones. Syria was suspended from the League of Arab States in November 2011. Furthermore, the League of Arab States introduced a number of restrictions against Syria. ibid 6–9.

1317 The European Union, Australia, Canada, Japan, Switzerland and the United States have adopted unilateral restrictive measures against the Russian Federation for its role in the destabilisation of Ukraine. ibid 9–11.

required opinio juris; thus, he argues in favour of the legality of third-party countermeasures.[1318]

Christian Hillgruber argues that the lack of effective enforcement mechanisms embedded in the human rights treaties implies that states implicitly agree to rely upon countermeasures.[1319] Hillgruber argues as follows: "Unless we wish to assume that the States wanted to create obligations under international law without any way of enforcing them, i.e. practically merely natural obligations, there is good reason to assume that human rights agreements implicitly grant each contracting State the right to respond to violations of the agreement by other States using any one of the entire range of 'self-help' instruments permitted under international law, i.e. by having recourse to reprisals."[1320] Furthermore, he claims that the permissibility of reprisals does not depend on the seriousness of a violation,[1321] concluding with respect to the question of the obligation to take third-party countermeasures: "Reprisals by third States are possible responses to certain violations of international law, but are by no means obligatory."[1322]

According to Andreas Paulus: "While there is much reason to be less than enthusiastic about the crude enforcement mechanism that is euphemistically termed 'countermeasures' by the ILC the permissibility of such countermeasures for the enforcement of obligations towards the international community as a whole is a necessary corollary of their legal nature."[1323] Criticising the Draft articles for the lack of legal certainty with respect to third-party countermeasures, Paulus has argued that "if countermeasures are permitted in cases of simple breach of a bilateral obligation, it is inconceivable to provide a lower threshold of protection to those obligations considered erga omnes or even jus cogens."[1324] However, Paulus has warned against the possible substitution of "community interests" with interests of individual states legitimised by philosophical speculations.[1325] According to him, the identification of "community

1318 ibid 11–15; Dawidowicz, 'Public Law Enforcement without Public Law Safeguards?' (n 372).

1319 Hillgruber (n 503) 273–278.

1320 ibid 274. This conclusion sounds even stronger in relation to the crime of genocide. The Genocide Convention prescribes in Article 1 a general obligation to "prevent and punish" the crime of genocide. Thus, Christian Hillgruber argues that third-party countermeasures are covered by this general obligation.

1321 ibid 277.

1322 ibid 291.

1323 Andreas Paulus, 'Whether Universal Values Can Prevail over Bilateralism and Reciprocity' in Antonio Cassese (ed), *Realizing Utopia: The Future of International Law* (Oxford University Press 2012) 90–91.

1324 ibid 101.

1325 ibid 91.

interests" and "universal values" requires a collective legitimate decision-making procedure.[1326]

These discussions reveal that the inconclusive text of the Draft articles has inspired a long-lasting scholarly debate on the legality of third-party countermeasures. Since unilateral human rights sanctions are third-party countermeasures in the sense outlined in the Draft articles, their legality is debatable.

Against this background, an argument advanced by Mortimer Sellers deserves our attention. Sellers argues in favour of using the term "sanction" to denote restrictive measures imposed on human rights grounds instead of "countermeasures."[1327] The distinction between the two terms, according to Sellers, is the following: "'Sanction' is best used of countermeasures undertaken primarily to enforce universal or public interests protected by international law, such as fundamental human rights. 'Countermeasure' (without further elaboration) indicates a legitimate measure taken under international law to protect one's own particular interests. The difference is a matter of emphasis, but meaningful, and worth preserving."[1328]

3 Economic Sanctions Targeting Human Rights Violations and the Immunities of Heads of States and Other High-Ranking Government Officials

In recent times, unilateral human rights sanctions have frequently targeted heads of states and other senior government officials. For instance, the Venezuela Defense of Human Rights and Civil Society Act of 2014 authorises the blocking of property belonging to, as well as the imposition of travel restrictions on, the current or former officials of the government of Venezuela, if these persons committed or were otherwise involved in human rights violations in Venezuela.[1329] In a similar vein, the United States introduced unilateral sanctions against commanders of the Burmese Security Forces for serious human rights abuses.[1330] More specifically, the Burmese military

1326 Paulus (n 1323).

1327 Sellers (n 1304) 481–482.

1328 ibid 482.

1329 Venezuela Defense of Human Rights and Civil Society Act of 2014, Public Law 113–278, Dec. 18, 2014, 128 Stat. 3011 Section 5.

1330 President of the United States of America. Executive Order 13818 of December 20, 2017. Blocking the Property of Persons Involved in Serious Human Rights Abuse or Corruption. (n 210).

official Maung Maung Soe was designated as the chief of the Burmese Army's Western Command, which was responsible for human rights atrocities committed against Rohingya population.[1331]

High-ranking government officials of Iran are also subject to various restrictions for human rights violations. For example, Ansar-e Hizballah was designated "for being an official of the Government of Iran or a person acting on behalf of the Government of Iran (including members of paramilitary organizations) who is responsible for or complicit in, or responsible for ordering, controlling, or otherwise directing, the commission of serious human rights abuses against persons in Iran or Iranian citizens or residents, or the family members of the foregoing."[1332]

The recent wave of the US sanctions against senior government officials has targeted the Saudi Arabian and Russian nationals. In particular, restrictive measures were imposed against the following individuals: Mohammed al Otaibi, former consul general of Saudi Arabia in Istanbul, for serious human rights abuses relating to the murder of Jamal Khashoggi at the consulate in Istanbul in October 2018, and Aslan Iraskhanov, head of the ministry of interior affairs for Grozny in the Chechen Republic of the Russian Federation, who is "credibly alleged to be responsible for the summary execution of 27 men" in his previous role as the head of the A.A. Kadyrov police unit.[1333] Previously, Zimbabwe's minister of state for national security, Owen Ncube was sanctioned for his involvement in gross violations of human rights.[1334]

1331 ibid.

1332 President of the United States of America. Executive Order 13553 of September 28, 2010. Blocking Property of Certain Persons With Respect to Serious Human Rights Abuses by the Government of Iran and Taking Certain Other Actions.

1333 'Public Designations of Current and Former Foreign Government Officials Due to Involvement in Gross Violations of Human Rights Under Section 7031(c) of the Department of State, Foreign Operations, and Related Programs Appropriations Act' (*United States Department of State*, 10 December 2019) <https://www.state.gov/public-designations-of-current-and-former-foreign-government-officials-due-to-involvement-in-gross-violations-of-human-rights-under-section-7031c-of-the-department-of-state-foreign-operations-and/>.

1334 'Public Designation of Owen Ncube, Due to Involvement in Gross Violations of Human Rights, under Section 7031(c) of the FY 2019 Department of State, Foreign Operations, and Related Programs Appropriations Act' (*United States Department of State*, 25 October 2019) <https://www.state.gov/public-designation-of-owen-ncube-due-to-involvement-in-gross-violations-of-human-rights-under-section-7031c-of-the-fy-2019-department-of-state-foreign-operations-and-related-programs-appropriati/>.

It is not only the United States that enacts such unilateral sanctions against the heads of states and senior government officials. Other states do so as well. In 2011, Switzerland decided to freeze the assets of the then-head of state Colonel Gadaffi as well as the assets of the Libyan Central Bank.[1335] In 2018, Switzerland imposed sanctions on Venezuela in alignment with the EU sanctions, including restrictions on the government officials responsible for grave human rights violations.[1336]

In November 2019, the European Union renewed sanctions targeting 25 individuals in official positions deemed responsible for human rights violations and/or for undermining democracy and the rule of law in Venezuela.[1337] In discussing the EU's targeted economic sanctions imposed on human rights grounds, Clara Portela has observed: "The focus on officials from state authorities shows that individual designations are employed to denounce state-led or state-sponsored abuses perpetrated against the civilian population."[1338]

Against this backdrop, the question that requires further elucidation is whether these restrictive measures impede immunities granted under international law to the heads of states and other high-ranking government officials. For our subsequent discussion, the distinction between the immunities of a head of state and the immunities of other high-ranking government officials should be drawn.

The immunity of a head of state encompasses immunity in a public capacity (in other words, "as a state") as well as personal immunity.[1339] In *Arrest Warrant of 11 April 2000*, the ICJ unequivocally concluded that "in international law it is firmly established that [...] certain holders of high-ranking office in a State, such as the Head of State [...] enjoy immunities from jurisdiction in other States, both civil and criminal."[1340] Without defining the exact scope of this immunity, the court strongly emphasised that the finding that certain actions encroach on immunity should be based on the assessment of whether such

---

1335 'Switzerland Freezes Gaddafi Assets' (*SWI swissinfo.ch*) <https://www.swissinfo.ch/eng/switzerland-freezes-gaddafi-assets/29581082>.

1336 'Sanktionen Gegenüber Venezuela' (*SECO – Staatssekretariat für Wirtschaft*) <https://www.seco.admin.ch/seco/de/home/seco/nsb-news.msg-id-70265.html>.

1337 'Venezuela: Council Renews Sanctions until 14 November 2020' (*Council of the European Union*) <http://www.consilium.europa.eu/en/press/press-releases/2019/11/11/venezuela-council-renews-sanctions-until-14-november-2020/>.

1338 Portela (n 24) 18.

1339 Fox and Webb (n 762) 544.

1340 *Arrest Warrant of 11 April 2000 (Democratic Republic of the Congo v. Belgium), Judgment* (n 804) [51].

actions hinder the performance of the duties by the holder of the high-ranking office.[1341] In *Certain Questions of Mutual Assistance in Criminal Matters,* the ICJ reiterated this view: "Thus the determining factor in assessing whether or not there has been an attack on the immunity of the Head of State lies in the subjection of the latter to a constraining act of authority."[1342] According to the ICJ jurisprudence, the issuance of an arrest warrant hinders the ability of the minister of foreign affairs to travel abroad and perform his duties and thus violates his entitlement to immunity,[1343] while the issuance of witness summons addressed to the acting head of state during his official visit to the state that issued these summons does not encroach on his immunities.[1344]

The scope of the personal immunity of a head of state remains debatable.[1345] Despite this, a few principles governing this personal immunity can be discerned. Personal immunity implies the inviolability of a head of state, covering their physical integrity,[1346] as well as the inviolability of their premises in a foreign state – at least during official visits.[1347]

Some scholars argue that the immunity granted under international law is invoked only in the course of court proceedings and, for this reason, unilateral economic sanctions that are, as a rule, imposed by the executive or legislative branch cannot infringe on the privileges accorded by this immunity.[1348] Although this is a tenable intellectual position, the counterargument is that if these immunity entitlements protect certain foreign holders of high-ranking government positions during court proceedings, the same standard of protection should also be guaranteed for executive decision-making. There is no unanimity on this subject.[1349]

1341 ibid [53]-[55].

1342 *Certain Questions of Mutual Assistance in Criminal Matters (Djibouti v. France), Judgment* (n 804) [170].

1343 *Arrest Warrant of 11 April 2000 (Democratic Republic of the Congo v. Belgium), Judgment* (n 804).

1344 *Certain Questions of Mutual Assistance in Criminal Matters (Djibouti v. France), Judgment* (n 804).

1345 On the various approaches to the personal immunity of a head of state, see Fox and Webb (n 762) 550.

1346 "Apart from physical attacks or interference, State practice is less certain as to the extent of the respect to be afforded to a Head of State, with protection, where afforded more attributable to courtesy or comity than obligation under international law." ibid 552.

1347 Watts (n 801).

1348 Ruys (n 11).

1349 For a more detailed discussion, see chapter 2, section 6. Unilateral economic sanctions and the immunities of states and state officials.

Bearing in mind our discussion of the scope of the immunities guaranteed to an acting head of state, we may conclude that unilateral human rights sanctions which entail travel restrictions on an acting head of state present a significant risk of infringing immunities accorded under international law. When it comes to restrictions such as the freezing of personal assets, there is no unanimity about whether these restraints can be covered by the rules on immunity from execution.[1350] Hence, the compatibility of asset freezes with immunity guarantees remains undefined.[1351]

The definition of the scope of the immunity of government officials poses even more vexed questions, namely: who is entitled to benefit from such immunity? And what is the scope of this immunity?

The ICJ's jurisprudence may shed light on the nature and scope of the immunity of government officials. The ICJ has acknowledged that heads of governments, as well as ministers of foreign affairs, are entitled to immunities.[1352] While ministers of foreign affairs are entitled to immunity guarantees, certain other categories of government officials cannot benefit from these guarantees. The ICJ affirms that "there are no grounds in international law upon which it could be said that the officials concerned [the procureur de la République and the Head of National Security] were entitled to personal immunities."[1353] The reason for this conclusion is the essentially internal nature of their functions.[1354] However, the ICJ also acknowledges that "other persons representing a State in specific fields may be authorized by that State to bind it by their statements in respect of matter falling within their purview."[1355] This pronouncement has

1350 For a more detailed discussion, see chapter 2, section 6. Unilateral economic sanctions and the immunities of states and state officials.

1351 Ruys (n 11); Ronzitti (n 11); Thouvenin and Grandaubert (n 771).

1352 "The Court would observe at the outset that in international law it is firmly established that, as also diplomatic and consular agents, certain holders of high-ranking office in a State, such as the Head of State, Head of Government and Minister for Foreign Affairs, enjoy immunities from jurisdiction in other States, both civil and criminal." *Arrest Warrant of 11 April 2000 (Democratic Republic of the Congo v. Belgium), Judgment* (n 804) [51].

1353 *Certain Questions of Mutual Assistance in Criminal Matters (Djibouti v. France), Judgment* (n 804) [194].

1354 ibid.

1355 The ICJ observed: "The Court notes, however, that with increasing frequency in modern international relations other persons representing a State in specific fields may be authorized by that State to bind it by their statements in respect of matters falling within their purview. This may be true, for example, of holders of technical ministerial portfolios exercising powers in their field of competence in the area of foreign relations, and even of certain officials." *Armed Activities on the Territory of the Congo (New Application: 2002)*

been interpreted by commentators as "expand[ing] the categories of high-ranking officials benefiting from immunity *ratione personae*."[1356]

The scope of the immunity of high-ranking government officials is not well defined in customary international law. That said, given the ICJ judgement in *Arrest Warrant of 11 April 2000*, it is beyond dispute that the ability to travel internationally is covered by such immunities.[1357] Furthermore, the court acknowledged that senior government officials enjoy jurisdictional immunity throughout their term of office, even if there are allegations that they might be responsible for grave violations of human rights.[1358]

This entails that unilateral human rights sanctions in the form of travel restrictions may encroach on the immunity of the high-ranking government officials and thus constitute a violation of international obligations of the state that imposes them. However, these immunities are guaranteed only to a subset of high-ranking government officials, whose functions are not of an essentially internal nature. Given that the scope of the immunity of high-ranking government officials remains ambiguous, the consistency of the other types of unilateral human rights sanctions, such as asset freezes, with immunity guarantees remains undefined.

Of particular importance for our discussion is the question of whether unilateral restrictive measures can impede immunities granted under international law and still be justified on the human right grounds. In other words, can human rights considerations trump immunities?

In answering these questions, the following conclusion of Peter-Tobias Stoll on the intricacies of the relations between human rights and immunity is worthy of consideration: "the argument has been made that human rights norms may trump the customary rules of State immunity in cases where they may be considered to form part of *jus cogens*, as would be the case, for instance,

---

(*Democratic Republic of the Congo v. Rwanda*), *Jurisdiction and Admissibility, Judgment* (n 1069) [47].

1356 Fox and Webb (n 762) 565.

1357 "In the performance of these functions, he or she is frequently required to travel internationally, and thus must be in a position freely to do so whenever the need should arise." *Arrest Warrant of 11 April 2000* (*Democratic Republic of the Congo v. Belgium*), *Judgment* (n 804) [53].

1358 "The Court accordingly concludes that the functions of a Minister for Foreign Affairs are such that, throughout the duration of his or her office, he or she when abroad enjoys full immunity from criminal jurisdiction and inviolability. That immunity and that inviolability protect the individual concerned against any act of authority of another State which would hinder him or her in the performance of his or her duties." ibid [54].

with regard to the prohibition of torture. Indeed, the peremptory nature of those norms may be considered to suggest that they should be given effect, and it is often concluded that this entails that State immunity does not apply in the cases at hand. However, as has been observed by the ECtHR and the ILC Working Group, there are hardly any cases where immunity has indeed been denied on those grounds. This line of argument draws a line between a human rights standard and the potential legal consequences of its violation, including a denial of State immunity. Seen from this perspective, the potential peremptory character of the former does not at once have an impact on State immunity."[1359]

In the previous chapter, we discussed whether a violation of peremptory norms (jus cogens) entails legal consequences for the application of immunities granted to the states, as well as high-ranking government officials under international law.[1360] Our analysis confirmed the view expressed by Peter-Tobias Stoll.

The analysis of the pertinent ICJ jurisprudence demonstrates that human rights considerations cannot trump immunities. In *Jurisdictional Immunities of the State*, the ICJ was confronted with the question of whether the entitlement to the immunity from jurisdiction can be overridden if the claim that gives rise to a dispute is a violation of jus cogens.[1361] Ruling on this contentious matter, the court distinguished between the substantive jus cogens norms and the procedural norms of state immunity and thus concluded that these two sets of norms are not in conflict.[1362] The court further concluded that "whether a State is entitled to immunity before the courts of another State is a question entirely separate from whether the international responsibility of that State is engaged and whether it has an obligation to make reparation."[1363]

In the same way, the ICJ underlined the difference between immunity and impunity by explicitly stressing that: "Immunity from criminal jurisdiction and individual criminal responsibility are quite separate concepts. While

1359 Stoll (n 750).

1360 For a more detailed discussion, see chapter 3, subsection 2.1 Jus cogens.

1361 The dispute was initiated by Germany as a challenge to the decisions of Italian courts, in which compensation was granted to the victims of the atrocities committed by the German armed forces that occurred in 1943–1945. *Jurisdictional Immunities of the State (Germany v. Italy: Greece intervening), Judgment* (n 786).

1362 ibid [93].

1363 ibid [100].

jurisdictional immunity is procedural in nature, criminal responsibility is a question of substantive law."[1364]

The European Court of Human Rights was reluctant to depart from the traditional tenets of international law, acknowledging that "the recent judgment of the ICJ in Germany v. Italy [...] – which must be considered by this Court as authoritative as regards the content of customary international law – clearly establishes that, by February 2012, no jus cogens exception to State immunity had yet crystallised."[1365]

These judgements, along with other court decisions, have sparked a debate among scholars about whether immunity entitlements can be curtailed by a human rights exception.[1366] While these theoretical discussions have not triggered changes in the practice of international courts, which are dominated by the procedural-substantive divide, the possibility of justifying unilateral economic sanctions that impede immunity entitlements on human rights grounds seems unfeasible.

4 Economic Sanctions Imposed on Human Rights Grounds and WTO Law

Starting from the early 2000s, legal scholars fiercely debated the relationship between human rights and international trade law.[1367] Thus, this discussion is hardly novel. To a large extent, the interest in the WTO on the part of human rights scholars can be explained by its effective dispute settlement system and the possibility of retaliating against a state that is not abiding by its

1364 *Arrest Warrant of 11 April 2000 (Democratic Republic of the Congo v. Belgium), Judgment* (n 804) [60].

1365 *Jones and Others v. the United Kingdom, Applications no 34356/06 and 40528/06* (ECtHR, 14 January 2014) [198].

1366 Costelloe (n 1155) 246–259; Ingrid Wuerth, 'International Law in the Post-Human Rights Era' (2017) 96 Texas Law Review 279; Dapo Akande and Sangeeta Shah, 'Immunities of State Officials, International Crimes, and Foreign Domestic Courts' (2010) 21 European Journal of International Law = Journal europeen de droit international 815; Alexander Orakhelashvili, 'Immunities of State Officials, International Crimes, and Foreign Domestic Courts: A Reply to Dapo Akande and Sangeeta Shah' (2011) 22 European Journal of International Law 849.

1367 The World Trade Forum held in 2001 was devoted to a discussion of the interlinkages between the two regimes – human rights law and international trade law. Frederick M Abbott, Christine Breining-Kaufmann and Thomas Cottier, *International Trade and Human Rights: Foundations and Conceptual Issues* (The University of Michigan Press 2006).

membership obligations.[1368] In the course of this debate, the WTO consistency of unilateral human rights sanctions was also discussed.[1369]

However that may be, there is a need to re-examine the relationship between unilateral human rights sanctions and international trade law. This enquiry is warranted for a number of reasons. First of all, states frequently rely upon unilateral human rights sanctions.[1370] Second, the overwhelming bulk of the literature on the subject dates back to the times when WTO jurisprudence on the public morals and the national security exceptions was non-existent.[1371] As a result, the possibility of justifying economic sanctions targeting human rights violations under these exceptions was not analysed in light of recent WTO jurisprudence. Third, in January 2019, Venezuela – facing a barrage of unilateral economic sanctions imposed by the US, including human rights sanctions – brought the first-ever complaint against unilateral human

1368 Writing in 2002 about human rights and multilateral trading system, Thomas Cottier argued that human rights scholars and activists linked human rights with international trade only recently and that this was not the case in the 1980s and early 1990s. Thomas Cottier, 'Trade and Human Rights: A Relationship to Discover' (2002) 5 Journal of International Economic Law 111. It is reasonable to assume that such a development could have been influenced by the outcomes of the Uruguay Round, the creation of a new institution – the WTO – and a substantial formalisation of the dispute settlement system. In a decentralised and fragmented system of public international law, a state might have various, at times overlapping or contradictory obligations. Taking into consideration the relatively weak enforcement of human rights norms and an effective WTO dispute settlement system, states might be more inclined to comply with international trade norms than their human rights obligations. Yet, at the same time, some scholars, such as Gabrielle Marceau, argue that there can be no conflict between the trade rules and international human rights obligations. Gabrielle Marceau, 'WTO Dispute Settlement and Human Rights' (2002) 13 European Journal of International Law 753.

1369 Cleveland (n 551); Cleveland (n 27); Carlos Manuel Vasquez, 'Trade Sanctions and Human Rights – Past, Present, and Future' (2003) 6 Journal of International Economic Law 797; Robert L Howse and Jared M Genser, 'Are EU Trade Sanctions on Burma Compatible with WTO Law' (2007) Michigan Journal of International Law 165; Jeroen Denkers, *The World Trade Organization and Import Bans in Response to Violations of Fundamental Labour Rights* (Intersentia 2008).

1370 According to the database in Economic Sanctions Reconsidered, approximately 20 per cent of economic sanctions included in that database were imposed on human rights grounds. Hufbauer and others (n 28).

1371 The first panel report in which the public morals clause was interpreted dates back to 2005. *Panel Report, United States – Measures Affecting the Cross-Border Supply of Gambling and Betting Services, WT/DS285/R, adopted 20 April 2005, as modified by Appellate Body Report WT/DS285/AB/R, DSR 2005:XII, p 5797*. The invocation of the national security exception was discussed in a panel report that dates back to 2019. *Panel Report, Russia – Measures Concerning Traffic in Transit* (n 7).

rights sanctions before the WTO.[1372] Due to the political pressure exerted on Venezuela, it decided not to proceed with its request to establish a panel, even though the request had been submitted.[1373]

Human rights sanctions can take various forms. For the subsequent analysis, I rely upon the classification of unilateral human rights sanctions introduced by Sarah Cleveland.[1374] In her view, these coercive measures might be classified as "tailored," "semi-tailored" and "general" trade sanctions.[1375] Tailored sanctions are imposed for human rights violations that occur in the process of production or use of goods.[1376] An example of such a restriction is Section 307 of the US Tariff Act that prohibits the import of the goods produced with the convict, forced or indentured labour.[1377] Semi-tailored sanctions are directed against goods that are more broadly associated with human rights violations,[1378] for instance, an import prohibition on products if the proceeds are used to finance military operations against ethnic minorities. The broadest category is general sanctions, which, according to Sarah Cleveland, are "the most common form of human rights trade measures."[1379] This subgroup includes economic sanctions employed to remedy human rights violations that are not related to international trade, such as genocide, the denial of basic human rights to certain groups of the population, the use of torture, etc. The concern that general sanctions can be used as a form of disguised protectionism is not groundless. Thus, their use should be strictly regulated.

General sanctions can take various forms: import and export bans on goods and services, restrictions on traffic in transit and goods in transit, asset freezes and other financial restrictions, visa restrictions, etc. Additionally, the termination of foreign development aid has been frequently employed by states to

1372 Iryna Bogdanova, 'WTO Dispute on the US Human Rights Sanctions Is Looming on the Horizon' (*EJIL: Talk!*, 31 January 2019) <https://www.ejiltalk.org/wto-dispute-on-the-us-human-rights-sanctions-is-looming-on-the-horizon/>.

1373 The United States did not engage in consultations and contended that it is not obliged to do so, given that it does not recognise the current Venezuelan government as legitimate. In response, Venezuela proceeded with the request to establish a panel. The United States refused to agree to the agenda proposed for the meeting and, as a result, the meeting was postponed. In the next DSB meeting, which took place on 11 April 2019, the issue was not on the agenda.

1374 Cleveland (n 27).

1375 ibid.

1376 ibid 138.

1377 ibid 138–139.

1378 ibid 140.

1379 ibid 142.

promote human rights in the developing and least developed countries.[1380] Foreign development aid is a voluntary commitment on the part of a particular state, and thus its termination is an act of retorsion.[1381] In the context of international trade relations, developed states, for example the EU Member States, provide additional market access advantages for the developing and in particular the least developed countries under the condition that those states comply with various human rights obligations.[1382] Otherwise, the preferences granted would be withdrawn.[1383]

Discussing the reasons behind unilateral human rights sanctions, Sarah Cleveland contends that these sanctions seek not only to punish rogue states for their human rights violations, but also to assist "in the international definition, promulgation, recognition, and domestic internalization of human rights norms."[1384] In another publication, Cleveland argues: "Unilateral human rights sanctions are employed by countries for a variety of reasons. They may be used to punish a foreign state for its human rights practices, to deprive a rogue state of needed goods or foreign currency, to express the sending state's outrage at human rights atrocities, to prevent a state's own markets from contributing to human rights violations, to morally distance a state from human rights violators, and to generate pressure for the adoption of multilateral action."[1385]

In chapter 2, we discussed the fact that unilateral economic sanctions violate various obligations embedded in the WTO Agreements.[1386] Assuming that general economic sanctions imposed on human rights grounds may take the same form as the unilateral economic sanctions discussed in chapter 2, there is no need to re-examine their WTO inconsistency, and we can rely upon the analysis presented before. The subsequent analysis focuses on the discussion of the possibility to justify unilateral economic sanctions imposed on human rights grounds. The public morals exception and the national security exception are

---

1380 For more information about the US policies in the 1990s, see Cleveland (n 551) 38–40.

1381 Ruys (n 4).

1382 "[…] additional tariff preferences (normally duty free treatment), were made available to developing countries committing to ratify and implement a list of human rights and good governance conventions." Lorand Bartels, 'The WTO Legality of the EU's GSP + Arrangement' (2007) 10(4) Journal of International Economic Law, 869.

1383 James Yap, 'Beyond 'Don't Be Evil': The European Union GSP + Trade Preference Scheme and the Incentivisation of the Sri Lankan Garment Industry to Foster Human Rights' (2013) 19(2) European Law Journal, 283.

1384 Cleveland (n 551) 6.

1385 Cleveland (n 27) 135.

1386 For a more detailed discussion, see section 7. Unilateral economic sanctions and WTO law.

reviewed, while the invocation of these two exceptions by the WTO Members to justify their unilateral human rights sanctions is shown to be highly likely.

4.1 *Justification under the Public Morals Exception*

The public morals exception reads as follows: "Subject to the requirement that such measures are not applied in a manner which would constitute a means of arbitrary or unjustifiable discrimination between countries where the same conditions prevail, or a disguised restriction on international trade, nothing in this Agreement shall be construed to prevent the adoption or enforcement by any contracting party of measures: (a) necessary to protect public morals."[1387] The GATT 1994 and the GATS stipulate a similar public morals exception.[1388] Hence, in the following analysis, I will refer to the GATT 1994, but the findings are also valid for the possibility of justifying human rights sanctions under the GATS exception.

According to well-established WTO jurisprudence, a WTO-inconsistent measure can be justified under the general exceptions on the condition that this measure falls under one of the listed exceptions and meets the requirements of the chapeau of Article XX of the GATT 1994.[1389] Thus, the analysis proceeds as follows: at the outset, the prerequisites required for a measure to be "necessary to protect public morals" are determined, and the possibility of human rights sanctions to comply with these prerequisites is discussed. Subsequently, the requirements of the chapeau of Article XX of the GATT 1994 are enumerated, and compliance with these requirements is assessed.

Before we proceed, the question of whether the public morals exception justifies inwardly directed or outwardly directed measures calls for further clarification.[1390] The text of the public morals exception does not prescribe any distinction, and WTO jurisprudence does not provide a straightforward

---

1387 Article XX(a) GATT 1994.

1388 The GATS stipulates the similar exception "(a) necessary to protect public morals or to maintain public order."

1389 This sequence of analysis was introduced by the AB in its first report. *Appellate Body Report, United States – Standards for Reformulated and Conventional Gasoline, WT/DS2/AB/R, adopted 20 May 1996, DSR 1996:I, p 3.*

1390 Definitions of inwardly directed and outwardly directed trade measures are arbitrary and imprecise. For instance, Steve Charnovitz framed these definitions in the following way: "This Article will employ the term 'outwardly-directed' to describe trade measures used to protect the morals of foreigners residing outside one's own country. Conversely, trade measures used to protect the morals of persons in one's own country will be described as 'inwardly-directed.'" In the meantime, Charnovitz recognised the arbitrariness of this distinction. Steve Charnovitz, 'The Moral Exception in Trade Policy' (1998) 38 Virginia Journal of International Law 689, 695–696.

answer. The WTO adjudicators examined the public morals clause in several disputes, such as *US – Gambling* and *China – Publications and Audiovisual Products*, and the regulations scrutinised in these disputes intended to protect the morals of the persons residing inside the state that introduced them.[1391] In *EC – Seal Products*, the import restrictions imposed had an impact on the protection of animal welfare outside of the European Union.[1392] Despite this, the parties to that dispute agreed that there was a "sufficient nexus" between the import ban, the public moral concerns and the activities addressed by the measure, and thus the AB did not elaborate on the issue.[1393] Notwithstanding the apparent significance of the question at hand, I argue that similar to the import ban in *EC – Seal Products*, unilateral economic sanctions imposed on human rights grounds might be implemented to protect the public morals of the WTO Member that imposed these restrictions. For this reason, any further discussion of the issue can be omitted.

4.1.1 The Definition of "Public Morals"

The majority of bilateral trade agreements signed after 1927 incorporated a moral exception clause, which was commonly drafted as "prohibitions or restrictions imposed on moral or humanitarian grounds."[1394] Hence, it is not a coincidence that the public morals exception was incorporated into the GATT 1947 and then integrated into the GATT 1994. Discussing the negotiating history of the GATT's moral clause, Steve Charnovitz provides numerous examples of the state practise that existed before the negotiations[1395] and acknowledges that "the moral exception was a response to the fact that many governments were banning imports and exports for moral or humanitarian reasons."[1396]

The final text of the public morals exception excludes any reference to trade restrictions imposed on "humanitarian grounds." Charnovitz illustrates the

1391 *Appellate Body Report, United States – Measures Affecting the Cross-Border Supply of Gambling and Betting Services, WT/DS285/AB/R, adopted 20 April 2005, DSR 2005:XII, p 5663 (and Corr1, DSR 2006:XII, p 5475); Appellate Body Report, China – Measures Affecting Trading Rights and Distribution Services for Certain Publications and Audiovisual Entertainment Products, WT/DS363/AB/R, adopted 19 January 2010, DSR 2010:I, p 3.*

1392 *Appellate Body Reports, European Communities – Measures Prohibiting the Importation and Marketing of Seal Products* (n 822).

1393 ibid [5.173].

1394 Charnovitz (n 1390) 708–709.

1395 The examples include anti-slavery treaties, the narcotics regime, international regime regulating trade in liquor and regime regulating traffic in obscene publications. ibid 710–716.

1396 ibid 710.

obscurity that emerged from this omission: "On the one hand, one might argue that 'public morals' subsumes both 'moral' and 'humanitarian' grounds. On the other hand, one might argue that 'humanitarian' grounds were intentionally left out of 'public morals.' The issue is an important one since humanitarian aims are more likely to be outwardly-directed than inwardly-directed."[1397]

The negotiating history of the clause sheds little light on the meaning of the ambiguous term "public morals,"[1398] of which the WTO adjudicators adopted an all-embracing and amorphous definition. The panel in *US – Gambling* asserted that "the term 'public morals' denotes standards of right and wrong conduct maintained by or on behalf of a community or nation."[1399] Furthermore, the panel observed that various factors might be considered to define the exact scope of "public morals." It was admitted that public morals "can vary in time and space, depending upon a range of factors, including prevailing social, cultural, ethical and religious values."[1400]

The panel acknowledged a WTO Member's right to determine "public morals" within its territory: "Members should be given some scope to define and apply for themselves the concepts of 'public morals' and 'public order' in their respective territories, according to their own systems and scales of values."[1401] This approach was reiterated when, in response to Canada's argument that similar moral concerns should be addressed in the same way, the AB pronounced: "Members may set different levels of protection even when responding to similar interests of moral concern."[1402] The WTO adjudicators upheld these conclusions in their subsequent jurisprudence.[1403]

1397 ibid 716–717.

1398 Charnovitz (n 1390); Mark Wu, 'Free Trade and the Protection of Public Morals: An Analysis of the Newly Emerging Public Morals Clause Doctrine' (2008) 33 The Yale Journal of International Law 215.

1399 *Panel Report, United States – Measures Affecting the Cross-Border Supply of Gambling and Betting Services* (n 1371) [6.465].

1400 ibid [6.461].

1401 ibid.

1402 *Appellate Body Reports, European Communities – Measures Prohibiting the Importation and Marketing of Seal Products* (n 822) [5.200].

1403 *Panel Report, China – Measures Affecting Trading Rights and Distribution Services for Certain Publications and Audiovisual Entertainment Products, WT/DS363/R and Corr1, adopted 19 January 2010, as modified by Appellate Body Report WT/DS363/AB/R, DSR 2010:II, p 261; Panel Reports, European Communities – Measures Prohibiting the Importation and Marketing of Seal Products* (n 825); *Panel Report, Colombia – Measures Relating to the Importation of Textiles, Apparel and Footwear, WT/DS461/R and Add1, adopted 22 June 2016, as modified by Appellate Body Report WT/DS461/AB/R, DSR 2016:III, p 1227; Panel Reports, Brazil – Certain Measures Concerning Taxation and Charges, WT/DS472/R, Add1 and Corr1*

As a result, WTO Members have been granted significant latitude to define their "public morals." Nonetheless, this latitude "does not excuse a responding party in dispute settlement from its burden of establishing that the alleged public policy objective at issue is indeed a public moral objective according to its value system."[1404]

A WTO Member that invokes the public morals exception is obliged to prove that the trade-restrictive measures introduced address the public morals of a particular society. To prove this, the Member can demonstrate that the objective of such measures reflects "standards of right and wrong conduct" in a particular society and that the trade restrictions are being implemented in order to achieve such an objective linked to public morality. To demonstrate this, factual evidence can be presented. For example, the panel in *EC – Seal Products* has assessed "the texts of the statutes, the legislative history, and other evidence regarding the structure and operation of the measure at issue."[1405] In other words, a WTO Member cannot simply introduce public morals as a defence without showing that this had been a domestic concern in the process of legislation, administration and adjudication of the measure challenged.[1406]

The all-encompassing definition of "public morals" allows WTO Members to argue that human rights sanctions pursue "public morals" objectives. A WTO Member can rely upon its obligations under human rights treaties, as well as domestic human rights standards to demonstrate that human rights considerations constitute "public morals." In this context, Gabrielle Marceau suggests that if a WTO Member justifies its human rights measures under the public morals clause, a panel can examine this Member's participation in the relevant human rights treaties.[1407] According to Gabrielle Marceau, such an examination has three goals: "1. As evidence of the 'importance of the values and common interests' protected by the measure; 2. As evidence of the efficacy of the chosen measure; and 3. As evidence of the good faith and consistent behaviour of the concerned member."[1408] Other scholars support this conclusion.[1409]

/ WT/DS497/R, Add1 and Corr1, adopted 11 January 2019, as modified by Appellate Body Reports WT/DS472/AB/R / WT/DS497/AB/R.

1404 *Panel Reports, Brazil – Certain Measures Concerning Taxation and Charges* (n 1403) [7.558].

1405 *Panel Reports, European Communities – Measures Prohibiting the Importation and Marketing of Seal Products* (n 825) [7.378] and fn 627 thereto.

1406 Thomas Cottier, 'The Implications of EC – Seal Products for the Protection of Core Labour Standards in WTO Law' in Henner Gött (ed), *Labour Standards in International Economic Law* (Springer 2018).

1407 Marceau (n 1368).

1408 ibid 791.

1409 "Human rights law is most likely to be raised by a party to a dispute as evidence supporting an assertion of fact." Rachel Harris and Gillian Moon, '"Gatt" Article XX and Human

4.1.2 An Analytical Framework for Assessing Whether Economic Sanctions Targeting Human Rights Violations Are "Necessary to Protect Public Morals"

The AB developed an analytical framework to assess if a disputed measure is "necessary to protect public morals." This analytical framework consists of two steps: the member must demonstrate that the measure in question has been adopted "to protect public morals" and that it is "necessary."[1410]

4.1.2.1 *The "Design Step" of the Analysis*

The AB was confronted with a need to interpret the meaning of "to protect" in *EC – Seal Products*. In this dispute, Canada argued that the requirement "to protect" entails that a risk to public morals must exist and a measure, which is designed "to protect public morals," shall address this risk.[1411] The EU opposed this view.[1412] The AB ruled that "to protect" in Article XX(a) does not require the existence of a risk to public morals.[1413]

Rights: What Do We Know from the First 20 Years?' (2015) 16 Melbourne Journal of International Law 432.

1410 *Appellate Body Reports, European Communities – Measures Prohibiting the Importation and Marketing of Seal Products* (n 822) [5.169]; *Panel Report, Colombia – Measures Relating to the Importation of Textiles, Apparel and Footwear* (n 1403) [7.293].

1411 "Canada 'extrapolate[s] that the test to be applied' in determining whether a measure falls within the scope of application of Article XX(a) includes three elements: (i) 'identification of a public moral'; (ii) 'identification of a risk to that public moral'; and (iii) 'establishing that a nexus exists between the challenged measure and the protection of the public moral against that risk in the sense that the measure is capable of making a contribution to the protection of that public moral.'" *Appellate Body Reports, European Communities – Measures Prohibiting the Importation and Marketing of Seal Products* (n 822) [2.28].

1412 "Contrary to Canada's arguments, the European Union submits that there is no requirement to assess the 'risk' to public morals in order to determine whether a measure falls within the scope of Article XX(a). Instead, such examination must be undertaken as part of the 'necessity' analysis because, where the risks that a measure purports to address are shown to be 'inexistent or negligible,' the measure will be found 'unnecessary.' Relying on a statement by the Appellate Body in Korea – Various Measures on Beef, the European Union argues that 'all that must be shown in order to establish that a measure falls within the scope of Article XX(a) is that the measure is designed to protect public morals.'" ibid [2.140].

1413 "However, the notion of risk in the context of Article XX(b) is difficult to reconcile with the subject matter of protection under Article XX(a), namely, public morals. While the focus on the dangers or risks to human, animal, or plant life or health in the context of Article XX(b) may lend itself to scientific or other methods of inquiry, such risk-assessment methods do not appear to be of much assistance or relevance in identifying and assessing public morals. We, therefore, do not consider that the term 'to protect,' when used in relation to 'public morals' under Article XX(a), required the Panel, as Canada contends, to

The panel in *Colombia – Textiles* examined whether restrictions were adopted "to protect public morals." At first, the panel assessed whether the policy objective pursued was covered by the policies to protect "public morals."[1414] The subsequent analysis focused on whether the measure itself is designed to achieve the declared public policy goal. In this context, the panel analysed the measure's "design, architecture and revealing structure."[1415] On appeal, the AB agreed with the sequence of the analytical steps, yet clarified that the requirement "to protect" should not be excessively restrictive.[1416]

WTO adjudicators consider a wide range of evidence in assessing whether a disputed measure is "designed" or "capable of" protecting public morals. This evidence includes "the texts of statutes and/or regulations, the measure's legislative history, the measure's objective, and other evidence regarding its content, structure, and expected operation."[1417]

Economic sanctions targeting human rights violations may be "designed to" protect or "capable of" protecting public morals if certain prerequisites are met. A WTO Member can demonstrate that protection of human rights is a matter of significant concern for its population. To support this assertion, a WTO Member can describe its participation in international human rights conventions and its internal laws and practices that exemplify the role of human rights considerations in a particular society.

Furthermore, the respondent state can explain how the domestic regulation introducing the measure being challenged, as well as the operation of the measure, contribute to achieving the stated goals. For instance, a complete import ban imposed against a state that commits grave human rights violations can protect the citizens of a sending state from being exposed to the risk of buying goods from a rogue state, i.e. of buying morally objectionable goods. Similar

---

identify the existence of a risk to EU public moral concerns regarding seal welfare." ibid [5.198].

1414 *Panel Report, Colombia – Measures Relating to the Importation of Textiles, Apparel and Footwear* (n 1403) [7.297].

1415 ibid [7.343].

1416 It was noted: "With respect to the analysis of the 'design' of the measure, the phrase 'to protect public morals' calls for an initial, threshold examination in order to determine whether there is a relationship between an otherwise GATT-inconsistent measure and the protection of public morals. If this initial, threshold examination reveals that the measure is incapable of protecting public morals, there is not a relationship between the measure and the protection of public morals that meets the requirements of the 'design' step." *Appellate Body Report, Colombia – Measures Relating to the Importation of Textiles, Apparel and Footwear, WT/DS461/AB/R and Add1, adopted 22 June 2016, DSR 2016:III, p 1131* [5.68].

1417 ibid [5.80].

arguments could be relied upon to justify a partial import ban. If export restrictions are imposed, a responding state can argue that these exports contribute to an ongoing human rights violation and thus that the measure addresses the concerns of its population with respect to grave human rights violations occurring abroad.

4.1.2.2 *The Necessity Test*

The AB explicitly emphasised that the assessment of a measure's necessity imposes a stricter standard than the evaluation of a measure's design.[1418] Earlier jurisprudence had introduced the following necessity test: "a necessity analysis involves a process of 'weighing and balancing' a series of factors, including the importance of the objective, the contribution of the measure to that objective, and the trade-restrictiveness of the measure."[1419] Moreover, a measure being challenged ought to be compared with possible alternatives.[1420]

Concerning the first analytical step, the panel in *Brazil – Taxation* clarified that "the more vital or important those interests or values are, the easier it would be to accept as 'necessary' a measure otherwise found to be inconsistent with the GATT 1994."[1421] A determination of a measure's contribution is a subsequent step. The AB emphasised that panels enjoy a certain latitude in conducting contribution analysis[1422] and that such an analysis "can be done either in quantitative or in qualitative terms."[1423] Regarding the trade restrictiveness of a questioned measure, the AB pronounced that "if a Member chooses to adopt a very restrictive measure, it will have to ensure that the measure is carefully designed so that the other elements to be taken into account in weighing and balancing the factors relevant to an assessment of the 'necessity' of the measure will 'outweigh' such restrictive effect."[1424] Moreover, a complainant

---

1418 "We do not see the examination of the 'design' of the measure as a particularly demanding step of the Article XX(a) analysis. By contrast, the assessment of the 'necessity' of a measure entails a more in-depth, holistic analysis of the relationship between the measure and the protection of public morals." ibid [5.70].

1419 *Appellate Body Report, Brazil – Measures Affecting Imports of Retreaded Tyres, WT/DS332/AB/R, adopted 17 December 2007, DSR 2007:IV, p 1527* [5.169].

1420 ibid.

1421 *Panel Reports, Brazil – Certain Measures Concerning Taxation and Charges* (n 1403) [7.525].

1422 *Appellate Body Reports, European Communities – Measures Prohibiting the Importation and Marketing of Seal Products* (n 822) [5.210].

1423 ibid [5.211].

1424 *Appellate Body Report, China – Measures Affecting Trading Rights and Distribution Services for Certain Publications and Audiovisual Entertainment Products* (n 1391) [310].

may demonstrate that less trade-restrictive alternatives were available.[1425] If a complainant determines such alternatives, a respondent is required to prove that those alternatives were not available.[1426] The final determination of whether a WTO-inconsistent measure is "necessary" to protect public morals not only requires a review of the four criteria mentioned above, but also entails a holistic weighing and balancing exercise.[1427]

Unilateral economic sanctions imposed to remedy grave human rights violations have an important objective. Since it is undeniable that the protection of human rights would be acknowledged as a valid objective, human rights sanctions meet the first requirement of the necessity analysis.

Assessing the measure's contribution to the objective pursued is the next step in the necessity analysis. Although panels enjoy a certain latitude in choosing an appropriate framework for the contribution analysis, the measure must contribute to the desired outcome. Unilateral human rights sanctions imposed to restrict market access (for example, a complete import ban) can effectively prevent such access and guarantee that the country's residents are not exposed to the risk of buying morally objectionable goods and/or services. To reach this conclusion, we assume that the benchmark for the contribution analysis is the effective restriction of market access to goods and/or services that are actually "morally objectionable." This argument may establish that there is a certain degree of contribution, if a complete import ban is introduced.

As in the previous example, the benchmark for the analysis of the contribution made by a partial import ban is the restriction of market access to "morally objectionable" goods and/or services. In this regard, the question that needs to be tackled is why certain goods/services that originate in a state that abuses human rights are "morally objectionable," while other goods/services are not. A WTO Member can argue that targeted categories of goods/services arouse

1425 The panel in Brazil – Taxation pointed out that "a complaining party must also demonstrate that the proposed alternative is less trade-restrictive, and contributes to the achievement of the pursued objective to an equal or greater extent than the challenged measure." *Panel Reports, Brazil – Certain Measures Concerning Taxation and Charges* (n 1403) [7.532].

1426 *Panel Report, Colombia – Measures Relating to the Importation of Textiles, Apparel and Footwear* (n 1403) [7.326].

1427 In this respect, the weighing and balancing exercise can be understood as "a holistic operation that involves putting all the variables of the equation together and evaluating them in relation to each other after having examined them individually, in order to reach an overall judgment." *Panel Reports, Brazil – Certain Measures Concerning Taxation and Charges* (n 1403) [7.534].

strong public feelings, and thus are "morally unacceptable." It ought to be noted that establishing any such finding would be a fact-intensive exercise.

Export bans on goods and/or services face greater hurdles when it comes to demonstrating their contribution to the protection of public morals. The argument that can be advanced is that such restrictions protect public morals by denying exports to a regime that disobeys the human rights of its nationals. The weak point of this reasoning is that the exact contribution of export restrictions to the protection of public morals remains uncertain. Import bans, by contrast, can effectively restrict market access and thus prevent residents from being exposed to "morally objectionable" goods or services. The same logic does not apply to export bans. Furthermore, export bans may even contribute to a further deterioration of the human rights conditions in the targeted country.

The next stage of the analysis is a determination of trade restrictiveness. The trade restrictiveness of unilateral human rights sanctions depends on whether there is a complete or a partial ban. It is reasonable to assume that a complete import/export ban, as the most trade-restrictive measure available to the WTO Members, must make a significant contribution to achieving the objectives pursued in order to be justified. Partial import or export bans are less trade restrictive.

An examination of alternative measures is the last step of the analysis. A complaining party bears the burden of proving that alternative measures, which guarantee the same level of protection and are less trade restrictive, are available. The complaining party may suggest such alternatives as labelling schemes that inform the consumers about the origin of goods/services and thus leave the question of whether or not to buy such products in the hands of consumers.

In light of the above, a subset of unilateral human rights sanctions such as a complete import ban on goods or services, or to a lesser degree a partial import ban, may be potentially justified as "necessary" for the protection of public morals. A few clarifications are warranted here. First of all, a WTO Member that intends to justify such measures under the public morals exception would be required to demonstrate that human rights constitute public morals in a particular society. This would be a fact-intensive exercise. Second, given that the goods or services whose importation might be restricted are not related to particular human rights violations, it might be burdensome to argue that any good from a particular state is "morally objectionable." Hence, any final finding on the possibility to justify general import bans hinges on numerous factual circumstances. Furthermore, the analysis above reveals that the requirements of the necessity test under the public morals exception might be too strict to allow export bans on human rights grounds.

4.1.3 Analysis under the Chapeau of Article XX

The test under the chapeau consists of three subsequent analytical steps.[1428] The first step is to identify whether the conditions are the same in the countries between which a measure allegedly discriminates. In the AB's view, "'conditions' relating to the particular policy objective under the applicable subparagraph are relevant for the analysis under the chapeau."[1429] A respondent bears the burden of proving that the conditions prevailing in different countries are not the same.[1430] The second step is to assess whether there is discrimination. Discrimination exists "when countries in which the same conditions prevail are differently treated."[1431] Finally, adjudicators must decide whether the discrimination is arbitrary or unjustifiable. This analysis "should focus on the cause of the discrimination, or the rationale put forward to explain its existence."[1432] According to the AB: "One of the most important factors in the assessment of arbitrary or unjustifiable discrimination is the question of whether the discrimination can be reconciled with, or is rationally related to, the policy objective with respect to which the measure has been provisionally justified under one of the subparagraphs of Article XX."[1433]

If human rights sanctions are imposed against a state which persistently violates human rights, then the situation prevailing in that particular state might be unprecedented. Put differently, a WTO Member which introduces such restrictions may argue that the scale and gravity of human rights violations occurring in a particular state demonstrates that the conditions in the countries between which a measure allegedly discriminates are not the same. Consequently, the application of such human rights sanctions does not "constitute a means of arbitrary or unjustifiable discrimination" under the chapeau of Article XX.

1428 *Appellate Body Reports, European Communities – Measures Prohibiting the Importation and Marketing of Seal Products* (n 822).

1429 ibid [5.300].

1430 "If a respondent considers that the conditions prevailing in different countries are not "the same" in relevant respects, it bears the burden of proving that claim." ibid [5.301].

1431 *Appellate Body Report, United States – Import Prohibition of Certain Shrimp and Shrimp Products, WT/DS58/AB/R, adopted 6 November 1998, DSR 1998:VII, p 2755* [165].

1432 *Appellate Body Report, Brazil – Measures Affecting Imports of Retreaded Tyres* (n 1419) [226].

1433 *Appellate Body Reports, European Communities – Measures Prohibiting the Importation and Marketing of Seal Products* (n 822) [5.306].

Our analysis reveals that only a subset of human rights economic sanctions may be potentially justified under the public morals exception. More specifically, import bans on goods/services may be potentially justified, the ability to justify export restrictions under the public morals exception is hampered by the stringent requirements of the necessity test developed in WTO jurisprudence. Yet any such justification would require the existence of strong public opinion rejecting "morally objectionable" goods/services that originate in a state that abuses human rights.

4.2 *Justification under the National Security Exception*

General human rights sanctions do not target goods and/or services related to human rights violations. For this category of restrictions, the national security exception may be the most feasible way of justifying them.

Below, I discuss the first two panel reports, in which the respondents invoked the national security exception enshrined in the WTO Agreements, in particular the GATT 1994 and the TRIPS Agreement. In light of the panels' findings, the possibility of justifying human rights economic sanctions under the national security exception is analysed.

4.2.1 The WTO Tribunals' Jurisdiction over the National Security Exception

The right of the WTO tribunals to adjudicate the national security exception has been debated extensively.[1434] In *Russia – Traffic in Transit,* the Russian Federation contended that the panel does not have jurisdiction over matters related to the national security interests.[1435] It was argued that the panel had no right to engage in the examination of the measures at issue and should limit its findings to the mere acknowledgement that Article XXI of the GATT 1994 had been invoked.[1436] Against this, Ukraine claimed that the security exception is an affirmative defence, which does not modify rules on jurisdiction.[1437] A number of third parties submitted their own views on whether the

1434 The GATT 1947 and WTO disputes in which Members expressed their desire to invoke this exception reveal that it was a contentious matter for the contracting parties. *Panel Report, Russia – Measures Concerning Traffic in Transit* (n 7).

1435 "Neither the Panel nor the WTO has jurisdiction over the matters related to the measures necessary for the protection of Member's national security interests. This is explicitly reflected in the wording of Article XXI of the GATT, leaving the necessity, the form, design and the structure of such measures within the sole discretion of the Member invoking the Article." ibid Addendum Annex C-3, [59].

1436 ibid Annex C-3, [61].

1437 ibid Annex C-1, [37]-[39].

panel had jurisdiction.[1438] The overwhelming majority showed little sympathy for the argument that the invocation of the security clause falls outside the jurisdiction of the WTO tribunals.[1439] The United States argued that the panel has jurisdiction to rule over the security exception, although the clause is non-justiciable.[1440]

Against this background, the panel started its analysis by ascertaining its jurisdiction to entertain the legal claims before it. The starting point of the panel's analysis was the reiteration of the principle that international courts and tribunals "possess inherent jurisdiction which derives from the exercise of their adjudicative function."[1441] As a result, the panels are entitled to decide their substantive jurisdiction.[1442] In line with this preliminary assertion, the panel delved into the relevant provisions of the DSU, only to conclude that the invocation of the security clause falls squarely within its terms of reference.[1443]

Yet, the matter did not rest there. Emphasising the "self-judging" nature of the clause, the Russian Federation maintained that the panel is deprived of its jurisdiction *ratione materiae* over the trade measures justified by this exception.[1444] The panel engaged in an interpretative exercise, which confirmed that some elements of the security clause are susceptible to judicial review.[1445] To buttress this interpretative outcome, the panel made ample use of the negotiating history of the International Trade Organization.[1446]

The conclusion that flows logically from the panel's findings is that neither is the panel deprived of the jurisdiction to review the invocation of the security exception, nor is the clause non-justiciable.[1447]

In *Saudi Arabia – IPRs*, the respondent invoked the national security exception prescribed by Article 73(b)(iii) of the TRIPS Agreement and argued that,

1438 *Panel Report, Russia – Measures Concerning Traffic in Transit* (n 7) Annex-D.

1439 Nine third-party Members were in favour of the panel's jurisdiction to rule over the issue. ibid Annex D.

1440 The distinction between justiciable and non-justiciable legal claims is deeply rooted in US constitutional law and dates back to Chief Justice Marshall's opinion in Marbury v. Madison. For more details, see Iryna Bogdanova, 'Adjudication of the GATT Security Clause: To Be or Not to Be, This Is the Question' (2019) WTI Working Paper 01/2019 <http://www.wti.org/research/publications/1208/adjudication-of-the-gatt-security-clause-to-be-or-not-to-be-this-is-the-question/>.

1441 *Panel Report, Russia – Measures Concerning Traffic in Transit* (n 7) [7.53].

1442 ibid.

1443 ibid [7.56].

1444 ibid [7.57].

1445 ibid [7.102].

1446 ibid [7.83] – [7.100].

1447 ibid [7.103].

based on Articles 3.4, 3.7 and 11 of the DSU, the panel should decline to make any findings or recommendations on the subject matter of that dispute.[1448] The panel cited the existing jurisprudence, in addition to examining Saudi Arabia's claims against the background of the factual circumstances that triggered the dispute,[1449] and expressed disagreement with the argument cited above, thus confirming that it cannot decline to exercise its jurisdiction and that the matter is justiciable.[1450]

4.2.2 The Scope of the "Self-Judging" Nature of the National Security Clause

In the majority of the disputes involving the national security clause, the crux of the discussion is the scope of latitude granted to WTO Members under the national security exceptions.[1451] The determination of this scope inevitably entails a discussion of the self-judging nature of the clause. The views advanced in this debate are diverse, ranging from the belief that the invocation of the security exception deprives panels and the AB of the power to adjudicate the merits of the dispute[1452] to a detailed analysis of the standards that must be developed to review its application.[1453]

The panel in *Russia – Traffic in Transit* sheds some light on the matter. In a way reminiscent of the efforts of WTO adjudicators to balance the trade and non-trade objectives of Article XX, the panel made laudable efforts to strike

---

1448 *Panel Report, Saudi Arabia – Measures concerning the Protection of Intellectual Property Rights, WT/DS567/R and Add., circulated to WTO Members on 16 June 2020 [appealed on 28 July 2020]* [7.8].

1449 ibid, [7.10] – [7.22].

1450 ibid, [7.23].

1451 Yoo and Ahn (n 820).

1452 "As the textual analysis of Article XXI (b) above indicates, invocation of the national security exception is a matter left to the discretion of a sanctioning member. Moreover, realpolitik demands that Members retain this sovereign prerogative even if additional multilateral checks against abuse are adopted in the future. National legislators believe that one of the surest ways to damage the WTO would be for it to attempt to encroach on this prerogative. Accordingly, as a practical matter, it is likely that a WTO panel, like the GATT panel in the United States-Nicaragua case, would interpret its terms of reference narrowly to exclude a ruling on the substantive Article XXI arguments." Raj Bhala, 'National Security and International Trade Law: What the GATT Says, and What the United States Does' (1998) 19 University of Pennsylvania Journal of International Economic Law 263, 279.

1453 Wesley Cann, Jr, 'Creating Standards and Accountability for the Use of the WTO Security Exception: Reducing the Role of Power-Based Relations and Establishing a New Balance Between Sovereignty and Multilateralism' (2001) 26 Yale Journal of International Law 413.

a balance between trade and national security.[1454] In doing so, the panel distinguished between the objective and subjective elements of the security clause, as well as identifying the scope of the reviewability of the subjective elements.[1455] The panel in *Saudi Arabia – IPRs* relied upon the same analytical framework to review the invocation of the national security exception enshrined in the TRIPS Agreement.[1456] My analysis starts with a discussion of the objective elements of the clause and proceeds with the review of the subjective elements as well as their reviewability.

4.2.2.1 *Objective Elements of the National Security Exception*

The security exception of Article XXI(b)(iii) of the GATT 1994 reads as follows:

> Nothing in this Agreement shall be construed: [...]
> (b) to prevent any contracting party from taking any action which it considers necessary for the protection of its essential security interests
> (iii) taken in time of war or other emergency in international relations; [...]

The Russian Federation contended that the prerequisite "taken in time of war or other emergency in international relations" requires a subjective assessment of a WTO Member and thus "cannot be doubted or re-evaluated by any other party or judicial bodies."[1457] Legal scholars had expressed this view before. For instance, Olivia Swaak-Goldman asserted that "the panel should not transpose its perception of the conflict for that of the invoking member, but it should examine whether from that member's perspective there is a situation that constitutes a time of war or other emergency in international relations."[1458]

1454 Iryna Bogdanova, 'The WTO Panel Ruling on the National Security Exception: Has the Panel "Cut" the Baby in Half?' (*EJIL:Talk!* 12 April 2019) www.ejiltalk.org/the-wto-panel-ruling-on-the-national-security-exception-has-the-panel-cut-the-baby-in-half/#more-17087.

1455 ibid.

1456 *Panel Report, Saudi Arabia – Measures concerning the Protection of Intellectual Property Rights* (n 1448) [7.241] – [7.242].

1457 "A statement by that Member that the measures taken are the actions which it considers necessary for the protection of its essential security interests taken in time of war or other emergency in international relations, as the case may be, is sufficient for that Member to benefit from the exception set out in Article XX(b) of the GATT. This assessment by a Member cannot be doubted or re-evaluated by any other party or judicial bodies, as the measures in question are not ordinary trade measures regularly assessed by the WTO panels." *Panel Report, Russia – Measures Concerning Traffic in Transit* (n 7) Annex C-4, [31].

1458 Olivia Q Swaak-Goldman, 'Who Defines Members' Security Interest in the WTO?' (1996) 9 Leiden Journal of International Law 361, 369.

Ukraine opposed this position, arguing that "the phrase 'taken in time of war or other emergency in international relations' is to be given an objective meaning by a panel, and that a WTO Member invoking Article XXI(b)(iii) cannot unilaterally determine whether such circumstances exist."[1459]

Confronted with the need to interpret Article XXI(b)(iii), the panel raised the question whether the wording "which it considers" qualifies the prerequisites enumerated in subparagraphs (i)-(iii).[1460] By relying upon the general rule of interpretation along with the negotiating history of the Charter of the International Trade Organization, the panel concluded that these subparagraphs establish objective elements that are amenable to objective determination.[1461] The arguments expressed in support of this position are discussed below.

4.2.2.1.1 The Logical Structure of the Provision and the Principle of Effective Interpretation (Effet Utile)

The panel pronounced that the subparagraphs (i)–(iii) "operate as limitative qualifying clauses" that restrain the discretion granted to WTO Members under the national security clause.[1462] Any other interpretation, in the panel's view, runs counter to the principle of effective interpretation.[1463] The panel's reference to the principle of effective interpretation, *effet utile*, is embedded in the somewhat rhetorical question: "And what would be the use, or *effet utile*, and added value of these limitative qualifying clauses in the enumerated subparagraphs of Article XXI(b), under such an interpretation [i.e. an interpretation leaving their determination exclusively to the discretion of the invoking Member]?"[1464]

The principle of effective interpretation, as elaborated by the WTO adjudicators, requires giving meaning and effect to all the terms of the treaty. In one of its early cases, the AB noted: "One of the corollaries of the 'general rule of interpretation' in the VCLT is that interpretation must give meaning and effect to all the terms of a treaty. An interpreter is not free to adopt a reading that would result in reducing whole clauses or paragraphs of a treaty to redundancy or inutility."[1465]

1459 *Panel Report, Russia – Measures Concerning Traffic in Transit* (n 7) Annex C-1, [47].
1460 ibid [7.63].
1461 ibid [7.101].
1462 ibid [7.65].
1463 ibid.
1464 ibid.
1465 *Appellate Body Report, United States – Standards for Reformulated and Conventional Gasoline* (n 1389) p. 23.

4.2.2.1.2 The General Rule of Interpretation

The panel relied upon the general rule of interpretation to support the findings that the existence of such circumstances as "war" and "emergency in international relations" is an objective fact amenable to objective determination.[1466] Furthermore, the chronological concurrence "taken in time of" is also an objective fact.[1467]

The panel equated the term "war" with an armed conflict,[1468] while defining "emergency in international relations" as "a situation of armed conflict, or of latent armed conflict, or of heightened tension or crisis, or of general instability engulfing or surrounding a state."[1469]

The views on the scope of the expression "other emergency in international relations" advanced by legal scholars long before the panel's pronouncements are very similar. In Michael Hahn's view, its meaning can range from a "hostile interaction between States involving the use of force to 'something more' than purely strained relations."[1470] Hannes Schloemann and Stefan Ohlhoff argued that "the situation in question must exceed ordinary political tensions between states, if not actually involve some kind of military threat."[1471] Raj Bhala warned against equating the expression "other emergency in international relations" with the acts of self-defence.[1472] The rationale underlying his warning has been captured in the following claim: "If the drafters of GATT meant to include only self-defense cases, then they would have said so expressly and, perhaps, even referenced the language in Article 51 of the UN Charter."[1473] Moreover, Bhala suggested the concept of a credible threat as a benchmark,[1474] claiming that "it is the implicit concept of a credible threat judged from the objective standpoint of a reasonable, similarly-situated government, coupled with the articulation of specific types of dangers that track one or more of the three clauses of the security exception."[1475] Panagiotis

---

1466 *Panel Report, Russia – Measures Concerning Traffic in Transit* (n 7) [7.71] and again reiterated [7.77].

1467 ibid [7.70] and again reiterated [7.77].

1468 ibid [7.72].

1469 ibid [7.76].

1470 Michael J Hahn, 'Vital Interests and the Law of GATT: An Analysis of GATT's Security Exception' (1991) 12 Michigan Journal of International Law 558, 589.

1471 Hannes L Schloemann and Stefan Ohlhoff, '"Constitutionalization" and Dispute Settlement in the WTO: National Security as an Issue of Competence' (1999) 93 The American Journal of International Law 424, 446.

1472 Bhala (n 1452).

1473 ibid 274.

1474 ibid 275.

1475 ibid.

Delimatsis and Thomas Cottier proposed the following criteria for defining the situations of emergency in international relations: "the threat should be imminent or the security measure should reflect a rapid response and action in order to deal with a dangerous situation that arose suddenly and recently. Measures taken in response to a terrorist attack perfectly fit this definition."[1476]

To buttress its conclusions, the panel considered the object and purpose of the GATT 1994 and the WTO Agreement. As the panel has aptly pointed out: "It would be entirely contrary to the security and predictability of the multilateral trading system established by the GATT 1994 and the WTO Agreements, including the concessions that allow for departures from obligations in specific circumstances, to interpret Article XXI as an outright potestative condition, subjecting the existence of a Member's GATT and WTO obligations to a mere expression of the unilateral will of that Member."[1477]

4.2.2.1.3 Negotiating History of the Charter of the International Trade Organization

The panel has made ample use of the negotiating history of the Charter of the International Trade Organization.[1478] It is noteworthy that it reveals the contracting parties' intent to agree to a political escape clause that is midway between a catch-all exception and a blanket ban on the use of trade restrictions in times of political turmoil.[1479] More specifically, the delegate for the United States reassured the delegate for the Netherlands about the need for a balanced approach towards the scope of the national security exception, stating: "I think there must be some latitude here for security measures. It is really a question of a balance. We have got to have some exceptions. We cannot make it too tight, because we cannot prohibit measures which are needed purely for security reasons. On the other hand, we cannot make it so broad that, under the guise of security, countries will put on measures which really have a commercial purpose. We have given considerable thought to it and this is the best we could produce to preserve that proper balance."[1480] Ironically,

1476 Panagiotis Delimatsis and Thomas Cottier, 'Article XIV bis GATS: Security Exceptions' in Rüdiger Wolfrum, Peter-Tobias Stoll, Clemens Feinäugle (eds.), *Max Planck Commentaries on World Trade Law: WTO – Trade in Services* (Martinus Nijhoff Publishers 2008) 329–348.

1477 *Panel Report, Russia – Measures Concerning Traffic in Transit* (n 7) [7.79].

1478 The panel analysed the preparatory work of the ITO Charter, which began in 1945. Before doing so, the panel referenced a number of AB reports, in which the AB relied upon the preparatory work as a supplementary means of treaty interpretation. For more, see *Panel Report, Russia – Measures Concerning Traffic in Transit* (n 7) footnote 157.

1479 ibid [7.89] – [7.93].

1480 ibid [7.93].

this statement stands in sharp contrast to the views expressed recently by the United States.[1481]

Overall, the Charter's negotiating history as it is reflected in the panel report substantiates the panel's findings that the balance of the security exception lies in a combination of objective and subjective elements with the objective parts being enumerated in the subparagraphs (i)–(iii). The panel in *Saudi Arabia – IPRs* endorsed this interpretation and relied upon the analytical framework developed in *Russia – Traffic in Transit.*

4.2.2.2 *The Subjective Elements of the National Security Clause and the Scope of Their Reviewability*

4.2.2.2.1 The Subjective Standard of Necessity – "Which It Considers Necessary"

The panel interpreted the wording "which it [a WTO Member] considers necessary" as granting unfettered discretion to the WTO Members to decide the necessity of the measures imposed to protect essential security interests.[1482]

WTO adjudicators frequently rely on the technique of cross-referencing,[1483] including instances of identical and similar treaty language.[1484] The technique of cross-referencing is not restricted to the text of a single agreement, and thus adjudicators make use of the legal rules of the other agreements as well.[1485] In the present dispute, Ukraine, as well as the European Union, advanced an argument that the wording "which it considers" shall be interpreted similarly to the interpretation of the language "if that party considers" made in another dispute.[1486] The language "if that party considers" contained in Article 22.3 of the DSU was interpreted as granting "a certain margin of appreciation, but that a decision by a Member was nevertheless subject to review by the

1481 'Russia – Measures Concerning Traffic in Transit (DS512), Third Party Executive Summary of the United States'; 'Russia – Measures Concerning Traffic in Transit (DS512), Third-Party Oral Statement of the United States of America.'

1482 *Panel Report, Russia – Measures Concerning Traffic in Transit* (n 7) [7.146] – [7.147].

1483 Isabelle Van Damme concludes that cross-referencing is a common interpretive technique for the WTO tribunals and points out that: "The use of cross-referencing is not solely a means of contextualizing the treaty language. It also serves to maintain consistency and coherence. Cross-referencing allows for the 'synchronizing' of the meaning of different treaty provisions and guarantees mutually consistent interpretations." Isabelle Van Damme, 'Treaty Interpretation by the WTO Appellate Body' (2010) 21 European Journal of International Law 605, 628.

1484 Isabelle Van Damme, *Treaty Interpretation by the WTO Appellate Body* (Oxford University Press 2009) Chapter 6.

1485 ibid Chapter 6.

1486 *Panel Report, Russia – Measures Concerning Traffic in Transit* (n 7) [7.147].

Arbitrators regarding whether the Member had considered the necessary facts objectively."[1487]

In addressing this legal claim, the present panel distinguished between the latter interpretation and the wording of "which it considers" in Article XXI(b)(iii), arguing: "The arbitrator's decision regarding the scope of review under Article 22.3 of the DSU was based on the fact that the discretion accorded to the complaining party under the relevant subparagraphs of that provision was subject to the obligation in the introductory words to Article 22.3 of the DSU, which provides that '[i]n considering what concessions or other obligations to suspend, the complaining party shall apply the following principles and procedures.' There is no equivalent obligation anywhere in the text of Article XXI that expressly conditions the discretion accorded to an invoking Member under the chapeau of Article XXI(b)."[1488]

Our enquiry into the WTO jurisprudence, where similar treaty language was interpreted, demonstrates that the self-judging standards are interpreted differently by the WTO tribunals. For instance, on another occasion, the panel ruled that although a WTO Member can be entrusted with a right to determine certain elements of the legal obligation, the exercise of this right is not unconstrained. The panel reached this conclusion in the *EC – Hormones* dispute, in which it had to interpret the wording "deemed appropriate by the Member." The panel pronounced that although the wording gives broad discretion to identify an appropriate level of protection, yet "in choosing a measure to achieve that appropriate level of protection Members have agreed to observe the provisions of Articles 2, 5.1 to 5.3 and 5.6."[1489]

By contrast, in *EC – Bananas III* the AB recognised a WTO Member's right "to be largely self-regulated." This interpretation was developed as a part of a broader argument that each WTO Member should be able to exercise its legal right to initiate a dispute when it considers such an action necessary.[1490]

1487 *The decision by the Arbitrator, European Communities – Regime for the Importation, Sale and Distribution of Bananas – Recourse to Arbitration by the European Communities under Article 22.6 of the DSU, WT/DS27/ARB/ECU, 24 March 2000, DSR 2000:V, p 2237.*

1488 *Panel Report, Russia – Measures Concerning Traffic in Transit* (n 7) [7.147].

1489 *Panel Report, EC Measures Concerning Meat and Meat Products (Hormones), Complaint by the United States, WT/DS26/R/USA, adopted 13 February 1998, as modified by Appellate Body Report WT/DS26/AB/R, WT/DS48/AB/R, DSR 1998:III, p 699* [8.164].

1490 "In EC – Bananas III, the Appellate Body found that Members are expected to be 'self-regulating' in deciding whether to initiate a WTO dispute, taking into account the wording of Article XXIII:1 of the GATT and Article 3.7 of the DSU." Graham Cook, *A Digest of WTO Jurisprudence on Public International Law Concepts and Principles* (First published, University Press 2015) 16.4 Self-Judging Standards.

4.2.2.2.2 The Subjective Standard of "Essential Security Interests"

The parties to the dispute disagreed on whether the determination of "essential security interests" is completely the WTO Member's prerogative or whether the panel is entitled to review the correctness of such determination.[1491]

The panel defined what interests might fall under the definition of "essential security interests" as "interests relating to the quintessential functions of the state, namely, the protection of its territory and its population from external threats, and the maintenance of law and public order internally."[1492] Yet, this definition should not lead us astray: the panel left the right to define what might constitute "essential security interests" to WTO Members.[1493] It has been pointed out that such determination "will depend on the particular situation and perceptions of the state in question, and can be expected to vary with changing circumstances."[1494]

Since the exercise of this discretion is prone to politicisation and abuse, the panel emphasised that it is subject to the principle of good faith.[1495] It implies an obligation to articulate such essential security interests sufficiently enough in order to demonstrate their veracity.[1496]

4.2.2.2.3 Relations between the Trade-Restrictive Measures and Essential Security Interests – "for the Protection of"

The panel set out the standard of "a minimum requirement of plausibility" between the essential security interests defined by the WTO Member and the measures implemented.[1497] Put differently, the measure should not be "implausible as measures protective of these interests."[1498] This standard of "implausible as measures protective of these interests" is comparable with the requirement "the measure is incapable of protecting public morals" as it was elucidated in the context of the public morals exception.[1499]

1491 *Panel Report, Russia – Measures Concerning Traffic in Transit* (n 7) [7.129].

1492 ibid [7.130].

1493 ibid [7.131].

1494 ibid.

1495 ibid [7.132]–[7.133].

1496 ibid [7.134].

1497 ibid [7.138].

1498 ibid.

1499 The AB clarified that the requirement "to protect public morals" should not be excessively restrictive: "If this initial, threshold examination reveals that the measure is incapable of protecting public morals, there is not a relationship between the measure and the protection of public morals that meets the requirements of the 'design' step." *Appellate Body Report, Colombia – Measures Relating to the Importation of Textiles, Apparel and Footwear* (n 1403) [5.68].

4.2.3 Can Economic Sanctions for Human Rights Violations Be Justified under the National Security Exception?

In their rulings on the national security exception, the panels acknowledged their jurisdiction to adjudicate its invocation and interpreted the scope of its self-judging nature. A few of their pronouncements should be recalled here. First and foremost, the prerequisite "taken in time of war or other emergency in international relations" sets an objective standard, which is amicable to review. Second, the term "emergency in international relations" was interpreted as "a situation of armed conflict, or of latent armed conflict, or of heightened tension or crisis, or of general instability engulfing or surrounding a state."[1500] Third, the expression "taken in time of" implies that there should be a temporal nexus between the measures undertaken and the existence of the emergency in international relations. Finally, the necessity requirement under the national security exception was reduced to "a minimum requirement of plausibility" between "essential security interests" and the trade-restrictive measures enacted.

In light of this, the national security exception might potentially justify unilateral human rights sanctions only if the human rights violations that provoked the imposition of the trade-restrictive measures constitute a situation of "emergency in international relations," which gives rise to a threat or instability "engulfing or surrounding a state." Conceivably, only gross human rights violations which occur in geographical proximity to the state that imposes the restrictive measures could meet such a high threshold.

The panel in *Russia – Traffic in Transit* referred to the UN Resolutions to substantiate the factual findings on the existence of tensions between Ukraine and the Russian Federation. In this connection, it should be noted that the conclusions of the Security Council on whether human rights violations could threaten international or regional peace and security vary significantly.[1501] As the analysis presented in the next chapter demonstrates, in some instances grave human rights violations have been recognised as a "threat to regional peace and security," on other occasions as a "threat to international peace and security."[1502] There were a number of instances where any pronouncement on the significantly deteriorating situations of human rights violations on the part of the Security Council was vetoed by its permanent members. This inconsistency in the practice of the Security Council increases uncertainty about the

---

1500 *Panel Report, Russia – Measures Concerning Traffic in Transit* (n 7) [7.76].

1501 For a more detailed discussion, see chapter 5, subsection 3.4 Grave human rights violations as a threat to international peace and security.

1502 ibid.

possibility of justifying economic sanctions for human rights violations under the national security exception.

Regarding the subjective elements of the national security clause, in particular, the minimum requirement of plausibility, it seems implausible for a state to argue that human rights violations occurring in a distant state might endanger its "essential security interests" and thus, raise serious national security concerns. In light of these considerations, I conclude that only a subset of unilateral human rights sanctions can be justified under the national security exception.

5 Conclusion

Unilateral human right sanctions are prone to similar legal contestations as unilateral economic sanctions imposed in pursuit of other objectives. These sanctions, despite being used as a tool to achieve the important societal objective of punishing human rights violations, may run counter a number of obligations under public international law. To illustrate this, I discussed the possible unlawfulness of unilateral human rights sanctions under the UN Charter, the legality of third-party countermeasures imposed to redress human rights violations and the relationship between unilateral human rights sanctions that target senior government officials and immunities accorded to these same officials under international law.

In the last part of this chapter, we examined the possibility of justifying unilateral human rights sanctions under the two exceptions enshrined in the WTO Agreements, namely the public morals exception and the national security exception. According to this analysis, these two exceptions might justify only a tiny fraction of unilateral human rights sanctions. Moreover, the possibility of justifying such unilateral restrictions under the public morals exception and the national security exception hinges on various contributory factors, meaning that some of these restrictions might violate the WTO obligations of the state that imposes them. Thus, we can conclude that the legality of unilateral human rights sanctions under public international law remains debatable.

PART 3

The Contribution of the Doctrine of Common Concern of Humankind to the International Protection of Human Rights

CHAPTER 5

The Doctrine of Common Concern of Humankind and Its Contribution to Enhancing Human Rights Protection

This part of the book explores the potential added value of conceptualising human rights as a Common Concern of Humankind. To this end, I trace the evolution of the doctrine of Common Concern of Humankind in this chapter. Subsequently, the suggested normative implications of the doctrine are discussed. Against this background, the application of the doctrine to situations of grave human rights violations is analysed. I conclude by outlining the potential contributions of the doctrine of Common Concern of Humankind to improving the international protection of human rights by resolving some of the many conceptual tensions and inconsistencies found in international law with respect to the use of unilateral sanctions and the enforcement of human rights, which are reflected in Parts 1 and 2 of this book.

1 The Evolution of the Doctrine of Common Concern of Humankind

The concept of common concern emerged in international environmental law in the late 1980s.[1503] In 1988, the UN General Assembly adopted a resolution in which it was acknowledged that "climate change is a common concern of mankind, since climate is an essential condition which sustains life on earth."[1504] In this regard, Frank Biermann points out that this new concept evolved from a similar concept of common interest.[1505] However, Biermann, along with Jutta Brunnée, shares the view that contrary to the notion of common interest the term "common concern" denotes the protection of those societal values that are essential for the survival of humankind.[1506]

1503 Frank Biermann, 'Common Concern of Humankind: The Emergence of a New Concept of International Environmental Law' (1996) 34 Archiv des Völkerrechts 426, 430.

1504 Protection of global climate for present and future generations of mankind UNGA Res 43/53 (December 6, 1988) UN Doc A/RES/43/53.

1505 Biermann (n 1503) 431.

1506 Biermann (n 1503); Jutta Brunnée, 'Common Interest – Echoes from an Empty Shell? Some Thoughts on Common Interest and International Environmental Law' (1989) 49 Zeitschrift für Ausländisches Öffentliches Recht und Völkerrecht 791.

Indeed, the concept of common concern emerged from the other similar concepts already recognised in international environmental law, such as "common interest"[1507] and the "common heritage of mankind."[1508] Despite the existence of similar concepts, the shift from these other concepts to common concern has far-reaching implications. The Draft International Covenant on Environment and Development describes these implications as follows: "The conclusion that the global environment is a matter of 'common concern' implies that it can no longer be considered as solely within the domestic jurisdiction of States due to its global importance and consequences for all. It also expresses a shift from classical treaty-making notions of reciprocity and material advantage, to action in the long-term interests of humanity."[1509]

The recognition of the concept of common concern by the UN General Assembly paved the way for its subsequent incorporation in the international treaties. The United Nations Framework Convention on Climate Change endorsed the concept, claiming that "change in the Earth's climate and its

1507 Stephen Stec describes the difference between the concept of "common interest" and "common concern" as follows: "The shift from 'common interest of states' to 'common concern of humankind' is notable. The former term is dependent on the common awareness of states with varying internal politics. The latter term implies values that are above and beyond the calculated interest of states." Stephen Stec, 'Humanitarian Limits to Sovereignty: Common Concern and Common Heritage Approaches to Natural Resources and Environment' (2010) 12 International Community Law Review 361.

1508 Antônio Augusto Cançado Trindade, *International Law for Humankind: Towards a New 'Jus Gentium'* (2nd rev. ed, M Nijhoff Publishers 2013) 344, 348, 352. The following features distinguish the concept of common concern from the concept of the common heritage of mankind: common concerns are not restricted to the areas beyond national jurisdiction, but also include the territories of sovereign states; the subjects of the common concern are matters that are of "concern" to humanity as a whole; the main focus of common concern is the equitable sharing of the burden of cooperation and problem-solving; the concept of common concern has a higher status than other similar concepts, such as common heritage, shared resources, etc., and thus obligations that derive from it are higher in the hierarchy. Jimena Murillo, 'Common Concern of Humankind and Its Implications in International Environmental Law' (2008) 5 Macquarie Journal of International and Comparative Environmental Law 133. In this regard, Jutta Brunnée points out: "whereas common heritage regimes are concerned with equitable sharing of benefits, common concern regimes focus on equitable sharing of the burdens of cooperation and problem solving." Jutta Brunnée, 'Common Areas, Common Heritage, and Common Concern' in Daniel Bodansky, Jutta Brunnée and Ellen Hey (eds.), *The Oxford Handbook of International Environmental Law* (First Edition, Oxford University Press 2007).

1509 International Union for Conservation of Nature and Natural Resources, 'Draft International Covenant on Environment and Development, Implementing Sustainability' 45 <https://sustainabledevelopment.un.org/content/documents/2443Covenant_5th_edition.pdf>.

adverse effects are a common concern of humankind."[1510] In a similar vein, the United Nations Convention on Biological Diversity acknowledges that "the conservation of biological diversity is a common concern of humankind."[1511] Plant genetic resources have also been defined as a common concern.[1512]

The most recent international agreement that expressly introduces the concept is the Paris Agreement.[1513] What is noteworthy is that the Paris Agreement not only reaffirms that climate change is a common concern of humankind, but also emphasises that the parties should respect and promote human rights and special needs of certain vulnerable groups, when taking action to address climate change.[1514] The idea of integrating environmental protection and human rights had been predicted a decade earlier by Laura Horn.[1515] In her opinion: "In fact it is preferable to aim at integrating the two fields of international law. This means that when decisions are taken on human rights questions, environmental interests (if relevant) are also taken into account. On the occasions that it is necessary to reconcile conflicts on human rights questions there must be some means of making representation available to environmental interests if these interests are also involved in the conflict. Similarly, human rights problems cannot be ignored when considering environmental issues."[1516]

In the last two decades, the literature has abounded in claims that various collective action problems should be acknowledged as a common concern. The following examples illustrate this trend. Jutta Brunnée and Andre Nollkaemper have advanced the argument that global environmental threats resulting from forest decline should be recognised as a common concern.[1517] The valuable contribution made by the concept to the problem of deforestation and non-sustainable management of forests was explained as follows: "Thus the concept

1510 United Nations Framework Convention on Climate Change (adopted 9 May 1992, entered into force 21 March 1994) S. Treaty Doc No. 102–38, 1771 UNTS 107.

1511 Convention on Biological Diversity (adopted 5 June 1992, entered into force 29 December 1993) UNTS vol. 1760 p. 79.

1512 International Treaty on Plant Genetic Resources for Food and Agriculture (adopted 3 November 2001, entered into force 29 June 2004) UNTS vol. 2400 p. 303.

1513 Paris Agreement (Dec. 13, 2015), in UNFCCC, COP Report No. 21, Addendum, at 21, UN Doc FCCC/CP/2015/10/Add 1 (Jan. 29, 2016).

1514 ibid.

1515 Laura Horn, 'The Implications of the Concept of Common Concern of a Human Kind on a Human Right to a Healthy Environment' (2004) 1 Macquarie Journal of International and Comparative Environmental Law 233.

1516 ibid 265.

1517 Jutta Brunnée and André Nollkaemper, 'Between the Forests and the Trees – An Emerging International Forest Law' (1996) 23 Environmental Conservation 307.

limits the sovereignty of forest-rich nations not in its 'ownership' dimension, but only in its 'use' dimension and only to the extent that their activities create a common concern, thereby affecting the interests of other states."[1518] Edith Brown Weiss contends that the availability and use of fresh water should be recognised as a common concern of humankind:[1519] "The recognition of the availability and use of fresh water as a 'common concern of humankind' could provide a basis for future legal instruments, guidelines, and best practices to address the growing range of transnational issues."[1520] Nadia Sanchez Castillo-Winckels favours acknowledging the degradation of atmospheric conditions as a common concern of humankind,[1521] an argument that is made in light of the ILC's decision to remove the concept of common concern of humankind from its Draft Guidelines on the Protection of the Atmosphere.[1522] The previous text of Draft Guideline 3 suggested that "[t]he atmosphere is a natural resource essential for sustaining life on Earth, human health and welfare, and aquatic and terrestrial ecosystems, and hence the degradation of the atmosphere is a common concern of humankind."[1523] The decision to avoid the concept of common concern was made despite the strong support for the concept expressed by the ILC's special rapporteur on the protection of the atmosphere, Professor Shinya Murase.[1524]

The concepts of common interest and common concern can also be applied beyond their traditional domain of international environmental law. For example, Professor Wolfgang Benedek contends that human rights constitute a common interest of all states, as well as a community interest to a broader group comprising various stakeholders.[1525] This opinion echoes Jutta Brunnée's belief that the concept of third-generation rights, known as solidarity rights, is

---

1518 ibid 309.

1519 Edith Brown Weiss, 'The Coming Water Crisis: A Common Concern of Humankind' (2012) 1 Transnational Environmental Law 153.

1520 ibid 163.

1521 Nadia Sanchez Castillo-Winckels, 'Why Common Concern of Humankind Should Return to the Work of the International Law Commission on the Atmosphere' (2016) 29 Georgetown Environmental Law Review 131.

1522 ILC, 'Report of the International Law Commission, UN Doc A/70/10' (2015) General Assembly Official Records Seventieth Session Supplement No. 10.

1523 Shinya Murase, 'Second Report on the Protection of Atmosphere UN Doc A/CN.4/681' (2015) 67th Session of the International Law Commission.

1524 Castillo-Winckels (n 1521).

1525 Wolfgang Benedek, 'Humanization of International Law, Human Rights and the Common Interest' in Wolfgang Benedek (ed), *The Common Interest in International Law* (Intersentia 2014).

closely linked to the concept of "common interest."[1526] The preamble to the Rome Statute of the International Criminal Court even goes a step further, declaring that "the most serious crimes of concern to the international community as a whole must not go unpunished and that their effective prosecution must be ensured by taking measures at the national level and by enhancing international cooperation."[1527] Yet, international human rights treaties do not incorporate references to the concept of common concern. Apart from the aforementioned examples, the use of the concept has been limited. Indeed, as Thomas Cottier accurately points out: "Recourse to the notion of concern has been limited to, or related to, regulatory areas of natural resource management and efforts to protect them from overexploitation and degradation."[1528]

Notwithstanding the significant attention paid in the scholarly literature to the concept of common concern, the majority of the scholars do not attribute normative implications to the concept. Several academics emphasise that the concept embodies the possibility for cooperation, as well as more active engagement on the part of civil society.[1529] Aline Jaeckel contends that the obligation to conserve plant biodiversity, which constitutes a common concern of humankind, justifies limitations on private intellectual property rights over plants and related processes.[1530] Frank Biermann, while acknowledging that the legal content and implications of the concept of common concern have not been determined, does not propose the missing content himself.[1531] Instead, he makes a number of observations on the visible ramifications of the concept's incorporation into the treaty law.[1532] These ramifications entail the establishment of the different standards of conduct that apply to various categories of states, the existence of the common concern obligations not confined to the states' own jurisdiction and the availability of various means to enforce such obligations.[1533] Jutta Brunnée asserts that two difficulties arise when it

1526 Jutta Brunnée points out that: "The concept [the third generation of rights] is closely linked to the concept explored in this article: the notion of an interest in the protection of certain values common to the international community which can only be safeguarded by international cooperation and through international law." Brunnée (n 1506).

1527 Rome Statute of the International Criminal Court (adopted 17 July 1998, entered into force 1 July 2002) UNTS vol. 2187 no. 38544.

1528 Cottier, 'The Principle of Common Concern of Humankind.' (n 18).

1529 Murillo (n 1508); Weiss (n 1519).

1530 Aline Jaeckel, 'Intellectual Property Rights and the Conservation of Plant Biodiversity as a Common Concern of Humankind' (2013) 2 Transnational Environmental Law 167.

1531 Biermann (n 1503).

1532 ibid.

1533 ibid.

comes to identifying and enforcing common concerns.[1534] The first is establishing an adequate international consensus that the problem is of common concern and the second is the need to clarify the precise legal ramifications of common concerns.[1535] In further developing the idea of possible legal implications of the common concern, Jutta Brunnée attaches great significance to cooperation between states: "It may be more helpful, therefore, to conceive of the concept of common concern as entitling, perhaps even requiring, all states to cooperate internationally to address the concern."[1536] Duncan French, for his part, notes that the concept of common concern entails the collective responsibility to act.[1537] French further elucidates the established implications of the common concern and discusses its future normative consequences.[1538] He concludes by emphasising that "common concern is much more than a political tool; it has both the content and normative longevity of a meaningful legal principle."[1539] In other publications, international legal scholars have confirmed that the legal implications of the concept of common concern remain undefined.[1540] Indeed, even the discussion of the concept during the 67th session of the ILC revealed that "the most common objection had been the undefined character of the concept and the uncertainty as to what legal obligations flowed from it."[1541]

The doctrine and principle of Common Concern of Humankind, which entails a number of well-defined normative obligations, was developed to dispel the uncertainty regarding the normative content of the concept of common concern.[1542] In my subsequent analysis, I rely upon the theoretical

1534 Brunnée (n 1508).

1535 ibid 565.

1536 ibid 566.

1537 Duncan French, 'Common Concern, Common Heritage and Other Global(-Ising) Concepts: Rhetorical Devices, Legal Principles or a Fundamental Challenge?' in Michael Bowman, Peter Davies and Edward Goodwin (eds.), *Research Handbook on Biodiversity and Law* (Edward Elgar 2016).

1538 ibid 350–356.

1539 ibid 356.

1540 "No clear definition of a common concern of mankind exists, nor does a final decision about its legal implications in international environmental law." Murillo (n 1508) 134. "Although the efforts to explain the concept of common concern of humankind have shed light on its content, discussions at the ILC and the Sixth Committee of the General Assembly show that the concept is still generally perceived to be insufficiently clear." Castillo-Winckels (n 1521).

1541 ILC, 'Provisional Summary Record of the 3246th Meeting, UN Doc A/CN.4/SR.3246' (2016) International Law Commission, sixty-seventh session (first part).

1542 Cottier, 'The Principle of Common Concern of Humankind.' (n 18).

framework of Common Concern of Humankind developed by Professor Thomas Cottier and others, which is discussed in numerous publications.[1543]

2 The Suggested Normative Implications of the Principle of Common Concern of Humankind

The identification of community interests that might be elevated to the status of common concerns begins with the process of claims and responses.[1544] As Cottier emphasises: "Whether or not a matter is deemed a common concern is open to initiatives, debate, approval or rejection in the diplomatic and legal process of law-making."[1545]

A problem constituting a common concern should be defined as follows: "it stands for the proposition of an important shared problem and shared responsibility, and for an issue which reaches beyond the bounds of a single community and state as a subject of international law."[1546] The recognition of a shared problem as a common concern entails that this problem "bear[s] the potential and risk to threaten international stability, peace and welfare."[1547] The suggested normative implications of the doctrine of Common Concern of Humankind are enumerated and described below.

2.1 *Duty to Cooperate*

One of the essential normative obligations that flows logically from the recognition of a shared problem as a matter of common concern is a duty to cooperate: "the very point of recognizing a matter to amount to a Common Concern of Humankind is to recognize the essential need to co-operate in the field concerned."[1548] Such a duty to cooperate comprises several elements. These elements include transparency and access to the relevant information, a duty to consult and negotiate, burden-sharing and differentiated responsibility, and

1543 Thomas Cottier and Sofya Matteotti, 'International Environmental Law and the Evolving Concept of "Common Concern of Mankind"' in Thomas Cottier, Olga Nartova and Sadeq Z Bigdeli (eds.), *International Trade Regulation and the Mitigation of Climate Change: World Trade Forum* (Cambridge University Press 2009); Cottier and Schefer (n 18); Cottier, Aerni and Karapinar (n 18); Cottier, 'The Principle of Common Concern of Humankind.' (n 18).

1544 Cottier, 'The Principle of Common Concern of Humankind.' (n 18).

1545 ibid 21.

1546 ibid 26.

1547 ibid 28.

1548 ibid 43.

cooperation in implementing international obligations.[1549] I will first briefly expound on these elements, before discussing how they might improve the international protection of human rights.[1550]

Transparency entails that states grant access to information that is pertinent to a matter acknowledged to be of common concern.[1551] This information includes both legal texts and the factual information that might be requested by other interested states.

The duty to consult and negotiate involves an obligation to engage in good faith negotiations with the objective of reaching an amicable agreement.[1552] The obligation to engage in good faith negotiations is further embodied in the obligation to provide reasons should such negotiations fail.[1553]

Burden-sharing and differentiated responsibility reflect the existing diversity of countries with respect to their levels of economic and social development, as well as their capacity to contribute to resolving matters of common concern. Cottier provides numerous examples of such burden-sharing and differentiated responsibility in international environmental law.[1554] The potential ramifications of this approach to the international protection of human rights are addressed below.[1555]

Cooperation in the implementation of international commitments is the last element of the general duty to cooperate, and it is of paramount importance for issues recognised as matters of common concern. This form of cooperation comprises cooperation in designing governmental policies, the exchange of information between the regulatory agencies in different countries, mutual assistance by administrative bodies and judicial assistance.[1556]

This proposed duty to cooperate originated in another recent development in international law – its gradual shift from the law of co-existence to the law of cooperation. This shift is reflected in scholarly debates,[1557] as well as in the pronouncements of the ICJ.[1558] Regarding the latter, in his declaration attached

1549 ibid 43–44.

1550 For more details, see this chapter, subsection 4.1 Reinforced duty to cooperate.

1551 Cottier, 'The Principle of Common Concern of Humankind.' (n 18) 43.

1552 ibid.

1553 ibid.

1554 ibid 44.

1555 For more details, see this chapter, subsection 4.1 Reinforced duty to cooperate.

1556 Cottier, 'The Principle of Common Concern of Humankind.' (n 18) 44.

1557 Ulrich Fastenrath and others (eds.), *From Bilateralism to Community Interest: Essays in Honour of Judge Bruno Simma* (Oxford University Press 2011).

1558 "Witness the proliferation of international organizations, the gradual substitution of an international law of cooperation for the traditional international law of co-existence, the emergence of the concept of 'international community' and its sometimes successful

to the court's advisory opinion, Judge Mohammed Bedjaoui declared: "the gradual substitution of an international law of co-operation for the traditional international law of co-existence [...]. A token of all these developments is the place which international law now accords to concepts such as obligations erga omnes, rules of jus cogens, or the common heritage of mankind."[1559] Another oft-quoted statement conveying a similar view is from Judge Weeramantry's separate opinion in the *Gabcikovo-Nagymaros* case: "We have entered an era of international law in which international law subserves not only the interests of individual States, but looks beyond them and their parochial concerns to the greater interests of humanity and planetary welfare."[1560]

2.2 *Obligation to Do One's Homework*

The term "homework" designates "a legal denomination to address a bulk of obligations under the principle of Common Concern of Humankind."[1561] Two core duties compose this obligation: the first is the duty to implement international obligations domestically and the second is the adoption of autonomous measures.[1562] Each of these requirements stands in need of further explanation.

The prescribed duty to implement international obligations does not alter existing obligations under general international law, and in particular the principle of *pacta sunt servanda*.[1563] To the contrary, it reinforces this obligation concerning the matters that have been acknowledged as a common concern,[1564] entailing a duty to allocate the necessary resources to implement international obligations that are relevant to a common concern.[1565]

The second duty is an obligation to adopt autonomous measures. By its very nature, this obligation entails a right to implement domestic laws or regulations conducive to the protection of matters recognised to be of common

---

attempts at subjectivization." 'Legality of the Threat or Use of Nuclear Weapons. Advisory Opinion, I.C.J. Reports 1996, p. 226; Declaration of President Bedjaoui' [13]; 'Gabcikovo-Nagymaros Project (Hungary/Slovakia), Judgment, I.C.J. Reports 1997, p. 7, Separate Opinion of Vice-President Weeramantry' 118.

1559 'Legality of the Threat or Use of Nuclear Weapons. Advisory Opinion, I.C.J. Reports 1996, p. 226; Declaration of President Bedjaoui' (n 1558) [13].

1560 'Gabcikovo-Nagymaros Project (Hungary/Slovakia), Judgment, I.C.J. Reports 1997, p. 7, Separate Opinion of Vice-President Weeramantry' (n 1558) 118.

1561 Cottier, 'The Principle of Common Concern of Humankind.' (n 18) 45.

1562 ibid.

1563 ibid.

1564 ibid.

1565 ibid.

concern.[1566] Notably, implementation of this type of regulation might have effects beyond the boundaries of a certain jurisdiction, and thus it has the potential to be extraterritorial.[1567] Oft-quoted examples of such laws are domestic laws regulating and conditioning market access for foreign goods and services based on criteria unrelated to their physical characteristics, e.g. their impact on the environment.[1568]

2.3 *Securing Compliance*

The suggested normative implications of the doctrine of Common Concern of Humankind are intended to address the lack of reciprocity in some fields of public international law, including international human rights law. Hence, the third constitutive obligation under the doctrine of Common Concern is a duty to secure compliance with international obligations that relate to a common concern.[1569] Thomas Cottier illustrates the need for this element of the normative framework as follows: "While the duty to cooperate offers carrots to comply, sticks are equally required to address free-riding and failing full compliance with duties incurred and promises made."[1570]

The right to act in order to protect community interests is premised on the customary international law of state responsibility codified by the ILC in the Draft articles.[1571] More precisely, Articles 48 and 54 of the Draft articles entitle non-injured states to invoke the responsibility of a state that infringes its international obligations.[1572] Indeed, due to the nature of the values protected under the doctrine of Common Concern, these values represent community interests, and thus should entail obligations erga omnes.[1573] However, as already discussed, the Draft articles do not grant a right to impose countermeasures, including economic countermeasures, on non-injured states.[1574] In the next section of this chapter, we will discuss the ramifications of this right to act to secure compliance with recognised common concerns for international human rights protection.[1575]

1566 ibid 45–46.
1567 ibid 46–47.
1568 ibid.
1569 ibid 48.
1570 ibid.
1571 ILC, 'Draft articles' (n 90).
1572 ibid.
1573 Cottier, 'The Principle of Common Concern of Humankind.' (n 18) 50.
1574 For more details, see chapter 2, section 3. The legality of unilateral economic sanctions under the Draft articles on Responsibility of States for Internationally Wrongful Acts.
1575 For more details, see subsection 4.3. An instrument for providing legality and legitimacy to unilateral economic sanctions.

It is envisaged that the fully-fledged doctrine of Common Concern should prescribe not only the right to act, but also the duty to act.[1576] The duty to act is the most intricate normative implication of the doctrine of Common Concern. The duty to act implies that a state, subject to the principle of proportionality, ought to adopt unilateral measures (e.g. economic sanctions in the form of trade restrictions) against a state that does not abide by its commitments to address common concerns.[1577] The principle of proportionally, in this context, implies that the actions directed at ensuring compliance with the obligations under the doctrine of Common Concern should be taken only when they are well suited and potentially effective.

The duty to act under the doctrine of Common Concern is similar to the duty to intervene in the ongoing atrocities prescribed by the principle of Responsibility to Protect (R2P).[1578] The rationale behind these obligations to act is identical, yet the prerequisites for action differ.[1579] Furthermore, the doctrine of Common Concern favours "equal treatment of comparable constellations."[1580] Such an approach implies that all pertinent factors need to be taken into account, and any determination that there is a duty to act should be made on a case-by-case basis.[1581] The value of such a duty to act is greater transparency and accountability in foreign affairs.[1582]

3 The Introduction of the Doctrine of Common Concern of Humankind into International Human Rights Law

In attempting to introduce the doctrine of Common Concern of Humankind into international human rights law, we must first identify human rights violations that can be considered matters of common concern and then discuss the normative implications of the doctrine and its added value for the international protection of human rights. The following sections of this chapter focus on identifying criteria that may provide a basis for recognising grave human rights violations as matters of common concern. Before we launch into those

1576 Cottier, 'The Principle of Common Concern of Humankind.' (n 18) 48–54.
1577 ibid 51.
1578 For more details, see chapter 3, subsection 4.1 Humanitarian intervention and Responsibility to Protect (R2P).
1579 The R2P entails a number of obligations and allows humanitarian intervention as the measure of last resort.
1580 Cottier, 'The Principle of Common Concern of Humankind.' (n 18) 53.
1581 ibid.
1582 ibid 54.

discussions, however, the reasons behind states' abuse of human rights ought to be examined.

3.1 *The Reasons behind States' Abuses of Human Rights*

Research in the social sciences has contributed significantly to explaining the reasons behind states' abuses of human rights, as well as to examining the efficiency of the various strategies to promote human rights protection. Emilie Hafner-Burton, who has been researching this subject for more than a decade, has summarised various strands of research into the causes, impact and remedies for human rights violations.[1583] According to her analysis of the existing literature, there are two central causes of human rights abuses: (1) violent conflicts and (2) weak or overly powerful state institutions.[1584] As Emilie Hafner-Burton points out: "The central insight about violent conflict is that it creates cycles of human rights abuse that are difficult to interrupt."[1585] Regarding the impact of state institutions, both the structure of governance and the capacity of state institutions influence the level of human rights protection.[1586] David Weissbrodt and Patrick Finnegan indicate the following four causes of human rights violations: (1) government behaviour and structure, (2) armed conflict, (3) economic factors and (4) psychological factors.[1587] At the same time, they note that this categorisation is artificial, since these causes may be deeply intertwined and mutually reinforcing.[1588]

The four strategies that may prevent and reverse human rights violations have been exhaustively discussed in the relevant literature, namely: military interventions; economic policies including trade, investment, aid and sanctions; international law; and information strategies.[1589] While there is no consensus on the effectiveness of economic sanctions, it is worth emphasising that a number of studies have demonstrated that "sanctions can successfully yield concessions to improve human rights in some circumstances."[1590] The overall conclusion is that human rights violations that originate from weak institutions could be remedied by cooperative strategies, whereas human rights

1583 Emilie M Hafner-Burton, 'A Social Science of Human Rights' (2014) 51 Journal of Peace Research 273.
1584 ibid.
1585 ibid 274.
1586 ibid 276.
1587 David Weissbrodt and Patrick Finnegan, 'Human Rights Conditions: What We Know and Why It Matters' (2019) 28(1) Minnesota Journal of International Law 1.
1588 ibid.
1589 ibid.
1590 ibid 279.

abuses provoked by conflicts or governmental policies could be redressed by restrictive measures, including economic sanctions.[1591]

International law scholars have expressed their views on the reasons behind the world's poor human rights record. In this regard, the views of Antonio Cassese are of particular interest. In describing the controversy between the aspiration of universal human rights, which dominated the minds of intellectuals after World War II, and the realities of the modern world, Cassese concludes that "not only do human rights continue to be violated if not unabated, with stunning frequency, but the values preached by Roosevelt and Cassin and enshrined in the Universal Declaration have also not trickled down to all states of our planet."[1592] Among the reasons for this state of affairs, Cassese emphasises the essential role of two factors: the "persistent impact of sovereignty, and the ineradicable role of self-interest."[1593] In Cassese's view, the enhancement of human rights protection should take a two-pronged approach, which implies the distinction of a core set of fundamental values from other values and improved compliance with these core values.[1594]

The international law literature, in which human rights are considered global public goods, supports these conclusions. At the outset, it must be noted that scholars recognise that human rights fall under the definition of global public goods.[1595] Daniel Bodansky concludes that the analytical contributions made

---

1591 Hafner-Burton (n 1583).

1592 Antonio Cassese, 'A Plea for a Global Community Grounded in a Core of Human Rights' in Antonio Cassese (ed), *Realizing Utopia: the Future of International Law* (Oxford University Press 2012) 138.

1593 ibid.

1594 ibid 139–143.

1595 According to this theory, global public goods are defined by two characteristics: non-rivalry and non-excludability. For more, see Paul A Samuelson, 'The Pure Theory of Public Expenditure' (1954) 36 The Review of Economics and Statistics 387. On human rights as global public goods: "The global public good of the protection of human rights is different. Our production relationships are not directly affected when people we do not know are raped, tortured, murdered, or otherwise brutalized, even on a massive scale. We do not experience their physical pain; our liberties are not infringed; our incomes do not fall. But are we emotionally harmed by these experiences, when they are brought to our attention? Do we feel shame when, having the wherewithal to intervene, we decline to do so? Would we prefer that there existed institutions that could be relied upon to protect people from such atrocities when their own governments fail to do so – or, perhaps worse, when their own governments instigate and perpetrate such deeds? Would we be willing to pay for such institutions? If the answer to these questions is yes, then our 'utility' relations are affected when what we perceive as being the basic rights of all humans are denied to some humans, even people we do not know. The very term, a 'crime against humanity,' implies a universal injury, rather than one suffered only by those directly affected. In this sense, the safeguarding of human rights, and the prevention of atrocities, most especially

by the concept of public goods to the study of international law are the acknowledgement that public goods can be produced in a different way and thus raise different governance challenges.[1596] With this in mind, Bodansky relies upon the classification of public goods developed by Scott Barrett[1597] in his discussion of which governance responses are required for aggregate-effort problems, weakest-link problems and single-best-effort problems.[1598] According to this classification, the international protection of human rights can be equated with weakest-link public goods, which can be provided on the condition that all states cooperate. Non-cooperative behaviour can be explained either by a lack of resources or by an explicit decision on the part of a state not to participate in the provision of this particular public good.[1599] The reasons underlying such uncooperative behaviour determine what would constitute an effective response: a lack of resources can be remedied by assistance programmes, while an unwillingness to cooperate may be offset by coercion, such as economic sanctions or military action.[1600] These strategies echo the conclusions reached by the social scientists discussed in the preceding paragraphs.

The doctrine of Common Concern and its normative implications discussed above particularly aim at remedying the deficiencies of international law that prevent it from contributing to the provision of global public goods. As Thomas Cottier stresses: "Depicting an issue as a common concern ideally leads to solving underlying problems in producing appropriate public goods."[1601] The suggested normative implications of the doctrine of Common Concern entail both enhanced international cooperation to address the instances of a lack of resources and mechanisms of enforcement, in order to coerce states to abide by their international obligations. Yet before we discuss the potential implications of introducing the doctrine into international human rights law, we need to identify human rights violations that ought to meet the criteria for being

genocide, is a global public good, perhaps the most fundamental global public good of all." Scott Barrett, *Why Cooperate?: The Incentive to Supply Global Public Goods* (Oxford University Press 2010) 118.

1596 Daniel Bodansky, 'What's in a Concept? Global Public Goods, International Law, and Legitimacy' (2012) 23 European Journal of International Law/Journal europeen de droit international 651, 658.

1597 Scott Barrett classifies the global public goods into several categories and identifies cooperation problems for each category of the global public good. These categories are: single best effort, weakest link, aggregate effort, mutual restraint, coordination. Barrett (n 1595).

1598 Bodansky (n 1596) 658–665.

1599 ibid 661–662.

1600 ibid 662.

1601 Cottier, 'The Principle of Common Concern of Humankind.' (n 18) 31.

recognised as matters of common concern. These criteria are: (1) human rights violations should impede the essence of a human right (*Kerngehalt*), which is protected under international human rights law, and (2) these violations should be systematic, and (3) they should threaten international peace and security. In the following sections, we will examine each of these criteria in turn.

3.2 *The Concept of the Essence of Human Rights* (Kerngehalt) *as a Threshold to Define Human Rights as a "Common Concern"*

The concept of the essence of human rights emerged in constitutional law. The relevant provision of the Basic Law for the Federal Republic of Germany stipulates that "in no case may the essence of a basic right be affected."[1602] In a similar vein, the concept of *Kerngehalt* is embedded in the Federal Constitution of the Swiss Confederation.[1603] More specifically, the Federal Constitution of the Swiss Confederation prescribes that "the essence of fundamental rights is sacrosanct."[1604] Commentators have emphasised that this concept "is in substance rooted in human dignity," the protection of which is guaranteed under Article 7 of the Federal Constitution of the Swiss Confederation.[1605] Regarding the rationale behind the concept of the essence of human rights in the Swiss constitutional law, legal scholars point out that: "Depending on the fundamental right in question, the Kerngehalt describes the sphere of constitutional protection, which cannot be limited under any circumstances by the state."[1606]

The concept of the essence of human rights underwent further development and recognition in the law of the European Union. The Charter of Fundamental Rights of the European Union incorporates the concept of *Kerngehalt* using the following language: "Any limitation on the exercise of the rights and freedoms recognized by this Charter must be provided for by law and respect the essence of those rights and freedoms."[1607] Moreover, this concept was further elaborated in the jurisprudence of the Court of Justice of the European Union (CJEU)[1608] and scholarly debates on the subject.[1609]

1602 Article 19(2) Basic Law for the Federal Republic of Germany, 23 May 1949.

1603 Federal Constitution of the Swiss Confederation of 18 April 1999.

1604 Article 36(4) ibid.

1605 Alexander Misic and Nicole Töpperwien, *Constitutional Law in Switzerland* (Kluwer Law International BV 2018) 197.

1606 ibid.

1607 Article 52(1) Charter of Fundamental Rights of the European Union, 2012/C 326/02.

1608 *Case C-362/14, Maximillian Schrems v. Data Protection Commissioner* [*2015*] *ECLI identifier: ECLI:EU:C:2015:650*.

1609 Tuomas Ojanen, 'Making the Essence of Fundamental Rights Real: The Court of Justice of the European Union Clarifies the Structure of Fundamental Rights under the Charter'

It is crucial to bear in mind that the concept of the essence of human rights is discussed in the context of the limitations imposed on human rights. In other words, limitations on human rights that could be considered legal and legitimate should not impair the essence of a particular right. In this regard, Koen Lenaerts, President of the CJEU, explains the concept of *Kerngehalt* as follows: "the concept of the essence of a fundamental right implies that every fundamental right has a 'hard nucleus' that guarantees to each and every individual a sphere of liberty that must always remain free from interference. That nucleus is, in my view, absolute in so far as it may not be subject to limitations."[1610]

Notwithstanding these developments, the concept of the essence of human rights remains underexplored in international human rights law. Pierre Thielbörger is one of the few legal scholars to have examined whether international human rights law acknowledges this concept and, if not, what alternatives are used instead.[1611] Professor Thielbörger reached the following conclusions. First and foremost, the concept of the "essence" of human rights is fragmented in international human rights law[1612] – more specifically: "For civil political rights, the concept must mainly be linked to notions of non-derogability and non-restrictability. For socioeconomic rights, the concept, while also partly being connected to non-restrictability, is most relevant in terms of guaranteeing an essential level of protection that States have to uphold immediately and independent of potential resource limitations."[1613] Secondly, the concept may apply to the macro level, as well as to the micro level.[1614] At the macro level, this concept presupposes that some human rights are so essential that their protection is of paramount significance.[1615] At the micro level, however, this concept applies to the core part of each right.[1616]

For our discussion of whether it is possible to transpose the normative implications of the doctrine of Common Concern onto international human

(2016) 12 European Constitutional Law Review 318; Maja Brkan, 'The Concept of Essence of Fundamental Rights in the EU Legal Order: Peeling the Onion to Its Core' (2018) 14 European Constitutional Law Review 332.

1610 Koen Lenaerts, 'Limits on Limitations: The Essence of Fundamental Rights in the EU' (2019) 20 German Law Journal 779, 781.

1611 Pierre Thielbörger, 'The "Essence" of International Human Rights' (2019) 20 German Law Journal 924.

1612 ibid.

1613 ibid 926.

1614 Thielbörger (n 1611).

1615 ibid 935.

1616 ibid 933.

rights law, the application of the concept of the "essence" of human right at both levels (macro and micro) is of the utmost importance. Thus, in order to define human rights violations that meet the criteria for being of common concern, we rely upon the concept of "essence" at both levels.

3.3 *Systematic Human Rights Violations as an Additional Criterion*

The recognition of human rights violations as a matter of common concern has several normative implications as discussed above. Despite acknowledging that every violation of human rights should be remedied, I suggest that the normative implications of the doctrine of Common Concern should apply only to systematic human rights violations. There is no one well-defined standard for deciding whether such violations are systematic, but in order to qualify as a matter of common concern, these violations should represent a persistent pattern of behaviour. This pattern can be measured with reference to the period of time during which the violations occurred or to the repetitive nature of the violations, implying that the violations have consistently been repeated. Hence, a certain level of flexibility is inherent in this criterion.

3.4 *Grave Human Rights Violations as a Threat to International Peace and Security*

The end of World War II symbolised a new era for human rights. There is no better way to illustrate this shift than to provide the following historical example. In 1933, during the meeting of the League of Nations, Goebbels, attempting to justify German's barbarous policies, declared: "Gentlemen, the Third German Reich is a sovereign State and we are masters of our own home. All that has been said by this individual is not your business. We do what we deem necessary with our own socialists, our pacifists and our Jews."[1617] Since then, a drastic change has occurred. The essence of this change has been captured by Michael Reisman who notes that "no serious scholar still supports the contention that internal human rights are 'essentially within the domestic jurisdiction of any State' and hence insulated from international law."[1618]

The discussion of the possible causal relationship between the protection of human rights and lasting peace gained traction in the aftermath of World War II. The reasons for this are enumerated by Charles Beitz: "it was believed that the war might have been avoided if there had been effective international

1617 Pellet (n 26) 723–724.

1618 Michael Reisman, 'Sovereignty and Human Rights in Contemporary International Law,' in Dinah Shelton (ed), *International protection of human rights* (Brill Nijhoff 2017) 387.

mechanism to identify and sanction violations of human rights in Nazi Germany."[1619] Recent studies conducted by social scientists endorse the view that the states that abuse human rights are more likely to go to war,[1620] on the grounds that "[t]he domestic norms and values that govern local conflict politics also shape (or perhaps mirror) how states operate at the international level when faced with the challenges of conflict. Violent social models at home may animate states in conflict to refuse peaceful settlements in favour of violent solutions."[1621]

International law scholars echo this view. For instance, Anne-Marie Slaughter emphasises that "states do not sign on to, or at least ratify and implement, human rights treaties solely for moral or even political reasons. Nor are they willing to send troops into battle solely for such reasons. On the contrary, governments increasingly understand that they often cannot afford to look the other way; that fundamental threats to their own security, whether from refugees, terrorists, the potential destabilization of an entire region, or a miasma of disease and crime, may well have their origins in conditions once thought to be within a state's exclusive domestic jurisdiction."[1622]

Despite these scholarly debates, the practice of the UN Security Council regarding recognition of grave human rights violations as a threat to international peace and security is ambiguous and inconclusive. The end of the Cold War coincided with the period when the Security Council started to recognise the existence of non-military threats to international peace and security. A number of Security Council resolutions explicitly stipulate that human rights violations which lead to massive cross-border refugee flows threaten international peace and security in the region.[1623] For example, condemning the ongoing repression of the Iraqi civilian population in parts of Iraq, the Security Council declared that it was "[g]ravely concerned by the repression of the Iraqi civilian population in many parts of Iraq, including most recently in Kurdish populated areas, which led to a massive flow of refugees towards and across international frontiers and to cross-border incursions, which threaten international peace and security in the region."[1624] Turkey and the Islamic Republic of Iran brought this issue to the attention of the Security Council,

1619 Beitz (n 914) 16.

1620 Hafner-Burton (n 1583) 275.

1621 ibid., reference to the research of Caprioli and Trumbore.

1622 Anne-Marie Slaughter, 'Sovereignty and Power in a Networked World Order' (2004) 40 Stanford Journal of International Law 283.

1623 UNSC Res 688 (5 April 1991) UN Doc S/RES/688.

1624 ibid.

claiming that the gravity of the situation and its negative implications constituted a threat to peace and security.[1625] Conversely, the representative of Iraq described the Security Council resolution as "a flagrant, illegitimate intervention in Iraq's internal affairs and a violation of Article 2 of the Charter of the United Nations."[1626]

Another humanitarian crisis described as a threat to international peace and security was the Haitian crisis.[1627] Without explicitly invoking Article 39 of the UN Charter, the Security Council expressed concern about the Haitian crisis, speaking of "the incidence of humanitarian crises, including mass displacements of population, becoming or aggravating threats to international peace and security."[1628]

In the first Security Council resolution acknowledging the genocide in Rwanda, the threat to peace and security was mentioned twice.[1629] The relevant part of the text of the resolution, reads as follows: "Deeply disturbed by the magnitude of the human suffering caused by the conflict and concerned that the continuation of the situation in Rwanda constitutes a threat to peace and security in the region."[1630] The same resolution imposed an arms embargo, with the preceding paragraph declaring that "the situation in Rwanda constitutes a threat to peace and security in the region."[1631] The subsequent resolution proclaimed that "the magnitude of the humanitarian crisis in Rwanda constitutes a threat to peace and security in the region."[1632] Security Council resolution 955 reiterated that the situation continued to constitute a threat to international peace and security.[1633]

During the crisis in eastern Zaire, the Security Council adopted resolution 1080, in which it determined that "the magnitude of the present humanitarian crisis in eastern Zaire constitutes a threat to peace and security in the

1625 UNSC, 'Provisional Verbatim Record of 2982 Meeting, UN Doc S/PV.2982' (1991).
1626 ibid 17.
1627 "On September 30, 1991, Haiti's democratically elected President, Je Bertrand Aristide, was overthrown by a coup d'etat headed by Lieutenant General Raoul Cédras and driven into exile in the United States (U.S.). The Haitian political crisis triggered a stream of refugees bound foremost for the U.S." Götz-Dietrich Opitz, 'Transnational Organizing and the Haitian Crisis, 1991–1994' (2002) 8 Journal of Haitian Studies 114.
1628 UNSC Res 841 (16 June 1993) UN Doc S/RES/841.
1629 UNSC Res 918 (17 May 1994) UN Doc S/RES/918.
1630 ibid.
1631 ibid.
1632 UNSC Res 929 (22 June 1994) UN Doc S/RES/929.
1633 UNSC Res 955 (8 November 1994) UN Doc S/RES/955.

region."[1634] The discussion of the crisis during the Security Council meeting revealed that a number of members considered the displacement of the refugees as a threat to regional peace and security. For example, the representative of Honduras stated: "My delegation would like to express its deep concern at the serious events in eastern Zaire, which have caused more than a million Burundian and Rwandese refugees to abandon their camps, thereby threatening peace and security in the Great Lakes region."[1635] A similar view was expressed by the representative of the Republic of Korea: "The looming humanitarian catastrophe, unless tackled properly by the international community now, is bound to have serious consequences, threatening peace and security in the entire Great Lakes region."[1636]

The situation in Kosovo was on the Security Council's agenda for some time. During the debate, a number of members expressed their concerns about the deterioration of the situation.[1637] The representative of Costa Rica expressed the view that the scale of human rights violations posed a threat to international peace and security.[1638] The representative of the United Kingdom, speaking on behalf of the European Union, emphasised that violence against the civilian population was unacceptable.[1639] The Russian Federation, by contrast, claimed that it was an internal affair of the Federal Republic of Yugoslavia,[1640] while the Chinese representative expressed similar views.[1641] The representative of Slovenia made the following statement in the course of the discussions: "State sovereignty is not absolute and that it cannot be used as a tool of denial of humanity resulting in threats to peace."[1642] The Canadian representative admitted the causal nexus between human rights violations and peace and security, claiming: "From Rwanda to Kosovo, there is mounting historical evidence which shows how internal conflicts which threaten human security spill over borders and destabilize entire regions. We have learned in Kosovo and from other conflicts that humanitarian and human rights concerns are not just internal matters. Therefore, unlike the delegation of China, Canada considers that such issues can and must be given new weight in the Council's

1634 UNSC Res 1080 (15 November 1996) UN Doc S/RES/1080.
1635 UNSC, 'UN Security Council, 3713th Meeting, UN Doc S/PV.3713' (1996).
1636 ibid.
1637 UNSC, 'UN Security Council, 3868th Meeting, UN Doc S/PV.3868' (1998).
1638 ibid 4.
1639 ibid 14–15.
1640 ibid 10.
1641 ibid 11–12.
1642 UNSC, 'UN Security Council, 4011th Meeting, UN Doc S/PV.4011' (1999) 11.

definition of security and in its calculus as to when and how the Council must engage."[1643]

Security Council resolution 1296 "*Protection of civilians in armed conflict*" reiterated the view that grave and systematic violations of human rights undermine peace and security.[1644] As the Security Council puts it: "the deliberate targeting of civilian populations or other protected persons and the committing of systematic, flagrant and widespread violations of international humanitarian and human rights law in situations of armed conflict may constitute a threat to international peace and security, and, in this regard, reaffirms its readiness to consider such situations and, where necessary, to adopt appropriate steps."[1645] The discussions during the 4109th Security Council meeting, which preceded the resolution's adoption, revealed diverging views on the issue. While several members endorsed the position that grave human rights violations could pose a threat to international peace and security,[1646] the representatives of the Russian Federation[1647] and Belarus[1648] were cautious and sceptical. Overall, these discussions revealed that a causal relationship does exist between egregious human rights violations and long-term instability, yet the question of what constitutes an appropriate response to such violations remains a major source of controversy among members.

Security Council resolution 1314 "*The children and armed conflict*" adopted on 11 August 2000 confirms that some violations of human rights may pose

1643 ibid 13.

1644 UNSC Res 1296 (19 April 2000) UN Doc S/RES/1296.

1645 ibid.

1646 For example, the French representative declared: "Finally, humanitarian crises can reach such degrees of seriousness that, as has just been emphasized, the response can only be a political one and, in certain circumstances, one that will also require the use of force in order to put an end to large-scale violations of human rights and international humanitarian law. Those violations in themselves threaten international peace and security and therefore fully justify the use of such action, in accordance with the United Nations Charter. That was the case in Kosovo. Under those circumstances, the Council cannot but exercise the responsibilities assigned to it under the Charter." UNSC, 'UN Security Council, 4109th Meeting, UN Doc S/PV.4109' (2000) 7.

1647 As the delegate from the Russian Federation argued: "The experience of recent years has shown that the prevention and settlement of humanitarian crises has a direct bearing on the maintenance of regional and international stability. But it is also clear that we cannot end violations of international humanitarian law by taking actions that themselves violate the Charter of the United Nations. Arbitrary military measures that sidestep the Security Council – including those taken under the pretext of preventing so-called humanitarian catastrophes – are not acceptable and can only worsen crises." ibid 15.

1648 ibid 22–23.

a threat to international peace and security.[1649] This conclusion was reached as follows: "the deliberate targeting of civilian populations or other protected persons, including children, and the committing of systematic, flagrant and widespread violations of international humanitarian and human rights law, including that relating to children, in situations of armed conflict may constitute a threat to international peace and security, and in this regard reaffirms its readiness to consider such situations and, where necessary to adopt appropriate steps."[1650] Despite the fact that this statement refers to situations of armed conflict, no distinction is made between the instances of internal conflict and conflicts involving several states.

In 2004, addressing the deteriorating situation in Haiti, the Security Council re-emphasised that a strong connection exists between refugee flows and threats to international peace and security.[1651] The relevant part of the resolution reads as follows: "the situation in Haiti constitutes a threat to international peace and security, and to stability in the Caribbean especially through the potential outflow of people to other States in the subregion."[1652] Security Council resolutions 1674 and 1738 reaffirmed the Council's determination that the human rights violations in situations of armed conflict may constitute a threat to international peace and security,[1653] while resolution 1674 emphasised the role of human rights in collective security: "Acknowledging that peace and security, development and human rights are the pillars of the United Nations system and the foundations for collective security and well-being, and recognizing in this regard that development, peace and security and human rights are interlinked and mutually reinforcing." Subsequently, resolution 1738 echoed these views.

In 2006–2007, when discussing the ongoing internal conflict in Myanmar, the members of the Security Council engaged in a heated debate.[1654] One

---

1649 UNSC Res 1314 (11 August 2000) UN Doc S/RES/1314.

1650 ibid.

1651 UNSC Res 1529 (29 February 2004) UN Doc S/RES/1529.

1652 ibid.

1653 The relevant part of the resolution states that "the deliberate targeting of civilians and other protected persons, and the commission of systematic, flagrant and widespread violations of international humanitarian and human rights law in situations of armed conflict, may constitute a threat to international peace and security, and, reaffirms in this regard its readiness to consider such situations and, where necessary, to adopt appropriate steps." UNSC Res 1674 (28 April 2006) UN Doc S/RES/1674; UNSC Res 1738 (23 December 2006) UN Doc S/RES/1738.

1654 During the 5526th meeting of the Security Council (SC), members were deliberating whether the crisis in Myanmar should be included in the agenda. UNSC, 'UN Security Council, 5526th Meeting, UN Doc S/PV.5526' (2006). In 2007, the SC debated the adoption

group of states contended that the internal conflicts, which had resulted in hundreds of thousands of internally displaced people and refugees, constituted a threat to international peace and security.[1655] By contrast, other members, such as China and Qatar, asserted that the crisis in Myanmar was an internal matter and therefore could not constitute a threat to international peace and security.[1656]

Security Council resolution 1894 "*On the protection of civilians in armed conflict*," adopted on 11 November 2009, further reinforced the Security Council's earlier claims that systemic, flagrant and widespread violations of international humanitarian and human rights law in situations of armed conflict may constitute a threat to international peace and security.[1657]

In 2017, in the course of the Security Council's debate on *Human rights and prevention of armed conflict*, the president, Mrs Haley, made the following statement: "I am here today to assert that the protection of human rights is often deeply intertwined with peace and security. The two things often cannot be separated. In case after case, human rights violations and abuses are not merely the incidental by-products of conflict, but the trigger of conflict. When a State begins to systematically violate human rights, it is a sign; it is a red flag; it is a blaring siren – one of the clearest possible indicators that instability and violence may follow and spill across borders. It is no surprise that the world's most brutal regimes are also the most ruthless violators of human rights."[1658]

---

of the draft resolution on the crisis in Myanmar, which was submitted by the United States and the United Kingdom. In the course of the debate, no consensus was reached among the permanent members of the Council, and therefore the resolution was not adopted. Despite this outcome, the discussions revealed a sharp divide on the question of when a humanitarian crisis can be taken to represent a threat to international peace and security. The representatives of China and Qatar emphasised that the crisis was an internal matter, the Russian Federation opposed the adoption of the resolution and the representative of South Africa expressed the view that the SC was overstepping its mandate by discussing the situation in Myanmar. The representatives of the United States, the United Kingdom and Slovakia expressed their concerns about the worsening of the ongoing crisis and its negative ramifications for international peace and security. UNSC, 'UN Security Council, 5619th Meeting, UN Doc S/PV.5619' (2007).

1655 UNSC, 'UN Security Council, 5526th Meeting, UN Doc S/PV.5526' (n 1654); UNSC, 'UN Security Council, 5619th Meeting, UN Doc S/PV.5619' (n 1654); UNSC, 'UN Security Council, 5753rd Meeting, UN Doc S/PV.5753' (2007); UNSC, 'UN Security Council, 5777th Meeting, UN Doc S/PV.5777' (2007).

1656 UNSC, 'UN Security Council, 5526th Meeting, UN Doc S/PV.5526' (n 1654); UNSC, 'UN Security Council, 5619th Meeting, UN Doc S/PV.5619' (n 1654); UNSC, 'UN Security Council, 5753rd Meeting, UN Doc S/PV.5753' (n 1655); UNSC, 'UN Security Council, 5777th Meeting, UN Doc S/PV.5777' (n 1655).

1657 UNSC Res 1894 (11 November 2009) UN Doc S/RES/1894.

1658 UNSC, 'UN Security Council, 7926th Meeting, UN Doc S/PV.7926' (2017).

This statement, together with the Security Council resolutions discussed above, reflect developments in this area, although some UN Members undermine these developments through their use of the veto power. For example, although events in Syria had been unfolding dramatically since 2011 and numerous reports from the region confirmed large-scale human rights violations, the response from the UN Security Council was blocked by members exercising their veto power. The draft resolution, which condemned the Syrian crackdown on protestors, was vetoed by the Russian Federation and China on 4 October 2011.[1659] The following month, during the meeting of the Security Council, the representative of Germany signalled the concern about the situation in Syria: "the Assistant Secretary-General for Human Rights voiced his appeal that we prevent the violent suppression of mass protests from developing into civil war. That was six months ago. Meanwhile, the situation in Syria has deteriorated. The Syrian regime is relying on repression. Unarmed civilians are continuously being killed."[1660] Despite well-reported instances of ongoing human rights atrocities and the growing number of victims, further attempts by the Security Council to adopt resolutions failed as a result of the veto power exercised by the Russian Federation and China.[1661] Only after chemical weapons were used against the civilian population, including women and children, was the Security Council resolution that required the verification and destruction of chemical weapons stockpiles in Syria adopted.[1662] Yet, this resolution does not address grave human rights violations. Other resolutions that were adopted condemned gross human rights violations, but without authorising collective sanctions or humanitarian intervention, limiting their demands to humanitarian access across conflict lines.[1663] However, even this demand to guarantee humanitarian access across conflict lines was ignored by the Syrian

1659 'Security Council Fails to Adopt Draft Resolution Condemning Syria's Crackdown on Anti-Government Protestors, Owing to Veto by Russian Federation, China' (n 8).

1660 UNSC, 'UN Security Council, 6650th Meeting, UN Doc S/PV.6650' (2011).

1661 On 4 February 2012, the adoption of the draft resolution condemning the violence in Syria was vetoed by the Russian Federation and China. 'Security Council Fails to Adopt Draft Resolution on Syria as Russian Federation, China Veto Text Supporting Arab League's Proposed Peace Plan' <https://www.un.org/press/en/2012/sc10536.doc.htm>. On 19 July 2012, the adoption of another draft resolution was vetoed by the Russian Federation and China. 'Security Council Fails to Adopt Draft Resolution on Syria That Would Have Threatened Sanctions, Due to Negative Votes of China, Russian Federation' <https://www.un.org/press/en/2012/sc10714.doc.htm>.

1662 UNSC Res 2118 (27 September 2013) UN Doc S/RES/2118.

1663 UNSC Res 2139 (22 February 2014) UN Doc S/RES/2139; UNSC Res 2165 (14 July 2014) UN Doc S/RES/2165; UNSC Res 2191 (17 December 2014) UN Doc S/RES/2191; UNSC Res 2258 (22 December 2015) UN Doc S/RES/2258.

government.[1664] There is no need to describe how this humanitarian catastrophe triggered massive refugee flows, in what was called the "refugee crisis."

The determination that gross violations of human rights might constitute a threat to international peace and security is made by the UN Security Council on a case-by-case basis with a significant political component, namely veto power. In this context, the practice of regional organisations is of particular interest, as illustrated by Principle 4(h) of the Constitutive Act of the African Union providing for "the right of the Union to intervene in a Member State pursuant to a decision of the Assembly in respect of grave circumstances, namely: war crimes, genocide and crimes against humanity."[1665] Judge Yusuf interprets this entitlement as follows: "should the UN Security Council fail to act, the grave circumstances in respect of which the AU is empowered to take military action, namely genocide, war crimes and crimes against humanity, may sometimes require the adoption of emergency measures, including military force, aimed at saving human lives. Even in such a situation, the AU may still not be considered to be in breach of its international obligations, so long as its action meets the conditions and criteria laid down in Articles 52 and 54 of the Charter, […] and thus becomes eligible for an ex post facto endorsement or subsequent acquiescence by the Security Council."[1666] This shows that certain regional organisations have acknowledged the causal relationship between grave human rights violations and threats to peace and security, enshrining such an acknowledgement into their constitutive documents.

One more observation is warranted here. International peace is a classic example of a global public good[1667] and was one of the driving forces behind closer economic cooperation and interdependence.[1668] However, international

1664 "So long as the parties to conflict continue to disregard their international legal obligations, I regret that we will continue to report on more and more senseless tragedies, despite the demands of Security Council resolutions 2139 (2013) and 2165 (2014), said Assistant Secretary-General for Humanitarian Affairs Kyung-wha Kang, briefing the 15-member body on behalf of Valerie Amos, Under-Secretary-General for Humanitarian Affairs and Emergency Relief Coordinator." 'Amid Unrelenting Violence, Syria's Warring Parties Must Increase Aid Agencies' Access into Hard-to-Reach Areas, Top Relief Official Tells Security Council' <https://www.un.org/press/en/2014/sc11622.doc.htm>.

1665 Organization of African Unity (OAU), Constitutive Act of the African Union, 1 July 2000.

1666 Abdulqawi A Yusuf, 'The Right of Forcible Intervention in Certain Conflicts' in Abdulqawi Yusuf and Fatsah Ouguergouz (eds.), *The African Union, Legal and Institutional Framework: a manual on the Pan-African organization* (Martinus Nijhoff 2012) 346–347.

1667 Peace is an example of a pure public good. Inge Kaul (ed), *Global Public Goods: International Cooperation in the 21st Century* (Oxford University Press 1999) 4.

1668 Whether economic cooperation positively impacts the peaceful settlement of disputes between nations is still a subject of ongoing debate, with both liberals and realists claiming dominance of their arguments. In the late 1990s and early 2000s number of

peace and security is a weakest-link global public good and therefore its provision depends on the efforts of the least capable states. Scott Barrett has emphasised that "the weakest state" could either be incapable or unwilling to provide global public goods.[1669] Furthermore, the provision of global public goods is based on cost–benefit analyses conducted by each state and if the costs incurred by a state are lower than the benefit obtained, that state might be willing to cooperate.[1670] In the case of global peace and security, the costs might be more obvious than the benefits, leading to a false conclusion that the costs dominate. Thus, even the theory of global public goods emphasises that cooperation between states is crucial for preserving international peace and security.

4 The Potential of the Principle of Common Concern of Humankind in International Human Rights Law

The application of the principle of Common Concern of Humankind to international human rights law is an attempt to introduce an idea of subsidiary responsibility for human rights protection imposed on the international community of states, which is channelled through the normative implications prescribed by the doctrine.[1671] In the present context, the principle makes a contribution to taking into account the focus on grave and systematic violations. The idea of subsidiarity is grounded in a belief that grave human rights violations should be acknowledged to represent a matter of common concern, and thus to call for a response from the international community.

The normative implications of the doctrine apply only to instances of grave and systematic human rights violations which potentially threaten

researchers strongly endorsed the liberal argument, even introducing models to prove the empirical validity of this assumption. Academics who supported this classical liberal argument included Professors John R Oneal and Bruce Russett, Håvard Hegre and many others. In his recent book *Economic Interdependence and War*, Dale C Copeland argues that economic interdependence, in particular trade and investment between states, could either promote peace or cause military conflict depending on the circumstances of a particular case ("trade expectations theory"). For more details, see Dale C Copeland, *Economic Interdependence and War* (Princeton University Press 2015).

1669 Barrett (n 1595).

1670 ibid.

1671 For more details on the allocation of the duties that relate to human rights protection, see Samantha Besson, 'The Bearers of Human Rights' Duties and Responsibilities for Human Rights: A Quite (R)Evolution?' (2015) 32 Social Philosophy and Policy 244.

international peace and security. Each of these qualifying criteria has been discussed above. Yet, it must also be pointed out that the violations of human rights that are recognised as jus cogens constitute a matter of common concern under all circumstances.[1672]

Furthermore, as mentioned above, the doctrine of Common Concern identifies the order of priority of responses to grave human rights violations. More precisely, international cooperation, or a multilateral response, is the preferred approach and unilateral measures are allowed only if a multilateral response is not successful. Another valuable contribution made by the doctrine of Common Concern is that it provides a foundation for recognising the legality and legitimacy of unilateral actions when a state intervenes to prevent grave human rights violations occurring on the territory of another state. As a matter of last resort, the doctrine not only entails a right to act, but also imposes a duty to respond to instances of grave and systematic human rights violations. This duty to act is conditional upon the failure of attempts at international cooperation and noncompliance with international human rights obligations on the part of the state under whose jurisdiction these violations occur. I outline below four main contributions made by the doctrine of Common Concern when it is transposed into the domain of international human rights law.

4.1 *Reinforced Duty to Cooperate*

Research conducted by social scientists confirms that grave human rights violations are motivated either by a lack of the resources necessary to guarantee better human rights standards or by a government's intention to deprive its citizens of human rights guarantees.[1673] A lack of resources also implies weak institutional structures.[1674] The same conclusion was reached by legal scholars who studied the deficiencies of international human rights protection through the lens of global public goods.[1675] By designating human rights or human rights protection as a global public good, legal scholars contend that a combination of carrots and sticks should be used to resolve the collective action problems that undermine effective protection of human rights.[1676]

The duty to cooperate prescribed under the doctrine of Common Concern comprises the duties imposed on a state that is in dire need of assistance and the corresponding duties of the other states, which are in a position to provide

1672 Cottier, 'Improving Compliance: Jus Cogens and International Economic Law' (n 1126).
1673 Hafner-Burton (n 1583).
1674 ibid.
1675 Barrett (n 1595); Bodansky (n 1596).
1676 Barrett (n 1595); Bodansky (n 1596).

such assistance. Acting in good faith, a state upon whose territory grave human rights violations occur must provide accurate information about an incident in a timely manner and explicitly request assistance. This exchange of information could be channelled through the Human Rights Council or other organisations, which might require introducing changes in the legal documents that regulate the operation of these organisations. Alternatively, the committees that are established under the core human rights treaties may be entrusted with a new duty to administer such requests for assistance.

The duty to cooperate inherently implies enhanced transparency between the states. This duty may reinforce the reporting obligation enshrined in the core human rights treaties and may empower civil society in a particular state to demand the submission of regular reports, if the state does not fulfil its international obligation to do so.

The doctrine of Common Concern also entails differentiated responsibility. In international human rights law, this differentiated responsibility may require compulsory educational and financial assistance provided by the states that are in a position to render such assistance to a state that requires it. Proponents of the counterargument might argue that there are numerous examples of such cooperative efforts, which are mainly pursued by the developed states with a good human rights record along with the institutions promoting human rights protection worldwide. The historical record bears witness to instances of international cooperation of this sort, particularly in cases of natural disasters. Yet, such assistance is, as a rule, voluntary and depends on the willingness of the other states to provide it. Thus, a potentially valuable contribution made by the doctrine of Common Concern is that it would require a state in need to explicitly communicate this need and to provide all the relevant information, while at the same time imposing a duty on the other states to cooperate with each other in their common efforts to address the request. Put differently, it reinforces existing practice by giving it the sense of a legal obligation. Consequently, the duty to cooperate provides a legal foundation for a particular behaviour by allocating duties and responsibilities between the various subjects of international law.

4.2 *The Domestication of International Human Rights Obligations*

In chapter 3, we discussed numerous empirical studies demonstrating that the ratification of human rights treaties does not inevitably result in the enhanced protection of human rights.[1677] This finding indicates that states are

1677 For more details, see subsection 1.7 The deficiencies of treaty-based enforcement mechanisms.

more willing to ratify international human rights treaties than to implement them domestically. Indeed, Oona Hathaway has analysed various motivations behind the states' desire to participate in human rights treaties and concluded that the improvement of human rights protection is not the only reason for such participation.[1678]

Furthermore, the core human rights treaties prescribe an obligation to report measures that have been taken to implement the commitments undertaken. As we have described in chapter 3, states frequently neglect their duty to report.[1679] The relevant committees send reminders to these states, but many of them remain unanswered.[1680]

The doctrine of Common Concern entails a duty to do one's homework, which implies that the states must implement their international commitments domestically. It entails a basic obligation and duty on the part of states to prevent, avoid and remedy systemic violations of human rights as a matter of international law. It offers a minimal standard, upon the basis of which more advanced protection of human rights under domestic constitutional law can be put in place. This duty is premised on one of the cornerstones of international law – *pacta sunt servanda*. Despite seeming simple, this obligation is of the utmost importance for non-reciprocal regimes, such as international human rights law. Discussing this non-reciprocity, Oona Hathaway notes: "After all, the major engines of compliance that exist in other areas of international law are for the most part absent in the area of human rights. Unlike the public international law of money, there are no 'competitive market forces' that press for compliance. And, unlike in the case of trade agreements, the costs of retaliatory noncompliance are low to nonexistent, because a nation's actions against its own citizens do not directly threaten or harm other states. Human rights law thus stands out as an area of international law in which countries have little incentive to police noncompliance with treaties or norms. As Henkin remarked, 'The forces that induce compliance with other law […] do not pertain equally to the law of human rights.'"[1681]

The duty to do one's homework may be channelled through various aspects of government policy, including trade policy. By way of illustration, a state may discriminate between the two products based on their process and production

1678 Oona A Hathaway, 'Why Do Countries Commit to Human Rights Treaties?' (2007) 51 Journal of Conflict Resolution 588.

1679 For more details, see subsection 1.7 The deficiencies of treaty-based enforcement mechanisms.

1680 ibid.

1681 Hathaway (n 1087) 1938.

methods (PPMs). This distinction is particularly relevant for goods or services produced in circumstances that violate the internationally recognised labour standards.[1682] Hence, imported products can be banned if they were produced in violation of the basic international labour standards. In this context, Thomas Cottier points out: "Yet, in principle, a WTO Member today is free to require compliance with core labour standards, or the ban on child labour, in treating imported products on the basis of such PPMs. To the extent that the making of a product (good or service) is related to the protection of these core values, compliance can be enforced by means of imposing necessary trade restrictions."[1683]

PPM-based trade restrictions have traditionally been criticised for creating favourable circumstances for economic protectionism. Indeed, this is a valid point that needs to be addressed here. The normative implications of the doctrine of Common Concern prescribe a sequential order for their realisation. Thus, the right to rely upon unilateral trade-restrictive measures that are PPM-based is conditional upon the fulfilment of the duty to cooperate, which should precede any trade restrictions.

With regard to the violation of jus cogens norms, which are recognised to constitute a matter of common concern *per se*,[1684] reliance upon the PPM-based distinction is not always practical. That is to say, human rights violations, which can be protected as jus cogens, as a rule, do not occur in the process of production and thus, as a rule, do not relate to a particular good or service.

The role of the doctrine of Common Concern is thus to address this absence of reciprocity by introducing the duty to give effect to international obligations in the domestic legal order in parallel to the duty to rely upon unilateral measures if the former duty is not complied with.

4.3 *An Instrument for Providing Legality and Legitimacy to Unilateral Economic Sanctions*

Unilateralism has always been a part of public international law. Indeed, public international law is characterised by the decentralised system of law enforcement, including measures of self-help. Discussing the role of unilateralism, Monica Hakimi has emphasised that unilateral actions could offer a possible solution to situations which "require regulating states that are uninterested in

1682 Cottier, 'The Implications of EC – Seal Products for the Protection of Core Labour Standards in WTO Law' (n 1406).

1683 Cottier, 'Improving Compliance: Jus Cogens and International Economic Law' (n 1126) 338.

1684 Cottier, 'Improving Compliance: Jus Cogens and International Economic Law' (n 1126).

being regulated or participating meaningfully in international governance."[1685] Furthermore, Monica Hakimi acknowledges that unilateral measures are not only a conventional instrument of enforcement, but also have a law-making function.[1686]

Coercive economic measures have played a significant role in enforcing public international law. Even though the leading international law scholars refused to acknowledge the existence of the right to be free from economic coercion in the 1980s,[1687] the 1990s[1688] or even today,[1689] the legal status of unilateral economic sanctions remains undefined.[1690] Moreover, a number of states are unwilling to accept the legality of unilateral coercive economic measures.[1691] Traditionally, there were two main arguments against unilateral measures, based on the interest in preserving sovereign equality of states and the implications of such measures for power politics.[1692] Regarding the latter, Alain Pellet has stated: "leaving aside the use of force, I am not convinced that there is more risk in admitting sanctions in pursuance of community interests than to recognize the lawfulness of countermeasures."[1693]

On this basis, it must be acknowledged that there is a divergence between the law and state practice. On the one hand, states frequently rely upon unilateral coercive economic measures to achieve a range of objectives, including human rights protection. In this regard, it is noteworthy that even the working group of the Human Rights Committee considered "extreme action involving reprisals and the use of sanctions" among the legal mechanisms for the enforcement of international human rights.[1694] On the other hand, the legality and legitimacy of such actions are disputed. Hence, there is an increasing need for disciplines to resort to unilateral actions that may potentially have a detrimental effect on targeted states and individuals.

1685 Hakimi (176) 108.

1686 Monica Hakimi focuses more on the law-making aspect of the unilateral coercive measures than on their role in enforcing international law norms. To substantiate her argument, Monica Hakimi provides examples of instances when the unilateral conduct of states "was a part of a broader effort to change the law" and, in fact, was successful. ibid 124.

1687 Damrosch (n 1302).

1688 Elagab (n 452).

1689 Tzanakopoulos (n 369).

1690 For a more detailed discussion, see chapter 2.

1691 ibid.

1692 Hakimi (n 176) 141–145.

1693 Pellet (n 26).

1694 Beitz (n 914) 24.

The doctrine of Common Concern not only prescribes a right to impose unilateral coercive measures, but it also sets out the limits of this right by allowing international intervention to redress systematic violations of the inalienable core contents of human rights. At the same time, it also entails a duty to act in such circumstances.[1695] However, this duty is triggered only if the situation of grave human rights violations meets the threshold for being recognised as a common concern and if the sovereign state on whose territory these violations occur neither engages in cooperation on the international level nor resolves the situation. Thus, the doctrine of Common Concern can legitimise only a tiny fraction of unilateral responses.

The contribution of the duty to act prescribed under the doctrine of Common Concern implies two outcomes that may seem to be contradictory. If certain prerequisites are met, this duty becomes compulsory for every state, and hence the state is under an international obligation to impose unilateral coercive measures to redress human rights violations abroad. Conversely, if these preconditions are not fulfilled, states cannot benefit from the presumption that these unilateral responses are legal and legitimate. Thus, this obligation is not an open-ended possibility to abuse unilateralism, but rather imposes a constraint on the use of economic coercion.

If the normative implications of the doctrine of Common Concern are endorsed, unilateral coercive economic measures imposed in accordance with it would be lawful. In particular, such restrictive actions would not contradict the principle of non-intervention enshrined in the UN Charter, in virtue of recognising grave human rights violations as the common concern of all states and not as a domestic matter. Moreover, such unilateral actions may be qualified as legitimate third-party countermeasures imposed on a state that does not comply with its international obligations. As regards coercive measures with extraterritorial effect, these restrictions ought to be legal since the acknowledgement that a common concern exists triggers subsidiary responsibility of all states. Furthermore, the doctrine of Common Concern, if it fully develops into a principle of law, has the potential to play a significant role in international adjudication.[1696] Consequently, it may inform the interpretation of the relevant provisions of WTO law. For example, grave human rights violations that reach the threshold for being a common concern could be interpreted as "other emergency in international relations" for the purposes of invoking the national security exception. Alternatively, the WTO tribunals,

1695 Cottier, 'The Principle of Common Concern of Humankind.' (n 18) 48–54.

1696 ibid 55.

when adjudicating whether unilateral economic sanctions imposed to redress grave human rights violations can be justified under the public morals exception may use the doctrine in their necessity analysis. Hence, general human rights sanctions might be acknowledged to be WTO consistent.

One issue that might be raised by opponents of the idea of introducing the normative framework of Common Concern is that there will be no institution responsible for supervising its functioning. Yet, it should be emphasised that in public international law the normative and institutional issues are often separated and this does not prevent the normative ideas from flourishing.

4.4 *An Instrument to Empower Civil Society*

Civil society is playing an increasingly powerful role in influencing domestic politics and demanding more transparency and accountability from governments globally. Research conducted by political scientists has underlined that the demands of the electorate can influence policy-makers to respond to grave human rights violations taking place elsewhere in the world.[1697] For example, scholars have demonstrated a positive correlation between the coverage of human suffering by the US media and the government's response in the form of economic sanctions.[1698]

In this context, Thomas Cottier envisions the role of the doctrine of Common Concern in assessing the accountability of governments as follows: "The obligation to give the reasons why measures are taken, or not taken, increases accountability of governments and transparency and informs domestic debate on foreign policy."[1699] In a similar vein, Daniel Bodansky has pointed out with respect to the role international law as an enabler of domestic changes that "[t]he existence of an international obligation gives domestic actors both within and outside government a 'hook' for their arguments. If an international obligation is incorporated into national law, the hook is legal in nature and can potentially be applied by courts. But even if not, international norms can provide a useful argument for domestic supporters."[1700] With this in mind,

1697 Elena V McLean and Taehee Whang, 'Designing Foreign Policy: Voters, Special Interest Groups, and Economic Sanctions' (2014) 51 Journal of Peace Research 589; Stephanie Chan, 'Principle Versus Profit: Debating Human Rights Sanctions' (2018) 19 Human Rights Review 45.

1698 Dursun Peksen, Timothy M Peterson and A Cooper Drury, 'Media-Driven Humanitarianism? News Media Coverage of Human Rights Abuses and the Use of Economic Sanctions' (2014) 58 International Studies Quarterly 855.

1699 Cottier, 'The Principle of Common Concern of Humankind.' (n 18) 54.

1700 Bodansky (n 1596) 660.

we anticipate that the doctrine of Common Concern may encourage various domestic actors to act to fully implement it in the field of human rights.

5 Conclusion

This chapter introduced the theoretical framework of the doctrine of Common Concern of Humankind and outlined its suggested normative implications. It argued that the normative implications of the doctrine apply only to instances of grave and systematic human rights violations which potentially threaten international peace and security.

The doctrine puts forward the idea of improved international cooperation between states with the aim of redressing instances of grave human rights violations. When applied to the international protection of human rights, the doctrine reinforces the existing international obligations under the core human rights treaties by prescribing a duty to do one's homework. Furthermore, the doctrine can legitimise economic sanctions imposed for human rights violations, as well as restrict their use if such coercive measures are politically motivated. A fully-fledged doctrine entails an obligation to act in order to redress grave human rights violations.

The chapter concludes that the emerging doctrine of Common Concern of Humankind offers a suitable framework for addressing the problem of non-reciprocal interests and redefining rights and obligations in the field of human rights.

Conclusion

The present study pursues several goals concurrently. The first objective is to demonstrate the abundance of state practice in employing unilateral economic sanctions against the background of their disputed legality and intricate relationship with various fields of international law. The second aim is to explore the role of unilateral economic sanctions in the context of the existing system of international human rights protection and the legality of economic sanctions targeting human rights violations under international law. The third and final aspiration is to study the normative implications of the principle of Common Concern of Humankind and to consider its application to situations of grave and systematic human rights violations for the purpose of improving international protection of human rights, *inter alia* through the legitimisation of unilateral human rights sanctions if certain preconditions are met.

The general conclusion of the analysis presented here is that the emerging principle of Common Concern of Humankind may contribute to enhanced protection of human rights, by reinforcing the duty to cooperate in situations of grave human rights violations, requiring the domestication of international human rights obligations and legitimising unilateral economic sanctions, which are employed to redress gross human rights violations that are recognised to constitute a matter of common concern. Moreover, the acknowledgement of this doctrine and principle could potentially empower domestic actors, thus influencing domestic politics through the demands of civil society for more transparency and accountability from governments globally.

The working hypothesis of this study is that the legality of unilateral economic sanctions is contested even when these restrictions pursue the goal of remedying gross human rights violations. Hence, the proposed framework of the doctrine of Common Concern of Humankind provides pathways for legitimising unilateral human rights sanctions. The main conclusions of this study conclusively prove the initial hypothesis. Other conclusions connected to the three objectives of this study are presented below.

1 States Are Increasingly Using Unilateral Economic Sanctions against the Background of Their Questionable Effectiveness and Disputed Legality

The history of economic coercion dates back to the times of ancient Greece. These early attempts to exert economic pressure were accompanied by the use

© IRYNA BOGDANOVA, 2022 | DOI:10.1163/9789004507890_008

of military force. The remarkable success of the economic sanctions imposed by the United States and the United Kingdom during World War I instilled political leaders with high hopes for their future potential. President Woodrow Wilson, anticipating the effectiveness of economic sanctions, called them a "hand upon the throat of the offending nation."[1701]

This enthusiasm was reflected in Article 16 of the Covenant of the League of Nations. This provision obligated states to impose economic sanctions against any member of the League that resorted to war, in violation of its obligations under the Covenant. Historians describe the rationale behind this obligation in terms of "[the] hope that the threat of facing universal economic sanctions would lead countries to reconsider before launching the war."[1702] However, the collective economic sanctions prescribed by the Covenant met the same fate as the League of Nations itself.[1703]

The Charter of the United Nations empowers the Security Council to authorise collective economic sanctions, which are binding on UN Member States. By the end of the Cold War, the Security Council had exercised this power twice. In the meantime, states habitually relied upon unilateral economic sanctions. These sanctions pursued a range of objectives, including behaviour modification, punishment or sending a signal to a targeted country or to a third country.[1704]

The practice of imposing unilateral economic sanctions inspired protracted legal debates about their legality and effectiveness. In chapter 1 of this book, major studies on the effectiveness of economic sanctions were analysed and presented, which emphasise that individual states are faced with the need to find a balance between the costs incurred and the potential success of economic sanctions.[1705] Another valuable contribution of this debate to present-day sanctioning policies is the finding that the "pain-gain" formula is not universally applicable. More specifically, the severity of the economic pain inflicted is not always proportional to the probability of a successful outcome. This conclusion provoked further discussions of the particular mechanisms through which the impact of economic sanctions is channelled. This new

1701 Wilson and Foley (n 55) 71.

1702 Dehne (n 64) 3.

1703 "In the cases of the Italian invasion of Ethiopia and the Japanese occupation of Manchuria, the League provided incapable of forcing recalcitrant members to do the League's bidding and thus was fundamentally unable to enforce international law as embodied in the League Covenant." ibid 6.

1704 Alexander (n 19) 10.

1705 Baldwin, *Economic Statecraft* (n 260); Baldwin, 'The Sanctions Debate and the Logic of Choice' (n 290).

approach enabled political scientists and economists to focus on the contribution of the various factors to the overall success of economic coercion. The results of these intellectual endeavours paved the way for more narrowly construed and efficient sanctioning programmes.

Unilateral economic sanctions are a grey area in public international law. Even the definition of the term "sanction" is controversial. From the perspective of public international law, various forms of economic restrictions may fall under such legal categories as retorsion, reprisal, countermeasures, third-party countermeasures and sanctions. The boundaries of these categories remain blurred.

Political considerations haunt the discussion of the legality of unilateral economic sanctions. Paradoxically, this strong divide between states is not reflected in state practice. Indeed, as illustrated in this study, even the staunchest opponents of such unilateral measures – the Russian Federation and China – rely upon unilateral sanctions to advance their foreign policy agenda.

This political rift laid the foundation for two legal arguments. First of all, it was contended that the use of economic coercion is prohibited under Article 2(4) of the UN Charter. This argument implies that the prohibition of the use of force enshrined in Article 2(4) also entails a prohibition on the use of economic force. While a few legal scholars endorse this position, the majority agree that the prohibition of the use of force should be interpreted narrowly. Second, it was argued that the principle of non-intervention is breached by states that rely upon unilateral economic sanctions. Our enquiry has shown that the numerous declarations adopted under the auspices of the UN do not shed much light on the legality of unilateral economic sanctions. Further analysis of the legal scholarship and ICJ pronouncements lend support to the conclusion that only coercive economic measures that intervene in the *domaine réservé* of a state may be taken to encroach on the principle of non-intervention. Despite this conclusion, the distinction between forms of economic coercion that can be defined as "pressure," "interference" or "intervention" is not clearly established.

Attempts to recognise the legality of unilateral economic sanctions revolve around the idea that these restrictive actions can be justified either as legal countermeasures or third-party countermeasures. Our analysis suggests that only a tiny subset of unilateral economic sanctions can be justified as legal countermeasures. This outcome is the logical result of the narrow definition of an injured state embedded in the Draft articles, as well as of the absence of an explicit entitlement to impose countermeasures granted to non-injured states. The legality of the third-party countermeasures – or "solidarity measures," as they are often referred to – has been the subject of an extensive legal debate. The final text of the Draft articles is equivocal regarding the legality of third-party countermeasures. The legal deliberations on these countermeasures that followed the adoption of the Draft articles confirmed the abundance of the state practice, and thus called into question the conclusions of the ILC that this practice is embryonic. Notwithstanding the voluminous literature on the subject, the matter is far from settled.

In their efforts to enhance the effectiveness of economic sanctions, states design them in ways that raise the question of their compatibility with the established principles of jurisdiction in international law. A strand of the literature discusses the unlawful extraterritoriality of unilateral economic sanctions. However, this literature focuses, as a rule, on a particular sanctions regime. In this study, I attempt to identify types of unilateral sanctions that are particularly prone to legal contestation as being unlawfully extraterritorial. The results of this enquiry demonstrate that there are different types of unilateral sanctions which are extraterritorial and which cannot be justified under the existing principles on ascertaining jurisdiction in international law.

Unilateral financial sanctions can also be unlawfully extraterritorial. In order to illustrate how unilateral US financial sanctions apply extraterritorially, we discussed a recent case that was decided by a US court. In that particular dispute, a US domestic court reaffirmed the jurisdiction of the United States over conduct that took place entirely abroad. A foreign national was accused of "violating U.S. law for agreeing with *foreign* persons in *foreign* countries to direct *foreign* banks to send funds transfers from *foreign* companies to other *foreign* banks for *foreign* companies."[1706] The only nexus that existed originated "out of the incidental involvement of a U.S. bank at some mid-point in the payment chain of a transaction that originated from a foreign country and occurred between two foreign entities."[1707] My analysis concluded that this newly emerged principle of ascertaining jurisdiction, which is called correspondent-bank account jurisdiction, is questionable.

The growing tendency to rely upon unilateral economic sanctions targeting central banks, heads of state and other high-ranking government officials was considered. The background against which sanctions of this kind have been evaluated are the immunities granted under international law to states, heads of state and senior government officials. The part of the study in which these legal questions were tackled concluded with the following observations. First and foremost, the extent to which state immunity guarantees protection to the

1706 'United States of America, Government v. Reza Zarrab, et al., Defendant No. S1 15 Cr. 867 (RMB) Memorandum of Law in Support of Defendant Reza Zarrab's Motion to Dismiss the Superseding Indictment, July 19, 2016' (n 694) 4.

1707 ibid 5.

assets of central banks is questionable. Second, the immunity of a head of state may potentially entail the freedom to travel abroad, and hence travel bans imposed on acting heads of state may violate this entitlement. It is debatable, however, whether freezing the assets of the acting head of state encroaches on immunity entitlements. Third, the scope of the immunities granted to other high-ranking government officials remains uncertain, and thus we are deprived of the possibility of making a definite pronouncement on whether unilateral economic sanctions infringe these immunities.

It is well established that various types of unilateral economic sanctions are inconsistent with the fundamental principles of WTO law. Our analysis confirmed that this conclusion stands, with one notable exception, namely that export restrictions on services are less prone to be identified as WTO inconsistent than other types of unilateral sanctions.

2 Faced with a Need to Respond to the Instances of Grave Human Rights Violations, States Impose Unilateral Sanctions Even Though Their Legality Is Not Yet Settled and Other Mechanisms of Human Rights Enforcement Exist

This study not only analysed the legality of unilateral economic sanctions irrespective of their objectives, but also conducted an analysis of the legality of unilateral economic sanctions imposed on human rights grounds. To set the context for this discussion, the international enforcement of human rights was examined.

Chapter 3 of this study was devoted to the analysis of the treaty-based mechanisms of international human rights enforcement, as well as to the contribution of the Human Rights Council and the Security Council to human rights protection. The protection of those human rights that have gained a special status, such as jus cogens and obligations erga omnes, was also discussed.

Our analysis revealed that the overwhelming majority of the core international human rights treaties (nine out of ten) prescribe an identical enforcement mechanism. The only obvious exception is the Convention on the Prevention and Punishment of the Crime of Genocide, which by its very nature cannot entail a reporting obligation or an individual complaints procedure. Nonetheless, this convention contains a compromissory clause that grants jurisdiction to the ICJ, and the court has been engaged in several disputes in which compliance with the obligations under this convention was adjudicated.

The enforcement mechanism of the core international human rights treaties comprises the reporting obligation, interstate and individual complaints procedures, an inquiry procedure and the possibility to initiate a dispute before the ICJ. Each of these elements suffers from a number of deficiencies that undermine the ultimate goal of improving human rights protection globally. By way of illustration, we should recall that states often neglect their reporting obligations or ignore the recommendations prepared by the human rights committees. The interstate complaints mechanism is not frequently used. For example, two complaints submitted by Qatar in March 2018 against Saudi Arabia and the UAE represented "the first time that a human rights treaty body receive[d] an inter-state communication."[1708] The individual complaints mechanism does not offer any effective remedy to the affected individuals. The disputes that were brought before the ICJ reflect the states' desire to protect their own citizens. Notably, the recent dispute initiated by the Gambia against Myanmar is the only exception.

Additional protection that is guaranteed to human rights that gained a special status of jus cogens or obligations erga omnes is hampered by the definitional ambiguity of both concepts. Furthermore, the normative implications of these concepts are not well defined.

To complete the picture of international human rights protection, the role of the Human Rights Council and the involvement of the Security Council were reviewed. I argued that the political nature of these bodies deprives them of the possibility to effectively respond to instances of appalling human rights atrocities. Indeed, the lack of a coordinated response to the events in Rwanda, Kosovo, Darfur and Syria offer evidence to support this contention.

In order to answer the question of whether unilateral economic sanctions imposed on human rights grounds are susceptible to the same legal contestations as other types of unilateral economic sanctions, the interrelations between these sanctions and diverse fields of international law was analysed. To begin with, the interrelations between unilateral human rights sanctions and the principle of non-intervention were examined. There is no one generally accepted opinion on the matter. The literature review confirmed that the sharp divide between developed and developing countries with respect to the lawfulness of unilateral economic sanctions, including human rights sanctions, still exists. This disagreement is clearly reflected in the voting patterns at the UN General Assembly, where a group of developing states have made countless attempts to adopt resolutions condemning unilateral economic sanctions as illegal instruments of pressure.

1708 'CERD Information Note on Inter-State Communications' (n 1107).

The impossibility of justifying unilateral human rights sanctions as legal countermeasures has been well described by James Crawford: “Human rights obligations are not, in the first instance at least, owed to particular states, and it is accordingly difficult to see how a human rights obligation could itself be the subject of legitimate countermeasures.”[1709] The legality of third-party countermeasures has been debated at length within the international community. Nonetheless, the voluminous literature on the subject does not provide absolute certainty on the legal status of third-party countermeasures.

Efforts to bring justice to victims of egregious human rights violations often result in economic sanctions imposed against heads of state, heads of government and other high-ranking government officials. The states imposing these measures contend that human rights norms trump the immunities granted to such individuals under customary international law. This study has shown that unilateral economic sanctions can indeed encroach on the immunities granted to the states, heads of state, and other senior government officials. However, the possibility of justifying these restrictions by invoking human rights considerations is far from settled. Existing ICJ jurisprudence, which is supported by the views of legal scholars, is sceptical of such a possibility.

Before we discuss the possibility of justifying unilateral human rights sanctions under the WTO exception clauses, one observation is warranted here. It should be noted that our analysis focuses on general economic sanctions, implying that these restrictive measures are not related to the process and production methods. General economic sanctions are trade-restrictive measures employed to remedy human rights violations, such as genocide, the denial of basic human rights and the use of torture, and are thus not related to particular goods or services.

The possibility of justifying WTO-inconsistent human rights sanctions under the public morals exception and the national security exception embedded in the WTO Agreements was analysed. Regarding the justification under the public morals exception, I concluded that the stringent requirements of the necessity test preclude a significant part of general economic sanctions from being justified under this exception clause. Thus, only a subset of general economic sanctions imposed on human rights grounds can be justified under the public morals exception.

The analysis of the panel’s pronouncements on the ambit of the self-judging nature of the national security exception reveals that the panel decided that

---

1709 Crawford (n 353) 692.

the clause has objective, as well as subjective elements. The broadest exception allows for the justification of trade-restrictive measures "taken in time of war or other emergency in international relations." The panel's definition of "other emergency in international relations" is broad. Nonetheless, one should bear in mind that the definition of "emergency in international relations" explicitly mentions that the situation that qualifies as an emergency should be "engulfing or surrounding a state." Thus, it remains unclear whether a WTO Member can impose unilateral economic sanctions to redress human right violations occurring far from its territory and to justify such measures under the national security exception. The inevitable conclusion that can be drawn from these findings is that the legality of the unilateral economic sanctions imposed on human rights grounds is debatable.

3 The Doctrine and Principle of Common Concern of Humankind May Contribute to the Enhanced Protection of Human Rights

The concept of common concern has been enshrined in numerous international agreements and declarations. Furthermore, over the past two decades, the literature has abounded in claims that various collective action problems ought to be acknowledged as common concerns. Despite these developments, the legal implications of the concept of common concern remain underdetermined.

Against this backdrop, the doctrine of Common Concern of Humankind, which entails a number of well-defined normative obligations, was developed by Professor Thomas Cottier and others.

The suggested normative implications include: a duty to cooperate, an obligation to do one's homework and obligations to secure compliance. These normative obligations apply only to the shared problems that can be defined as a common concern. More specifically, a problem that constitutes a common concern "stands for the proposition of an important shared problem and shared responsibility, and for an issue which reaches beyond the bounds of a single community and state as a subject of international law."[1710]

The doctrine of Common Concern of Humankind applies only to a subset of human rights violations. Specifically, the following criteria should be fulfilled: human rights violations should impede the essence of human right

1710 Cottier, 'The Principle of Common Concern of Humankind.' (n 18) 26.

(*Kerngehalt*), which is protected under international human rights law; these violations should be systematic; and they should threaten international peace and security.

The application of the doctrine of Common Concern of Humankind to international human rights law is an attempt to introduce an idea of subsidiary responsibility for human rights protection that is imposed on the international community. The main contributions of the doctrine of Common Concern when it is transposed into the international human rights law are: a reinforced duty to cooperate, the domestication of international human rights obligations, an instrument to provide legality and legitimacy to unilateral economic sanctions and a tool to empower civil society. The reinforced duty to cooperate entails an obligation on the part of the states lacking the necessary resources to guarantee a minimum level of human rights protection to communicate their need and imposes an obligation on the states that are in a position to provide assistance to do so. The domestication of international human rights obligations requires the full implementation of international commitments in the domestic sphere. This includes conditioning market access by requiring that imported goods and services are produced in a way that respects minimum standards of human rights protection. Furthermore, the doctrine can legitimise economic sanctions imposed on human rights grounds and can restrict their use if the coercive measures in question are politically motivated. A fully-fledged doctrine entails an obligation to act in order to redress grave human rights violations.

Bibliography

Table of Cases

PCIJ Cases

The case of the SS Lotus (*France v. Turkey*) (Merits) PCIJ (1927) Rep Series A No 10.

ICJ Cases

Ahmadou Sadio Diallo (Republic of Guinea v. Democratic Republic of the Congo), Preliminary Objections, Judgment, I.C.J. Reports 2007, p. 582.

Ahmadou Sadio Diallo (Republic of Guinea v. Democratic Republic of the Congo), Merits, Judgment, I.C.J. Reports 2010, p. 639.

Application of the Convention on the Prevention and Punishment of the Crime of Genocide (Bosnia and Herzegovina v. Serbia and Montenegro), Judgment, I.C.J. Reports 2007, p. 43.

Application of the Convention on the Prevention and Punishment of the Crime of Genocide (Croatia v. Serbia), Judgment, I.C.J. Reports 2015, p. 3.

Application of the Convention on the Prevention and Punishment of the Crime of Genocide, Preliminary Objections, Judgment, I.C.J. Reports 1996, p. 595.

Application of the Convention on the Prevention and Punishment of the Crime of Genocide (Croatia v. Serbia), Preliminary Objections, Judgment, I.C.J. Reports 2008, p. 412.

Application of the Convention on the Prevention and Punishment of the Crime of Genocide (The Gambia v. Myanmar), Request for the indication of provisional measures, Order, January 23, 2020.

Application of the International Convention for the Suppression of the Financing of Terrorism and of the International Convention on the Elimination of All Forms of Racial Discrimination (Ukraine v. Russian Federation). Preliminary Objections, Judgment, I.C.J. 2019.

Application of the International Convention on the Elimination of All Forms of Racial Discrimination (Georgia v. Russian Federation), Preliminary Objections, Judgment, I.C.J. Reports 2011, p. 70.

Application of the International Convention on the Elimination of All Forms of Racial Discrimination (Qatar v. United Arab Emirates) Request for the Indication of Provisional Measures Order, June 14, 2019.

Armed Activities on the Territory of the Congo (Democratic Republic of the Congo v. Uganda), Judgment, I.C.J. Reports 2005, p. 168.

Armed Activities on the Territory of the Congo (New Application: 2002) (Democratic Republic of the Congo v. Rwanda), Jurisdiction and Admissibility, Judgment, I.C.J. Reports 2006, p. 6.

Arrest Warrant of 11 April 2000 (Democratic Republic of the Congo v. Belgium), Judgment, I.C.J. Reports 2002, p. 3.

Barcelona Traction, Light and Power Company, Limited, Judgment, I.C.J. Reports 1970, p. 3.

Certain Iranian Assets (Islamic Republic of Iran v. United States of America), Preliminary Objections, Judgment, I.C.J. Reports 2019, p.7.

Certain Questions of Mutual Assistance in Criminal Matters (Djibouti v. France), Judgment, I.C.J. Reports 2008, p. 177.

Corfu Channel case, Judgment of April 9th, 1949: I.C.J. Reports 1949, p. 4.

East Timor (Portugal v. Australia), Judgment, I.C.J. Reports 1995, p.90.

Gabcikovo-Nagymaros Project (Hungary/Slovakia), Judgment, I.C.J. Reports 1997, p. 7.

Jurisdictional Immunities of the State (Germany v. Italy: Greece intervening), Judgment, I.C.J. Reports 2012, p. 99.

Military and Paramilitary Activities in and against Nicaragua (Nicaragua v. United States of America) Merits, Judgment I.C.J. Reports 1986, p. 14.

Questions relating to the Obligation to Prosecute or Extradite (Belgium v. Senegal), Judgment, I.C.J. Reports 2012, p. 422.

United States Diplomatic and Consular Staff in Tehran, Judgment, I.C.J. Reports 1980, p. 3.

ICJ Advisory Opinions

Legal Consequences of the Construction of a Wall in the Occupied Palestinian Territory, Advisory Opinion, ICJ Reports 2004, p 136.

Reservations to the Convention on Genocide, Advisory Opinion: ICJ Reports 1951, p 15.

ICJ Documents

'Gabcikovo-Nagymaros Project (Hungary/Slovakia), Judgment, I.C.J. Reports 1997, p. 7, Separate Opinion of Vice-President Weeramantry.'

'International Court of Justice, Armed Activities on the Territory of the Congo (Democratic Republic of the Congo v. Rwanda), Application Instituting Proceedings, June, 23, 1999.'

'International Court of Justice. Ahmadou Sadio Diallo (Republic of Guinea v. Democratic Republic of the Congo). Application Instituting Proceedings. December 28, 1998.'

'International Court of Justice. Application of the Convention on the Prevention and Punishment of the Crime of Genocide (Croatia v. Serbia). Application Instituting Proceedings, July 2, 1999.'

'International Court of Justice. Application of the Convention on the Prevention and Punishment of the Crime of Genocide (Croatia v. Serbia). Counter-Memorial of Serbia, December 1, 2009.'

'International Court of Justice. Application of the Convention on the Prevention and Punishment of the Crime of Genocide (The Gambia v. Myanmar). Application Instituting Proceedings and Request for the Indication of Provisional Measures, November 11, 2019.'

'International Court of Justice. Application of the International Convention for the Suppression of the Financing of Terrorism and of the International Convention on the Elimination of All Forms of Racial Discrimination (Ukraine v. Russian Federation). Application Instituting Proceedings, January 16, 2017.'

'International Court of Justice. Application of the International Convention for the Suppression of the Financing of Terrorism and of the International Convention on the Elimination of All Forms of Racial Discrimination (Ukraine v. Russian Federation). Preliminary Objections Submitted by the Russian Federation, September 12, 2018.'

'International Court of Justice. Application of the International Convention for the Suppression of the Financing of Terrorism and of the International Convention on the Elimination of All Forms of Racial Discrimination (Ukraine v. Russian Federation). Written Statement of Observations and Submissions on the Preliminary Objections of the Russian Federation Submitted by Ukraine, January 14, 2019.'

'International Court of Justice. Application of the International Convention on the Elimination of All Forms of Racial Discrimination (Qatar v. United Arab Emirates). Application Instituting Proceedings, June 11, 2018.'

'International Court of Justice. Application of the International Convention on the Elimination of All Forms of Racial Discrimination (Qatar v. United Arab Emirates). Order, May 2, 2019.'

'International Court of Justice. Application of the International Convention on the Elimination of All Forms of Racial Discrimination (Qatar v. United Arab Emirates). Request for the Indication of Provisional Measures of the United Arab Emirates, March 22, 2019.'

'International Court of Justice. Armed Activities on the Territory of the Congo (Democratic Republic of the Congo v. Burundi). Application Instituting Proceedings, June 23, 1999.'

'International Court of Justice. Certain Iranian Assets (Islamic Republic of Iran v. United States of America). Application Instituting Proceedings, June 14, 2016.'

'International Court of Justice. Certain Iranian Assets (Islamic Republic of Iran v. United States of America). Preliminary Objections Submitted by the United States of America.'

'International Court of Justice. Questions Relating to the Seizure and Detention of Certain Documents and Data (Timor-Leste v. Australia). Memorial of Timor-Leste.'

'Legality of the Threat or Use of Nuclear Weapons. Advisory Opinion, I.C.J. Reports 1996, p. 226; Declaration of President Bedjaoui.'

WTO Dispute Settlement Reports

Appellate Body Report, Argentina – Measures Relating to Trade in Goods and Services, WT/DS453/AB/R and Add1, adopted 9 May 2016, DSR 2016:II, p 431.

Appellate Body Report, Brazil – Measures Affecting Imports of Retreaded Tyres, WT/DS332/AB/R, adopted 17 December 2007, DSR 2007:IV, p 1527.

Appellate Body Report, China – Measures Affecting Trading Rights and Distribution Services for Certain Publications and Audiovisual Entertainment Products, WT/DS363/AB/R, adopted 19 January 2010, DSR 2010:I, p 3.

Appellate Body Report, Colombia – Measures Relating to the Importation of Textiles, Apparel and Footwear, WT/DS461/AB/R and Add1, adopted 22 June 2016, DSR 2016:III, p 1131.

Appellate Body Report, Japan – Taxes on Alcoholic Beverages, WT/DS8/AB/R, WT/DS10/AB/R, WT/DS11/AB/R, adopted 1 November 1996, DSR 1996:I, p 97.

Appellate Body Report, United States – Import Prohibition of Certain Shrimp and Shrimp Products, WT/DS58/AB/R, adopted 6 November 1998, DSR 1998:VII, p 2755.

Appellate Body Report, United States – Measures Affecting the Cross-Border Supply of Gambling and Betting Services, WT/DS285/AB/R, adopted 20 April 2005, DSR 2005:XII, p 5663 (and Corr1, DSR 2006:XII, p 5475).

Appellate Body Report, United States – Standards for Reformulated and Conventional Gasoline, WT/DS2/AB/R, adopted 20 May 1996, DSR 1996:I, p 3.

Appellate Body Reports, China – Measures Related to the Exportation of Rare Earths, Tungsten, and Molybdenum, WT/DS431/AB/R / WT/DS432/AB/R / WT/DS433/AB/R, adopted 29 August 2014, DSR 2014:III, p 805.

Appellate Body Reports, China – Measures Related to the Exportation of Various Raw Materials, WT/DS394/AB/R / WT/DS395/AB/R / WT/DS398/AB/R, adopted 22 February 2012, DSR 2012:VII, p 3295.

Appellate Body Reports, European Communities – Measures Prohibiting the Importation and Marketing of Seal Products, WT/DS400/AB/R / WT/DS401/AB/R, adopted 18 June 2014, DSR 2014:I, p 7.

Contracting Parties to the GATT 1947, 'Twenty-Second Meeting, GATT/CP.3/SR.22, p. 9; II/28, Request of Czechoslovakia for Decision under Article XXIII' (1949).

Decision by the Arbitrator, European Communities – Regime for the Importation, Sale and Distribution of Bananas – Recourse to Arbitration by the European Communities under Article 22.6 of the DSU, WT/DS27/ARB/ECU, 24 March 2000, DSR 2000:V, p 2237.

Panel Report, Brazil – Measures Affecting Imports of Retreaded Tyres, WT/DS332/R, adopted 17 December 2007, as modified by Appellate Body Report WT/DS332/AB/R, DSR 2007:V, p 1649.

Panel Report, Canada – Certain Measures Concerning Periodicals, WT/DS31/R and Corr1, adopted 30 July 1997, as modified by Appellate Body Report WT/DS31/AB/R, DSR 1997:I, p 481.

Panel Report, China – Certain Measures Affecting Electronic Payment Services, WT/DS413/R and Add1, adopted 31 August 2012, DSR 2012:X, p 5305.

Panel Report, China – Measures Affecting Trading Rights and Distribution Services for Certain Publications and Audiovisual Entertainment Products, WT/DS363/R *and Corr1, adopted 19 January 2010, as modified by Appellate Body Report* WT/DS363/AB/R, DSR *2010:II, p 261.*

Panel Report, Colombia – Indicative Prices and Restrictions on Ports of Entry, WT/DS366/R *and Corr.1, adopted 20 May 2009,* DSR *2009:VI, p. 2535.*

Panel Report, Colombia – Measures Relating to the Importation of Textiles, Apparel and Footwear, WT/DS461/R *and Add1, adopted 22 June 2016, as modified by Appellate Body Report* WT/DS461/AB/R, DSR *2016:III, p 1227.*

Panel Report, EC *Measures Concerning Meat and Meat Products (Hormones), Complaint by the United States,* WT/DS26/R/USA, *adopted 13 February 1998, as modified by Appellate Body Report* WT/DS26/AB/R, WT/DS48/AB/R, DSR *1998:III, p 699.*

Panel Report, Mexico – Measures Affecting Telecommunications Services, WT/DS204/R, *adopted 1 June 2004,* DSR *2004:IV, p 1537.*

Panel Report, Russia – Measures Concerning Traffic in Transit, WT/DS512/R *and Add1, adopted 26 April 2019.*

Panel Report, Saudi Arabia – Measures concerning the Protection of Intellectual Property Rights, WT/DS567/R *and Add., circulated to* WTO *Members on 16 June 2020 [appealed on 28 July 2020].*

Panel Report, United States – Import Prohibition of Certain Shrimp and Shrimp Products, WT/DS58/R *and Corr1, adopted 6 November 1998, as modified by Appellate Body Report* WT/DS58/AB/R, DSR *1998:VII, p 2821.*

Panel Report, United States – Measures Affecting the Cross-Border Supply of Gambling and Betting Services, WT/DS285/R, *adopted 20 April 2005, as modified by Appellate Body Report* WT/DS285/AB/R, DSR *2005:XII, p 5797.*

Panel Report, United States – Restrictions on Imports of Cotton and Man-made Fibre Underwear, WT/DS24/R, *adopted 25 February 1997, as modified by Appellate Body Report* WT/DS24/AB/R, DSR *1997:I, p. 31.*

Panel Reports, Brazil – Certain Measures Concerning Taxation and Charges, WT/DS472/R, *Add1 and Corr1 /* WT/DS497/R, *Add1 and Corr1, adopted 11 January 2019, as modified by Appellate Body Reports* WT/DS472/AB/R / WT/DS497/AB/R.

Panel Reports, European Communities – Measures Prohibiting the Importation and Marketing of Seal Products, WT/DS400/R *and Add1 /* WT/DS401/R *and Add1, adopted 18 June 2014, as modified by Appellate Body Reports* WT/DS400/AB/R / WT/DS401/AB/R, DSR *2014:II, p 365.*

Panel Reports, European Communities – Regime for the Importation, Sale and Distribution of Bananas, WT/DS27/R/ECU *(Ecuador) /* WT/DS27/R/GTM, WT/DS27/R/HND *(Guatemala and Honduras) /* WT/DS27/R/MEX *(Mexico) /* WT/DS27/R/USA *(US), adopted 25 September 1997, as modified by Appellate Body Report* WT/DS27/AB/R, DSR *1997:II, p 695 to* DSR *1997:III, p 1085.*

United States – Trade measures affecting Nicaragua, Report by the Panel (unadopted), Doc L/6053, 13 October 1986.

Arbitral Awards

Case concerning the Air Service Agreement of 27 March 1946 between the United States of America and France [1978] 18 RIAA 417.

Responsibility of Germany arising out of damage caused in the Portuguese colonies of southern Africa (Naulilaa incident), 2 RIAA 1025 (Award of July 31, 1928).

European Court of Human Rights

Jones and Others v. the United Kingdom, Applications no 34356/06 and 40528/06 (ECtHR, 14 January 2014).

Magnitskiy and Others v. Russia App no 32631/09 and 53799/12 (ECtHR, 27 August 2019).

CJEU Cases

Case C-362/14 Maximillian Schrems v. Data Protection Commissioner [2015] ECLI identifier: ECLI:EU:C:2015:650.

Case T-253/02 Chafiq Ayadi v. Council of the European Union [2006] European Court Reports 2006 II-02139 ECLI identifier: ECLI:EU:T:2006:200.

Case T-306/01 Ahmed Ali Yusuf and Al Barakaat International Foundation v. Council of the European Union and Commission of the European Communities [2005] European Court Reports 2005 II-03533 ECLI identifier: ECLI:EU:T:2005:331.

Case T-315/01 Yassin Abdullah Kadi v. Council of the European Union and Commission of the European Communities [2005] European Court Reports 2005 II-03649 ECLI identifier: ECLI:EU:T:2005:332.

Case T-49/04 Faraj Hassan v. Council of the European Union and Commission of the European Communities [2006] European Court Reports 2006 II-00052 ECLI identifier: ECLI:EU:T:2006:201.

Joined cases C-399/06 P and C-403/06 P Faraj Hassan v. Council of the European Union and European Commission (C-399/06 P) and Chafiq Ayadi v. Council of the European Union (C-403/06 P) [2009] European Court Reports 2009 I–11393 ECLI identifier: ECLI:EU:C:2009:748.

Joined cases C-402/05 P and C-415/05 P Yassin Abdullah Kadi and Al Barakaat International Foundation v. Council of the European Union and Commission of the European Communities [2008] European Court Reports 2008 I–06351 ECLI identifier: ECLI:EU:C:2008:461.

Cases before the US Courts

Deborah D Peterson, et al, Plaintiffs-Appellees, v. Islamic Republic of Iran, et al, Defendants-Appellants, 758 F3d 185 [2014] United States Court of Appeals, Second Circuit No. 13-2952-CV.

Filartiga v. Pena-Irala, 630 F2d 876 (2d Cir 1980) United States Court of Appeals, Second Circuit.

Fulmen Company v. Office of Foreign Assets Control, 'United States District Court for the District of Columbia, Case No. 18–2949, Memorandum Opinion, Mar. 31, 2020.'

Licci v. Lebanese Canadian Bank, SAL [2016] Court of Appeals for the Second Circuit No. 15-1580.

Morrison v. National Australia Bank Ltd 561 US 247 [2010] Supreme Court of the United States No. 08–1191.

United States of America, Government, v. Reza Zarrab, et al, Defendant Decision & Order [2016] SDNY No. S1 15 Cr. 867 (RMB).

United States v. Aluminum Co of America 148 F2d 416 (1945) Circuit Court of Appeals, 2nd Cir.

United States v. Banki [2012] 2d Cir 685 F.3d 99.

United States v. Budovsky [2015] SDNY 13-cr-368 (DLC).

United States v. Homa International Trading Corp [2004] 2d Cir 387 F.3d 144.

Cases before Other National Courts

Bouzari v. Islamic Republic of Iran, OJ No 2800 [2004] Ontario Court of Appeal Toronto, Ontario Docket No. C38295.

Ferrini v. Federal Republic of Germany, judgment No 5044/2044 [2003] 87 Riv Dirit Internazionale 539 (Italian Supreme Court (Corte di Cassazione)).

Jones v. Ministry of the Interior of the Kingdom of Saudi Arabia (EWCA Civ 1394).

Prefecture of Voiotia v. Federal Republic of Germany Case No 11/2000 (Areios Pagos (Hellenic Supreme Court)).

Table of Legislation

International Treaties

Charter of the United Nations (adopted June 26, 1945, entered into force October 24, 1945) UNTS 1 XVI.

Convention Against Torture and Other Cruel, Inhuman or Degrading Treatment or Punishment (adopted December 10, 1984, entered into force June 26, 1987) UNTS vol. 1465 p. 85.

Convention on Biological Diversity (adopted June 5, 1992, entered into force December 29, 1993) UNTS vol. 1760 p. 79.

Convention on the Elimination of All Forms of Discrimination Against Women (adopted December 18, 1979, entered into force September 3, 1981) UNTS vol. 1249 p. 13.

Convention on the Prevention and Punishment of the Crime of Genocide (adopted December 9, 1948, entered into force January 12, 1951) UNTS vol. 78 p. 277.

Convention on the Rights of Persons with Disabilities (adopted December 13, 2006, entered into force May 3, 2008) UNTS vol. 2515 p. 3.

Convention on the Rights of the Child (adopted November 20, 1989, entered into force September 2, 1990) UNTS vol. 1577 p. 3.

DSU, Dispute Settlement Rules: Understanding on Rules and Procedures Governing the Settlement of Disputes, Marrakesh Agreement Establishing the World Trade Organization, Annex 2, 1869 UNTS 401.

GATS: General Agreement on Trade in Services, Apr. 15, 1994, Marrakesh Agreement Establishing the World Trade Organization, Annex 1B, 1869 UNTS 183.

GATT 1994: General Agreement on Tariffs and Trade 1994, Apr. 15, 1994, Marrakesh Agreement Establishing the World Trade Organization, Annex 1A, 1867 UNTS 187.

International Convention for the Protection of All Persons from Enforced Disappearance (adopted December 20, 2006, entered into force December 23, 2010) UNTS vol. 2716 p. 3.

International Convention on the Elimination of All Forms of Racial Discrimination (adopted December 21, 1965, entered into force January 4, 1969) UNTS vol. 660 p. 195.

International Convention on the Protection of the Rights of All Migrant Workers and Members of their Families (adopted December 18, 1990, entered into force July 1, 2003) UNTS vol. 2220 p. 3.

International Covenant on Civil and Political Rights (adopted December 16, 1966, entered into force March 23, 1976) UNTS vol. 999 p. 171.

International Covenant on Economic, Social and Cultural Rights (adopted December 16, 1966, entered into force January 3, 1976) UNTS vol. 993 p. 3.

International Treaty on Plant Genetic Resources for Food and Agriculture (adopted November 3, 2001, entered into force June 29, 2004) UNTS vol. 2400 p. 303.

League of Nations, Covenant of the League of Nations, 28 April 1919.

Organization of African Unity (OAU), Constitutive Act of the African Union, 1 July 2000.

Paris Agreement in UNFCCC, COP Report No. 21, Addendum at 21 UN Doc FCCC/CP/2015/10/Add 1 (adopted December 12, 2015, entered into force November 4, 2016).

Rome Statute of the International Criminal Court (adopted July 17, 1998, entered into force July 1, 2002) UNTS vol. 2187 no. 38544.

United Nations Framework Convention on Climate Change (adopted May 9, 1992, entered into force March 21, 1994) S. Treaty Doc No. 102–38, 1771 UNTS 107.

Vienna Convention on the Law of Treaties (adopted May 23, 1969, entered into force January 27, 1980) 1155 UNTS 331.

Constitutions, Statutes and Bills

31 C.F.R. § 583 Global Magnitsky Sanctions Regulations.

31 C.F.R. § 584 Magnitsky Act Sanctions Regulations.

Amendments to the Law on Amending the Obligation to Leave and Prohibition on Entry Act 262 SE, adopted 08.12.2016.

Autonomous Sanctions (Russia, Crimea and Sevastopol) Specification 2015 Made under Regulations 4, 5B and 5C of the Autonomous Sanctions Regulations 2011.

Autonomous Sanctions Amendment (Magnitsky-style and Other Thematic Sanctions) Bill 2021. https://parlinfo.aph.gov.au/parlInfo/download/legislation/bills/s1326_third-senate/toc_pdf/2116121.pdf;fileType=application%2Fpdf.

Basic Law for the Federal Republic of Germany, 23 May 1949.

Commission Delegated Regulation (EU) 2018/1100 of 6 June 2018 amending the Annex to Council Regulation (EC) No 2271/96 protecting against the effects of extra-territorial application of legislation adopted by a third country, and actions based thereon or resulting therefrom 2018 (OJ L).

Commission Implementing Regulation (EU) 2016/218 of 16 February 2016 amending Council Regulation (EC) No 314/2004 concerning certain restrictive measures in respect of Zimbabwe 2016 (OJ L).

Commission Implementing Regulation (EU) 2018/1101 of 3 August 2018 laying down the criteria for the application of the second paragraph of Article 5 of Council Regulation (EC) No 2271/96 protecting against the effects of the extra-territorial application of legislation adopted by a third country, and actions based thereon or resulting therefrom 2018 (OJ L).

Comprehensive Iran Sanctions, Accountability, and Divestment Act of 2010, Public Law 111–195, July 1, 2010, 124 Stat. 1312.

Council Decision 2012/35/CFSP of 23 January 2012 amending Decision 2010/413/CFSP concerning restrictive measures against Iran 2012 (OJ L).

Council Decision 2014/512/CFSP of 31 July 2014 concerning restrictive measures in view of Russia's actions destabilising the situation in Ukraine 2014 (OJ L).

Council Decision 2019/797/CFSP of 17 May 2019 concerning restrictive measures against cyber-attacks threatening the Union or its Member States 2019 (OJ L).

Council Decision 2020/1127/CFSP of 30 July 2020 Amending Decision (CFSP) 2019/797 concerning restrictive measures against cyber-attacks threatening the Union or its Member States 2020 (OJ L).

Council Decision 2020/1999/ CFSP of 7 December 2020 concerning restrictive measures against serious human rights violations and abuses 2020 (OJ L).

Council Decision 2021/481/ CFSP of 22 March 2021 amending Decision (CFSP) 2020/1999 concerning restrictive measures against serious human rights violations and abuses (OJ L).

Council Implementing Regulation (EU) 2021/478 of 22 March 2021 implementing Regulation (EU) 2020/1998 concerning restrictive measures against serious human rights violations and abuses (OJ L).

Council Regulation (EC) No 2271/96 of 22 November 1996 protecting against the effects of the extra-territorial application of legislation adopted by a third country, and actions based thereon or resulting therefrom 1996 (OJ L).

Council Regulation (EU) No 168/2012 of 27 February 2012 amending Regulation (EU) No 36/2012 concerning restrictive measures in view of the situation in Syria 2012 (OJ L).

Council Regulation (EU) No 2019/796 of 17 May 2019 concerning restrictive measures against cyber-attacks threatening the Union or its Member States 2019 (OJ L).

Council Regulation (EU) No 2020/1125 of 30 July 2020 Implementing Regulation (EU) 2019/796 concerning restrictive measures against cyber-attacks threatening the Union or its Member States 2020 (OJ L).

Council Regulation (EU) No 2020/1998 of 7 December 2020 concerning restrictive measures against serious human rights violations and abuses 2020 (OJ L).

Council Regulation (EU) No 269/2014 of 17 March 2014 concerning restrictive measures in respect of actions undermining or threatening the territorial integrity, sovereignty and independence of Ukraine 2014 (OJ L).

Council Regulation (EU) No 36/2012 of 18 January 2012 concerning restrictive measures in view of the situation in Syria and repealing Regulation (EU) No 442/2011 2012 (OJ L).

Criminal Finances Act 2017.

Cuban Assets Control Regulations 31 CFR § 515.207 Entry of vessels engaged in trade with Cuba.

Cuban Assets Control Regulations 31 CFR Part 515.

Cuban Liberty and Democratic Solidarity (LIBERTAD) Act of 1996, Pub. L. No. 104–114, 110 Stat. 785 (1996) (codified at 22 U.S.C. §§ 6021–6091).

Export Control Act 2002, July 24, 2002.

Federal Constitution of the Swiss Confederation of 18 April 1999.

Iran and Libya Sanctions Act of 1996, Public Law 104–172, August 5, 1996, 110 Stat. 1541.

Iran Threat Reduction and Syria Human Rights Act of 2012, Public Law 112–158, August 10, 2012, 126 Stat. 1214.

Iranian Transactions and Sanctions Regulations 31 CFR Part 560.

Justice for Victims of Corrupt Foreign Officials Act (Sergei Magnitsky Law) (S.C. 2017, c. 21) 2017.

Regulation (EU) 2021/821 of the European Parliament and of the Council of 20 May 2021 setting up a Union regime for the control of exports, brokering, technical assistance, transit and transfer of dual-use items (recast) 2021 (OJ L).

Republic of Lithuania Law on the Legal Status of Aliens 29 April 2004 No. IX–2206.

Resolution of the Government of the Russian Federation No. 778 of 7 August 2014 'On measures concerning implementation of the Presidential Decree as of 6 August 2014 No. 560 On applying of certain special economic measures in order to ensure safety of the Russian Federation.'

Sanctions and Anti-Money Laundering Act 2018.
Special Economic Measures (Ukraine) Regulations. SOR/2014–60. March 17, 2014.
The Cyber (Sanctions) (EU Exit) Regulations 2020 No. 597 (2020).
The Decree of the President of the Russian Federation on August 6, 2014 No. 560 'On the application of certain special economic measures to ensure the security of the Russian Federation' (Указ Президента Российской Федерации от 06.08.2014 г. No.560 О применении отдельных специальных экономических мер в целях обеспечения безопасности Российской Федерации).
The Global Human Rights Sanctions Regulations 2020 No. 680 (2020).
The Global Magnitsky Human Rights Accountability Act, Public Law 114–328, title XII, Dec. 23, 2016, 130 Stat. 2533.
The Iranian Financial Sanctions Regulations 31 CFR part 561.
The Sergei Magnitsky Rule of Law Accountability Act of 2012, Public Law 112–208, title IV, Dec. 14, 2012, 126 Stat. 1502.
Trade Act of 1974, Public Law 93–618, January 3, 1975, 88 Stat.
Venezuela Defense of Human Rights and Civil Society Act of 2014, Public Law 113–278, Dec. 18, 2014, 128 Stat. 3011.

Table of Other Legal Sources

Annex I to the Prosecution's Provision of the Supporting Document of the Referral Submitted by the Government of Venezuela, ICC Doc. ICC-01/20-4-AnxI, 04 March 2020 (Situation in the Bolivarian Republic of Venezuela II). https://www.icc-cpi.int/Pages/record.aspx?docNo=ICC-01/20-4-AnxI .
Charter of Economic Rights and Duties of States, UNGA Res 39/163 (17 December 1984) UN Doc A/RES/39/163.
Charter of Fundamental Rights of the European Union, 2012/C 326/02.
Commonwealth of Australia. Senate. Hansard. Tuesday, 3 August, 2021. https://parlinfo.aph.gov.au/parlInfo/download/chamber/hansards/cc2b3d91-d8ca-4ed3-a179-cce9561bc86e/toc_pdf/Senate_2021_08_03_8996.pdf;fileType=application%2Fpdf.
Council of the EU, 'Declaration by the High Representative on behalf of the EU on the alignment of certain third countries concerning restrictive measures against cyber-attacks threatening the Union or its member states' (2 July 2019).
Council of the EU, 'Guidelines on Implementation and Evaluation of Restrictive Measures (Sanctions) in the Framework of the EU Common Foreign and Security Policy,' Annex to Doc No 5664/18 (4 May 2018).
Council of the EU, EU Best Practices for the Effective Implementation of Restrictive Measures, Doc. 8519/18 (4 May 2018), https://data.consilium.europa.eu/doc/document/ST-8519-2018-INIT/en/pdf.
Declaration of the Rights of the Child UNGA (20 November 1959) UN Doc A/RES/1386(XIV).

Declaration on Principles of International Law concerning Friendly Relations and Cooperation among States in accordance with the Charter of the United Nations, UNGA Res 2625 (24 October 1970) UN Doc A/RES/2625(XXV).

Declaration on the Inadmissibility of Intervention and Interference in the Internal Affairs of States, UNGA Res 36/103 (December 1981) UN Doc A/RES/36/103.

Declaration on the Inadmissibility of Intervention in the Domestic Affairs of States and the Protection of Their Independence and Sovereignty, UNGA Res 2131 (21 December 1965) UN Doc A/RES/2131(XX).

European Parliament, Resolution of 20 May 2021 on Chinese countersanctions on EU entities and MEPS and MPS (2021/2644(RSP)). https://www.europarl.europa.eu/doceo/document/TA-9-2021-0255_EN.html.

Geneva Declaration of the Rights of the Child of 1924, adopted Sept. 26, 1924, League of Nations O.J. Spec. Supp. 21.

ILC, 'Draft Articles on Responsibility of States for Internationally Wrongful Acts, (2001), UN Doc. A/56/10.'

ILC, 'Peremptory Norms of General International Law (Jus Cogens). Text of the Draft Conclusions and Draft Annex Provisionally Adopted by the Drafting Committee on First Reading. UN Doc A/CN.4/L.936' (2019).

ILC, 'Provisional Summary Record of the 3246th Meeting, UN Doc A/CN.4/SR.3246' (2016) International Law Commission, sixty-seventh session (first part).

ILC, 'Report of the International Law Commission on the Work of Its First Session' (12 April 1949) UN Doc A/CN.4/13 and Corr. 1–3.

ILC, 'Report of the International Law Commission, UN Doc A/70/10' (2015) General Assembly Official Records Seventieth Session Supplement No. 10.

Martti Koskenniemi, 'Fragmentation of International Law: Difficulties Arising from the Diversification and Expansion of International Law: Report of the Study Group of the International Law Commission.' (2006).

Note by the Secretary-General, 'Economic Measures as a Means of Political and Economic Coercion against Developing Countries.' (1993) UN Doc A/48/535.

Office of Foreign Assets Control, General License No. 1 'Authorizing Certain Transactions with the Federal Security Service' (February 2, 2017) https://home.treasury.gov/system/files/126/cyber_gl1.pdf.

Office of Foreign Assets Control, General License No. 1B 'Authorizing Certain Transactions with the Federal Security Service' (March 2, 2021) https://home.treasury.gov/system/files/126/cyber_gl1b.pdf.

President of the United States of America. Executive Order 13553 of September 28, 2010. Blocking Property of Certain Persons With Respect to Serious Human Rights Abuses by the Government of Iran and Taking Certain Other Actions.

President of the United States of America. Executive Order 13573 of May 18, 2011. Blocking Property of Senior Officials of the Government of Syria.

President of the United States of America. Executive Order 13582 of August 17, 2011. Blocking Property of the Government of Syria and Prohibiting Certain Transactions With Respect to Syria.

President of the United States of America. Executive Order 13660 of March 6, 2014. Blocking Property of Certain Persons Contributing to the Situation in Ukraine.

President of the United States of America. Executive Order 13661 of March 16, 2014. Blocking Property of Additional Persons Contributing to the Situation in Ukraine.

President of the United States of America. Executive Order 13694 of April 1, 2015. Blocking the Property of Certain Persons Engaging in Significant Malicious Cyber-Enabled Activities.

President of the United States of America. Executive Order 13757 of December 28, 2016. Taking Additional Steps to Address the National Emergency with Respect to Significant Malicious Cyber-Enabled Activities.

President of the United States of America. Executive Order 13818 of December 20, 2017. Blocking the Property of Persons Involved in Serious Human Rights Abuse or Corruption.

President of the United States of America. Executive Order 13850 of November 1, 2018. Blocking Property of Additional Persons Contributing to the Situation in Venezuela.

President of the United States of America. Executive Order 13884 of August 5, 2019. Blocking Property of the Government of Venezuela.

President of the United States of America. Executive Order 13902 of January 10, 2020. Imposing Sanctions With Respect to Additional Sectors of Iran.

President of the United States of America. Executive Order No. 12,513, 50 Fed. Reg. 18,629 (May 1, 1985). Prohibiting Trade and Certain Other Transactions Involving Nicaragua.

Protection of global climate for present and future generations of mankind UNGA Res 43/53 (December 6, 1988) UN Doc A/RES/43/53.

Report of the Secretary-General, 'Compilation of Guidelines on the Form and Content of Reports to Be Submitted by States Parties to the International Human Rights Treaties UN Doc HRI/GEN/2/REV.6' (2009).

Shinya Murase, 'Second Report on the Protection of Atmosphere UN Doc A/CN.4/681' (2015) 67th Session of the International Law Commission.

Special Rapporteur Sir Humphrey Waldock, 'Second Report on the Law of Treaties, Doc A/CN.4/156 and Add.1–3' (Yearbook of the International Law Commission, Volume II 1963).

SR 946.231.176.72 Verordnung Vom 27. August 2014 Über Massnahmen Zur Vermeidung Der Umgehung Internationaler Sanktionen Im Zusammenhang Mit Der Situation in Der Ukraine <https://www.admin.ch/opc/de/classified-compilation/20142202/index.html>.

The Declaration of the Russian Federation and the People's Republic of China on the Promotion of International Law (2016) <https://www.mid.ru/foreign_policy/news/-/asset_publisher/cKNonkJE02Bw/content/id/2331698>.

The Settlement Agreement between Ericsson Inc. and Ericsson, and the U.S. Department of the Treasury Office of Foreign Assets Control (OFAC). <https://www.treasury.gov/resource-center/sanctions/CivPen/Documents/20180606_ericsson_settlement.pdf>.

UN Committee against Torture, 'Report of the Committee against Torture. UN Doc A/73/44' (2018) General Assembly Official Records Seventy-third Session Supplement No. 44.

UN Committee on Economic, Social and Cultural Rights, 'Committee on Economic, Social and Cultural Rights, UN Doc E/2018/22, E/C.12/2017/3' (2018) Economic and Social Council Official Records Supplement No. 2.

UN Committee on Enforced Disappearances, 'Report of the Committee on Enforced Disappearances, UN Doc A/73/56' (2018) General Assembly Official Records Seventy-third Session Supplement No. 56.

UN Committee on the Elimination of Racial Discrimination, 'Report of the Committee on the Elimination of Racial Discrimination, UN Doc A/73/18' (2018) General Assembly Official Records Seventy-third Session Supplement No. 18.

UN Human Rights Committee, 'Report of the Human Rights Committee, UN Doc A/73/40' (2018) General Assembly Official Records Seventy-third Session Supplement No. 40.

UNCHR Res 2005/80 (21 April 2005) UN Doc E/CN.4/RES/2005/80.

UNGA Res 66/253 B The situation in the Syrian Arab Republic (7 August 2012) UN Doc A/RES/66/253 B.

UNGA Res 75/181 Human rights and unilateral coercive measures (28 December 2020) UN Doc A/RES/75/181.

UNGA Res 799 Request for the codification of the principles of international law governing State responsibility (7 December 1953) UN Doc A/RES/799.

UNGA Sixth Committee (25th Session) Summary record of the 1179th meeting (24 September 1970) UN Doc A/C.6/SR.1179.

UNGA, 'Responsibility of States for Internationally Wrongful Acts. Compilation of Decisions of International Courts, Tribunals and Other Bodies' (2016) UN Doc A/71/80.

UNGA, United Nations Convention on Jurisdictional Immunities of States and Their Property, 2 December 2004, A/RES/59/38.

UNGA Res 2160 (30 November 1966) UN Doc A/RES/2160 (XXI).

UNGA Res 51/242 (26 September 1997) UN Doc A/RES/51/242.

UNGA Res 60/251 (3 April 2006) UN Doc A/RES/60/251.

UNGA Res 68/262 Territorial integrity of Ukraine (27 March 2014) UN Doc A/RES/68/262.

UNHRC, 'Report of the Special Rapporteur on the Negative Impact of Unilateral Coercive Measures on the Enjoyment of Human Rights' (2015) UN Doc A/HRC/30/45.

UNHRC Thematic study of the Office of the United Nations High Commissioner for Human Rights on the impact of unilateral coercive measures on the enjoyment of human rights, including recommendations on actions aimed at ending such measures. (11 January 2012) UN Doc A/HRC/19/33.

UNHRC, 'Institution-Building of the United Nations Human Rights Council, UN Doc A/HRC/RES/5/1' (2007).

UNHRC Res 27/21 (3 October 2014) UN Doc A/HRC/RES/27/21.

UNHRC Res 40/16 (8 April 2019) UN Doc A/HRC/RES/40/16.

U.S. Department of Commerce, Bureau of Industry and Security, 15 C.F.R. § 744 Addition of Entities to the Entity List, Final Rule (16 May 2019).

U.S. Department of Commerce, Bureau of Industry and Security, 15 C.F.R. § 744 Addition of Certain Entities to the Entity List and Revision of Entries on the Entity List, Final Rule (19 Aug. 2019).

U.S. Department of Commerce, Bureau of Industry and Security, 15 C.F.R. Parts 736, 744 and 762, Addition of Huawei Non-U.S. Affiliates to the Entity List, the Removal of Temporary General License, and Amendments to General Prohibition Three (Foreign-Produced Direct Product Rule).

U.S. Department of Commerce, Bureau of Industry and Security, 15 C.F.R. § 730, 732, 736, and 744 Export Administration Regulations: Amendments to General Prohibition Three (Foreign-Produced Direct Product Rule) and the Entity List, Interim final rule (15 May 2020).

United Nations Declaration on the Elimination of All Forms of Racial Discrimination, UNGA Res 1904 (20 November 1963) A/RES/1904.

United States of America v. Huawei Technologies Co., LTD, Huawei Device USA Inc., Skycom Tech Co. LTD., Wanzhou Meng, No 1:18-cr-00457, Indictment, August 22, 2018.

United States of America v. Huawei Technologies Co., LTD, Huawei Device USA Inc., Skycom Tech Co. LTD., Wanzhou Meng, No 1:18-cr-00457, Superseding Indictment, January 24, 2019.

United States of America, Government v. Mehmet Hakan Atilla, Defendant No. S4 15 Cr. 867 (RMB) Government's Memorandum of Law in Opposition to Defendant Mehmet Hakan Atilla's Motions to Dismiss the Superseding Indictment and for Severance, October 16, 2017.

United States of America, Government v. Reza Zarrab, et al., Defendant No. S1 15 Cr. 867 (RMB) Memorandum of Law in Support of Defendant Reza Zarrab's Motion to Dismiss the Superseding Indictment, July 19, 2016.

United States of America, Government v. Reza Zarrab, et al., Defendant No. S1 15 Cr. 867 (RMB) Government's Memorandum of Law in Opposition to Defendant Reza

Zarrab's Motions to Dismiss the Indictment and to Suppress Evidence, August 8, 2016.

United States of America, Government v. Reza Zarrab, et al., Defendant No. S1 15 Cr. 867 (RMB) Sealed Indictment, December 15, 2015.

United States of America, Government v. Reza Zarrab, et al., Defendant No. S2 15 Cr. 867 (RMB) Superseding Indictment, November 7, 2016.

United States of America, Government v. Reza Zarrab, et al., Defendant No. S3 15 Cr. 867 (RMB) Superseding Indictment, April 7, 2017.

United States of America, Government v. Reza Zarrab, et al., Defendant No. S4 15 Cr. 867 (RMB) Memorandum of Law in Support of Defendant Mehmet Hakan Atilla's Motion to Dismiss Superseding Indictment S4, or Alternatively for Severance, October 9, 2017.

United States of America, Government v. Reza Zarrab, et al., Defendant No. S4 15 Cr. 867 (RMB) Superseding Indictment, September 6, 2017.

UNSC Enclosure Improving fair and clear procedures for a more effective United Nations sanctions system. UN Doc A/67/557, S/2012/805 (9 November 2012) https://www.un.org/ga/search/view_doc.asp?symbol=A/67/557.

UNSC Res 134 (1 April 1960) UN Doc S/RES/134.

UNSC Res 181 (7 August 1963) UN Doc S/RES/181.

UNSC Res 202 (6 May 1965) UN Doc S/RES/202.

UNSC Res 216 (12 November 1965) UN Doc S/RES/216.

UNSC Res 217 (20 November 1965) UN Doc S/RES/217.

UNSC Res 221 (9 April 1966) UN Doc S/RES/221.

UNSC Res 418 (4 November 1977) UN Doc S/RES/418.

UNSC Res 460 (21 December 1979) UN Doc S/RES/460.

UNSC Res 569 (26 July 1985) UN Doc S/RES/569.

UNSC Res 661 (6 August 1990) UN Doc S/RES/661.

UNSC Res 665 (25 August 1990) UN Doc S/RES/665.

UNSC Res 666 (13 September 1990) UN Doc S/RES/666.

UNSC Res 670 (25 September 1990) UN Doc S/RES/670.

UNSC Res 688 (5 April 1991) UN Doc S/RES/688.

UNSC Res 700 (17 June 1991) UN Doc S/RES/700.

UNSC Res 757 (30 May 1992) UN Doc S/RES/757.

UNSC Res 841 (16 June 1993) UN Doc S/RES/841.

UNSC Res 917 (6 May 1994) UN Doc S/RES/917.

UNSC Res 918 (17 May 1994) UN Doc S/RES/918.

UNSC Res 929 (22 June 1994) UN Doc S/RES/929.

UNSC Res 955 (8 November 1994) UN Doc S/RES/955.

UNSC Res 1080 (15 November 1996) UN Doc S/RES/1080.

UNSC Res 1296 (19 April 2000) UN Doc S/RES/1296.

UNSC Res 1314 (11 August 2000) UN Doc S/RES/1314.
UNSC Res 1529 (29 February 2004) UN Doc S/RES/1529.
UNSC Res 1674 (28 April 2006) UN Doc S/RES/1674.
UNSC Res 1730 (19 December 2006) UN Doc S/RES/1730.
UNSC Res 1738 (23 December 2006) UN Doc S/RES/1738.
UNSC Res 1894 (11 November 2009) UN Doc S/RES/1894.
UNSC Res 1904 (17 December 2009) UN Doc S/RES/1904.
UNSC Res 2118 (27 September 2013) UN Doc S/RES/2118.
UNSC Res 2139 (22 February 2014) UN Doc S/RES/2139.
UNSC Res 2165 (14 July 2014) UN Doc S/RES/2165.
UNSC Res 2191 (17 December 2014) UN Doc S/RES/2191.
UNSC Res 2231 (20 July 2015) UN Doc S/RES/2231.
UNSC Res 2253 (17 December 2015) UN Doc S/RES/2253.
UNSC Res 2255 (22 December 2015) UN Doc S/RES/2255.
UNSC Res 2258 (22 December 2015) UN Doc S/RES/2258.
UNSC, 'Provisional Verbatim Record of 2982 Meeting, UN Doc S/PV.2982' (1991).
UNSC, 'UN Security Council, 3713th Meeting, UN Doc S/PV.3713' (1996).
UNSC, 'UN Security Council, 3868th Meeting, UN Doc S/PV.3868' (1998).
UNSC, 'UN Security Council, 4011th Meeting, UN Doc S/PV.4011' (1999).
UNSC, 'UN Security Council, 4109th Meeting, UN Doc S/PV.4109' (2000).
UNSC, 'UN Security Council, 5526th Meeting, UN Doc S/PV.5526' (2006).
UNSC, 'UN Security Council, 5619th Meeting, UN Doc S/PV.5619' (2007).
UNSC, 'UN Security Council, 5753rd Meeting, UN Doc S/PV.5753' (2007).
UNSC, 'UN Security Council, 5777th Meeting, UN Doc S/PV.5777' (2007).
UNSC, 'UN Security Council, 6650th Meeting, UN Doc S/PV.6650' (2011).
UNSC, 'UN Security Council, 7926th Meeting, UN Doc S/PV.7926' (2017).
WTO, Russia – Measures Concerning the Importation and Transit of Certain Ukrainian Products. Request for Consultations by Ukraine, Document WT/DS532/1, G/L/1189 G/TFA/D1/1, G/SPS/GEN/1582, 19 October 2017.
WTO, Russia – Measures Concerning Traffic in Transit (DS512), Third Party Executive Summary of the United States.
WTO, Russia – Measures Concerning Traffic in Transit (DS512), Third-Party Oral Statement of the United States of America.
WTO, Ukraine – Measures Relating to Trade in Goods and Services, Request for Consultations by the Russian Federation, Document WT/DS525/1, G/L/1179 S/L/414, G/TBT/D/50 G/LIC/D/52, G/SPS/GEN/1549, 1 June 2017.
WTO, United Arab Emirates – Measures Relating to Trade in Goods and Services, and Trade-Related Aspects of Intellectual Property Rights. Request for Consultations by Qatar. Document WT/DS526/1, G/L/1180 S/L/415, IP/D/35, 4 August 2017.

WTO, United States – Measures Relating to Trade in Goods and Services. Request for Consultations by Venezuela. Document WT/DS574/1, G/L/1289, S/L/420, 8 January 2019.

WTO, United States – Measures Relating to Trade in Goods and Services. Request for the Establishment of a Panel by Venezuela. Document WT/DS574/2, 15 March 2019.

WTO, United States – The Cuban Liberty and Democratic Solidarity Act. Request for the Establishment of a Panel by the European Communities. Document WT/W38/2, 8 October 1996.

Указ Президента України №82/2019, 'Про Рішення Ради Національної Безпеки і Оборони України Від 19 Березня 2019 Року' (*Офіційне інтернет-представництво Президента України*) <https://www.president.gov.ua/documents/822019-26290>.

Указ Президента України від 14.05.2018 No.126/2018, 'Про Рішення Ради Національної Безпеки і Оборони України Від 2 Травня 2018 Року "Про Застосування Та Скасування Персональних Спеціальних Економічних Та Інших Обмежувальних Заходів (Санкцій)"' (*Законодавство України*) <https://zakon.rada.gov.ua/go/126/2018>.

Bibliography of Secondary Sources

Abashidze A and Koneva A, 'The Process of Strengthening the Human Rights Treaty Body System: The Road towards Effectiveness or Inefficiency?' (2019) 66 Netherlands International Law Review 357.

Abbott FM, Breining-Kaufmann C and Cottier T, *International Trade and Human Rights: Foundations and Conceptual Issues* (The University of Michigan Press 2006).

Adlung R, 'Export Policies and the General Agreement on Trade in Services' (2015) 18 Journal of International Economic Law 487.

Akande D and Shah S, 'Immunities of State Officials, International Crimes, and Foreign Domestic Courts' (2010) 21 European journal of international law = Journal europeen de droit international 815.

Akande D, Akhavan P, and Bjorge E, 'Economic Sanctions, International Law, and Crimes Against Humanity: Venezuela's ICC Referral' (2021) 115(3) American Journal of International Law 493.

Alexander K, *Economic Sanctions: Law and Public Policy* (Palgrave Macmillan 2009).

Allen SH, 'Political Institutions and Constrained Response to Economic Sanctions' (2008) 4 Foreign Policy Analysis 255.

Amid Unrelenting Violence, Syria's Warring Parties Must Increase Aid Agencies' Access into Hard-to-Reach Areas, Top Relief Official Tells Security Council <https://www.un.org/press/en/2014/sc11622.doc.htm>.

Amnesty International, *Amnesty International Report 2017/2018: The State of the World's Human Rights*. (Amnesty International UK 2018).

Anglin DG, 'Unilateral Independence in Southern Rhodesia' (1964) 19 International Journal 551.

Austin D, 'Sanctions and Rhodesia' (1966) 22 World Today 106.

Axworthy L, 'RtoP and the Evolution of State Sovereignty' in Jared Genser and Irwin Cotler (eds), *The Responsibility to Protect: the promise of stopping mass atrocities in our time* (Oxford University Press 2012).

Baek BS, 'Economic Sanctions Against Human Rights Violations' (2008) Cornell Law School Inter-University Graduate Student Conference Papers <https://scholarship.law.cornell.edu/lps_clacp/11>.

Baldwin DA, *Economic Statecraft* (Princeton University Press 1985).

Baldwin DA, 'The Sanctions Debate and the Logic of Choice' (1999) 24 International Security 80.

Baldwin DA, 'Prologamena to Thinking about Economic Sanctions and Free Trade' (2003) 4 Chicago Journal of International Law 271.

Baldwin DA and Pape RA, 'Evaluating Economic Sanctions' (1998) 23 International Security 189.

Banton M, *International Action against Racial Discrimination* (Clarendon Press 1996).

Banton M, *What We Now Know About Race and Ethnicity* (1st ed., Berghahn Books 2018).

Barigazzi J, 'EU to Prepare Magnitsky-Style Human Rights Sanctions Regime' *POLITICO* (9 December 2019) <https://www.politico.eu/article/eu-to-prepare-magnitsky-style-human-rights-sanctions-regime/>.

Barlyn S, 'Deutsche Bank to Pay $258 Million to Settle U.S. Sanctions Case – NYDFS' *Reuters* (4 November 2015) <https://www.reuters.com/article/us-deutsche-bank-penalty-idUSKCN0ST2J720151104>.

Barrett S, *Why Cooperate?: The Incentive to Supply Global Public Goods* (Oxford University Press 2010).

Bartels L, 'The WTO Legality of the EU's GSP + Arrangement' (2007) 10(4) Journal of International Economic Law, 869.

Beaucillon C, 'Practice Makes Perfect, Eventually? Unilateral State Sanctions and the Extraterritorial Effects of National Legislation' in Natalino Ronzitti (ed), *Coercive Diplomacy, Sanctions and International Law* (Brill Nijhoff 2016).

Bechky PS, 'Sanctions and the Blurred Boundaries of International Economic Law' (2018) 83 Missouri Law Review 1.

Beeson M, 'Geoeconomics Isn't Back – It Never Went Away' (22 August 2018) <https://www.lowyinstitute.org/the-interpreter/geoeconomics-isnt-back-never-went-away>.

Beitz CR, *The Idea of Human Rights* (Oxford University Press 2009).

Bellamy AJ and Paul DW, 'The New Politics of Protection? Côte d'Ivoire, Libya and the Responsibility to Protect' (2011) 87 International Affairs (Royal Institute of International Affairs 1944-) 825.

Benedek W, 'Drago-Porter Convention (1907),' *Max Planck Encyclopedia of Public International Law* [*MPEPIL*] https://opil.ouplaw.com/view/10.1093/law:epil/9780199231690/law-9780199231690-e733.

Benedek W, 'Humanization of International Law, Human Rights and the Common Interest' in Wolfgang Benedek (ed), *The common interest in international law* (Intersentia 2014).

Bentham M and Moore-Bridger B, 'Assad family cash frozen after dictator's niece found living in London' *Evening Standard* (18 April 2019) https://www.standard.co.uk/news/crime/assad-family-cash-frozen-after-dictator-s-niece-found-living-in-london-a4121211.html.

Bertram A, 'The Economic Weapon as a Form of Peaceful Pressure' (1931) 17 Transactions of the Grotius Society 139.

Besson S, 'The Bearers of Human Rights' Duties and Responsibilities for Human Rights: A Quite (R)Evolution?' (2015) 32 Social Philosophy and Policy 244.

Bhala R, 'National Security and International Trade Law: What the GATT Says, and What the United States Does' (1998) 19 University of Pennsylvania Journal of International Economic Law 263.

Bianchi A, 'Human Rights and the Magic of Jus Cogens' (2008) 19 European Journal of International Law 491.

Biermann F, 'Common Concern of Humankind: The Emergence of a New Concept of International Environmental Law' (1996) 34 Archiv des Völkerrechts 426.

Biersteker TJ, 'Targeted sanctions and individual human rights' (Winter 2009–10) 65(1) International Journal 99.

Biersteker TJ, Eckert SE and Tourinho M, 'Thinking about United Nations targeted sanctions' in Thomas Biersteker, Sue E. Eckert, and Marcos Tourinho (eds), *Targeted sanctions: the impacts and effectiveness of United Nations action* (Cambridge University Press 2016).

Biglaiser G and Lektzian D, 'The effect of sanctions on U.S. Foreign direct investment' (2011) 65(3) International Organization, 531.

Black I, 'Barack Obama Offers Iran "new Beginning" with Video Message' *The Guardian* (20 March 2009) <https://www.theguardian.com/world/2009/mar/20/barack-obama-video-iran>.

Blackwill RD and Harris JM, *War by Other Means: Geoeconomics and Statecraft* (The Belknap Press of Harvard University Press 2016).

Blanchard J-MF and Ripsman NM, 'A Political Theory of Economic Statecraft' (2008) 4 Foreign Policy Analysis 371.

Blum YZ, 'Economic Boycotts in International Law' (1977) 12 Texas International Law Journal 5.

Bodansky D, 'What's in a Concept? Global Public Goods, International Law, and Legitimacy' (2012) 23 European Journal of International Law/Journal europeen de droit international 651.

Bogdanova I and Callo-Müller MV, 'Unilateral Cyber Sanctions: Between Questioned Legality and Normative Value' (2021) 54 Vanderbilt Journal of Transnational Law 911.

Bogdanova I and Callo-Müller MV, 'Unilateral Economic Sanctions to Deter and Punish Cyber-Attacks: Are They Here to Stay?' (*EJIL: Talk!*, 7 December 2021), https://www.ejiltalk.org/unilateral-economic-sanctions-to-deter-and-punish-cyber-attacks-are-they-here-to-stay/.

Bogdanova I, 'Adjudication of the GATT Security Clause: To Be or Not to Be, This Is the Question' (2019) WTI Working Paper 01/2019 http://www.wti.org/research/publications/1208/adjudication-of-the-gatt-security-clause-to-be-or-not-to-be-this-is-the-question/.

Bogdanova I, 'Reshaping the Law of Economic Sanctions for Human Rights Enforcement: The Potential of Common Concern of Humankind' in Thomas Cottier and Zaker Ahmad (eds.), *The Prospects of Common Concern of Humankind in International Law* (Cambridge University Press 2021) doi:10.1017/9781108878739.008.

Bogdanova I, 'Targeted Economic Sanctions and WTO Law: Examining the Adequacy of the National Security Exception' (2021) 48(2) Legal Issues of Economic Integration 171.

Bogdanova I, 'The WTO Panel Ruling on the National Security Exception: Has the Panel "Cut" the Baby in Half?' (*EJIL:Talk!*, 12 April 2019) www.ejiltalk.org/the-wto-panel-ruling-on-the-national-security-exception-has-the-panel-cut-the-baby-in-half/#more-17087.

Bogdanova I, 'Turning Crisis into Opportunity: Unfolding Ukraine's Trade Potential with the Canada-Ukraine Free Trade Agreement' (2021) VIII(2) East/West Journal of Ukrainian Studies 151. doi.org/10.21226/ewjus561.

Bogdanova I, 'WTO Dispute on the US Human Rights Sanctions Is Looming on the Horizon' (*EJIL: Talk!*, 31 January 2019) https://www.ejiltalk.org/wto-dispute-on-the-us-human-rights-sanctions-is-looming-on-the-horizon/.

Boscariol JW, 'An Anatomy of a Cuban Pyjama Crisis: Reconsidering Blocking Legislation in Response to Extraterritorial Trade Measures of the United States' (1999) 30 Law and Policy in International Business 439.

Bown CP, 'The US-China Trade War and Phase One Agreement' (2021) Peterson Institute for International Economics Working paper 21–2 https://www.piie.com/sites/default/files/documents/wp21-2.pdf.

Briggs HW, *The Doctrine of Continuous Voyage* (Johns Hopkins Press 1926).

Brkan M, 'The Concept of Essence of Fundamental Rights in the EU Legal Order: Peeling the Onion to Its Core' (2018) 14 European Constitutional Law Review 332.

Brosche H, 'The Arab Oil Embargo and United States Pressure against Chile: Economic and Political Coercion and the Charter of the United Nations' (1974) 7 Case Western Reserve Journal of International Law 3.

Brownlie I, *Principles of Public International Law* (7th ed., Oxford University Press 2008).

Brunnée J and Nollkaemper A, 'Between the Forests and the Trees – an Emerging International Forest Law' (1996) 23 Environmental Conservation 307.

Brunnée J, 'Common Interest – Echoes from an Empty Shell? Some Thoughts on Common Interest and International Environmental Law' (1989) 49 Zeitschrift für Ausländisches Öffentliches Recht und Völkerrecht 791.

Brunnée J, 'Common Areas, Common Heritage, and Common Concern' in Daniel Bodansky, Jutta Brunnée and Ellen Hey (eds), *The Oxford Handbook of International Environmental Law* (First Edition, Oxford University Press 2007).

Brunnée J, 'The Prohibition on Torture: Driving Jus Cogens Home?' (2010) 104 Proceedings of the ASIL Annual Meeting 454.

Brzoska M, 'Design and Implementation of Arms Embargoes and Travel and Aviation Related Sanctions' (BICC Publications 2001) <https://www.bicc.de/publications/publicationpage/publication/design-and-implementation-of-arms-embargoes-and-travel-and-aviation-related-sanctions-results-of-t/>.

Buergenthal T, 'International Human Rights: Need for Further Institutional Development' (2018) 50 Case Western Reserve Journal of International Law 9.

Burke-White WW, 'Adoption of the Responsibility to Protect' in Jared Genser and Irwin Cotler (eds), *The Responsibility to Protect: the promise of stopping mass atrocities in our time* (Oxford University Press 2012).

Byers M, 'Conceptualising the Relationship between Jus Cogens and Erga Omnes Rules' (1997) 66 Nordic Journal of International Law 211.

Callejón C, Kemileva K and Kirchmeier F, *Treaty Bodies' Individual Communication Procedures: Providing Redress and Reparation to Victims of Human Rights Violations* (Académie de droit international humanitaire et de droits humains à Genève 2019).

Company RC, 'U.S.-Turkish Relations in the Arms Embargo Period 1974–1980' (ProQuest Dissertations Publishing 1984).

Canada judge delays extradition hearings in win for Huawei executive, *The Guardian* (21 April 2020) https://www.theguardian.com/world/2021/apr/21/meng-wanzhou-extradition-hearings-huawei-cfo.

Cann, Jr. W, 'Creating Standards and Accountability for the Use of the WTO Security Exception: Reducing the Role of Power-Based Relations and Establishing a New Balance Between Sovereignty and Multilateralism' (2001) 26 Yale Journal of International Law 413.

Cao L, 'Currency Wars and the Erosion of Dollar Hegemony' (2016) 38 Michigan Journal of International Law.

Cardwell R and Kerr WA, 'Can Export Restrictions Be Disciplined Through the World Trade Organisation?' (2014) 37 The World Economy 1186.

Carter BE, 'International Economic Sanctions: Improving the Haphazard U.S. Legal Regime' (1987) 75 California Law Review 1159.

Carter BE, *International Economic Sanctions: Improving the Haphazard U.S. Legal Regime* (Cambridge University Press 1988).

Cassese A, 'A Plea for a Global Community Grounded in a Core of Human Rights' in Antonio Cassese (ed), *Realizing utopia: the future of international law* (Oxford University Press 2012).

Castillo-Winckels NS, 'Why Common Concern of Humankind Should Return to the Work of the International Law Commission on the Atmosphere' (2016) 29 Georgetown Environmental Law Review 131.

Caytas JD, 'Weaponizing Finance: U.S. and European Options, Tools, and Policies' (2017) 23 Columbia Journal of European Law 441.

CERD Information Note on Inter-State Communications <https://www.ohchr.org/EN/NewsEvents/Pages/DisplayNews.aspx?NewsID=23566&LangID=E>.

Chan S, 'Principle Versus Profit: Debating Human Rights Sanctions' (2018) 19 Human Rights Review 45.

Chandler MM, 'The Interpretation and Effect of Article 16 of the Covenant of the League of Nations. Dissertation University of Chicago' (1936).

Charlesworth H and Larking E, 'Introduction: The Regulatory Power of the Universal Periodic Review' in Hilary Charlesworth and Emma Larking (eds), *Human Rights and the Universal Periodic Review: Rituals and Ritualism* (Cambridge University Press 2015).

Charnovitz S, 'The Moral Exception in Trade Policy' (1998) 38 Virginia Journal of International Law 689.

Chilton AS and Posner EA, 'Respect for Human Rights: Law and History' (2016) SSRN Electronic Journal <https://www.ssrn.com/abstract=2815272>.

Cleveland S, 'Norm Internalization and U.S. Economic Sanctions' (2001) 26 Yale Journal of International Law 1.

Cleveland S, 'Human Rights Sanctions and International Trade: A Theory of Compatibility' (2002) 5 Journal of International Economic Law 133.

Convention on the Rights of Persons with Disabilities (CRPD) (*un.org*) <https://www.un.org/development/desa/disabilities/convention-on-the-rights-of-persons-with-disabilities.html>.

Cook G, *A Digest of WTO Jurisprudence on Public International Law Concepts and Principles* (First published, University Press 2015).

Cooper J, *Raphael Lemkin and the Struggle for the Genocide Convention* (Palgrave Macmillan 2008).

Copeland DC, *Economic Interdependence and War* (Princeton University Press 2015).

Cortright D, Lopez GA and Conroy RW, *The Sanctions Decade: Assessing UN Strategies in the 1990s* (L Rienner 2000).

Costelloe D, *Legal Consequences of Peremptory Norms in International Law* (Cambridge University Press 2017).

Cottier T and Matteotti S, 'International Environmental Law and the Evolving Concept of "Common Concern of Mankind"' in Thomas Cottier, Olga Nartova and Sadeq Z Bigdeli (eds), *International trade regulation and the mitigation of climate change: World Trade Forum* (Cambridge University Press 2009).

Cottier T and Schefer KN, 'Responsibility to Protect (R2P) and the Emerging Principle of Common Concern' (2012) NCCR Working Paper 2012/29.

Cottier T et al., 'The Principle of Common Concern and Climate Change' (2014) 52 Archiv des Völkerrechts 293.

Cottier T et al., 'The Principle of Proportionality in International Law: Foundations and Variations' (2017) 18 The Journal of World Investment & Trade 628.

Cottier T, 'Trade and Human Rights: A Relationship to Discover' (2002) 5 Journal of International Economic Law 111.

Cottier T, 'Improving Compliance: Jus Cogens and International Economic Law' in den Maarten Heijer and Harmen van der Wilt (eds), *Netherlands Yearbook of International Law 2015: Jus Cogens: Quo Vadis?* (TMC Asser Press 2016).

Cottier T, 'The Implications of EC – Seal Products for the Protection of Core Labour Standards in WTO Law' in Henner Gött (ed), *Labour standards in international economic law* (Springer 2018).

Cottier T, 'The Principle of Common Concern of Humankind' in Thomas Cottier and Zaker Ahmad (eds.), *The Prospects of Common Concern of Humankind in International Law* (Cambridge University Press 2021).

Cowden M, *Children's Rights: From Philosophy to Public Policy* (Palgrave Macmillan 2016).

Coyne CJ, *Doing Bad by Doing Good: Why Humanitarian Action Fails* (Stanford Economics and Finance 2013).

Craven M, 'Humanitarianism and the Quest for Smarter Sanctions' (2002) 13 European Journal of International Law 43.

Crawford J, *State Responsibility: The General Part* (Cambridge University Press 2013).

Damme IV, *Treaty Interpretation by the WTO Appellate Body* (Oxford University Press 2009).

Damme IV, 'Treaty Interpretation by the WTO Appellate Body' (2010) 21 European Journal of International Law 605.

Damrosch LF, 'Politics Across Borders: Nonintervention and Nonforcible Influence Over Domestic Affairs' (1989) 83 American Journal of International Law 1.

Dawidowicz M, 'Public Law Enforcement without Public Law Safeguards? An Analysis of State Practice on Third-Party Countermeasures and Their Relationship to the UN Security Council' (2007) 77 British Yearbook of International Law 333.

Dawidowicz M, 'Third-Party Countermeasures: A Progressive Development of International Law?' (2016) Questions of International Law.

Dawidowicz M, *Third-Party Countermeasures in International Law* (Cambridge University Press 2017).

Degener T and Begg A, 'From Invisible Citizens to Agents of Change: A Short History of the Struggle for the Recognition of the Rights of Persons with Disabilities at the United Nations' in Valentina Della Fina, Rachele Cera and Giuseppe Palmisano (eds), *The United Nations Convention on the Rights of Persons with Disabilities: A Commentary* (Springer International Publishing 2017).

Dehne PA, *After the Great War: Economic Warfare and the Promise of Peace in Paris 1919* (Bloomsbury Academic 2019).

Delanis JA, "Force' under Article 2(4) of the United Nations Charter: The Question of Economic and Political Coercion' (1979) 12 Vanderbilt Journal of Transnational Law.

Delimatsis P and Cottier T, 'Article XIV bis GATS: Security Exceptions' in Rüdiger Wolfrum, Peter-Tobias Stoll, Clemens Feinäugle, (eds), *Max Planck Commentaries on World Trade Law, WTO – Trade in Services* (Leiden/Boston: Martinus Nijhoff Publishers, 2008).

Denkers J, *The World Trade Organization and Import Bans in Response to Violations of Fundamental Labour Rights* (Intersentia 2008).

Donnan S and Hille K, 'Russia Threatens US with WTO Action over Crimea Sanctions' *Financial Times* (16 April 2014) <https://www.ft.com/content/5418ad46-c57c-11e3-97e4-00144feabdc0>.

Doraev M, 'The "Memory Effect" of Economic Sanctions against Russia: Opposing Approaches to the Legality of Unilateral Sanctions Clash Again' (2015) 37 University of Pennsylvania Journal of International Law 355.

Doxey MP, *Economic Sanctions and International Enforcement* (2nd ed., Macmillan Press 1980).

Drezner DW, *The Sanctions Paradox: Economic Statecraft and International Relations* (Cambridge University Press 1999).

Drezner DW, 'Bargaining, Enforcement, and Multilateral Sanctions: When Is Cooperation Counterproductive?' (2000) 54 International Organization 73.

Drezner DW, 'Sanctions Sometimes Smart: Targeted Sanctions in Theory and Practice' (2011) 13 International Studies Review 96.

Drezner DW, 'Targeted sanctions in a world of global finance' (2015) 41 International Interactions 755.

Drury AC, 'Revisiting Economic Sanctions Reconsidered' (1998) 35 Journal of Peace Research 497.

Dunning TS, 'D'Amato in a China Shop: Problems of Extraterritoriality with the Iran and Libya Sanctions Act of 1996' (1998) 19 U. Pa. J. Int'l L. 169.

Dupont P-E, 'Countermeasure and Collective Security: The Case of the EU Sanctions against Iran' (2012) 17 Journal of Conflict and Security Law 301.

Early BR and Spice R, 'Economic Sanctions, International Institutions, and Sanctions Busters: When Does Institutionalized Cooperation Help Sanctioning Efforts?' (2015) 11 Foreign Policy Analysis 339.

Eaton J and Engers M, 'Sanctions' (1992) 100 Journal of Political Economy 899.

Eckert SE and Biersteker TJ, 'Due Process and Targeted Sanctions.' (Watson Institute for International Studies, Brown University 2012).

Eckert SE, 'The Use of Financial Measures to Promote Security' (2008) 62 Journal of International Affairs 103.

Efing M, Goldbach S, and Nitsch V, 'Freeze! Financial sanctions and bank responses' (2018) Deutsche Bundesbank Discussion Paper No 45/2018.

Egle S, 'The Learning Curve of Sanctions – Have Three Decades of Sanctions Reform Taught Us Anything Chester James Taylor Award 2011' (2010) 19 Currents – International Trade Law Journal 34.

Eichengreen B, *Exorbitant Privilege: The Rise and Fall of the Dollar* (Oxford University Press 2011).

Elagab OY, *The Legality of Non-Forcible Counter-Measures in International Law* (Clarendon Press 1988).

Elagab OY, 'Coercive Economic Measures Against Developing Countries' (1992) 41 International and Comparative Law Quarterly 682.

Ellings RJ, *Embargoes and World Power: Lessons from American Foreign Policy* (Westview Press 1985).

Elliott KA, 'Assessing UN Sanctions after the Cold War: New and Evolving Standards of Measurement. (UN Sanctions: New Dilemmas and Unintended Consequences)' (2009) 65 International Journal 85.

Emery C, 'The Transatlantic and Cold War Dynamics of Iran Sanctions, 1979–80' (2010) 10 Cold War History 371.

Emmenegger S and Döbeli T, 'Extraterritorial Application of US Sanctions Law' in Andrea Bonomi and Krista Nadakavukaren Schefer (eds), *US Litigation Today: Still a Threat For European Businesses or Just a Paper Tiger? Conference proceedings from the 29th Journée de droit International privé du 23 juin 2017*, vol 85 (Schulthess Verlag 2018).

Emmenegger S, 'Extraterritorial Economic Sanctions and Their Foundation in International Law' (2016) 33 Arizona Journal of International and Comparative Law 631.

Espa I, *Export Restrictions on Critical Minerals and Metals: Testing the Adequacy of WTO Disciplines* (Cambridge University Press 2015).

European Commission Acts to Protect the Interests of EU Companies Investing in Iran as Part of the EU's Continued Commitment to the Joint Comprehensive Plan of Action (*European Commission*) <https://ec.europa.eu/commission/presscorner/detail/en/IP_18_3861>.

'Factbox: U.S. Sanctions on Venezuela's Oil Industry' *Reuters* (30 January 2019) <https://www.reuters.com/article/us-venezuela-politics-usa-sancti ons-fact-idUSKCN1PN34I>.

Fairley HS, 'Between Scylla and Charybdis: The U.S. Embargo of Cuba and Canadian Foreign Extraterritorial Measures Against It' (2010) 44 The International Lawyer 887.

Fan L-S, 'The Economy and Foreign Trade of China' (1973) 38 Law and Contemporary Problems 249.

Fariss CJ, 'Respect for Human Rights Has Improved Over Time: Modeling the Changing Standard of Accountability' (2014) 108 The American Political Science Review 297.

Fassbender B, 'Targeted Sanctions and Due Process. The Responsibility of the UN Security Council to Ensure That Fair and Clear Procedures Are Made Available to Individuals and Entities Targeted with Sanctions under Chapter VII of the UN Charter, Study Commissioned by the United Nations Office of Legal Affairs.' (2006).

Fastenrath U and others (eds), *From Bilateralism to Community Interest: Essays in Honour of Judge Bruno Simma* (Oxford University Press 2011).

Felbermayr G et al., 'The Global Sanctions Data Base' (4 August 2020) https://voxeu.org/article/global-sanctions-data-base.

Filkins D, 'A Mysterious Case Involving Turkey, Iran, and Rudy Giuliani' *The New Yorker* (14 April 2017) <https://www.newyorker.com/news/news-desk/a-mysterious-case-involving-turkey-iran-and-rudy-giuliani>.

Finnish Court Rejects Rotenberg's Suit against Nordic Banks *Reuters* (13 January 2020) <https://www.reuters.com/article/finland-russia-sanctions-idUSL8N29I260>.

Flicker SM, Fiebig J and Manley K, 'United States of America v. Reza Zarrab: The Long Reach of U.S. Sanctions May Have Just Gotten Longer' *Paul Hastings LLP* https://casetext.com/analysis/united-states-of-america-v-reza-zarrab-the-long-reach-of-us-sanctions-may-have-just-gotten-longer-1.

Foreign, Commonwealth & Development Office. *Press release.* UK sanctions perpetrators of gross human rights violations in Xinjiang, alongside EU, Canada and US. (22 March 2021) https://www.gov.uk/government/news/uk-sanctions-perpetrators-of-gross-human-rights-violations-in-xinjiang-alongside-eu-canada-and-us.

Foreign & Commonwealth Office. *Press Release.* UK announces first sanctions under new global human rights regime. (6 July 2020) https://www.gov.uk/government/news/uk-announces-first-sanctions-under-new-global-human-rights-regime.

Fox B, 'Poland Demands WTO Challenge over Russia Food Ban' (20 August 2014) <https://euobserver.com/news/125295>.

Fox H and Webb P, *The Law of State Immunity* (Revised and Updated Third Edition, Oxford University Press 2015).

Freedman R, 'The United Nations Human Rights Council: More of the Same?' (2013) 31 Wisconsin International Law Journal 208.

Freifeld K, 'U.S. Reveals ZTE Settlement Details, Ban Still in Place' *Reuters* (11 June 2018) <https://www.reuters.com/article/us-usa-trade-china-zte-idUSKBN1J72GK>.

French D, 'Common Concern, Common Heritage and Other Global(-Ising) Concepts: Rhetorical Devices, Legal Principles or a Fundamental Challenge?' in Michael Bowman, Peter Davies and Edward Goodwin (eds), *Research Handbook on Biodiversity and Law* (Edward Elgar 2016).

Galtung J, 'On the Effects of International Economic Sanctions: With Examples from the Case of Rhodesia' (1967) 19 World Politics 378.

Giegerich T, 'Retorsion,' *Max Planck Encyclopedia of Public International Law* [*MPEPIL*] (2011) http://opil.ouplaw.com/view/10.1093/law:epil/9780199231690/law-9780199231690-e983.

Giumelli F, 'Understanding United Nations targeted sanctions: an empirical analysis' (2015) 91(6) International affairs 1351.

Giumelli F, Hoffmann F and Książczaková A, 'The when, what, where and why of European Union sanctions' (2021) 30(1) European Security 1.

Global Affairs Canada. *News release*. Canada joins international partners in imposing new sanctions in response to human rights violations in Xinjiang. (22 March 2021) https://www.canada.ca/en/global-affairs/news/2021/03/canada-joins-international-partners-in-imposing-new-sanctions-in-response-to-human-rights-violations-in-xinjiang.html.

Gozzi G, 'The "Discourse" of International Law and Humanitarian Intervention' (2017) 30 Ratio Juris 186.

Grant TD, 'Annexation of Crimea' (2015) 109 American Journal of International Law 68.

Griffin J, 'Discrepancies Between the Best Philosophical Account of Human Rights and the International Law of Human Rights' (2001) 101 Proceedings of the Aristotelian Society 1.

Griffin J, 'Human Rights and the Autonomy of International Law' in Samantha Besson and John Tasioulas (eds), *The philosophy of international law* (Oxford University Press 2010).

Groll E, 'Turkish Gold Dealer Pleads Guilty in Politically Explosive Sanctions Trial' *Foreign Policy* <https://foreignpolicy.com/2017/11/28/turkish-gold-dealer-pleads-guilty-in-politically-explosive-sanctions-trial-iran-zarrab-erdogan/>.

Guchteneire P de and Pécoud A, 'Introduction: The UN Convention on Migrant Workers' Rights,' in Ryszard Cholewinski, Paul de Guchteneire and Antoine Pecoud (eds), *Migration and Human Rights: The United Nations Convention on Migrant Workers' Rights* (Cambridge University Press 2009).

Hafner-Burton EM and Tsutsui K, 'Human Rights in a Globalizing World: The Paradox of Empty Promises' (2005) 110 The American Journal of Sociology 1373.

Hafner-Burton EM and Tsutsui K, 'Justice Lost! The Failure of International Human Rights Law to Matter Where Needed Most' (2007) 44 Journal of Peace Research 407.

Hafner-Burton EM, 'A Social Science of Human Rights' (2014) 51 Journal of Peace Research 273.

Hahn MJ, 'Vital Interests and the Law of GATT: An Analysis of GATT's Security Exception' (1991) 12 Michigan Journal of International Law 558.

Hakimi M, 'Unfriendly Unilateralism' (2014) 55 Harvard International Law Journal 105.

Halberstam D and Stein E, 'The United Nations, the European Union, and the King of Sweden: Economic Sanctions and Individual Rights in a Plural World Order' (2009) 46 Common Market Law Review 13.

Harris C, 'Note of the Month. Political and Economic Effects of Sanctions on Rhodesia.' (1967) 23 The World Today 1.

Harris R and Moon G, '"Gatt" Article XX and Human Rights: What Do We Know from the First 20 Years?' (2015) 16 Melbourne Journal of International Law 432.

Hathaway OA, 'Do Human Rights Treaties Make a Difference?' (2002) 111 The Yale Law Journal 1935.

Hathaway OA, 'Why Do Countries Commit to Human Rights Treaties?' (2007) 51 Journal of Conflict Resolution 588.

Have N van der, 'The Proposed EU Human Rights Sanctions Regime: A First Appreciation' (2020) 1 Security and Human Rights 1.

Hehir A, 'NATO's "Humanitarian Intervention" in Kosovo: Legal Precedent or Aberration?' (2009) 8 Journal of Human Rights 245.

Heinegg WH von, 'Blockade,' *Max Planck Encyclopedia of Public International Law* [*MPEPIL*] (2015) <http://opil.ouplaw.com/view/10.1093/law:epil/9780199231690/law-9780199231690-e252>.

Henkin L, 'Kosovo and the Law of "Humanitarian Intervention"' (1999) 93 The American Journal of International Law 824.

Hill DW, 'Estimating the Effects of Human Rights Treaties on State Behavior' (2010) 72 The Journal of Politics 1161.

Hillgruber C, 'The Right of Third States to Take Countermeasures' in Christian Tomuschat and Jean-Marc Thouvenin (eds), *The Fundamental Rules of the International Legal Order* (Martinus Nijhoff Publishers 2006).

Hilpold P, 'From Humanitarian Intervention to Responsibility to Protect: Making Utopia True?' in Ulrich Fastenrath at el (ed), *From Bilateralism to Community Interest: Essays in Honour of Bruno Simma* (Oxford University Press 2011).

Hofer A, 'The Developed/Developing Divide on Unilateral Coercive Measures: Legitimate Enforcement or Illegitimate Intervention?' (2017) 16 Chinese Journal of International Law 175.

Holt H, 'The League to Enforce Peace' (1917) 7 Proceedings of the Academy of Political Science in the City of New York 65.

Horn L, 'The Implications of the Concept of Common Concern of a Human Kind on a Human Right to a Healthy Environment' (2004) 1 Macquarie Journal of International and Comparative Environmental Law 233.

Hovell D, 'Due Process in the United Nations' (2016) 110 The American Journal of International Law 1.

Hovell D, 'Unfinished Business of International Law: The Questionable Legality of Autonomous Sanctions' (2019) 113 ajil Unbound 140.

Howse RL and Genser JM, 'Are EU Trade Sanctions on Burma Compatible with WTO Law' (2007) Michigan Journal of International Law 165.

Hoyos C, 'Big Oil Groups Implicated in Oil-for-Food Scandal' (28 October 2005) <https://www.ft.com/content/1f250dd4-47de-11da-a949-00000e2511c8>.

Huawei and 68 Affiliates Added to US Department of Commerce Entity List (*EU Sanctions*, 21 May 2019) https://www.europeansanctions.com/2019/05/huawei-and-68-affiliates-added-to-us-department-of-commerce-entity-list/.

'Huawei CFO Wanzhou Meng Admits to Misleading Global Financial Institution' (*The United States Department of Justice*, 24 September 2021) https://www.justice.gov/opa/pr/huawei-cfo-wanzhou-meng-admits-misleading-global-financial-institution.

Huawei finance chief Meng Wanzhou arrested in Canada, *BBC News* (6 December 2018), https://www.bbc.com/news/business-46462858.

Hufbauer GC, Schott JJ and Elliott KA, *Economic Sanctions Reconsidered: History and Current Policy* (Institute for International Economics 1985).

Hufbauer GC, Schott JJ and Elliott KA, *Economic Sanctions Reconsidered* (3rd ed, Peterson Institute for International Economics 2007).

Inquiry into Whether Australia Should Examine the Use of Targeted Sanctions to Address Human Rights Abuses. <https://www.aph.gov.au/Parliamentary_Business/Committees/Joint/Foreign_Affairs_Defence_and_Trade/MagnitskyAct>.

International Bar Association, 'Report of the IBA Task Force on Extraterritorial Jurisdiction' (2009).

International Commission on Intervention and State Sovereignty, 'The Responsibility to Protect: Report of the International Commission on Intervention and State Sovereignty' (2001).

International Union for Conservation of Nature and Natural Resources, 'Draft International Covenant on Environment and Development, Implementing Sustainability' <https://sustainabledevelopment.un.org/content/documents/2443Covenant_5th_edition.pdf>.

Ishay MR, *The Human Rights Reader: Major Political Essays, Speeches and Documents From Ancient Times to the Present* (2nd edition, Routledge 2007).

Jaeckel A, 'Intellectual Property Rights and the Conservation of Plant Biodiversity as a Common Concern of Humankind' (2013) 2 Transnational Environmental Law 167.

Jamnejad M and Wood M, 'The Principle of Non-Intervention' (2009) 22 Leiden Journal of International Law 345.

Jazairy I, 'Unilateral Economic Sanctions, International Law, and Human Rights' (2019) 33 Ethics & International Affairs 291.

Johnson K, Freifeld K and Landauro I, 'Societe Generale to Pay $1.4 Billion to Settle Cases in the U.S.' *Reuters* (19 November 2018) https://www.reuters.com/article/us-usa-fed-socgen-idUSKCN1NO26B.

Johnson LH, III, 'The Business of War: Trading with the Enemy in English and Early American Law' (1974) 118(5) Proceedings of the American Philosophical Society 459.

Joint Statement on Crimea by President of the European Council Herman Van Rompuy and President of the European Commission José Manuel Barroso. Brussels, 18 March 2014. euco 63/14.

Jones L, *Societies under Siege: Exploring How International Economic Sanctions (Do Not) Work* (First edition, Oxford University Press 2015).

Joseph S and Kyriakakis J, 'The United Nations and Human Rights,' in Sarah Joseph (ed), *Research handbook on international human rights law* (Edward Elgar 2010).

Joseph S, *Blame It on the WTO?: A Human Rights Critique* (Oxford University Press 2011).

Joseph S, *Blame It on the WTO?: A Human Rights Critique* (Oxford University Press 2013).

Joyner C, 'Boycott,' *Max Planck Encyclopedia of Public International Law* (2009) <https://opil.ouplaw.com/oxlaw/entryview/viewoxlawoxchap/10.1093$002flaw:epil$002f9780199231690$002flaw-9780199231690-e258>.

Junxiang M and Xi S, 'Strength of Review and Scale of Response: A Quantitative Analysis of Human Rights Council Universal Periodic Review on China' (2017) 23 Buffalo Human Rights Law Review 1.

Kälin W and Künzli J, *The Law of International Human Rights Protection* (1st publ., Oxford University Press 2009).

Kälin W and Künzli J, *The Law of International Human Rights Protection* (Second edition, Oxford University Press 2019).

Kälin W, 'Ritual and Ritualism at the Universal Periodic Review: A Preliminary Appraisal' in Hilary Charlesworth and Emma Larking (eds), *Human Rights and the Universal Periodic Review: Rituals and Ritualism* (Cambridge University Press 2015).

Katselli Proukaki E, *The Problem of Enforcement in International Law: Countermeasures, the Non-Injured State and the Idea of International Community* (Routledge 2011).

Katzenstein S, 'Dollar Unilateralism: The New Frontline of National Security' (2015) 90 Indiana Law Journal 293.

Katzman K, 'The Iran Sanctions Act (ISA),' (2007) crs Report for Congress rs20871.

Kaul I (ed), *Global Public Goods: International Cooperation in the 21st Century* (Oxford University Press 1999).

Keith LC, 'The United Nations International Covenant on Civil and Political Rights: Does It Make a Difference in Human Rights Behavior?' (1999) 36 Journal of Peace Research 95.

Klasfeld A, 'Bygone US Sentence of Turkish Banker Hakan Atilla Affirmed,' *Courthouse News Service* (20 July 2020) https://www.courthousenews.com/bygone-us-sentence-of-turkish-banker-hakan-atilla-affirmed/.

Klasfeld A, 'Out of Prison, Ex-Halkbank Manager Appeals Bygone Sentence' (16 December 2019) https://www.courthousenews.com/out-of-prison-ex-halkbank-manager-appeals-bygone-sentence/.

Kolb R, *The International Law of State Responsibility: An Introduction* (Edward Elgar Publishing 2017).

Kreutz J, 'Hard Measures by a Soft Power? Sanctions Policy of the European Union 1981–2004' (2005) Bonn International Center for Conversion, paper 45 1.

Krommendijk J, 'The (In)Effectiveness of UN Human Rights Treaty Body Recommendations' (2015) 33 Netherlands Quarterly of Human Rights 194.

Lam SL, 'Economic Sanctions and the Success of Foreign Policy Goals: A Critical Evaluation' (1990) 2 Japan & The World Economy 239.

Lange J and Torbati Y, 'UBS to Pay $1.7 Mln Settlement over Sanctions Case – U.S. Treasury' *Reuters* (27 August 2015) https://www.reuters.com/article/ubs-group-settlement-idUSL1N1121WN20150827.

Lau S, 'China Slaps Retaliatory Sanctions on EU Officials' *politico* (22 March 2021) https://www.politico.eu/article/china-slaps-retaliatory-sanctions-on-eu-officials/.

Lau TJ, 'Triggering Parent Company Liability under United States Sanctions Regimes: The Troubling Implications of Prohibiting Approval and Facilitation' (2004) 41 American Business Law Journal 413.

Lauterpacht H, 'Boycott in International Relations' (1933) 14 British Yearbook of International Law 125.

Lektzian D and Patterson D, 'Political Cleavages and Economic Sanctions: The Economic and Political Winners and Losers of Sanctions' (2015) 59 International Studies Quarterly 46.

Lemkin R, *Axis Rule in Occupied Europe: Laws of Occupation, Analysis of Government, Proposals for Redress* (Carnegie Endowment for International Peace 1944).

Lemkin R, 'Genocide as a Crime under International Law' (1947) 41 The American Journal of International Law 145.

Lenaerts K, 'Limits on Limitations: The Essence of Fundamental Rights in the EU' (2019) 20 German Law Journal 779.

Lesaffer R, 'Kellogg-Briand Pact (1928),' *Max Planck Encyclopedia of Public International Law* [*MPEPIL*] <https://opil.ouplaw.com/view/10.1093/law:epil/9780199231690/law-9780199231690-e320>.

Lester M, 'Helsinki Court Dismisses Boris Rotenberg's Sanctions Case' *EU Sanctions* (15 January 2020) https://www.europeansanctions.com/2020/01/helsinki-court-dismisses-boris-rotenbergs-sanctions-case/.

Lester M, 'China adopts new export control law' *EU Sanctions* (19 October 2020) https://www.europeansanctions.com/2020/10/china-adopts-new-export-control-law/.

Lin TCW, 'Financial Weapons of War' (2016) 100 Minnesota Law Review 1377.

Love B, 'Companies Caught in EU-US Sanctions Crossfire' (30 January 2020) <https://www.ft.com/content/97a75318-16a8-11ea-b869-0971bffac109>.

Lowenfeld AF, 'Trade Controls for Political Ends: Four Perspectives' (2003) 4 Chicago Journal of International Law 355.

Lowenfeld AF, *International Economic Law* (2nd ed., Oxford University Press 2008).

Luttwak EN, 'From Geopolitics to Geo-Economics: Logic of Conflict, Grammar of Commerce' (1990) The National Interest 17.

MacAskill E, 'Oil-for-Food Report Condemns "corrupt" UN' *The Guardian* (7 September 2005) https://www.theguardian.com/world/2005/sep/07/iraq.ewenmacaskill.

Macikenaite V, 'China's economic statecraft: the use of economic power in an interdependent world' (2020) 9(2) Journal of Contemporary East Asia Studies 108 https://www.tandfonline.com/doi/full/10.1080/24761028.2020.1848381?scroll=top&needAccess=true.

Making Targeted Sanctions Effective. Guidelines for the Implementation of UN Policy Options. (Peter Wallensteen et al. eds., Uppsala University, Department of Peace and Conflict Research, 2003).

Marceau G, 'WTO Dispute Settlement and Human Rights' (2002) 13 European Journal of International Law 753.

Marceau G, 'WTO and Export Restrictions' (2016) 50 Journal of World Trade (Law-Economics-Public Policy) 563.

Martin LL, *Coercive Cooperation: Explaining Multilateral Economic Sanctions* (Princeton University Press 1992).

McLean EV and Whang T, 'Designing Foreign Policy: Voters, Special Interest Groups, and Economic Sanctions' (2014) 51 Journal of Peace Research 589.

McMahon E and Ascherio M, 'A Step Ahead in Promoting Human Rights? The Universal Periodic Review of the UN Human Rights Council' (2012) 18 Global Governance: A Review of Multilateralism and International Organizations 231.

Meyer JA, 'Second Thoughts on Secondary Sanctions' (2009) 30 University of Pennsylvania Journal of International Law 905.

Milanovic M and Schmitt MN, 'Cyber Attacks and Cyber (Mis)information Operations During a Pandemic' (2020) 11 Journal of National Security Law & Policy 247.

Milanovic M, 'Norm Conflict in International Law: Whither Human Rights?' (2009) 20 Duke Journal of Comparative & International Law 69.

Miles T, 'U.S. Objection over Venezuela Threatens to Halt WTO Trade Disputes' *Reuters* <https://www.reuters.com/article/us-usa-trade-venezuela-wto/u-s-venuezela-spat-threatens-to-halt-wto-trade-disputes-idUSKCN1R71KJ>.

Miller D, 'Distributing Responsibilities' (2001) 9 Journal of Political Philosophy 453.

Miller DH and Butler NM, *The Drafting of the Covenant* (G P Putnam's sons 1928).

Milne B, *Rights of the Child: 25 Years After the Adoption of the UN Convention* (Springer International Publishing 2015).

Minister of Foreign Affairs Mandate Letter https://pm.gc.ca/en/mandate-letters/2019/12/13/minister-foreign-affairs-mandate-letter.

Misic A and Töpperwien N, *Constitutional Law in Switzerland* (Kluwer Law International bv 2018).

Mitchell AD, 'Sanctions and the World Trade Organization' in Larissa van den Herik (ed), *Research Handbook on UN Sanctions and International Law* (Cheltenham, Edward Elgar Publishing, 2017).

Morijn J, 'Reforming United Nations Human Rights Treaty Monitoring Reform' (2011) 58 Netherlands International Law Review 295.

Mueller J and Mueller K, 'Sanctions of Mass Destruction' (1999) 78 Foreign Affairs 43.

Murillo J, 'Common Concern of Humankind and Its Implications in International Environmental Law' (2008) 5 Macquarie Journal of International and Comparative Environmental Law 133.

Muse RL, 'A Public Internation Law Critique of the Extraterritorial Jurisdiction of the Helms-Burton Act (Cuban Liberty and Democratic Solidarity (Libertad) Act of 1996)' (1996) 30 The George Washington Journal of International Law and Economics 207.

Neier A, 'Sanctions and Human Rights' (2015) 82:4 Social research 875.

Nesbitt M, 'Canada's Unilateral Sanctions Regime under Review: Extraterritoriality, Human Rights, Due Process, and Enforcement in Canada's Special Economic Measures Act' (2016) 48(2) Ottawa Law Review 507.

Neumayer E, 'Do International Human Rights Treaties Improve Respect for Human Rights?' (2005) 49 The Journal of Conflict Resolution 925.

Neuwirth RJ and Svetlicinii A, 'The Economic Sanctions over the Ukraine Conflict and the WTO: 'Catch-XXI' and the Revival of the Debate on Security Exceptions' (2015) 49 Journal of World Trade 891.

Neuwirth RJ and Svetlicinii A, 'The Current EU/US–Russia Conflict over Ukraine and the WTO: A Preliminary Note on (Trade) Restrictive Measures' (2016) 32 Post-Soviet Affairs 237.

Nolte G, 'From Dionisio Anzilotti to Roberto Ago: The Classical International Law of State Responsibility and the Traditional Primacy of a Bilateral Conception of Inter-State Relations' (2002) 13 European Journal of International Law 1083.

Noortmann M, *Enforcing International Law: From Self-Help to Self-Contained Regimes* (Ashgate 2005).

Nooruddin I, 'Modeling Selection Bias in Studies of Sanctions Efficacy' (2002) 28 International Interactions 57.

Nossal KR, 'Knowing When to Fold: Western Sanctions against the USSR 1980–1983' (1988) 44 International Journal 698.

Nurnberger RD, 'The United States and Idi Amin: Congress to the Rescue' (1982) 25 African Studies Review 49.

O'Connell ME, 'Debating the Law of Sanctions' (2002) 13 European Journal of International Law 63.

ohchr | Special Procedures of the Human Rights Council (*ohchr.org*) <https://www.ohchr.org/EN/HRBodies/SP/Pages/Welcomepage.aspx>.

Ojanen T, 'Making the Essence of Fundamental Rights Real: The Court of Justice of the European Union Clarifies the Structure of Fundamental Rights under the Charter' (2016) 12 European Constitutional Law Review 318.

Opinion | The Oil-for-Food Failures *The New York Times* (8 September 2005) <https://www.nytimes.com/2005/09/08/opinion/the-oilforfood-failures.html>.

Opitz G-D, 'Transnational Organizing and the Haitian Crisis, 1991–1994' (2002) 8 Journal of Haitian Studies 114.

Orakhelashvili A, 'Immunities of State Officials, International Crimes, and Foreign Domestic Courts: A Reply to Dapo Akande and Sangeeta Shah' (2011) 22 European Journal of International Law 849.

Oyer H, 'The Extraterritorial Effects of U.S. Unilateral Trade Sanctions and Their Impact on U.S. Obligations under NAFTA' (1997) 11 Florida Journal of International Law 429.

Paarlberg RL, 'Lessons on the Grain Embargo' (1980) 59 Foreign Affairs 144.

Paddeu FI, 'Countermeasures,' *Max Planck Encyclopedia of Public International Law* [*MPEPIL*] <https://opil.ouplaw.com/view/10.1093/law:epil/9780199231690/law-9780199231690-e1020?prd=OPIL>.

Pape RA, 'Why Economic Sanctions Do Not Work' (1997) 22 International Security 90.

Pape RA, 'When Duty Calls: A Pragmatic Standard of Humanitarian Intervention' (2012) 37 International Security 41.

Pattison J, *Humanitarian Intervention and the Responsibility to Protect: Who Should Intervene?* (Oxford University Press 2010).

Paulus A, 'Jus Cogens in a Time of Hegemony and Fragmentation – An Attempt at a Re-Appraisal' (2005) 74 Nordic Journal of International Law 297.

Paulus A, 'Whether Universal Values Can Prevail over Bilateralism and Reciprocity' in Antonio Cassese (ed), *Realizing Utopia: The Future of International Law* (Oxford University Press 2012).

Peksen D, Peterson TM and Drury AC, 'Media-Driven Humanitarianism? News Media Coverage of Human Rights Abuses and the Use of Economic Sanctions' (2014) 58 International Studies Quarterly 855.

Pellet A and Miron A, 'Sanctions,' *Max Planck Encyclopedia of Public International Law* [*MPEPIL*] <https://opil.ouplaw.com/view/10.1093/law:epil/9780199231690/law-978 0199231690-e984?prd=OPIL>.

Pellet A, 'Unilateral Sanctions and International Law. A Proposal for a New Commission on Unilateral Sanctions and International Law.' (2015) 76 Yearbook of Institute of International Law.

Perlow GH, 'Taking Peacetime Trade Sanctions to the Limit: The Soviet Pipeline Embargo' (1983) 15 Case Western Reserve Journal of International Law 253.

Petri PA, 'United States – China Technological Rivalry' (22 August 2019) https://ssrn .com/abstract=3441035.

Pifer S, 'Crimea: Six Years after Illegal Annexation' (*Brookings*, 17 March 2020) https:// www.brookings.edu/blog/order-from-chaos/2020/03/17/crimea-six-years-after-ille gal-annexation/.

Poh A, *Sanctions with Chinese Characteristics: Rhetoric and Restraint in China's Diplomacy* (Amsterdam University Press 2021).

Pollmann M, 'What's Driving Japan's Trade Restrictions on South Korea?' <https://thed iplomat.com/2019/07/whats-driving-japans-trade-restrictions-on-south-korea/>.

Portela C, 'Targeted sanctions against individuals on grounds of grave human rights violations – impact, trends and prospects at EU level' (2018) Study commissioned by the European Parliament's Subcommittee of Human Rights 1.

Posner EA, *The Twilight of Human Rights Law* (Oxford University Press 2014).

'President of Ukraine by His Decree Put into Effect the Decision of the National Security and Defense Council of Ukraine "On the Imposition of Personal Special Economic and Other Restrictive Measures (Sanctions)" – National Security and Defense Council of Ukraine' https://www.rnbo.gov.ua/en/Diialnist/2764.html?PRINT.

Press Release, Government proposes new sanctions act (18 December 2020) https:// www.regjeringen.no/en/aktuelt/new-sanctions-act/id2815141/.

Press Statement, U.S. Imposes Visa Restrictions on Certain Employees of Chinese Technology Companies that Abuse Human Rights (July 15, 2020) https://2017-2021 .state.gov/u-s-imposes-visa-restrictions-on-certain-employees-of-chinese-technol ogy-companies-that-abuse-human-rights/index.html.

Public Designation of Owen Ncube, Due to Involvement in Gross Violations of Human Rights, under Section 7031(c) of the FY 2019 Department of State, Foreign Operations, and Related Programs Appropriations Act (*United States Department of State*, 25 October 2019) <https://www.state.gov/public-designation-of-owen-ncube -due-to-involvement-in-gross-violations-of-human-rights-under-section-7031c-of -the-fy-2019-department-of-state-foreign-operations-and-related-programs-appr opriati/>.

Public Designations of Current and Former Foreign Government Officials Due to Involvement in Gross Violations of Human Rights Under Section 7031(c) of the

Department of State, Foreign Operations, and Related Programs Appropriations Act (*United States Department of State*, 10 December 2019) <https://www.state.gov/public-designations-of-current-and-former-foreign-government-officials-due-to-involvement-in-gross-violations-of-human-rights-under-section-7031c-of-the-department-of-state-foreign-operations-and/>.

Qatar, 'An Inter-State Communication against the Kingdom of Saudi Arabia' https://www.ohchr.org/EN/NewsEvents/Pages/DisplayNews.aspx?NewsID=23566&LangID=E.

Qatar, 'An Inter-State Communication against the United Arab Emirates' <https://www.ohchr.org/EN/NewsEvents/Pages/DisplayNews.aspx?NewsID=23566&LangID=E>.

Quigley J, *The Genocide Convention: An International Law Analysis* (Ashgate 2006).

Ragazzi M, *The Concept of International Obligations Erga Omnes* (Clarendon Press 1997).

Rathbone M, Jeydel P and Lentz A, 'Sanctions, Sanctions Everywhere: Forging a Path through Complex Transnational Sanctions Laws' (2013) 44 Georgetown Journal of International Law 1055.

Reilly J, 'China's Unilateral Sanctions' (2012) 35 The Washington Quarterly 121.

Reisman WM, 'Kosovo's Antinomies' (1999) 93 The American Journal of International Law 860.

Reisman WM, 'Sanctions and International Law. Keynote Address: The Cuban Embargo and Human Rights.' (2008) 4 Intercultural Human Rights Law Review 13.

Reisman WM, 'Sovereignty and Human Rights in Contemporary International Law.' in Dinah Shelton (ed), *International protection of human rights* (Brill Nijhoff 2017).

Rej A, 'Australian Parliamentary Committee Recommends Global Magnitsky Type Legislation' The Diplomat (7 December 2020) https://thediplomat.com/2020/12/australian-parliamentary-committee-recommends-global-magnitsky-type-legislation/.

Roberts A, Choer Moraes H and Ferguson V, 'The Geoeconomic World Order' (*Lawfare*, 19 November 2018) https://www.lawfareblog.com/geoeconomic-world-order.

Roberts A, Choer Moraes H and Ferguson V, 'Toward a Geoeconomic Order in International Trade and Investment' (2019) 22 Journal of International Economic Law 655.

Ronzitti N, 'Sanctions as Instruments of Coercive Diplomacy: An International Law Perspective' in Natalino Ronzitti (ed), *Coercive Diplomacy, Sanctions and International Law* (Brill Nijhoff 2016).

Rotblat C, 'Weaponizing the Plumbing: Dollar Diplomacy, Yuan Internationalization, and the Future of Financial Sanctions' (2017) 21 ucla J Int'l L Foreign Aff 311.

Ruffert M, 'Reprisals,' *Max Planck Encyclopedia of Public International Law* [*MPEPIL*] (2015) http://opil.ouplaw.com/view/10.1093/law:epil/9780199231690/law-9780199231690-e1771.

Ruys T and Ryngaert C, 'Secondary Sanctions: A Weapon out of Control? The International Legality of, and European Responses to, US Secondary Sanctions' (2021) British Yearbook of International Law 1.

Ruys T, 'Sanctions, Retorsions and Countermeasures: Concepts and International Legal Framework' in Larissa Van den Herik (ed), *Research Handbook on UN Sanctions and International Law* (Edward Elgar Publishing 2017).

Ruys T, 'Non-UN Financial Sanctions against Central Banks and Heads of State: In Breach of International Immunity Law?' (*ejil: Talk!*, 12 May 2017) https://www.ejiltalk.org/non-un-financial-sanctions-against-central-banks-and-heads-of-state-in-breach-of-international-immunity-law/.

Ruys T, 'Immunity, Inviolability and Countermeasures – A Closer Look at Non-UN Targeted Sanctions' in Tom Ruys and Nicolas Angelet (eds), *The Cambridge Handbook of Immunities and International Law* (Cambridge University Press 2019).

Ryngaert C, 'Extraterritorial Export Controls (Secondary Boycotts)' (2008) 7 Chinese Journal of International Law 625.

Ryngaert C, *Jurisdiction in International Law* (Second edition, Oxford University Press 2015).

Saeima Approves Proposed Sanctions against the Officials Connected to the Sergei Magnitsky Case (*saeima.lv*) <https://www.saeima.lv/en/news/saeima-news/26575-saeima-approves-proposed-sanctions-against-the-officials-connected-to-the-sergei-magnitsky-case>.

Safaryan H, 'Implementation of the Import Substitution Policy – Further Developments' (2015) https://cms.law/en/rus/publication/implementation-of-the-import-substitution-policy-further-developments.

Samuelson PA, 'The Pure Theory of Public Expenditure' (1954) 36 The Review of Economics and Statistics 387.

Sanctions (*United Nations Security Council*) <https://www.un.org/securitycouncil/sanctions/information>.

Sanger DE, 'Wal-Mart Canada Is Putting Cuban Pajamas Back on Shelf' *The New York Times* (14 March 1997) <https://www.nytimes.com/1997/03/14/business/wal-mart-canada-is-putting-cuban-pajamas-back-on-shelf.html>.

Sanktionen Gegenüber Venezuela (*SECO – Staatssekretariat für Wirtschaft*) <https://www.seco.admin.ch/seco/de/home/seco/nsb-news.msg-id-70265.html>.

Saul M, 'Identifying Jus Cogens Norms: The Interaction of Scholars and International Judges' (2015) 5 Asian Journal of International Law 26.

Savin A, 'In Finland, the Court Rejected the Claim of Billionaire Boris Rotenberg to Scandinavian Banks' *24-my.info* (14 February 2019) <https://www.24-my.info/in-finland-the-court-rejected-the-claim-of-billionaire-boris-rotenberg-to-scandinavian-banks/>.

Schefer KN, *Social Regulation in the WTO: Trade Policy and International Legal Development* (Edward Elgar 2010).

Schloemann HL and Ohlhoff S, '"Constitutionalization" and Dispute Settlement in the WTO: National Security as an Issue of Competence' (1999) 93 The American Journal of International Law 424.

Schreiber AP, 'Economic Coercion as an Instrument of Foreign Policy: U.S. Economic Measures Against Cuba and the Dominican Republic' (1973) 25 World Politics 387.

Schwartzkopff F, Pohjanpalo K and Meyer H, 'Russian Oligarch Rotenberg Files Lawsuit Against Nordic Banks' *Bloomberg.com* (19 October 2018) <https://www.bloomberg.com/news/articles/2018-10-19/russian-oligarch-rotenberg-files-lawsuit-against-nordic-banks>.

Scovazzi T and Citroni G, *The Struggle against Enforced Disappearance and the 2007 United Nations Convention* (Brill Nijhoff 2007).

Security Council Fails to Adopt Draft Resolution Condemning Syria's Crackdown on Anti-Government Protestors, Owing to Veto by Russian Federation, China <https://www.un.org/press/en/2011/sc10403.doc.htm>.

Security Council Fails to Adopt Draft Resolution on Syria as Russian Federation, China Veto Text Supporting Arab League's Proposed Peace Plan <https://www.un.org/press/en/2012/sc10536.doc.htm>.

Security Council Fails to Adopt Draft Resolution on Syria That Would Have Threatened Sanctions, Due to Negative Votes of China, Russian Federation https://www.un.org/press/en/2012/sc10714.doc.htm.

Seelke CR, 'Venezuela: Overview of U.S. Sanctions,' Congressional Research Service (CRS) updated January 22, 2021.

Sellers MNS, 'Economic Sanctions against Human Rights Violations' in Laura Picchio Forlati and Linos-Alexander Sicilianos (eds.), *Economic Sanctions in International Law* (Brill Academic Publishers 2004).

Shagina M, 'Japan's Sanctions Policy Vis-à-Vis Russia,' Sasakawa Peace Foundation, https://spfusa.org/wp-content/uploads/2018/09/Forum-No.-15-Shagina-Sep-25.pdf.

Shelton D, 'Normative Hierarchy in International Law' (2006) 100 The American Journal of International Law 291.

Silverstone PH, 'The Export Control Act of 1949: Extraterritorial Enforcement' (1959) 107 University of Pennsylvania Law Review 331.

Simma B and Müller AT, 'Exercise and Limits of Jurisdiction' in James Crawford and Martti Koskenniemi (eds), *The Cambridge Companion to International Law* (Cambridge University Press 2012).

Simma B and Wessendorf N (eds), *The Charter of the United Nations: A Commentary* (3rd ed., Oxford University Press 2012).

Simmons BA, *Mobilizing for Human Rights: International Law in Domestic Politics* (Cambridge University Press 2009).

Sir Arthur Watts, 'Heads of Governments and Other Senior Officials,' *Max Planck Encyclopedia of Public International Law* [*MPEPIL*] https://opil.ouplaw.com/view/10.1093/law:epil/9780199231690/law-9780199231690-e1417.

Sir Arthur Watts, 'Heads of State,' *Max Planck Encyclopedia of Public International Law* [*MPEPIL*] https://opil.ouplaw.com/view/10.1093/law:epil/9780199231690/law-9780199231690-e1418?prd=EPIL.

Skidmore D and Gates W, 'After Tiananmen: The Struggle over U.S. Policy toward China in the Bush Administration' (1997) 27(3) Presidential Studies Quarterly 514.

Slaughter A-M, 'Sovereignty and Power in a Networked World Order' (2004) 40 Stanford Journal of International Law 283.

Spanogle JA, 'Can Helms-Burton be challenged under WTO?' (1998) XXVII Stetson Law Review 1313.

Ssenyonjo M, *Economic, Social and Cultural Rights in International Law* (Hart Publishing 2009).

Standard Chartered Agrees Settlement with New York Regulator *BBC News* (14 August 2012) <https://www.bbc.com/news/business-19253666>.

Standard Chartered to Pay $1bn for Breaching Iran Sanctions *BBC News* (9 April 2019) <https://www.bbc.com/news/business-47872318>.

Stantchev S, 'The Medival Origins of Embargo as a Policy Tool' (2012) 33 History of Political Thought 373.

Statement of the Prosecutor of the International Criminal Court, Mrs Fatou Bensouda, on the Referral by Venezuela Regarding the Situation in Its Own Territory <https://www.icc-cpi.int/Pages/item.aspx?name=200217-otp-statement-venezuela>.

Status of Ratification Interactive Dashboard <https://indicators.ohchr.org/>.

Stec S, 'Humanitarian Limits to Sovereignty: Common Concern and Common Heritage Approaches to Natural Resources and Environment' (2010) 12 International Community Law Review 361.

Stoll P-T, 'State Immunity,' *Max Planck Encyclopedia of Public International Law* [*MPEPIL*] <https://opil.ouplaw.com/view/10.1093/law:epil/9780199231690/law-9780199231690-e1106>.

Stoll P, et al., 'Extraterritorial sanctions on trade and investments and European responses' (2020) Study requested by the European Parliament's Committee on International Trade.

Stürchler N, *The Threat of Force in International Law* (1st publ., Cambridge University Press 2007).

Subedi SP, *The Effectiveness of the UN Human Rights System: Reform and the Judicialisation of Human Rights* (Routledge 2017).

Sveaass N, 'The United Nations Convention Against Torture and Other Cruel, Inhuman or Degrading Treatment or Punishment: The Absolute Prohibition and the Obligation to Prevent' in Metin Başoğlu (ed), *Torture and Its Definition In International Law: An Interdisciplinary Approach* (Oxford University Press 2017).

Swaak-Goldman OQ, 'Who Defines Members' Security Interest in the WTO?' (1996) 9 Leiden Journal of International Law 361.

Switzerland Freezes Gaddafi Assets (*SWI swissinfo.ch*) <https://www.swissinfo.ch/eng/switzerland-freezes-gaddafi-assets/29581082>.

Talmon S, 'Jus Cogens after Germany v. Italy: Substantive and Procedural Rules Distinguished' (2012) 25 Leiden Journal of International Law 979.

Tams CJ, *Enforcing Obligations 'Erga Omnes' in International Law* (Cambridge University Press 2005).

Targeted Financial Sanctions: A Manual for Design and Implementation: Contributions from the Interlaken Process (Thomas J Watson Jr Institute for International Studies 2001).

The Doctrine of Continuous Voyages (1916) St. Louis L. Rev. 259.

The Use of Nonviolent Coercion: A Study in Legality under Article 2(4) of the Charter of the United Nations' (1974) 122 University of Pennsylvania Law Review 983.

Thielbörger P, 'The "Essence" of International Human Rights' (2019) 20 German Law Journal 924.

Thouvenin J-M and Grandaubert V, 'The Material Scope of State Immunity from Execution' in Tom Ruys and Nicolas Angelet (eds), *The Cambridge Handbook of Immunities and International Law* (Cambridge University Press 2019).

Thouvenin J-M, 'International Economic Sanctions and Fundamental Rights: Friend or Foe?' in Norman Weiß and Jean-Marc Thouvenin (eds.), *The Influence of Human Rights on International Law* (Springer 2015).

Tomuschat C, *Human Rights: Between Idealism and Realism* (3rd ed, Oxford University Press 2014).

Tostensen A and Bull B, 'Are Smart Sanctions Feasible?' (2002) 54 World Politics 373.

Trindade AAC, *International Law for Humankind: Towards a New 'Jus Gentium'* (2nd rev. ed, M Nijhoff Publishers 2013).

Tsebelis G, 'Are Sanctions Effective? A Game-Theoretic Analysis' (1990) 34 Journal of Conflict Resolution 3.

Turck N, 'The Arab Boycott of Israel' (1977) 55 Foreign Affairs 472.

Turkish Banker Convicted of Conspiring to Evade U.S. Sanctions Against Iran and Other Offenses (*The United States Department of Justice*, 3 January 2018) <https://www.justice.gov/opa/pr/turkish-banker-covicted-conspiring-evade-us-sanctions-against-iran-and-other-offenses>.

Turkish Banker Mehmet Hakan Atilla Sentenced To 32 Months For Conspiring To Violate U.S. Sanctions Against Iran And Other Offenses (*The United States Department of Justice*, 16 May 2018) <https://www.justice.gov/usao-sdny/pr/turkish-banker-mehmet-hakan-atilla-sentenced-32-months-conspiring-violate-us-sanctions>.

Tzanakopoulos A, 'The Right to Be Free from Economic Coercion' (2015) 4 Cambridge International Law Journal 616.

U.S. Customs and Border Protection. *Press Release*. The Department of Homeland Security Issues Withhold Release Order on Silica-Based Products Made by Forced

Labor in Xinjiang. (24 June 2021) https://www.cbp.gov/newsroom/national-media-release/department-homeland-security-issues-withhold-release-order-silica.

U.S. Department of Commerce. *Press Release*. Commerce Department Adds Five Chinese Entities to the Entity List for Participating in China's Campaign of Forced Labor Against Muslims in Xinjiang. (24 June 2021) https://www.commerce.gov/news/press-releases/2021/06/commerce-department-adds-five-chinese-entities-entity-list.

U.S. Department of State, 'Infographics: December 9-10 2020 Global Magnitsky Program Designations' (2020) https://www.state.gov/wp-content/uploads/2020/12/Infographic_v1.8-508.pdf.

U.S. Department of the Treasury. *Press Release*. Treasury Sanctions Chinese Government Officials in Connection with Serious Human Rights Abuse in Xinjiang. (22 March 2021) https://home.treasury.gov/news/press-releases/jy0070.

Updated Blocking Statute in Support of Iran Nuclear Deal Enters into Force (*European Commission*) https://ec.europa.eu/commission/presscorner/detail/en/IP_18_4805.

Vardi N, 'Feds Arrest Turkish Banker For Conspiring With Trader Reza Zarrab To Violate Sanctions Against Iran' *Forbes* <https://www.forbes.com/sites/nathanvardi/2017/03/28/feds-arrest-turkish-banker-for-violating-u-s-sanctions-against-iran/>.

Vasquez CM, 'Trade Sanctions and Human Rights – Past, Present, and Future' (2003) 6 Journal of International Economic Law 797.

Vattel E de, *The Law of Nations, or, Principles of the Law of Nature, Applied to the Conduct and Affairs of Nations and Sovereigns, with Three Early Essays on the Origine and Nature of Natural Law and on Luxury* (Béla Kapossy and Richard Whatmore eds, Indianapolis, Liberty Fund 2008).

Venezuela: Council Renews Sanctions until 14 November 2020 (*Council of the European Union*) <http://www.consilium.europa.eu/en/press/press-releases/2019/11/11/venezuela-council-renews-sanctions-until-14-november-2020/>.

Vidmar J, 'Rethinking Jus Cogens After Germany v. Italy: Back to Article 53?' (2013) 60 Netherlands International Law Review 1.

Volcker PA, Goldstone RJ and Pieth M, 'Independent Inquiry Committee into the United Nations Oil-for-Food Programme. Interim Report, February 3, 2005.'

Volcker PA, Goldstone RJ and Pieth M, 'Independent Inquiry Committee into the United Nations Oil-for-Food Programme. Second Interim Report. March 29, 2005.'

Volcker PA, Goldstone RJ and Pieth M, 'Independent Inquiry Committee into the United Nations Oil-for-Food Programme. Third Interim Report. August 8, 2005.'

Volcker PA, Goldstone RJ and Pieth M, 'Independent Inquiry Committee into the United Nations Oil-for-Food Programme. The Management of the United Nations Oil-For-Food Programme. September 7, 2005.'

Volcker PA, Goldstone RJ and Pieth M, 'Independent Inquiry Committee into the United Nations Oil-for-Food Programme. Manipulation of the Oil-For-Food Programme by the Iraqi Regime. October 27, 2005.'

Volkov M, 'United States, European Union, United Kingdom and Canada Coordinate Further Sanctions Against Belarus' *JD Supra* (21 December 2021) https://www.jdsupra.com/legalnews/united-states-european-union-united-2693437/.

Wakabayashi D and Rappeport A, 'Huawei C.F.O. Is Arrested in Canada for Extradition to the U.S.' *The New York Times* (5 December 2018) https://www.nytimes.com/2018/12/05/business/huawei-cfo-arrest-canada-extradition.html.

Weber PM and Stępień B, 'Conform or challenge? Adjustment strategies of sanction-torn companies' (2020) 43 The World Economy 3006.

Webster G et al., 'Mapping U.S. – China Technology Decoupling' (27 August 2020) Stanford Freeman Spogli Institute for International Studies White Paper.

Weiss EB, 'The Coming Water Crisis: A Common Concern of Humankind' (2012) 1 Transnational Environmental Law 153.

Weissbrodt D and Finnegan P, 'Human Rights Conditions: What We Know and Why It Matters' (2019) 28(1) Minnesota Journal of International Law 1.

Welt C and others, 'U.S. Sanctions on Russia. Congressional Research Service, Report R45415' (2020).

Wertheim S, 'The League That Wasn't: American Designs for a Legalist-Sanctionist League of Nations and the Intellectual Origins of International Organization, 1914–1920' (2011) 35 Diplomatic History 797.

Wet E de, 'Jus Cogens and Obligations Erga Omnes' in Dinah Shelton (ed), *The Oxford Handbook of International Human Rights Law* (2013).

Wilson W and Foley H, *Woodrow Wilson's Case for the League of Nations* (Princeton University Press; Humphrey Milford/Oxford University Press 1923).

Winkler HR, 'The Development of the League of Nations Idea in Great Britain, 1914–1919' (1948) 20 The Journal of Modern History 95.

World Report 2018: Events of 2017 (2018) <https://www.hrw.org/sites/default/files/world_report_download/201801world_report_web.pdf>.

Wu M, 'Free Trade and the Protection of Public Morals: An Analysis of the Newly Emerging Public Morals Clause Doctrine' (2008) 33 The Yale Journal of International Law 215.

Wu M, 'China's Export Restrictions and the Limits of WTO Law' (2017) 16 World Trade Review 673.

Wuerth I, 'International Law in the Post-Human Rights Era' (2017) 96 Texas Law Review 279.

Wuerth I, 'Immunity from Execution of Central Bank Assets' in Tom Ruys and Nicolas Angelet (eds), *The Cambridge Handbook of Immunities and International Law* (Cambridge University Press 2019).

Yap J, 'Beyond 'Don't Be Evil': The European Union GSP + Trade Preference Scheme and the Incentivisation of the Sri Lankan Garment Industry to Foster Human Rights' (2013) 19(2) European Law Journal, 283.

Yoo JY and Ahn D, 'Security Exceptions in the WTO System: Bridge or Bottle-Neck for Trade and Security?' (2016) 19 Journal of International Economic Law 417.

Yusuf AA, 'The Right of Forcible Intervention in Certain Conflicts' in Abdulqawi Yusuf and Fatsah Ouguergouz (eds), *The African Union, legal and institutional framework: a manual on the Pan-African organization* (Martinus Nijhoff 2012).

Zarate JC, *Treasury's War: The Unleashing of a New Era of Financial Warfare* (Public Affairs 2013).

Zemanek K, 'The Metamorphosis of Jus Cogens: From an Institution of Treaty Law to the Bedrock of the International Legal Order?' in Enzo Cannizzaro (ed), *The Law of Treaties Beyond the Vienna Convention* (Oxford University Press 2011).

Zoller E, *Peacetime Unilateral Remedies: An Analysis of Countermeasures* (Transnational Publishers 1984).

Zwingel S, *Translating International Women's Rights: The CEDAW Convention in Context* (Palgrave Macmillan 2016).

Index

www.ingramcontent.com/pod-product-compliance
Lightning Source LLC
Chambersburg PA
CBHW071327230926
51849CB00002B/329
* 9 7 8 9 0 0 4 5 0 7 8 8 3 *